CU000925354

THE SPIRIT OF MEDIEVAL ENGLISH
POPULAR ROMANCE

LONGMAN MEDIEVAL AND RENAISSANCE LIBRARY

General editors:

Charlotte Brewer, Hertford College, Oxford *N. H. Keeble*, University of Stirling

THE SPIRIT OF MEDIEVAL ENGLISH POPULAR ROMANCE

EDITED BY

AD PUTTER AND JANE GILBERT

An imprint of **Pearson Education**

Harlow, England · London · New York · Reading, Massachusetts · San Francisco
Toronto · Don Mills, Ontario · Sydney · Tokyo · Singapore · Hong Kong · Seoul
Taipei · Cape Town · Madrid · Mexico City · Amsterdam · Munich · Paris · Milan

Pearson Education Limited
Edinburgh Gate
Harlow
Essex CM20 2 JE
England

and Associated Companies throughout the world

Visit us on the world wide web at:
http://pearsoneduc.com

First published 2000

© Pearson Education Limited 2000

All rights reserved; no part of this publication may be reproduced,
stored in a retrieval system, or transmitted in any form or by any
means, electronic, mechanical, photocopying, recording, or otherwise
without either the prior written permission of the Publishers or a
licence permitting restricted copying in the United Kingdom issued by
the Copyright Licensing Agency Ltd, 90 Tottenham Court Road,
London W1P 0LP.

ISBN 0 582 29880 6 CSD
ISBN 0 582 29888 1 PPR

British Library Cataloguing-in-Publication Data
A catalogue record for this book is available from the British Library

Library of Congress Cataloging-in-Publication Data
The spirit of medieval English popular romance / edited by Ad Putter and Jane Gilbert.
    p.   cm. — (Longman medieval and Renaissance library)
    Includes bibliographical references and index.
    ISBN 0–582–29880–6 (alk. paper) — ISBN 0–582–29888–1 (pbk.: alk. paper)
    1. English literature—Middle English, 1100–1500—History and criticism.
2. Romances, English—History and criticism.   3. Popular literature—English—
History and criticism.   4. Popular culture—England—History—To 1500.   5. Tales,
Medieval—History and criticism.   I. Putter, Ad.   II. Gilbert, Jane.   III. Series.

PR321.S65   2000
823′.109—dc21   00–020189

Typeset by 35 in 11/13 pt Baskerville MT
Produced by Pearson Education Asia Pte Ltd.
Printed in Singapore

CONTENTS

PREFACE

The Middle English popular romances are today accessible to readers in numerous editions and anthologies. The number of recent student editions of popular romances is particularly gratifying, even as it shows up how little literary critics have managed to say about them. Why, readers might want to know, should we bother at all with popular romances? The embarrassment surrounding that question perhaps explains the predominance in romance studies of scholarship on manuscripts, editorial problems, and textual history – scholarship which can proceed very well without requiring from its practitioners any belief in the aesthetic value of popular romances, and which has accordingly done little to alter their reputation as poetic disasters.

The aim of this collection is to help bring these romances back into the arena of critical discussion. Each contributor has been asked to develop an interpretation of one particular Middle English romance to reveal the interests it holds for modern literary criticism. No restrictions have been imposed on methodology or on the traffic of ideas between disciplines. The result is a volume with a wide spectrum of approaches: historicist, narratological, psychoanalytical, and others. That, we think, is how it should be. For if popular romance is ever to regain some of the vitality it possessed in medieval times, it will need to be read with all the resourcefulness and theoretical awareness that characterizes literary criticism today.

For the benefit of non-specialists the contributors have also been asked to introduce the romance of their choice by briefly setting out the relevant information concerning dates of composition, audience, manuscripts, sources, and relevant secondary criticism. The general introduction does the same for the genre of popular romance as a whole. The first part, 'A Historical Introduction', discusses the medieval context of popular romances; the second, 'A Theoretical Introduction', explores the modern reception of popular romances and the interpretive possibilities opened up by developments in literary theory.

It is to be hoped that, by offering readings of as well as introductions to popular romances, this book may both suggest appropriate strategies of interpretation and serve as a starting point for further analytical approaches.

We should like to thank Elizabeth Archibald, Charlotte Brewer, John Burrow, Tony Edwards, Jill Mann, Maldwyn Mills, Rhiannon Purdie and James Simpson for their comments on sections of this book. The index was compiled by Demelza Curnow, and financed by a grant from the Arts Faculty Research Fund of the University of Bristol. We thank them and the staff at Pearson Education.

A.P.

J.G.

NOTE ON REFERENCES AND ABBREVIATIONS

The reference system adopted for *secondary sources* is the author–year system. When more than one work by the same author appeared in the same year, the year of publication is followed by a, b, c, etc. In the case of authors with the same surname, we also give the initial. Full bibliographical details for the author–year references can be found by checking the integrated bibliography at the end of this book. In the case of *primary sources*, full bibliographical details appear in notes at the end of each chapter as well as in the bibliography. References to Chaucer, Langland, *Sir Gawain and the Green Knight,* and Malory are to the standard editions as listed in the bibliography of primary sources. We have modernized the orthography of thorns and yoghs in all Middle English citations. References to Sigmund Freud are to *The Standard Edition of the Complete Psychological Works of Sigmund Freud,* ed. James Strachey, 24 vols (London: Hogarth Press, 1953–74), abbreviated as *SE.*

The following abbreviations are also used:

CCM	*Cahiers de civilisation médiévale*
CFMA	Classiques français du Moyen Age
ChR	*Chaucer Review*
EETS o.s.	Early English Text Society, original series
EETS e.s.	Early English Text Society, extra series
MAE	*Medium Aevum*
MED	*Middle English Dictionary*
MLR	*Modern Language Review*
MS	*Mediaeval Studies*
NM	*Neuphilologische Mitteilungen*
N&Q	*Notes and Queries*
OED	*Oxford English Dictionary*
PMLA	*Publications of the Modern Language Association of America*
RMS	*Reading Medieval Studies*
SATF	Société des anciens textes français
SP	*Studies in Philology*
STS	Scottish Text Society
TLF	Textes littéraires français
YES	*Yearbook of English Studies*

A Historical Introduction

AD PUTTER

The difficulty of being precise about the authorship and audience of the Middle English popular romances is largely due to the fact that the narratives that are conventionally brought together under this term are an extremely varied group. The first volume of the *Manual of the Writings in Middle English*, devoted to 'The Romances' (Severs 1967), lists over a hundred medieval narratives, from *King Horn* (1225) to Lord Berners' *Arthur of Little Britain* (before 1533), and a cursory glance at this list should suffice to persuade anyone that the category of 'romance' is loose and fuzzy at the edges.

The resemblances shared by the overwhelming majority of romances are very broad: romances usually end happily with the restoration of an order that was disrupted at the beginning of the story; the cast is aristocratic, consisting of knights and kings, queens and ladies; the setting is idealized, often supernatural.[1] Such general resemblances of course hardly demarcate the genre, and they pale into insignificance when compared with the striking resemblances shown by members of various branches within the romance family. Thus some romances tell of the self-fulfilment of a knight in adventures of love and chivalry (e.g. *Sir Launfal*, *Sir Degaré*, *Sir Perceval of Galles*); some trace the fortuitous wanderings of calumniated, exiled or abandoned ladies (*Emaré*, *Lay le Freine*, *Le Bone Florence*); others deal with outlaw heroes (*Gamelyn*, *The Gest of Robyn Hode*), or with classical legends (*The Seege of Troy*, *King Alisaunder*); some are based on, or call themselves, 'Breton lays' (*Sir Orfeo*, *Lai le Freine*, *Sir Degaré*); while still other romances contain a strong didactic or penitential impulse (*Sir Isumbras*, *Robert of Sicily*, and the first fragment of the *Awntyrs off Arthure*). Subdivisions could easily be multiplied. Arthurian romances, homiletic romances, society romances, crusading romances, family romances, penitential romances, exemplary romances, Charlemagne romances: these are some examples of subgenres that critics

1

have at one time or another found useful. However, it should be noted that in the indeterminate field of romance the areas occupied by these subgenres are likewise unbounded and overlapping: *Sir Launfal* is at the same time a 'Breton lay', a 'chivalric romance', and an 'Arthurian romance'; *Sir Isumbras* is a 'penitential romance', but also a 'family romance', with plenty of crusading to boot. For the sake of convenience, strict definitions and demarcations of 'romance' and its family branches can be proposed, but such conceptual borders are, and always have been, blurred: sharp dividing lines can be imposed but they cannot convincingly be demonstrated. In Wittgenstein's terminology, romance is a 'family-resemblance' category: we should think of them as forming a complex network of relationships and similarities, not as a set that can be defined on the basis of specific properties common to each of its members (Wittgenstein 1953, 31–2).

We can spare ourselves the trouble of agonizing needlessly about problems of definition if we accept that we have inherited the word 'romance', with all its vagueness, from those who talked before us. Indeed, the use of 'romance' as a generic label goes back to the medieval period. In Middle English 'romance' originally designated 'romance languages' (especially French), but English writers of the fourteenth century first began to use it to single out narratives containing fanciful, miraculous, amorous or chivalrous matter (Strohm 1977). But 'romaunce' never was a precise generic marker. Thus the fourteenth-century poet of a *Life of St Gregory*, who announced to his listeners that he would 'ariht biginne romauncen of this ilke song', evidently thought of this saint's life as a kind of 'romance' (Hoops 1929, 35). The term was also extended to works which literary historians today might prefer to call chronicles or epics. Geoffrey Chaucer uses it, for example, of a history of Thebes (*Troilus and Criseyde*, II, 100). The categorical inexactness of 'romance' is further reflected in manuscript compilations, in which a saint's life is sometimes found in the middle of a sequence of romances (Thompson 1983, 118), and in which romances are sometimes found in the middle of chronicles or religious material (Guddat-Figge 1976, 39–40). The vexed questions that exercise critics today – how to separate romance from chronicles and saints' lives – are thus bound up with the earliest usages of the word; in an important sense, they are not 'our' problem.

We shall say more about the implications of the adjective 'popular' that often qualifies the romances to which this book is devoted, but for the moment let us simply note that 'popular' is not a magic word that suddenly imposes uniformity on the romances it specifies. The meaning of 'popular' is largely negative (*not* courtly, *not* aristocratic), and since the romances read by the English aristocracy of the Middle Ages were predominantly in French, all Middle English romances could be called 'popular'. Alliterative romances (particularly *Sir Gawain and the Green Knight*), Chaucer's 'romances', Gower's tales and the prose romances of the fifteenth century, including Malory's *Morte D'Arthur*, are sometimes cited as exceptions to the rule that Middle English romances are 'popular' as a matter of course, but the coincidence that the exceptions are all greatly admired raises the suspicion that 'popular' and 'courtly' are disguised value judgements, masquerading as objective statements about audience or 'tone'.

Even if we can legitimately isolate the romances of Chaucer, Gower, Malory, *Sir Gawain* and the fifteenth-century prose romances, the 'popular romances' remain a heterogeneous group, and it is no surprise that there has been much debate about the kind of audience and the mode of composition and reception that we should envisage for them. For newcomers to this debate, the opposing views could be described as follows:

1. Popular romances are the improvised compositions of minstrels. They were recited orally at feasts and festivals, intended for the ears of ordinary folk, for the 'people' (whence the designation 'popular' romances).
2. So-called popular romances were composed and copied for the amusement and edification of the newly literate classes – not the lower orders, but the gentry and the prosperous middle classes who formed the market for the trade in vernacular books in the later medieval period.

These two positions – let us call them the 'romantic' and the 'revisionist' positions – really only mark out the extreme poles of the debate. In practice critics situate themselves somewhere in between these two poles, though they usually betray marked inclinations towards one or the other.

The view one takes of the qualities of popular romance, such as its formulaic style, depends a great deal on these inclinations. Critics have long noted the profusion of stock phrases and tags, which are usually found in popular romances as solutions to specific metrical challenges (Baugh 1959; Wittig 1978). For example, the word 'knyght' repeatedly calls forth the rhyming phrase 'strong in fyght'; knights and ladies are not simply 'glad' but 'glad and blythe', and consequently thank God 'many a sythe'. The 'romantic' treats these tags and formulas as evidence of minstrel improvisation, as the instinctive resource of a performer who must keep the story going without the aid of a written text. For the 'revisionist', however, they betray the hand of the hack professional who draws liberally from the stock of conventional lines and phrases to ease the work of written composition or translation.

So which of these two positions is more persuasive, the 'romantic' or the 'revisionist'? The next section looks at the various kinds of evidence that have been brought to bear on this question, first of all the evidence of surviving romance manuscripts.

The Manuscript Evidence

The study of the manuscripts in which the Middle English romances have come down to us has provided the main impulse behind the revisionist view of popular romances.[2] About three-fifths of existing romances from the thirteenth and fourteenth centuries are extant in four miscellanies in which romances are anthologized with material of a strong didactic or religious cast (McSparran and Robinson 1979, vii). These four manuscripts also contain most of the romances discussed by the contributors to this collection. The earliest is the famous Auchinleck manuscript (Edinburgh, National Library of Scotland, Advocates' 19.2.1), copied in the first half of the fourteenth century.[3] From the fifteenth century come three other notable manuscript miscellanies containing Middle English romances: the so-called Thornton manuscript (Lincoln Cathedral Library, MS 91);[4] Cambridge University Library (CUL), Ff.2.38;[5] and finally London, British Library, Cotton Caligula A.ii.[6]

The first three of these four manuscript collections are available in facsimile editions;[7] and the idea that minstrels might have carried these romance collections with them on their journeys will have lost all its attraction to anyone who has ever lifted any of these facsimiles off the shelf. A few portable romance manuscripts, such as might theoretically have served as repertoire books for minstrels, do exist. The two most significant ones are Lincoln's Inn, MS 150 (containing versions of *Libeaus Desconus*, *King Alisaunder*, *Arthour and Merlin* and *The Seege of Troy*) and Oxford, Bodleian Library, Ashmole 61 (containing *Sir Isumbras*, *Earl of Toulous*, *Libeaus Desconus*, *Sir Cleges* and *Orfeo*). The small format of these two manuscripts – transportable in a holster, and hence known as 'holster books' – led earlier scholars to claim them as minstrel manuscripts, but recent research has effectively undermined this argument (Guddat-Figge 1976, 30–36; Hirsch 1977; Taylor 1991). In the later medieval period, manuscripts of the holster format were in common use as account books, and could be acquired ready-bound from commercial bookshops. For anyone wishing to compile an anthology of texts for family entertainment, the holster-book format would have seemed a logical choice, and the extended use of holster books for literary miscellanies may reveal more about the consequences of the spread of literacy than about the contents of the minstrel's travel bag. A close look at the contents of the two manuscripts casts further doubts on the minstrel hypothesis. The A-version of *Piers Plowman*, contained in the Lincoln's Inn manuscript (*c*.1410), would seem an unlikely choice for a minstrel recitation, and George Kane describes the hand as typical of 'provincial guild or corporation documents and private correspondence, expert but unpretentious' (Kane 1988, 10–11).

4

MS Ashmole 61, referred to by Kane as a 'minstrel's book' (Kane 1988, 11), again has precious little to do with minstrels.[8] The writer of Ashmole 61 (*c*.1450), who signs himself Rate, was probably a professional scribe, and this particular manuscript seems to have been put together for a provincial Leicestershire family. Accompanying the romances in this volume are saints' lives, courtesy books and various moral exempla. A comparable collection of the same date is National Library of Scotland, Advocates' 19.3.1, which contains the same mixture of romances (*Sir Gowther*, *Sir Isumbras* and *Sir Amadace*) and pious and didactic material, and which was probably also intended as a one-volume library for a small landowning family, the Sherbrookes of Oxton, Nottinghamshire.[9] On the evidence of their mixed contents, the four major romance miscellanies (Auchinleck, Thornton, CUL Ff.2.38 and Cotton Caligula A.ii) may also have served as reading books for family entertainment, devotion and practical instruction.

The medieval popular romances are often found in the entertainment sections of such household miscellanies, where they form remarkably similar clusters.[10] These recurrent clusters of romances are interesting for two reasons. First, they justify the premise that, despite their differences, Middle English popular romances may be considered as a group, since they were often treated as such by their earliest compilers. Second, they suggest that the exemplars which medieval copyists had at their disposal often comprised a standard selection of contemporary bestsellers. The commercial overtones of this description are deliberate, for there is evidence to link some romance manuscripts with commercial 'bookshops'.[11] The entrepreneur of a bookshop would employ professional or semi-professional scribes to produce manuscripts or, more often, 'booklets' or fascicles. A selection of independent booklets, some filled with romances, others with instructional or devotional material, would be bound up later to the taste of the individual customer (Pearsall and Cunningham 1977, ix). The earliest romance miscellany that can be associated with commercial production is the Auchinleck manuscript (Loomis 1942). Derek Pearsall has described the romances in it as the competent work of professional hacks, some of whom may have worked in close association with a London bookshop (Pearsall 1977, 145–6). The texts of three romances discussed in this collection – *Sir Degaré*, *Sir Orfeo* and *Lai le Freine* – possibly offer evidence of 'hack work' by Auchinleck scribes or versifiers. Thus the prologue to *Lai le Freine* in the Auchinleck manuscript seems to have been taken verbatim from the opening of *Sir Orfeo* (or vice versa); the scribes also churned out several versions of *Sir Degaré*, each embellished to varying degrees with lines lifted from *Lai le Freine*, *Bevis of Hampton* and *Guy of Warwick* (Jacobs 1982). The original programme of decorated miniatures further suggests that the Auchinleck manuscript was a book 'to be looked at and read by the private reader', who may have been 'an aspirant middle-class citizen, perhaps a wealthy merchant' (Pearsall and Cunningham 1977, vii–viii). The pattern of borrowings from popular romances in Chaucer's parodic *Tale of Sir Thopas* makes it possible that one of the early readers of the Auchinleck manuscript was Geoffrey Chaucer (Loomis 1940).

For the earliest owners of some of the other key miscellanies – Cotton Caligula A.ii, CUL Ff.2.38, Egerton 2862 – we should probably also look to the prosperous bourgeoisie or the middling landowners. Not that these miscellanies need necessarily have been the products of commercial bookshops. Manuscripts circulated among friends and relatives, and favourite texts might be copied by the head or the chaplain of a household and so become part of a new family reading book. The Lincoln Thornton appears to have been an amateur production of this kind.[12] Robert Thornton, a fifteenth-century Yorkshire gentleman, compiled his manuscript over a number of years from a number of different exemplars (some of southern, others of northern origin) as they became available locally.[13] A more modest example of an amateur collection is the so-called Ireland–Blackburn manuscript (*c*.1450, now Princeton University Library, Robert Taylor Collection), which contains *Sir Amadace*, the *Avowing of Arthur*, the *Awntyrs of Arthur* as well as an assortment of memoranda relating to the manor of Hale in Lancashire. The romances were probably copied for the entertainment of the Ireland family who held the manor of Hale. Like Robert Thornton, the Irelands of Hale belonged to the country gentry, who along with prosperous merchants and artisans formed a major constituent of the audience for Middle English popular romance.

The revisionist drift of the manuscript evidence will have been apparent: the prime audience to emerge from it is not 'the people', but the prosperous middle classes and the provincial gentry who had the money to buy books and the education to read them; the mode of reception is reading (whether private or within the family circle); the transmission is scribal (professional or amateur); and the minstrel can be dismissed as an irrelevance: 'There was no minstrel dropping in, at whose dictation Thornton wrote' (Brewer and Owen 1975, ix). Further evidence could be adduced in support of the revisionist case. Thus there can be no doubt that some Middle English romances such as *William of Palerne, Ywain and Gawain* and *Ipomadon A* are not improvised minstrel compositions, for they are so closely based on Old French originals that the translators must have had the French text in front of them. If these poets were not clerics, they were certainly bookish.[14] An isolated but nevertheless suggestive piece of evidence is a sheet of parchment with a fragmentary draft of the Middle English romance *Sir Ferumbras*, complete with authorial revisions and corrections, which has survived by accident in the book covers of Oxford, Bodleian, Ashmole 33. On the other side of the sheet, the same author wrote a document (dated 1377) dealing with ecclesiastical business in the diocese of Exeter. The poet of *Sir Ferumbras* must have been a cleric in or around Exeter.[15]

The revisionists, in short, have an excellent case, based on the hard evidence of extant manuscripts. The problem is that the 'hard evidence' is partial: manuscripts were written and they were read; that they are not going to give us evidence of minstrel recitations or memorial composition was predictable from the start. And what might make us suspicious about some revisionist claims is the convenience with which things that lie beyond the scope of codicological evidence are declared never to have existed. Thus the editors of the Auchinleck facsimile propose that the Auchinleck romances were in fact composed and translated by the scribes themselves. The editors of the Thornton facsimile extrapolate from the history of this manuscript that Middle English tail-rhyme romances 'were consciously written to be read, even if read aloud. The manuscript was the essential vehicle, and there is little evidence for actual oral transmission, as opposed to a style that was designed to allow oral delivery or even merely imitated it' (Brewer and Owen 1975, xi). The life of popular romances has shrunk to fit the small world of the medieval codex: they are born in the scriptorium, and cannot reproduce without the assistance of scribes.

Anyone unpersuaded by the revisionist case, however, faces the difficult task of producing evidence for phenomena which are by their very nature ephemeral. What would evidence of minstrel composition and oral transmission look like, and how persuasive is it? The following section addresses these questions.

Minstrels and Memorial Transmission

One type of evidence is the stories which romances tell about themselves. To read Middle English romance is to be repeatedly buttonholed by an 'I' who calls for attention and may even demand a cup of ale at the end of a fitt.[16] The inscribed narrative situation is typically that of a someone reciting a poem to a large audience of listeners. It has often been objected that this inscribed situation may be part and parcel of the literary fiction (Taylor 1992), and in some instances this is manifestly true. But there also exists strong corroborating evidence for oral circulation, suggesting that these 'minstrel phrases' may on occasion have been literal as well as conventional. In his *Chronicle* of 1338, Robert Mannyng stated he did not wish his work to become fodder for minstrels – 'I made noght for no disours, / ne for no seggers, no harpours' (75–6) – and complained about their inability to remember the lines of *Sir Tristrem*, his personal favourite (101–4).[17] And Mannyng is not alone in linking Middle English romance with minstrels. The *Laud Troy Book* (*c*.1400) mentions a host of romances about heroes such as Bevis, Guy, King Richard, Perceval and Tristrem, who owe their fame to professional reciters: '. . . gestoures ofte dos of hem gestes, / At mangeres and at grete ffestes' (39–40).[18] Also revealing are the disparaging comments about romances in the *Speculum vitae* (*c*.1370, attributed to William of Nassyngton), which speaks disparagingly of minstrels 'That make spekyng in mony a place / Of Octovian and Isanbrace / And of many other gestes' (38–40).[19]

Such descriptions of minstrel activity cast doubt on the revisionist claim that 'there is little evidence for actual oral transmission', although it should be remembered that the *gestour*'s performance may well have been a public reading from a written text of a romance. The alliterative poet of 'The Lament for Sir John Berkeley' remembers with nostalgia how this fourteenth-century provincial knight entertained his guests with such pastimes as 'romance reading'. Anyone visiting his manor of Wymondham (in Leicestershire)

> . . . myght haf metes manerly and mirthes amonge,
> And of his semli servandes sembland and songe,
> Daliance of damisels to driue away tho day,
> To rede him oright romance were redi on aray.
>
> (41–4)[20]

Romances were read out aloud by ladies and household servants, and professional *disours* may also have based their performances on a script. Even so, this would imply an audience more numerous and socially diverse than the bourgeois family to which the manuscript evidence points. 'The Lament for Sir John Berkeley' asks us to imagine instead a large gathering of distinguished guests and friends who join the *familia* in the medieval sense of the word: the lord's relations and children, his household servants, and his armed following. The poem also reminds us that written texts and oral recitation often went hand in hand in the medieval period. Most manuscripts still existed to serve the ears of listeners (Chaytor 1966, 10);[21] and, paradoxically, written texts often served the purpose of channelling a romance back into oral circulation (Bradbury 1994, 48).

Medieval romances were thus 'published' not only in print but also by being recited, and, contrary to revisionist claims, we must assume that this oral mode of publication played a major part in the transmission of our surviving romances. The most convincing evidence comes from the variations in the texts of romances that survive in more than one manuscript.

The traditional way of explaining textual variation – which has served us very well in textual criticism of Chaucer and Langland – is that scribes copying from written exemplars make predictable errors: for example, harder words are likely to be substituted by easier ones, look-alike letters may generate misreadings, the eye may skip a word or a line, the scribe may consciously improve or censor the copy-text. The difficulty faced by many editors of popular romances is that the scale and typology of variation are very different and difficult to explain in terms of scribal copying alone (Edwards 1991). William Holland's research on the text of *Arthour and Merlin* illustrates the problem (Holland 1973). The earliest text of this romance is that of the Auchinleck manuscript, which is probably not far removed from the lost original, a translation of the French Vulgate *Merlin*. But when Holland compared the Auchinleck version with the text of the romance in a later fifteenth-century version, the result was startling. Although the story had changed little and the same incidents were recounted in roughly the same order, the wording had changed dramatically. In a sample of 500 lines, only ten lines were exactly identical in the two manuscript versions. Admittedly, a long chain of scribal copying can be responsible for introducing numerous variant readings, but such a process cannot plausibly explain a retention rate of only two per cent of the original text. It would appear that at some stage in its textual history *Arthour and Merlin* was reproduced not from a written exemplar but from memory.

While such scale of variation is on occasion attributable to drastic authorial or scribal redaction, recent research indicates that the nature of the textual variation often argues against this. The sound principle from which this research has proceeded is that people who are reconstituting a text from memory are prone to different kinds of mistakes and interventions than people who are copying a text from a written exemplar. In the latter case, corruption is likely to be induced by the chunk of text that the scribe sees (or thinks he sees) in front of him; in the case of memorial reproduction, however, the text that can induce departures from the original is not bounded by the reproducer's visual range but by the range of his memory. Thus a verbal or thematic similarity between two episodes remote from one another in the text may lead to confusion or substitution when stories are reproduced from memory (Rubin 1995, 36).

This fusion of distant episodes by conscious or unconscious association has been documented for a number of Middle English romances,[22] and a case for memorial transmission could plausibly be made for others. The romance of *Eger and Grime* is a case in point. In 1497, King James IV of Scotland is known to have paid 'tua fithelaris' for singing the romance, and memorization is probably responsible for some of the variations between the surviving witnesses, on the one hand the Percy Folio and on the other the early printed editions (Huntington–Laing).[23] Although the plot has remained fairly stable in the different witnesses, the scale of variation is staggering, as a simple line-count reveals (Percy Folio: 1474, Huntington–Laing: 2860). A comparison of the texts also reveals numerous instances of the migration of lines, passages or motifs across hundreds of lines. I have space for only one example. The early prints describe the hospitality received by Grime after his duel with Sir Graysteel as follows:

> The wine bottle he took in hand,
> He set it to his head and drank,
> And said, the Lady serveth [deserves] thank,
> *For there was neither aile nor wine*
> *That came to me in so good time.*
>
> (1634–8; italics mine)

The last two lines of this passage are found in the Percy Folio at a much earlier point in the story, when Eger tells Grime how, after fighting Graysteel, he received hospitality in a castle and was fortified by a drink served by the Lady of the Castle:

> Shee gaue me drinke for to restore,
> for neere hand was I killed before;
> *then was never alle [ale] nor wine*
> *came to me in soe good a time.*
>
> (245–8)

Leaving aside the question of which of these readings is more authentic, we are probably faced with a case of 'memorial transfer': a similarity in situation (the heroes are given a drink by the Lady of the Castle) appears to have triggered the transfer of a couplet from one place to another. This and other long-distance transfers presuppose a transmitter who carried the whole romance in his head and reproduced it from memory.

Armed with such evidence of memorial transmission, the romantics can take their case against the revisionists one step further: romances were indeed recited in public, sometimes by professional entertainers; they were intended not simply for 'family reading' but for *familia* listening. Moreover, transmission from memory is apparent from both the scale and the kind of variation in the texts of many popular romances. Romances survived not only by being copied or read, but by being orally recited and stored in living memories. This is not to say that the surviving texts of memorially transmitted romances are to be regarded as transcripts of minstrel improvisations. Possibly romances were reconstructed from notes or from memory by someone who had heard a reading from a written romance. And possibly romances were passed on as jokes and nursery rhymes are today – by being told to others (repeatedly if necessary). If the memorization of lengthy romances seems hard to imagine today, the prologue of the thirteenth-century *chanson de geste* *La Bataille Loquifer* (about 4000 lines) is instructive. It tells us that Jendeus de Brie composed the poem ('les vers an trova', 3041); that he refused to teach the poem to anyone, but that on his deathbed he bequeathed it to his son ('a son fil la laissa', 3046); the son passed it on to Count William, who subsequently had it written down in a book ('en .I. livre la mist', 3049); this so distressed the son that he fell ill and never regained health.[24] The suggestion is clearly that before the romance was fixed in writing the transmissions were oral.

The prologue of *Sir Tristrem* from the Auchinleck manuscript presents us with a comparable textual history:

> I was at Ertheldoun [sic]
> With Tomas spak Y thare;
> Ther herd Y rede in roune
> Who Tristrem gat and bare,
> Who was king with croun,
> And who him fosterd yare,
> And who was bold baroun,
> As thar elders ware.
> Bi yere
> Tomas telles in toun
> This aventours as thai ware.
> (1–11)[25]

If this can be taken at face value, the poet of *Sir Tristrem* was Thomas of Erceldoune, a shadowy figure elsewhere associated with the court of King Alexander III of Scotland. The narrator claims that he learned the poem after hearing Thomas recite it;[26] and he is now in turn telling that story to an assembled group of listeners (e.g. 199: 'Rewthe mow ye *here*').

Like the poet of *La Bataille Loquifer*, the *Tristrem*-poet may obviously have made this story up; probably he did.[27] What counts is that the stories which these texts tell about themselves are *presented* as true, and so cannot have struck their contemporary audience as unbelievable. The prologues reveal to us a culture where – even if Thomas of Erceldoune and Jendeus de Brie never passed on their compositions by word of mouth – it was thought plausible that poets would.

Conclusion

Given the strength of both the revisionist and the romantic cases, we are obviously not in a position to resolve the debate by selecting one side of the story. The history of Middle English romances is simply more complex and diverse than either the romantic or the revisionist interpretation will allow. The heroes of this history are minstrels as well as professional scribes, book-dealers, and clerics; the supporting cast is the newly literate bourgeoisie and gentry as well as the assembled gathering at a feast; and the setting comprises the family living room as well as the manor hall. We began this chapter by noting that the Middle English romances vary greatly in subject matter; we can now see that the same is true for the circumstances in which they were composed and received.

However, the problem is not simply that we cannot generalize from one Middle English romance to the other; it is that we cannot even generalize about a single romance. Thus the romance of *Emaré* probably started life as a translation or loose adaptation of a French lay (now lost). Like *Lai le Freine*, a fairly faithful adaptation of one of Marie de France's lays, *Emaré* may have been composed quill in hand, but the state in which the text has survived suggests that it was subsequently transmitted from memory, perhaps by a minstrel.[28] However, the only known terminus of its journeys through medieval England was a written manuscript, Cotton Caligula A.ii, which was possibly produced by a commercial bookshop (Richardson 1965, xi). In this manuscript it survives alongside other romances, including *Sir Launfal*, but also a Latin chronicle, an English medical treatise and a form of confession in prose. These last companion pieces were presumably meant to be read, and there is no reason to assume a different mode of consumption for the romances in this manuscript (Guddat-Figge 1976, 50).

The romance of *Sir Degaré* also moves in and out of revisionist and romantic scenarios.[29] The first redactions of this romance (and possibly its composition) were undertaken in association with the commercial bookshop that produced the Auchinleck manuscript, in which the earliest text of *Degaré* survives. But while the prosperous bourgeois family that owned Auchinleck could have read the text of *Degaré* in manuscript, the romance also passed into oral tradition. Evidence for this comes from the version of *Degaré* in Oxford, Bodleian Library, Rawlinson Poetry 34, which contains errors that show that the text had undergone memorization. And at the same time that the London printing houses were tidying up the text for publication, the story of *Degaré* continued to be orally transmitted, witness the debased text of the romance in the Percy Folio.

In the course of its textual history one and the same romance could thus assume very different social forms. In the same way, romances composed by bookish authors might sooner or later become part of a minstrel's repertoire, as happened to *King Alisaunder* (Smithers, 1957, II, 11–12). Conversely, a romance in oral transmission might later be edited and adapted by a scribe for an upmarket audience of readers, as happened to *The Seege of Troy* in Harley MS 525 (Pearsall 1965, 93). This fluidity is only to be expected in the Middle Ages, when literate and oral traditions still co-existed. Romances passed easily from the hands of readers to the memories of minstrels or listeners, and from the oral recitations of minstrels or amateurs back into the writings of scribes.

If the case of Thomas Chestre is anything to go by, the poets of Middle English romances must have inhabited the same hybrid oral and literate world. Unlike most of his colleagues, Thomas Chestre escaped from anonymity, because he named himself at the end of *Sir Launfal*: 'Thomas Chestre made thys tale, / Of the noble knyght Syr Launfale' (1939–40).[30] Chestre was active in the second half of the fourteenth century. A. J. Bliss speculated that he may have been Chaucer's personal friend, since Chaucer was intimately familiar with Thomas Chestre's romances (Bliss 1958). Intriguingly, one 'Thomas de Chestre' is mentioned along with Chaucer and others in a list of soldiers ransomed by Edward III in 1360 during the Hundred Years' War.[31] It would be nice to think that this 'Thomas de Chestre' entertained Chaucer with his romances in his period of captivity, though the surname 'Chester' is so common that the identification must remain speculative. We can be slightly more confident in our knowledge that Thomas Chestre authored three surviving popular romances: *Libeaus Desconus*, *Sir Launfal* and *Octavian* (southern version).[32]

There is disagreement about whether these narratives should be regarded as the work of a *disour* (Mills 1962, 109) composing from memory, or as the output of 'yet another "mediaeval hack writer"' (McSparran 1979, 55, quoting Slover 1931) who cobbled together his romances by the cut-and-paste method. The conflicting views evoke the familiar set of oppositions (minstrel/hack writer; oral/literate; memory/writing), but again the evidence on either side is so wholly convincing that both must be right – and wrong if they believe that these oppositions have any purchase on Chestre or his age.

That Chestre was literate need not be doubted. McSparran has shown, for instance, that some differences between *Octavian* and its Old French source point to Chestre's intermittent access to a text of this romance (McSparran 1979, 49). Probably, Chestre wrote down his compositions, as his claim that he 'made thys tale' in *Sir Launfal* implies.[33] On the other hand, many differences between Chestre's originals and his adaptation strongly suggest that he normally had his sources not in his eye but in his mind. In the case of *Sir Launfal*, for example, Chestre probably drew not on a written text of his main source (*Sir Landevale*) but on his memory of it. Comparing *Sir Launfal* with *Landevale*, Stephen Knight has shown that Chestre's verbal recall is secure only in the case of the rhyme words (Knight 1969). In the rest of the lines Chestre preserves the sense, while the wording differs dramatically. It is an empirical fact that rhyme (or alliteration) helps to lodge words in memory, and that without such mnemonic support, people will retain the sense but not the letter (Rubin 1995, 75). The operations of memory would readily explain the differences and the similarities between *Sir Launfal* and *Sir Landevale*. Mills's research on *Octavian* confirms that this poet tended to work with texts in his brain.[34] Thus in his account in *Octavian* of a fight between a knight and an ape, Chestre added the following curious detail:

> The ape thorgh clodys and also hys schert,
> Brayde of hys pappys.
>
> (335–6)[35]

The Old French source, also known as *Octavian*, has nothing equivalent, yet the same detail is found earlier on in the French romance where it forms part of the empress's nightmare:

> . . . un aeigle l'auoit aerse
> Et l'abatoit tot en trauerse,
> Et ses mameles esrachoit.
>
> (251–3)

(An eagle had attacked her and thrown her down, and torn out her breasts.)

Not unlike the case of memorial transfer in *Eger and Grime*, a recurrence in theme (an animal attacks) has given rise to the transposition of textual material. Maldwyn Mills gives many more examples of such fusions of originally distinct motifs in Chestre's oeuvre, and reasonably concludes that they 'could only have taken place in a work composed from memory' (Mills 1962, 91). And the extent of that memory might have made a professional minstrel jealous. Among his minor sources we can number a version of *Graelent* and numerous English romances (*Arthour and Merlin*, *Sir Tristrem*, *Guy of Warwick*, *Lai le Freine* and *Landevale*). Verbal and thematic similarities between the story he was working on and these other romances again appear to have activated Chestre's memory of this extraneous material, and by conscious or unconscious association lines or plot motifs from minor sources found a place in Chestre's intertextual mosaic.

Do these facts make Chestre a '*disour*' or a 'professional hack writer'? If the former, he was a literate *disour* who wrote down his romances and had access to written sources; if the latter, he had memorized a substantial number of romances, which he re-composed from memory. Like the texts of Middle English romances, their composers refuse to be confined to a world that is either literate or oral, for the simple reason that their world was both.

The way beyond the deadlock in the debate between the romantics and the revisionists therefore lies not in any attempt to reconcile their contradictions but, more challengingly, in the attempt to imagine ourselves back in a culture for which the terms oral/written, reading/recitation, minstrel/scribe, *disour*/hack writer were not yet contradictory as they seem to us. As Nancy Mason Bradbury puts it:

> The history of romances bears out Brian Stock's claim that the great transition of the Middle Ages 'was not so much from oral *to* written as from an earlier state, predominantly oral, to various combinations of oral *and* written.' By embodying the combined effects of improvisation, memory, performance, and writing, the romances re-enact for us the complexities of late medieval orality and literacy.
>
> (Bradbury 1994, 41)[36]

A Theoretical Introduction

JANE GILBERT

The first half of this introduction discussed what we know of the historical circumstances of Middle English popular romances' production, transmission and reception. This second half is concerned with their evaluation within literary criticism. To say that this evaluation has been unfavourable would be putting the case mildly. I shall outline below in more detail the charges levelled against the popular romances. For the moment, suffice it to say that the usual answer to the question 'why should literary critics read Middle English popular romances?' is that they are medieval cultural artefacts, and that as medievalists, we should be interested in every aspect of that culture. This argument, however worthy, has notably failed to convince. Life, medievalist literary critics generally seem to have felt, is too short to waste time on such mediocrities; there is more important work to be done on quality texts.

The times, however, are changing. In recent years, the popular romances have aroused more interest, and interest of differing sorts. Critics have begun to ask about the sorts of meanings we might uncover in the romances, and about the reading methods which would be appropriate to them. The essays in this volume form part of this new movement. Each gives detailed consideration to a particular romance, posing it questions, listening to its answers. What emerges, apart from interpretations of specific texts, is a range of new reasons and new methods for reading the popular romances. In this theoretical introduction, I wish to suggest some contexts in which those readings can fruitfully be placed: the contexts of modern thinking on the 'popular', of medieval studies, and of the contemporary institution and practice of literary criticism.

Popular Culture

What concerns me here is not what 'popular' meant in the Middle Ages, but what it means today. What is at stake for modern critics in the designation 'popular'? To answer this question, we need to look at how the terms 'popular' and 'popular culture' have been used. My analysis, which draws on work done under the aegis of sociology and of cultural studies (a discipline established with the specific aim – among others – of studying the popular), reveals three main, relevant senses of 'popular culture', and I shall examine these in turn, before situating in relation to them the critical reception of the Middle English popular romances.

A useful starting point in such matters remains Raymond Williams's *Keywords*, a historical account of the connotations carried by numerous ideologically charged terms. Williams begins his discussion of the word 'popular' with the statement: '**Popular** was originally a legal and political term, from *popularis*, L – belonging to the people' (Williams 1983, 236). Neutral and technical in its origins, the term nevertheless quickly acquired a pejorative sense, with the additional meanings of ' "low" or "base" ' (Williams 1983, 236) attested from the sixteenth century. It is clear that for this earlier sense to have evolved into the modern meaning, which Williams gives as ' "widely favoured" or "well-liked" ' (Williams 1983, 236; meanings attested from the late eighteenth century onwards), a major shift in political affiliation must have occurred. An elitist contempt for the great unwashed has been transformed into a democratic approval for the favourites of the many. For the first time, with the appearance of the modern meaning, '**Popular** was being seen from the point of view of the people rather than from those seeking favour or power from them' (Williams 1983, 237).

Despite this general semantic shift, the pejorative sense of 'popular' lingers on today in the context of culture:

> **Popular culture** was not identified by *the people* but by others, and it still carries two older senses: inferior kinds of work (cf. **popular literature**, **popular press** as distinguished from *quality press*); and work deliberately setting out to win favour (**popular journalism** as distinguished from *democratic journalism*, or **popular entertainment**); as well as the modern sense of well-liked by many people, with which, of course, in many cases, the earlier senses overlap. The sense of **popular culture** as the culture actually made by people for themselves is different from all these.
>
> (Williams 1983, 237)

The first of these 'older senses' gives the key to what is perhaps the most common usage of the term 'popular culture'. Popular culture is inferior, substandard culture: 'a residual category, there to accommodate cultural texts and practices which fail to meet the required standards to qualify as high culture' (Storey 1993, 7). According to this view, the artistic conception motivating popular culture is crude and its execution incompetent, while the conceptual value is negligible: popular culture presents simple ideas in a simple way. Completely opposed to this version of popular culture, indeed its photographic negative, is the construct I will call 'quality culture'. Quality cultural products are viewed as aesthetically sophisticated and skilfully executed, conceptually subtle and far-sighted, often politically exploratory or liberal (in contrast to the supposed unimaginative conservatism of popular culture). Despite being purportedly apolitical, the distinction between popular and quality culture centrally incorporates an element of social class: by definition, 'popular culture' is enjoyed primarily by 'the people', while quality culture is the preserve of a social and intellectual elite. 'The people' here are thus constructed negatively, by what they lack: aesthetic discrimination and conceptual sophistication. In this first, 'substandard' version, then, 'popular culture' is a nexus in which the inferior aesthetic standard of the work reflects and reinforces the low social and cultural status of the audience.

The second 'older sense' which, Williams proposes, is still often given to 'popular culture' is that of 'work deliberately setting out to win favour'. This 'mass culture theory' draws on the 'substandard', but takes it further, and has a somewhat different attitude towards the popular. The 'substandard' theory views popular culture with a sort of benign disdain. Lowly as it is, popular culture is appropriate to humble souls who would find grander fare indigestible. It may even be construed as paying a sort of homage to quality culture by recognizing its own inferiority, 'knowing its place' (and keeping 'the people' in theirs). The mass theory, by contrast, considers popular culture to be harmful both to its consumers and to society as a whole; and, moreover, to be deliberately, strategically so. 'Mass produced for mass consumption' (Storey 1993, 10), this culture is above all commercial. Seeking to sell its products to the greatest possible number, it strives to produce a sort of cultural lowest common denominator: characterless, weightless pap which will offend none and be acceptable to all. It is also politically manipulative, endeavouring to persuade its audience to accept a particular political system, or to whip it up in support of a particular cause. In this view, the aesthetic inferiority of popular culture is no accident but a strategy. Mass culture's formulaic, unchallenging and simplistic nature is a key element in its goal of reducing its audience to undiscriminating passivity, a state in which it will literally and figuratively 'buy' any product aimed at it. The intentions of the person behind the production here become an issue. Whereas the quality work is created by an artist motivated by a love of art for art's sake, the popular work is produced by an unscrupulous cynic, whose goal is the dumbing down of an entire population.[37] In the mass theory of popular culture, 'popular = mass = debased' (Ashley 1997, 35).

Both the substandard and mass theories of popular culture are generally invoked in support of specific political agendas. There is no exclusive alliance with left or right: both theories lend themselves equally to a frankly snobbish disdain for the lower orders and to a Marxian insistence on the false consciousness instilled in the people by ideology.[38] Whereas the 'substandard' view tends to regard the distinction between popular and quality culture as having existed in every historical period of the West, however, the 'mass' version generally goes hand in hand with nostalgia for a golden age before industrialization and urbanization. The popular culture which existed prior to these developments is supposed to have been something quite other, and much more positively valuable; mass culture is considered to represent the degradation undergone by the popular as a result of modern Western social forms.

A third definition of popular culture has an almost contrary sense to the first two: in it, audience, politics and aesthetics are all quite differently valued. The audience of undiscriminating clods postulated by the substandard and mass theories is replaced with one capable of both aesthetic and conceptual discrimination. Furthermore, this popular audience is viewed approvingly as the salt of the earth, at once the most important and the most worthy element of society. Popular culture becomes the authentic voice of this audience, beyond an officialdom which would suppress it: this is the meaning of Williams's 'culture actually made by people for themselves'. An aesthetic revaluation of sorts accompanies this political revision. The people's culture expresses the people's native genius, and is praised for qualities such as vitality, vigour, even virility. The art (as it may in this version be considered) thus produced is acclaimed as powerful and elemental, rawly primitive and monumental (terms with less pejorative connotations than 'crude', but which designate substantially similar things).[39] This third notion of popular culture we shall call the 'folk' version.[40] It often includes an idealization of the past similar to that seen in mass culture theory: thus, folk culture may be seen as the product (exclusively or primarily) of the pre-industrial period, with all popular culture produced since that time being debased. When folk is admitted to exist in the present it is generally in implicit or explicit resistance to modern, debased (often 'mass') culture.[41] The folk culture theory can be employed in the service of a conservative politics nostalgic for a time of order and settled hierarchy or, equally well, in the context of a faith in the people's irrepressible revolutionary potential.[42]

Popular Romance

These, then, are the principal senses in which the term 'popular culture' is encountered today.[43] Which is carried in the phrase, 'Middle English popular romances'? There is no straightforward answer. Certain romances have been viewed as 'popular' in one sense, others as 'popular' in a different sense. If we are to generalize, however, we may say that the popular romances as a group were at one time approached as 'folk' productions, but have more recently been viewed as 'substandard', and even 'mass' works. As is well known, modern study and appreciation of medieval culture began as an interest in folk art. It originated in the Romantic revaluation of northern European and medieval culture in reaction against the Renaissance and classical periods, which had privileged southern Europe and classical antiquity and had designated the medieval north 'Gothic' (a word originally carrying much the same overtones as our modern 'vandal'). The Romantic aesthetic gave a new value to what were seen as qualities native to the north, among them creative disorder, intimacy with nature and a particular version of masculinity. Whereas a writer such as Chaucer was quickly recognized as an elite and official writer in touch with Italian developments (a perception which simultaneously added to and subtracted from his value), popular works were considered to be authentic expressions of the spirit of the Germanic peoples of northern Europe. The popular romances were celebrated as precious survivals of an age wherein flourished virtues and aims, forms of art and society, lost to modern man.[44]

Although praise for the vigour and vitality of some romances is still occasionally to be found, the appreciation of them as folk culture is at present effectively no more: it is itself a relic of a former age. As the folk perception has faded, so the less ambivalent view of the popular romances as substandard has spread. Many of the contributors to this volume draw attention to the poor reputation of the romance they are studying; others could have done the same. In this century at least, the popular romances have been characterized above all negatively, by their failure to meet such desirable literary criteria as formal complexity and conceptual sophistication.[45] They have also been defined by their audience, similarly considered second-rate by comparison with that which sponsored and enjoyed the quality works we prize today. Popular romances have been the less interesting to the literary critic because their audience is said to have no significant overlap with that of quality romance. Within this general view of the popular romances as substandard there have appeared at times – and perhaps appear increasingly – elements specifically characteristic of the 'mass' model. For example, the hack professional scribe, trotting out work after work designed solely to give his patrons undemanding pleasure, bears striking similarities to the producer of the modern popular novel.[46] Also reminiscent of the 'mass' model is the view that the political function of the Middle English romances is to sell or 'euphemize' chivalric life to a squirarchy bound to admire its glamour from a safe social distance (Knight 1986b). In this perspective, the most that a popular romance can offer the modern critic is a glimpse of the mentality of its consumers, medieval England's lumpen lowbrows.[47]

These have been the traditional approaches to the Middle English popular romances. In recent years, however, such approaches have inspired growing dissatisfaction, and this dissatisfaction has in turn led to the development of new treatments and methodologies. Elitism and nostalgia are disappearing from the literary criticism of popular romances, as is the old focus on their 'poor' or 'primitive' aesthetic quality. These changes are in line with modern intellectual currents, which have brought a new interest in popular culture of many sorts and from many sources. The historically and theoretically specific textual readings in this volume are examples of these new directions. In the remainder of this introduction, I wish to outline how, in my view, these essays contribute to the ongoing task of reflecting on the construct known as 'Middle English popular romance'. I shall concentrate on two areas identified above as central to the appreciation of any production designated as part of popular culture: audience and artistic value.

Audience

Whereas they may differ on the question of aesthetic value, all the concepts of the 'popular' described above posit an audience 'of the people'. Some meat is put on the bones of 'the people' by the Historical Introduction to this volume. It will be clear from that discussion that the different circumstances of circulation and transmission of the romances imply a variety of different audiences, both for the genre as a whole and potentially for individual works. It will also be clear that popular romance audiences were not only drawn from the lower social ranks, but might also include those of higher status. The highest, even: Hasler cites James IV of Scotland, on record as having paid for a performance of 'Graysteil', probably a version of *Eger and Grime*. For the same reason, these audiences were not necessarily ignorant of or unable to appreciate finer productions: some works produced for the court filtered down the echelons of society (as, we know, did Chaucer's); some popular works evidently filtered up. Socially and aesthetically, some popular romance audiences at least also had 'quality'.

If historical audiences are difficult to categorize, things are still more complicated when it comes to audience as an interpretative criterion – which is my primary concern here. Critics of many different persuasions invoke the responses of audience or reader in support of particular interpretations of a text. The range of phenomena referred to is vast. It covers a huge scale, extending from the idealized, literary-critical concept of the implied reader constructed by and in the text, to any of the specific, concrete groups of listeners who may have formed the actual, historical audience at a particular performance (whether contemporary with the text or later), with any number of points in between these two extremes.[48] The responses of these various 'audiences' to any single text will not necessarily be the same; indeed, they may be sharply contrasting.[49] Determining the reactions of these distinct audiences requires different methodologies: a hermeneutic approach is needed to reconstruct the 'implied reader', whereas actual listeners and readers require investigation through external evidence. Thus, any number of critical approaches may be signified by (often apparently subtly) different inflections of the single term 'audience'.[50]

Even among those critics who take the historical audience as the basis of their interpretations, there is disagreement: which of various 'historical audiences' is most significant? At a simple level, this may be a matter of focus. For example, Stephen Greenblatt illustrates the difference of New Historicism from older historicist ways of reading by contrasting the appearance of a performance of Shakespeare's *Richard II* in the context of the attempted rebellion led by the Earl of Essex with Dover Wilson's carefully documented assertion that the play would be read by contemporaries as 'a hymn to Tudor order' (Greenblatt 1982, 4). Where Dover Wilson takes as the centre of his interpretative method the (generalized, implicit) Elizabethan audience, New Historicism replaces this with a series of particular Elizabethan audiences. Plurality and concreteness take over from singularity and abstraction; at the same time, the political focus of the interpretation shifts, from consensus and order to conflict and resistance. When New Historicism adduces historical evidence of audience response, then, it is with a particular agenda in mind: its practitioners do not seek only to endorse existing readings, but to find new ones.[51] Hence, different historical (and differently historical) audiences may be highlighted, depending on the type of interpretation which attracts the critic in question.[52] Whatever the historical truth about an audience, any construction of it will necessarily have resonances for and engage with the political investments of today's intellectual elite.

To posit an audience is thus to engage with questions of reading as well as of history. And the designation of the popular romances' audience as one 'of the people' has, for the most part, had a deadening effect on interpretation of the texts. The task which presses on critics today – of finding different interpretative frameworks for the romances – is therefore likely to require a renegotiation of the question of audience. This is the challenge: to construct new reading-positions while respecting the available historical evidence. In the essays collected here, the reader will nowhere find the stereotypical views of the popular romance audience: as a harmonious community of all ranks; as lower-rank simpletons incapable of discrimination; as passive consumers easily manipulated. Although the contributors to this volume do not all comment explicitly on audience, each of them finds a way of reading which allows the text to be other than artistically inept, and thus steps beyond the dominant modern stereotype of the popular work. They treat the romances as strategic interventions, in which power relations are negotiated, reinforced and challenged. The texts' social positions are shown to be complex: evidently marginal to aristocratic culture, yet in different ways deeply involved with aristocratic ideology. In my view, the essays collected here illustrate three main variants of this involvement, which may be classified as follows: the critique of dominance; the critique of marginality; and the intricate interweaving of the popular and the elite.

Without subscribing to the 'folk' theory of popular culture, we can recognize that works designated as 'popular' may offer a perspective somewhat different from that of strictly elite productions. They may even provide grounds for a critique of such productions. In this volume, the essays by McDonald and Hasler show how some popular romances can be used, precisely by virtue of their position on the periphery of aristocratic ideology, to uncover what such ideology sets out to hide. Both critics analyse the system of homosocial male bonding and exchange of women which underlies the myth of 'courtly love', despite that myth's claim to elevate women to a position of authority. McDonald refers to work in anthropology and economics to show how *The Seege of Troye* reveals that the lady desired and sought by questing knights takes her greatest value not from erotic interest, but from economic and social considerations: she is an object to be bartered for wealth, a prize in a power game played out between men. Discussing *Eger and Grime* (a romance apparently appreciated by medieval connoisseurs but considered by modern critics to be a failure), Hasler analyses how the text's very incoherences reveal that courtly love and chivalric activity are mystifications of a basic political programme: the consolidation of male bonds and the subordination of women. Hasler's psychoanalytic approach goes further, however, showing how *Eger* also lays bare the anxiety about emptiness and loss which this programme generates, and which lies beneath even the most assertive of chivalric texts. In both these analyses, the old charge that popular romances lack subtlety and delicacy is exploited, but diverted from its traditional use of shoring up the distinction between popular and quality works. It is argued that exploitation is at the heart of the courtly agenda; texts of greater 'quality', more securely lodged within aristocratic circles than are the 'popular' works, appear above all to be more successful in covering their ideological tracks.

Shippey uses *Gamelyn* to make a similar point about Chaucer, perhaps the archetypal 'quality' writer of medieval English literature. Drawing on both external and internal evidence, Shippey shows how Chaucer's consistently unfavourable representations of the yeomanry are part of a political struggle. Yeomen and well-connected civil servants like Chaucer are 'class enemies' competing for a similar position and similar patronage, and each group, in its way, exerts itself in aggression against the other. Chaucer's political position is thus argued to be that of an upwardly mobile bureaucrat attempting to harness aristocratic prestige and prejudice against an enemy which, while threatening to his own group, presents no risk to the aristocracy itself. It is perhaps not surprising that academics, who today occupy social positions similar to Chaucer's in his time, have found his snobbery about yeomen and popular romances immensely congenial, and have reproduced his bias in their contemptuous pronouncements on romances such as *Gamelyn*.[53] As Shippey suggests, the 'father of English poetry' may also be the father of some of our prejudices.[54]

It is fairly certain that we will not hear, in those Middle English popular romances which survive, the unmediated voice of radically marginalized, oppressed groups: the fact that a romance was committed to writing already bespeaks a certain level of privilege. However, as the essays in this volume show, the social groups whose specific concerns are addressed by many popular romances are often not in the most powerful or central positions of their society. Without necessarily being produced exclusively for such persons, a text can nevertheless offer certain insights into their social condition. Whereas some romances speak for distinct classes (as *Gamelyn* does for the yeomanry), others appear to put forward the interests of persons who formed part of the dominant group, but were relatively disenfranchised within that group. When the interests of such persons were not served by quality texts, 'popular' style might offer an opportunity for expressing their exclusion from full power and full representation.[55] We can take the example of women, since they feature in many of the essays in this volume. Women formed part of romance audiences at all levels of medieval society (Meale 1994), from the elite to the lowly. As argued by McDonald and Hasler (and as increasingly recognized in recent years), however, the courtly ideology espoused by the aristocracy and voiced in quality romance texts did women little service. Several of the contributors here demonstrate the mismatch in the romances they study between the female subject and the masculine order. Archibald shows how, in what can be read as a form of passive resistance, *Lai le Fresne* does not – or refuses to – reinscribe narrative expectations which express male but not female experience; while Spearing draws on feminist readings of classic Hollywood cinema to argue that Heurodis's abduction by fairies in *Sir Orfeo* is a metaphor for madness produced in her by a male system which does not fit her needs. My own essay draws attention to the distance which separates woman from 'the feminine', and analyses how the heroine of *Sir Tristrem* manipulates her society's repressive constitution of femininity so that it works against itself and serves her ends. Writing on *The Awntyrs off Arthure*, Robson argues that both the physicality and the femaleness of the dead body at the heart of the narrative remain so difficult to assimilate – so basically unacceptable – that they tend to slip from sight even in analyses which set out to focus on them.

All these interpretations show how partial and male-centred conventional interpretations of the romances studied have been. By implicitly reconstructing what may have been the experience of the women who formed a large part of the medieval romance audience, these essays at once offer a new, female-centred 'implied reader' and break down the boundary which traditionally separates that internal, critical construction from the external, historical audience.[56] Such readings can, of course, adduce little conclusive historical evidence in their cause; but, as the Historical Introduction above shows in relation to oral performance, we ought not to dismiss audiences we know existed, simply because they have left few traces and are therefore frustratingly difficult of access. If the argument is true for audience as a historical category, it is even more true where the interpretative category is concerned.

Popular romances as a group were once considered to be simple and trite, but the essays in this volume paint a very different picture. On close study, a multiplicity of inscribed reader-positions and ideological identifications emerges from these texts. The sheer complexity of the implications baffles attempts to place the texts within a reductive opposition between 'popular' and 'quality'. Perhaps the most striking examples exposed here are in the essays of Fowler, Diamond and Simpson. In *Sir Isumbras*, the subject of Fowler's essay, the hero begins as a knight before becoming a pauper, pilgrim, blacksmith, a knight once more, and finally a king. What relationships to an audience might we posit here? Fowler shows how the concern for consent and dominion runs through the text, appearing in the varied contexts of conquest, marriage, creed and penance. The mixture of theological, aristocratic, domestic and legal perspectives here complicates our determination of the text's origin(s), destination(s) and meaning(s). Similar complexity is analysed in Diamond's discussion of *William of Palerne*. Diamond draws out the effects of the poem's difference from its French source: for example, of the descriptions of common life which were added or amplified. The distinctive treatment accorded by the English poet to the cast of characters extends the poem's implied readership across different levels of society. This produces a communitarian ethos which apparently allows both sympathetic contact between classes and a certain social mobility. Although the poem defines nobility as an ethical ideal to which people of any rank may attain, it finally resolves in favour of the existing hierarchy. The vision of a happy community in which all fulfil their allotted duties has often been ascribed to the popular romances; ironically, it appears here under the patronage of Earl Humphrey de Bohun as the expression of a deeply conservative, aristocratic ideology.

The notion that so-called 'popular' romances necessarily espouse an obviously 'popular' ideology is further debunked here in Simpson's essay. Simpson analyses the relations pertaining between proper name, property and propriety as a way of unpacking the political positions of three romances. These are united by their narrative theme of anonymous adventuring, but strikingly different in other respects: *Sir Degaré* is 'popular' and the *Folie Tristan d'Oxford* 'courtly', while Malory's 'Tale of Sir Gareth of Orkney' could be considered to be ambiguously placed within this opposition.[57] Although *Degaré* and 'Gareth' appear to be questioning the equation of noble birth with moral worth by setting up narratives in which an anonymous man has to prove his value independently of his genealogy, their supposedly self-made heroes ultimately turn out to have been noble all along. Thus the qualities they have demonstrated throughout the narrative merely confirm the superiority aristocratic blood affords. Only the courtly *Folie* fails to subscribe to the aristocratic myth of innate nobility. Here, proper name is used to undermine the notion of property, which (as Simpson shows) it supposedly guarantees: Tristan, unlike Degaré or Gareth, is condemned from birth to be forever dispossessed.

In each of these essays, a principal point of interest is the intermingling of elements we ascribe to different social classes. It emerges that aristocratic male ideology can be put to a range of uses, none of which necessarily has the interests of aristocratic men exactly at heart. The relationship of 'popular' to 'quality' is clearly more complex than has generally been admitted.

Artistic Value

Over the past half-century, there has been an increasing tendency to question the conventional Western artistic canon. The charge has been made that the absence from that canon of almost any figure who is not (to cite the familiar list) European, white, Christian, heterosexual, male and of a certain social standing, is neither accidental nor insignificant. Commentators have shown how traditional Western aesthetics operates in terms of social class, gender, sexuality, religion, race and ethnicity.[58] Aesthetic theory has been shown to be inseparable from issues of power, cultural practices and productions to be at once an effective political tool and an important arena for political struggle. Pierre Bourdieu's monumental 'social critique of the judgement of taste' (the subtitle of Bourdieu 1984) in France demonstrates how even apparently individual preferences (such as whether a sunset or cabbages would make the more beautiful photograph) function as codes which situate the chooser within the gradations of the social hierarchy. Our every judgement is a 'distinction' in the sense that it distinguishes the social group to which we belong from the other groups that surround us.[59]

As the canon has been subjected to revision, so have methods of interpretation and evaluation. In former times, aesthetic value was supposed to be a constant, its criteria applicable equally to all historical periods and to all societies. In those days, the critic's job was twofold: to contribute to the ongoing task of articulating the timeless, universal features of true art, and to study particular works with the aim of determining their place on the scale of absolute value. This project is now generally considered to be outdated. Today, the terms governing artistic endeavour are believed to be culturally specific, neither transparent to the eye of a godlike observer (white, male and so on: the critic comes from the same mould as the canonical artist), nor necessarily inferior to the criteria that godlike observer himself espouses. Different social groups – both groups occupying different positions within a society and groups belonging to other societies – may use different aesthetic conventions, and these conventions can mark their difference, and even their dissent, from the politically dominant group. If works produced in this way are read solely in the light of the conventions familiar to the dominant group, however, then they may well appear unintelligible or of poor quality.[60] Certain critical approaches thus reinforce the cultural supremacy of the dominant group: their application to the culture of the dominated will tend to reproduce the view of that culture as inferior, even if such reproduction is not part of the critic's conscious agenda. Culture cannot help but be at once a weapon and a battleground in the struggle for social status; we must therefore examine with care our approaches to it. Today, those working on cultural texts of all sorts acknowledge the need to elaborate new ways of reading in order to realize the design of appreciating unfamiliar or dominated cultures positively. One of the most interesting and rewarding developments of recent literary criticism has been the search for approaches which will facilitate these projects. The methods developed for use in these areas often leave evaluation aside altogether. This does not marginalize them within literary criticism: on the contrary, most work on canonical texts today also prefers to explore what and how texts mean – using, for example, historicist, post-structuralist or psychoanalytic approaches – rather than to assess their artistic value.

A further incentive for questioning the distinction between quality and popular culture must be the difficulty of establishing that distinction in practice. Practitioners of cultural studies delight in pointing out the problems which beset the unwary person who attempts to decide in which category many individual texts should be placed (one of many examples is Storey 1993, 8–10). If the decision is a problematic one as regards contemporary texts, it is the more difficult where the past is concerned. Stuart Hall argues that we cannot assume that because a work or practice may be considered 'popular' in one society at one historical moment, it should be so considered at other moments or in other societies. For Hall, what is permanent is the 'opposition which constantly structures the domain of culture into the "popular" and the "non-popular"' (Hall 1981, 234).[61] Although its specific content changes, the opposition itself is constantly renewed, supported as it is by a wide range of institutions and their practices (such as education and literary criticism).

In the case of medieval romance, the problem of classification is complicated by the introduction of another term: the courtly. Designating as it does at once high artistic value and an audience of elevated social rank, 'courtliness' in a text is to some extent synonymous with 'quality'. In another context, however, courtliness means something quite specific: a certain setting, characters and events in the narrative, a particular system of values evoked, a precise set of expectations in the audience. The resulting slippage between these usages of the words 'popular' and 'courtly' is neatly illustrated by the debate between critics about whether Earl Humphrey de Bohun, to whom *William of Palerne* is dedicated, did or did not take an active interest in this romance. Readers who have liked the romance have labelled it 'courtly' and have played up its association with its prestigious dedicatee, while readers who consider the romance 'banal' argue that it 'comes nearer to the popular romances' and conclude that 'perhaps it was intended for the kitchen staff'.[62] On either side of the argument, the seemingly empirical question of *William of Palerne*'s audience, its courtliness or popularity, has ultimately been decided by the critic's taste.

Further slippage is made possible by the fact that, while the words 'courtly' and 'popular' purport to describe objective matters subject to ongoing literary and historical scholarship, they also form part of our present-day vocabulary of social distinction (and few if any critics are immune to anxieties about status). In theory, we all know full well that medieval *courtoisie* is not modern courtesy. In practice, however, the transfer of values does tend to occur, especially in the generally little regarded domain of popular romance. Here deprecation is the order of the day, and at times it seems to matter little what sources of disparagement are drawn upon. In her essay here, Stokes investigates in detail the meanings of 'popular' and 'courtly' in two particular instances by means of a close comparison between the popular English *Sir Launfal* and the courtly French *Lanval*. Her conclusions reveal points at which modern critics have occasionally, and no doubt unwittingly, exported their own notions of politeness into their assessments of the text. *Launfal* emerges as less skilful, but Stokes shows that the spirit of materialism (nowadays considered vulgar, 'of the people'), which critics have found in *Launfal*, is actually espoused openly and unembarrassedly by the courtly Marie de France. By drawing attention to the contradictory ways in which the words 'popular' and 'courtly' are used, and by outlining the senses in which Marie's *Lanval* could be described as more 'popular' than *Launfal* (on account of *Lanval*'s wider dissemination and its unabashed economic realism), Stokes's essay shows us that such slippage can be avoided by careful attention to what one sees and to how one expresses it.

The courtly is the dominant other of medieval popular romance, influencing its reception in many ways. As several of the contributors to this volume note (Diamond, Archibald, McDonald, Shippey), the perception of quality is to some extent a function of genre, and a contributing factor in the deprecation of the popular romances' artistic worth has been the fact that they do not fit standard modern definitions of medieval romance. As is also noted, these definitions have typically privileged courtly romance; when popular romances are mentioned, it is chiefly as unclassifiable monstrosities, failed or lacking in some crucial respect. More recently, however, such prescriptiveness has lost critical favour. It is acknowledged as absurd for critics to impose an externally derived pattern onto an existing body of texts and then to dismiss as inadequate or anomalous those texts which do not fit that pattern. The essays included here find meaning in, rather than outside of, the conventions used by the romances themselves. One approach is via comparison with courtly texts. As it is shown by the essays of Archibald, Stokes, Simpson and Shippey, this method does not necessarily imply simple consent to the commonly accepted criteria of courtly romance: it can open up new, much more precise ways of reading both popular and quality works. A radical and strikingly successful solution to the search for new contextual frameworks in which to read the romances is demonstrated by Spearing: his essay draws on film studies to find a method and an analogue appropriate to *Sir Orfeo*, thus showing how enriching can be the comparison of popular cultural artefacts from two very different periods. A further strategy for allowing the popular romances to be meaningful is to tackle head-on the poor reputation of particular works, and demonstrate that the incoherences and inconsistencies which supposedly riddle these texts appear primarily when they are insensitively read. Diamond, Shippey, Simpson and Stokes all follow this path: they show how the texts they discuss, even if not great art, are intelligent and competent works which achieve plausible ends with a certain degree of skill. Alternatively, what is usually seen as the romances' lack of courtliness may be transformed into the basis for a positive reading: thus Hasler, McDonald and Robson all argue that the romances they study express a critique of the courtly system which is not hampered but enabled by the texts' reputed insufficiencies – their aporias and lack of connectedness. Putter goes a step further with the failures of narrative structure and characterization commonly seen in *Emaré*. His study of repetition in the poem brings together narratological, philosophical and psychoanalytic perspectives to suggest alternative ways of understanding how the narrative might work and to give the characters a psychological depth which yet does not stem from conventional (and anachronistic) notions of individuality. Here, as throughout the collection, there are significant implications for the reading of other medieval narratives.

All these approaches allow the Middle English popular romances to be meaningful by suspending or reworking conventional aesthetic criteria. Time and again, it is evident that the greatest obstacle to appreciating the Middle English popular romances is a restricted definition of aesthetic value which, too often, confirms a pre-existing prejudice about their worthlessness. The contributors to this volume use up-to-date, non-evaluative critical methods, which allow them to study both what and how the romances mean; thus the interpretations elaborated here bring out the strongest, not the weakest, sides of these texts.

I am not, however, urging the abandonment of quality as a criterion in literary criticism. On the contrary, the essays collected here illustrate how far the enterprise of constructing the meaning of a text depends on a certain presumption of competence. Each contributor takes their text seriously, in the sense that they accord it the same degree of respect – and disrespect

– they would bring to a 'quality' product. Endeavouring to discover the programme and principles that lie behind a work requires us to assume that the work is at least reasonably successful in its own terms. To come to a text with the opposite assumption, of the inferiority of its design and poverty of its execution (as Middle English popular romances have so often been approached), is a sure route to missing altogether any point the text may have. Only if we are willing to risk presupposing a basic competence will we ever be able to revise our aesthetic principles to the extent necessary if we are to understand works produced in cultural contexts different from our own. In particular, the sorts of meaning discussed in the previous section – the meanings of those who are not the dominant group – depend on such a presupposition, without which they will remain incoherent or eccentric. We need, therefore, to find ways of talking about popular works having positive qualities which are yet not wholly contained within the ideological nexus here called 'quality'. This need will not be met if we refuse to discuss the issue altogether.

In another respect, too, the spectre of quality is not so simply exorcized. Most critics do what they do because they enjoy the works they read, and works which are beautifully written afford a special pleasure. Whereas popular works typically elicit from the critic either silence or laughter (Ashley 1997, 1–5), quality texts nourish a rich multiplicity of appreciative critical discourses. The *raison d'être* of criticism was traditionally the discernment of quality, and even when this project is apparently put aside, the desire for quality tends to return in disguised forms. Even those who call vociferously for the abolition of the canon often find it harder to break away from it in practice than in theory. Raymond Williams, for example, wrote for the most part on canonical authors and texts, while advocating the study of popular works as a central project of democratic criticism. In a different vein, the 'low' culture of popular works is not infrequently approached via the 'high' culture of esoteric theory. Thus Slavoj Žižek, one of the most high-profile of contemporary cultural studies practitioners, makes it clear that, when he 'indulg[es] in the idiotic enjoyment of popular culture' (Žižek 1991, viii), his real object is to explicate the difficult and prestigious theories of Lacan. This statement confirms the 'mass' theory of popular culture as degraded, while redeeming the loss of intellectual status potentially involved in writing about that 'idiotic' culture by superimposing onto it a highly sophisticated and complex theoretical framework. An alternative strategy often employed in order to reconcile the study of popular culture with academic dignity is to elevate the non-canonical text under investigation to canonical status, insisting that it does in fact meet accepted aesthetic criteria. What is claimed to be the abandonment of the traditional canon often turns out to be its extension, as ever more quality is discovered where one might least expect it. Such a practice constitutes no critique of the canon *per se*, but instead confirms it. In these various ways, criticism of popular culture demonstrates time and again that it is not so easy to renounce what Bourdieu calls 'cultural capital'. Although we may give up aesthetic criteria once held dear, 'quality', in a barely reconstructed version of old-fashioned 'high' culture, tends to creep back in by one means or another.

For all these reasons, I should like to propose a different way of approaching the issue of quality, via the work of Gayatri Chakravorty Spivak. Working in the context of post-colonialism, Spivak argues that the benefits that imperialism can confer – such as an elite education straddling different worlds, and a lingua franca enabling communication with people from other colonized countries – are not to be despised (only those who are in no danger of losing privilege can afford the luxury of disdaining it). Third World intellectuals (such as Spivak herself) need not – indeed cannot – reject altogether the culture of imperialism if they are to exercise an effective critique of imperialism. The task is therefore to exploit the positive potential offered by imperialism, while yet retaining a distance from the intellectual and emotional positions that imperialism normally implies. In Spivak's own terms, what is required is 'a persistent critique of what one cannot not want' (Landry and MacLean 1996, 28). Adapting this model, I wish to suggest that 'quality' may be something that literary critics 'cannot not want'. Because the nexus of 'quality' combines aesthetic, intellectual, institutional and social concerns, it is the principal mediator of professional self-respect and prestige for critics. The desire for 'quality' would thus be inherent in the discipline of literary criticism, one of its conditions of possibility. Its practitioners would not be able to cast this desire aside without ceasing to be literary critics (becoming, perhaps, cultural critics instead).[63] If this model is accepted, then our goal should not be the rejection of quality as such, but the persistent critique of quality and of the desire for it – each of which should be regarded as integral to a structure that, as literary critics, we 'cannot not (wish to) inhabit' (Spivak 1993, 284). This imperative addresses all critics alike, both those who wish to do away with the notion of literary value and those who wish to preserve it.

Notes

1   On the common characteristics of the Middle English romances see Everett 1955 and Hume 1974. Finlayson 1980–81 thinks the term 'romance' should be restricted to narratives about knights riding forth to achieve adventure. On this definition, almost half of the texts conventionally referred to as 'romances'

would have to be excluded from the corpus. On the problems raised by Finlayson's definition of romance see also Archibald, pp. 41–2 below.

2 An essential resource for the study of romance manuscripts is Gisela Guddat-Figge's *Catalogue of Manuscripts Containing Middle English Romances* (1976). See also Meale 1994.

3 Apart from saints' lives, homiletic material, religious and humorous poems, the Auchinleck manuscript contains the romances of *King Tars*, *Amis and Amiloun*, *Sir Degaré*, *Floris and Blanchefleur*, *Guy of Warwick*, *Bevis of Hampton*, *Arthour and Merlin*, *Lai le Freine*, *Roland and Vernagu*, *Otuel*, *King Alisaunder*, *Sir Tristrem*, *Sir Orfeo*, *Horn Child* and *Richard Coer de Lyon*.

4 This miscellany of religious, instructive and secular works contains the *Prose Alexander*, *Alliterative Morte Arthure*, *Octavian* (northern version), *Isumbras*, *Earl of Toulous*, *Sir Degrevant*, *Sir Eglamour*, *Awntyrs off Arthure* and *Perceval of Galles*.

5 The romances *Earl of Toulous*, *Sir Eglamour*, *Sir Triamour*, *Octavian*, *Bevis of Hampton*, *Guy of Warwick*, *Le Bone Florence*, *Robert of Sicily* and *Sir Degaré* occupy the final section of this manuscript, which is otherwise devoted to literature of moral improvement.

6 This, too, contains a mixture of the practical, the devotional and the entertaining. The romances in it are *Eglamour of Artois*, *Octavian* (southern version), *Launfal*, *Libeaus Desconus*, *Emaré*, *Seege of Jerusalem*, *Chevalere Assigne* and *Isumbras*.

7 *Auchinleck Manuscript: National Library of Scotland, Advocates' MS 19.2.1*, ed. Derek Pearsall and I. C. Cunningham (London: Scolar Press, 1977) *Thornton Manuscript (Lincoln Cathedral MS 91)*, ed. Derek Brewer and A. E. B. Owen (London: Scolar Press, 1975) and *Cambridge University Library, MS Ff.2.38*, ed. Frances McSparran and P. R. Robinson (London: Scolar Press, 1979). All three editions contain valuable introductions dealing with questions of audience and authorship.

8 The manuscript has received detailed attention in Blanchfield 1991 and 1996.

9 On Advocates' 19.3.1 see Hardman 1978 and Turville-Petre 1983.

10 Thus the virtually unbroken sequence of romances in CUL Ff.2.38 – *Earl of Toulous*, *Eglamour*, *Sir Triamour*, *Octavian*, *Bevis of Hampton*, *Seven Sages*, *Guy of Warwick*, *Le Bone Florence*, *Robert of Sicily* and *Sir Degaré* – is reminiscent of a cluster in the Auchinleck manuscript: *Sir Degaré*, *Seven Sages*, *Floris and Blanchefleur*, *Guy of Warwick* and *Bevis of Hampton*. The list of seven romances contained in the late fourteenth-century romance anthology London, British Library, Egerton 2862 produces the same effect of *déjà vu*. With Auchinleck it shares *Richard Coer de Lyon*, *Bevis of Hampton*, *Sir Degaré*, *Floris and Blanchefleur* and *Amis and Amiloun*; and with CUL Ff.2.38 it shares *Degaré*, *Bevis* and *Eglamour*. Romances in post-medieval manuscripts still come in the same kinds of sequences. Thus Oxford, Bodleian, Douce 261 (dated 1564, now MS Bodley 21835) contains, in addition to the unique text of the *Jeaste of Sir Gawain*, the usual run of old-time favourites: *Sir Isumbras*, *Sir Degaré* and *Sir Eglamour*. The roll-call of romances in the Percy Folio, British Library, Add. MS 27879 (*c*.1650) – *Sir Lambewell* (a couplet version of the *Launfal* story), *Eger and Grime*, *Merline* (a version of *Arthour and Merlin*), *Sir Triamore*, *Eglamore*, *Sir Degree* (a debased version of *Sir Degaré*) and

Libius Disconius – is also reminiscent of the contents of medieval romance-anthologies (Rogers 1991).

11 The term 'bookshop' is used here as a convenient shorthand for a nexus of commercial bookmaking activities which were, in reality, not highly centralized. As argued by Doyle and Parkes 1978 and Shonk 1985, the commercial production of vernacular books was usually undertaken by a bookdealer or scribe who subcontracted work to independent scribes, illuminators and binders. Of the romance volumes mentioned above, Guddat-Figge signals the possibility of commercial production for the following: Auchinleck, Egerton 2862, Cotton Caligula A.ii and CUL Ff.2.38.

12 For information on this manuscript see Brewer and Owen 1975 and Thompson 1983.

13 Thus one exemplar, containing the *Alliterative Morte Arthur* and the *Privity of the Passion*, originated from Lincolnshire, while the series of romances copied consecutively by Thornton – *Octavian*, *Sir Isumbras* and the *Earl of Toulous* – may well have come from a booklet exemplar of the kind produced professionally in secular *scriptoria* (Thompson 1983, 119).

14 The strongest case for the clerical authorship of many surviving Middle English romances is Baugh 1950.

15 The fragment and the memorandum are printed in *Sir Ferumbras*, ed. Sidney J. Herrtage, EETS e.s. 34 (London: Trübner, 1879). For a discussion see Shepherd 1989.

16 See Baugh 1967 for examples.

17 Robert Mannyng of Brunne, *The Chronicle*, ed. Idelle Sullens (Binghamton, NY: Medieval and Renaissance Texts and Studies, 1996).

18 *Land Troy Book*, ed. J. E. Wülfing, EETS o.s. 121, 122 (London: Trübner, 1902).

19 Quoted in Baugh 1950, 10.

20 Thorlac Turville-Petre, ed., 'The Lament for Sir John Berkeley', *Speculum* 57 (1982), 332–9. It should be noted that the Middle English phrase 'reden romaunce' need not imply 'reading' in our sense, but is also found in the sense of 'telling a story' (Hoops 1929, 37–9).

21 Cf. Gower, *Confessio Amantis* II, 877–8: 'Min *Ere* with a good pitance / Is fedd of redinge of romance': *The English Works of John Gower*, ed. G. C. Macaulay, EETS e.s. 89, 91 (London: Oxford University Press, 1900–01).

22 Traces of apparent memorial transmission have been detected in at least one version of the following romances: *King Alisaunder* (Smithers 1957, II, 11–12), *Awntyrs off Arthure* (Allen 1987), *Arthour and Merlin* (Holland 1973), *Sir Isumbras* (Reichl 1991), *Beves of Hamtoun*, *Guy of Warwick* (Baugh 1959), *Libeaus Desconus* (Mills 1969), *Sir Degrevant* (Casson 1949, xvii–xxi), *King Horn* (Quinn and Hall 1982; McGillivray 1990), *Sir Orfeo*, *Seege of Troy*, *Floris and Blanchefleur* (McGillivray 1990), *Sir Degaré* (Jacobs 1995, 63, 96, 98, 108) and *Richard Coer de Lyon* (Baugh 1967, 30–31).

23 *Eger and Grime*, ed. J. R. Caldwell (Cambridge, MA: Harvard University Press, 1933), p. 6. For further discussion of the text and logic of this romance see Antony J. Hasler's essay in this collection.

24 *La Bataille Loquifer*, ed. Monica Barnett (Oxford: Society for the Study of Medieval Languages and Literature, 1975). The possible identities of Jendeus de Brie and Count William are discussed at pp. 29–30 of this edition.

25 *'Lancelot of the Laik' and 'Sir Tristrem'*, ed. Alan Lupack, TEAMS (Kalamazoo, MI: Medieval Institute Publications, 1994).

26 Probably a public recital is meant: 'in toun' (10) usually means 'in company' in these contexts.

27 The attribution to the Scottish poet Thomas of Erceldoune may be spurious, since the dialect of the poem is not Scottish (McIntosh 1989). There may be some confusion with the Anglo-Norman 'Thomas' who wrote the *Tristan* on which *Tristrem* is based. The spelling 'Ertheldoun', presumably due to confusion of t and c, points to a stage of scribal transmission in the history of the text.

28 On *Emaré* and Cotton Caligula A.ii see Guddat-Figge 1976, 50 and Thompson 1996. The orality of this romance is discussed below, pp. 161–2, 176.

29 This paragraph is based on the thorough study of the textual history of *Degaré* by Jacobs 1995.

30 *Sir Launfal*, ed. A. J. Bliss (London: Nelson, 1960).

31 *Chaucer Life-Records*, ed. Martin M. Crow and Clair C. Olson (Oxford: Oxford University Press, 1966), p. 24. The discovery is due to Burrow 1986.

32 The case for common authorship is argued by Mills 1962.

33 Such signatures are associated with written texts. Cf. the colophon in *Havelok* 2998–3000 – 'Seye a Pater Noster stille / For him that haueth the rym maked, / And ther-fore fele nihtes waked' – where the last line suggests written composition.

34 The example and the citation from the French *Octavian* are drawn from Mills 1962.

35 *Octavian Imperator*, ed. Frances McSparran (Heidelberg: Winter, 1979).

36 Bradbury's reference is to Stock 1983, 9.

37 These accusations are often aimed less at the actual person who produces the popular work than at its sponsor or patron: for instance, at the media mogul rather than the journalist.

38 Williams 1958 remains the best introductory discussion of the 'culture and civilization' tradition represented by Matthew Arnold, F. R. and Q. D. Leavis. An important right-wing deployment of mass culture theory occurred in the United States during the 1940s and 1950s, in the contexts of McCarthyism and the Cold War; see Storey 1993, 33–40. Exponents of the Marxian version include some of those critics associated with the Frankfurt School, such as Adorno.

39 In this way of thinking, quality productions are generally viewed ambivalently, or even condemned. They tend to be deprecated for, for instance, their aesthetic sterility and artificiality (as opposed to the organic naturalness of popular culture), and their political conformity or restrictiveness (against the freedom and spontaneity of the popular). Within this theory, even when quality culture is considered ultimately superior, it is still thought to lack something important, which folk culture possesses.

40 For a commentary on the term 'folk', see Williams 1983, 136–7. Although in writings reflecting on popular culture 'folk' is often used with the meaning I give it here, it should be noted that it is not always given this sense.

41 The equation mass = debased, quoted above, holds here too. 'Popular', however, is differently aligned, being opposed to 'mass' instead of identified with it. Thus, for folk culture theory, if mass = debased, popular (as folk) = non-debased.

42 Examples of the former use in the context of the Middle Ages are given in Chandler 1970. Where the latter use is concerned, perhaps the most famous example is Bakhtin's discussion of the sixteenth-century French writer Rabelais, with the influential idea of 'carnival' which emerged from it. According to Bakhtin, the folk culture of the Middle Ages provided for ordinary medieval people a 'nonofficial, extraecclesiastical and extrapolitical' dimension to their lives, 'a second world and a second life outside officialdom' (Bakhtin 1984, 6). Stallybrass and White 1986, 1–26, contains a sophisticated summary of the debate on the politics of carnival.

43 Storey 1993, 6–17, gives three more senses. It should be noted that within cultural studies, where the term 'popular culture' is today most reflected upon, all these senses are generally seen as specifically modern: 'what all these defini-tions have in common is the insistence that whatever else popular culture might be, it is definitely a culture that only emerged following industrialization and urbanization. . . . Before industrialization and urbanization, Britain had two cultures: a common culture which was shared, more or less, by all classes, and a separate elite culture produced and consumed by the dominant classes in society' (Storey 1993, 16–17). Although practitioners of cultural studies are no doubt correct to insist on a radical historical shift occurring in the wake of the Industrial Revolution, their account of pre-modern Britain is strikingly reminiscent of the nostalgic folk construction of a communitarian past. It is also reductive, in a depressingly familiar way: the pre-modern is constructed as a blank space characterized by the absence of all the features of modernity, which therefore not only can but must be approached without modern intel-lectual constructs. See Aers 1992 for a critique of this view.

44 In their essays in this volume, Hasler and Simpson discuss the ambivalence among earlier commentators. Eighteenth- and early nineteenth-century inter-est in the popular romances is examined in detail in Johnston 1964. On the political investments of medievalism and medieval studies, see also Williams 1958, 130–58; Chandler 1970; Girouard 1981; Patterson 1987, 3–39; Cantor 1991; and the essays in Bloch and Nichols 1996 (especially relevant is John Ganim's 'The Myth of Medieval Romance', 148–66).

45 Several of the contributors to this volume list examples of features considered desirable by literary critics but supposedly or actually lacking in many of the popular romances. These lists include: originality, self-consciousness, irony, stylistic density, explicit ethical complexity, resistance to narrative closure and historical specificity. There have of course been attempts to provide neutral definitions of the popular romances, such as Pearsall 1965 and Strohm 1971,

1977 and 1980. Although precise and scholarly, these have nevertheless failed to overturn the prevailing representation of the romances in criticism.

46   Over and again we are told that particular romances are guilty of being clichéd and overly conventional, of lacking ambiguity, of exploiting their audience's worst instincts, of mediocrity and of escapism: all identified by Stuart Hall and Paddy Whannel as characteristics ascribed to mass culture today (Hall and Whannel 1964, 365–70; reprinted in Ashley 1997, 49–52).

47   Thus, the 'revisionist' model of popular romance transmission and reception outlined in the Historical Introduction above has evident connections with mass culture theory. Affiliations are less obvious in the case of the 'romantic' model. Once clearly associated with folk culture theory, it fell into neglect when that theory lost favour among medievalists. Of late, however, the romantic model has been revived (as the above Introduction itself bears witness) in a revised and modernized form which manifests some of the features of the contemporary, positive appreciation of popular culture, and also some features of mass culture theory.

48   A useful discussion in a medieval context of Peter J. Rabinowitz's distinction between actual, authorial and narrative audiences is Krueger 1993, 24–8. Krueger's book as a whole contains useful reflections on questions of audience in relation to Old French verse romance.

49   To take a celebrated example, Radway 1984 shows how modern 'popular romances' – mass-produced romantic fiction – can be used by their actual readers in ways which differ from and even combat the conformist message implied in them.

50   It is worth noting that many of the interpretative issues often couched in terms of audience or reader are also frequently broached through the figure of the writer. I chose to concentrate on audience here principally for its special relation to the 'popular'.

51   In the medieval context see, for instance, Strohm 1992, Fradenburg 1991, Patterson 1987.

52   The proposed historical audience may even occasionally turn out to be subordinate to the interpretation, which in fact precedes it. A striking example has recently been furnished within the field of Old French literature. It was long thought that the genres of *fabliaux* and *chansons de geste* had popular audiences not dissimilar to those of the Middle English popular romances. (The opposition between popular and quality romance in Middle English is uncannily similar in many respects to that between *chanson de geste* and *roman* in Old French, on which see Kay 1995, especially 1–21.) This view has, however, been revised in recent years. The supposedly historical 'popular' audiences have been shown to be above all a hypostatization of modern critical judgements, themselves informed by modern ideas about what is coarse and vulgar (and therefore 'of the people'). A similar point is made below by McDonald.

53   In this volume, Diamond, Shippey, Simpson and Stokes all comment on the investments critics as a class have in deprecating the romances. Interestingly, a suspicion that the popular writer is hostile towards intellectuals emerges from

much writing on modern popular fiction. Thus Queenie Leavis complains that contemporary popular fiction teaches its public to 'despise the profession of letters' (Leavis 1932, 52; excerpts in Ashley 1997, 36–9, 38).

54 A further connection between Chaucer and the popular romances lies in the fact that the fortunes of the latter can be tracked to some extent via critical discussion of *Sir Thopas*, the tale begun by Chaucer the pilgrim as his Canterbury offering, but interrupted by the Host. *Sir Thopas* has been variously read as an affectionate or a satirical parody of the popular romance; it may express either Chaucer's poetic debt towards the genre, or his rejection of it, or his desire to transcend it. See Tigges 1990 for an overview of the text's recent critical history, and a balanced assessment.

55 Commentators on popular culture recognize that the aesthetic inferiority of the popular product is generally an inevitable social fact caused by the exclusion of its producers and consumers from the opportunities offered by wealth and education. At other times, however, the same style may be a deliberate choice made by the most privileged (as in the case of the naïve art produced by European modernist painters). Brett 1986, 7–26, offers a subtle discussion of the various modalities of popular style. He usefully emphasizes that such popular culture is not necessarily rooted in the past, but may represent new stylistic directions; the very notion of 'tradition' is not infrequently claimed as the exclusive property of the official regime.

56 This presumptive link is one of a number of approaches which feminist critics have used in order to give some historical grounding to female-sensitive readings; a book-length example is Krueger 1993.

57 Although, as noted in the Historical Introduction above, prose romances are not generally considered to be popular, Malory is thought to have been familiar with a number of popular romances: see P. J. C. Field 1979 and 1991, Kennedy 1981. Riddy 1987 treats Malory in the context of a variety of popular works. P. J. C. Field 1982 has further argued for Malory's authorship of the popular *The Wedding of Sir Gawain and Dame Ragnell*. (All the essays by Field cited in this note are reprinted in P. J. C. Field 1998.)

58 To take an example from the area best known to me: a useful collection of feminist reflections can be found in the section on the academy and the canon in Showalter 1985b. On the difficulties of accommodating feminist perspectives within one branch of medieval studies, see E. Jane Burns, Sarah Kay, Roberta L. Krueger and Helen Solterer, 'Feminism and the Discipline of Old French Studies: *Une Bele Disjointure*', 225–66 in Bloch and Nichols 1996.

59 In Bourdieu's work, 'distinction' also designates a combination of aesthetic and social criteria similar to that I here call 'quality'; thus Bourdieu writes of 'works of distinction'. While I wish to draw on Bourdieu's analysis, I have chosen the term 'quality' in order to mark the difference in principle (without going into the specific and varied differences) of the context with which I am concerned: that of Anglo-American literary criticism.

60 The point is illustrated by the essays of Archibald, Robson and Spearing. As described above, each argues that important elements of certain texts make

little sense when interpreted within standard norms, but come startlingly into focus once they are seen as rejections of the usual narrative patterns as being inadequate to express women's interests. The failure of Fresne's life to follow expected paths, Heurodis's incoherent alienation and the vividly disgusting corpse of Guinevere's mother all inscribe the unintelligibility of female desires and experiences when read through traditional, male-centred grids.

61 Thus, for the cultural studies practitioner, the object should be not 'a mere descriptive inventory – which may have the negative effect of freezing popular culture into some timeless descriptive mould – but the relations of power which are constantly punctuating and dividing the domain of culture into its preferred and its residual categories . . . : to put it bluntly and in an oversimplified form – what counts is the class struggle in and over culture' (Hall 1981, 234–5).

62 The quotation is from Pearsall 1977, 157. For a brief history of the reception of *William of Palerne* see Diamond's essay below.

63 Literary critics' engagement with 'quality' would thus be 'not an unquestioned good but a negotiation with enabling violence' (Spivak 1993, 283). The power of the word 'violence' may seem ill-suited to apply to literary criticism. However, I am quoting here from a book which addresses specifically the teaching of literature in American universities; and the words just quoted follow a discussion of the need to change the canon (Spivak 1993, 270–78).

CHAPTER ONE

Lai le Freine: The Female Foundling and the Problem of Romance Genre*

ELIZABETH ARCHIBALD

The Middle English *Lai le Freine*, a fairly close rendering of Marie de France's Breton lay of the same title, survives in only one fragmentary version preserved in the Auchinleck manuscript, National Library of Scotland, Advocates' 19.2.1, which contains a large number of Middle English narratives usually described as romances, as well as many religious and didactic texts.[1] In the following plot summary, square brackets indicate passages which are missing from the Middle English text, and are reconstructed on the basis of Marie's version.

> A lady comments maliciously that a neighbour who has just borne twin sons must have committed adultery; this remark upsets both her own husband and the new parents. Soon after this the critical lady herself bears twin daughters; greatly embarrassed, she asks the midwife to kill one, [but her maid proposes that it be exposed instead] and leaves it in an ash tree near a convent, with a ring and a rich cloth. The convent porter finds the child; named Le Freine after the ash tree in which she was found, she is raised as the abbess's niece. When she grows up she asks the abbess about her parents and siblings, and is told how she was found with the ring and the cloth.
>
> A rich knight, Sir Guroun, hears of the girl's charms and visits the convent; he falls in love with Freine and asks her to live with him, and she leaves with him (taking her tokens with her). All his people love and admire Freine, but his knights urge him to marry a lord's daughter and have legitimate children. His chosen bride is, unknown to all, Freine's sister.

* I am grateful to the editors and to Professor A. S. G. Edwards for their valuable comments on an earlier version of this essay.

[Freine is sad, but presides graciously over the arrangements for the wedding; thinking the covers on the bridal bed inadequate, she puts her own cloth on it. When the bride and her mother enter the room, the mother recognizes the cloth and inquires where it came from. Freine explains, and shows the ring too. The mother swoons, then tells her husband the truth about her twin daughters and how she exposed one (she adds that the cloth and the ring were his courtship presents to her). The bishop annuls the marriage, and Freine becomes Guroun's wife; her sister is married to a suitable knight.]

The French and English versions of the story are very close, as far as it is possible to tell given the incomplete English text (see Spearing 1990a). One significant difference, however, is that the English version begins with a prologue commenting on the Breton lay as a genre. The same prologue is attached to *Sir Orfeo* in two fifteenth-century manuscripts, and was probably included in the Auchinleck version, though it has not survived there (Pearsall and Cunningham 1977, xi); Spearing calls it 'an all-purpose lay prologue' (Spearing 1990a, 126). It includes a summary of subjects characteristic of the genre, in the manner of Marie's prologue to her collection of lays:

> Sum bethe of wer & sum of wo,
> & sum of ioie and mirthe also,
> & sum of trecherie & of gile,
> of old auentours that fel while;
> & sum of bourdes & ribaudy,
> & mani ther beth of fairy.
> Of al thinge[s] that men seth,
> mest o loue for sothe thai beth.
> (5–12)

Pearsall notes that the next text in the Auchinleck manuscript, the pious Charlemagne romance *Roland and Vernagu*, also seems to have begun with a prologue (of which only four lines survive); he suggests that the compiler(s) of the manuscript included these prologues as 'a broad and enthusiastic introduction . . . suitable for new and untutored readers', such as 'the aspirant middle-class citizen, perhaps a wealthy merchant' who probably commissioned it (Pearsall and Cunningham 1977, viii and x).[2]

But this catalogue of typical Breton lay themes is not very helpful to us today in considering the genre of *Lai le Freine*, particularly since we do not know what aspects of the story were emphasized in the lost ending. It is only marginally about treachery or guile; it is not about adventure or 'bourdes & ribaudy' or 'faerie'; and the love story is somewhat unconventional. Marie de France tends not to point morals at the end of her lays, and her *Fresne* is

40

no exception to this principle. It finishes with the information that when the story got out, after both sisters were married, the lay was composed and named after Fresne. In the other surviving Breton lays in Middle English, the happy ending is usually followed only by a brief prayer (Chaucer's *Franklin's Tale*, which ends on an interrogative note, is unusual in this respect, as in so many others).

The Auchinleck manuscript, written about 1330, is remarkable for the number of romances it contains: eighteen, if one includes *The Seven Sages of Rome*, and counts the three parts of the story of Guy of Warwick as separate romances (Pearsall and Cunningham 1977, viii; Shonk 1985, 75–6). Critics have accepted *Lai le Freine* unquestioningly in this generic group; although they acknowledge that Breton lays are not exactly the same as romances, the differences are not considered particularly significant (Mehl 1968, 40–44; Barron 1987, 191). It appears in some modern romance anthologies, as do other texts which can be described (or describe themselves) as Breton lays: for instance, *Lai le Freine*, *Sir Launfal* and *Sir Orfeo* are all included in Donald Sands's collection *Middle English Verse Romances*, a popular teaching text.[3] But can *Lai le Freine* – or indeed any medieval narrative of adventure with a female protagonist – be described as a romance, in the sense that modern critics give the term?

Medieval romance is notoriously hard to define, but it can be said with relative confidence that most definitions presuppose a male protagonist, and adventures or achievements only possible for a man. John Finlayson's summary is representative: 'there is a more or less agreed paradigm of the fundamental narrative activity of the genre, namely that the knight-hero rides forth either to seek adventure or to accomplish an established task' (Finlayson 1979, 1). Such definitions not only exclude female protagonists, but also obscure the frequent focus in medieval romance on families (Archibald 1990 and 1996). Stephen Knight is one of the few critics to discuss the family theme in romance, which is in fact, as he notes, 'very common and very rich' (Knight 1986b, 110 and 112; see also Brewer 1980, Vitz 1989, 96–125, and Maddox 1991). Many texts categorized today as romances describe the separation and eventual reunion of parents and children; recognition scenes are frequent and were clearly popular, and the quest for identity is a recurrent theme, as Northrop Frye notes in his study of the romance genre, where he puns on the meanings of 'descent' in his chapter 'Themes of Descent' (Frye 1976). It is striking that the Auchinleck manuscript includes two very different narratives of separated families besides *Freine*. It begins with the legendary life of Pope Gregory, the product of sibling incest who is exposed as a baby but survives to marry his unrecognized mother; discovery of their relationship leads him to do rigorous penance for many years, after which he is chosen as pope.[4] It also includes

Sir Degaré, the story of a foundling who becomes a knight and narrowly avoids committing both incest and parricide before the final happy family reunion.[5]

When children are separated at an early age from their parents, they are usually foundlings, whether they have been carried off by wild beasts (as in *Sir Eglamour*), or deliberately exposed by one or both of their parents (as in *Sir Degaré*).[6] John Boswell has shown in *The Kindness of Strangers*, his important study of the exposure of children in antiquity and the Middle Ages, that children were indeed frequently abandoned, though he argues that parents in fact hoped their babies would be found and reared (Boswell 1989). In the romances, of course, these babies are always found, and grow up to have distinguished chivalric careers and eventually to be reunited with their long-lost parents, who are royal or aristocratic.[7] But chivalric careers are only available to men. What happens when the foundling protagonist is a girl? What kind of adventures can she have? How many such stories have survived? Female protagonists are usually passive, in accordance with the conventions of medieval romance: can the heroine remain at the centre of the narrative even if she does not have many adventures? Are Le Freine and her literary sisters, among whom we might number Emaré and Constance, as well as Griselda (with whom she is often compared), automatically excluded by gender from being romance protagonists?[8] Or should we change our modern definitions of the genre to include these stories of separated families and victimized women which were so disturbingly popular in the Middle Ages?

In this essay I shall first discuss the very few other medieval narratives known to me which include a female foundling, and then compare the plot structure of *Lai le Freine* with romances (and cautionary tales) about male foundlings. Next I shall consider the adaptation of the story in *Galeran de Bretagne*, a French romance dating from the late twelfth or early thirteenth century; it is clearly based on Marie's *Fresne*, but adds many conventional motifs and focuses much more on the hero, in order to fulfil the expectations of romance.[9] Finally I shall look at *Lai le Freine* as a narrative which concentrates almost exclusively on women, and which is very hard to categorize generically.

Very few other medieval romances or quasi-romances have female foundlings as protagonists. I exclude heroines separated from their families who are isolated and marginalized socially, unprotected by husband or father, but do know or suddenly remember who they really are, such as Tarsia in *Apollonius of Tyre* (the source of Shakespeare's *Pericles*), Nicolette in *Aucassin et Nicolette*, and the protagonists of the popular narratives about falsely accused queens or daughters harassed by incestuous fathers.[10] According to these strict standards, I know of only one female foundling other than Freine. She

42

is the mother of the hero of the Icelandic *Hrólfs saga Kraka*; her story in-cludes the incest motif which so often appears in stories of male foundlings, but otherwise it is strikingly lacking in incident and adventure.[11]

King Helgi of Denmark forces the German queen Olof to sleep with him, to avenge a dishonour she has previously inflicted on him. After Helgi leaves, Olof bears a daughter for whom she feels nothing; she names the baby Yrsa after a dog, and gives her to a peasant family to rear. Yrsa tends their sheep; one day her biological father Helgi, disguised as a beggar but acting like a knight in a pastourelle, meets her, falls in love with her, detects her noble birth from her eyes, and carries her off against her will. Olof hears of this, but does nothing to stop the marriage, hoping that it will bring shame on her enemy Helgi.

Yrsa and Helgi live very happily together and have a son, Hrólf, the hero of the saga, who grows up to do great deeds. Olof is irritated by the fame of both father and son, so she goes to visit them and when Yrsa (who knows that the queen has been involved in her upbringing) inquires about her true parentage, suspecting rightly that she cannot be the child of peasants, Olof spitefully reveals the truth. Yrsa is horrified both at Olof's villainy and at her own incestuous marriage. Helgi would be quite happy for the marriage to continue, but Yrsa insists on leaving him, and later marries another king who eventually kills Helgi when he tries to retrieve Yrsa.

Yrsa's role in this story is largely passive. Like many heroines she is abducted, though, unusually, she enjoys a long and happy marriage with her abductor. In this case, family reunion proves to be disastrous: Yrsa's parents hate each other, and her mother has always known where she is, but does not want to claim her; her father does turn out to be a king, but he is also her husband. Yrsa does have some control – it is she who decides to leave Helgi. But her main function in this story, which is closer to epic than to romance, is to be the mother of the hero Hrólf, and there is relatively little interest in her own feelings. Nor is there a strong sense of sin: the context is not Christian, Yrsa's horror at her incest is not expressed in religious terms, and although Helgi's death is in some sense the result of his transgression, he is not presented explicitly as a sinner who deserved his fate.

Yrsa and Freine seem to be the only heroines in medieval narratives who are separated from their parents at birth, and do not discover their true identity till they are adults. In both stories this ignorance introduces the possibility of incest, which is also a feature of many stories about the expos-ure of male babies, as we shall see. Let us now compare the pattern of the plot in the story of Freine with the patterns in romances about male found-lings, and in the cautionary tales of Judas and Gregorius, which were well known and influential in the later Middle Ages. This comparison will show how uneventful Freine's story is.

I want to start the comparison when the protagonist grows up. In most of the stories of male foundlings, the first crucial turning point in the plot comes with a discovery about parentage – not the whole truth, for otherwise there could be no problematic encounters with the biological parents, but enough to pique the protagonist's curiosity or stir him to action of some sort, which will inevitably, though without his awareness, lead him to one or both of his parents. So Judas and Gregorius learn from a quarrel with a foster-brother that they are not the children of the adults who are rearing them; Gregorius demands to be knighted and goes out to look for his parents, and Judas flees to Jerusalem where he works for the ruler. Degaré is raised by a hermit and when he is twenty is given the tokens found with him; he sets out to find his family. We are not told how Degrebelle, Eglamour's son, learns about his origins, but his shield shows a griffin carrying a child, representing his own separation from his mother; he leaves home to win a bride in a tournament, and on discovering that she is his mother becomes her champion. Not all male protagonists actively look for their parents when they grow up, but they all leave their foster-homes and make a significant change in their lives.

Freine, on the other hand, takes the initiative in asking the abbess about her origins when she is grown up (241–50); there is no quarrel or reason for this other than innocent curiosity, presumably, since she is being passed off as the abbess's niece. The abbess tells her how she was found and gives her the tokens found with her, a cloth and a ring.

> The abbesse hir in conseyl toke,
> to tellen hir hye nought forsoke,
> hou hye was founden in al thing,
> & tok hir the cloth and the ring,
> & bad hir kepe it in that stede;
> and ther whiles sche liued so sche dede.
>
> (245–50)

Her reaction to this revelation is not given; it is not a turning point in the plot (though it is immediately after this that she meets Guroun). She simply stays in the convent – how could she go off alone and look for her parents?[12] Perhaps a sense of identity and lineage is less important to women in these stories, who take on the identity of the men they marry. In his famous discussion of the childhood fantasy of being separated from parents who are rich and important, Freud comments that this is more common in boys than in girls, since 'In this respect the imagination of girls is apt to show itself much weaker' (Freud 1959a, 238).

Male foundlings may have various rite-of-passage adventures during the search for their parents – they may kill a dragon or a giant, or rescue a damsel in distress – but the next major plot twist that we expect is an unwitting encounter with a parent. In *Eglamour* and *Degaré* the foundling wins the hand of his unrecognized mother as a tournament prize; Gregorius rescues his from being besieged by an unwelcome suitor, and then marries her at the urging of her barons. Sometimes the marriage is consummated and continues for some time before the true relationship is revealed (as in *Gregorius*, an exemplary text where a motive must be established for profound contrition and rigorous penance); in the romances the recognition takes place on the wedding night so that the incest is averted, as in *Eglamour* and *Degaré*. This incestuous marriage, however brief, introduces a recognition scene, and sets the protagonist on a new course, whether secular or spiritual. In religious tales which urge contrition and renunciation of the world, the discovery of the incest between mother and son is usually the crisis which drives the protagonist to attempt some kind of penance: Judas (who has already killed his father) becomes a follower of Jesus, though he cannot avert his destiny as the betrayer of the Messiah; but Gregorius's sincere contrition and harsh penance lead to his election as pope. In the secular narratives of adventure, however, the hero is determined to find his father, and the crucial peripeteia is the fight between them. In *Eglamour* it is the father who wins; in *Degaré* the two are equally matched. The fight leads to a second recognition scene (often by means of a token, a sword or a ring), and thus to the happy ending in which the separated lovers can marry at last, and their son is given a safely exogamous bride. This typically chivalric episode of a fight between father and son which foregrounds exclusively masculine qualities establishes not only the lineage but also the maturity and prowess of the erstwhile foundling.

In *Freine*, however, there is no hint of either parent–child incest or parricide (or even matricide); after the revelation that she is a foundling, the only significant change in the heroine's life is that a suitor persuades her to leave the convent and live with him (in Marie's version, as we have seen, the discovery of her origins is subordinated to this much more momentous event). In terms of the structure of the plot this might be seen as the equivalent of the incestuous marriage at the centre of the stories of Gregorius, Judas, Degrebelle and Degaré. But instead of introducing a dramatic recognition scene and a major shift in the direction of the narrative, the liaison of Freine and Guroun continues uneventfully and happily till such time as his barons pressure him to make a suitable marriage and provide an heir. Even this crisis apparently fails to provoke a reaction in the heroine (the fragment ends at the arrival of the new bride, before Freine's generous decoration of the bridal chamber). If we assume that Freine behaves like her French counterpart, she does not create a scene but behaves with admirable un-selfishness, like Griselda. The recognition scene and family reunion are motivated by near-miss incest, as in many stories of male foundlings – but whereas these men marry their mothers, here the incest is at one remove from the heroine, since it is the marriage of her lover to her sister. This constituted incest according to the very broad definition current in the later Middle Ages: any sexual encounter, however casual and brief, was thought to create 'one flesh' between the partners, and thus to establish a relation-ship between their two families which would prevent intermarriage (see Brundage 1987, 194–5). But this sort of incest is much less shocking (to medieval as well as modern sensibilities) than the mother–son marriage of the male foundling romances. In other stories of foundlings, the hero's first marriage (to his mother) must be annulled, and if he marries again, his bride is not a major character in the romance; but Freine and Guroun, who have lived together for so long, do (we assume) marry legitimately in the end, and it is the shadowy twin sister for whom another bridegroom must be found.[13] There is no other lover waiting in the wings for Freine, nor any ecclesiastical censure for her affair.

Unlike the heroines of the other stories mentioned above (with the pos-sible exception of Yrsa), Freine has a remarkably calm and uneventful life. She does not leave the convent where she is raised until Guroun takes her to his court, where she stays for the rest of the narrative. She never has to deal with the problem of pregnancy. She is never abducted, or threatened with violence of any kind. The unhappiness of her rejection by Guroun lasts a very short time, compared with the happiness and stability of her life before and afterwards. She does not spend many years without a partner, like the heroines in *Eglamour* and *Degaré* who for at least fifteen years are unclaimed tournament prizes while their lost sons grow up. She does not spend any time as an outcast, wandering unprotected, like Constance and her analogues, or socially marginalized, like Nicolette or Tarsia. She does not suffer during the period in which she and Guroun live together, as Griselda does in the first years of her marriage. She does not inspire a warrior to great deeds on her behalf, or rely on God for protection. She does not need any of the resourcefulness of Tarsia or Nicolette. It is her beauty and virtue which attract Guroun, but they do not cause any com-plications, as in the case of Griselda. The only test she has to pass is that of behaving well when Guroun decides to marry someone else, but this is not a test deliberately set by Guroun, and Freine's good behaviour is not dir-ectly responsible for the happy ending, as in the case of Griselda. Rather it is the extraordinary coincidence that the bride is her sister, and that her mother sees and recognizes the precious cloth which Freine has generously spread on the bridal bed. This happy twist of fate can hardly be equated

with the chivalric prowess which brings about the recognition scenes between father and son in the romances, or the contrition and painful penance of Gregorius in the exemplum.

The story of Freine focuses to an unusual degree on women's experience
– perhaps because the French lay was written by a woman, and perhaps
also because women often seem to have more central and active roles in
Breton lays. Several of Marie's lays concentrate on the heroine rather than
the hero, in spite of their titles – *Yonec*, *Eliduc* – and so does Chaucer's
Franklin's Tale. This is also true of the Middle English *Freine*, as far as we
can tell. The mother plays a crucial part at beginning and end; we hear
extremely little from the father.[14] It is in fact the mother's story as well as
Freine's, and rather than being read as a romance, it could plausibly be
linked to exemplary stories of a woman failing to confess some dreadful sin
– often incest or infanticide – who is eventually persuaded to confess (and
often dies immediately afterwards).[15] *Lai le Freine* too presumably ended, as
Marie's version does, with a confession and absolution, though in a domestic and secular setting: the wife confesses and the husband absolves her
through his joy at regaining the daughter he did not know he had lost. The
reunion of separated lovers or spouses which often occurs in romance narratives of male foundlings (*Eglamour*, *Degaré*), and also in the Incestuous
Father/Accused Queen stories, is here doubled, and Freine's story is eclipsed
or replaced by her mother's, which forms the frame of the narrative.[16]
Freine's parents are properly married and have never been physically separated, but the mother's confession seems to mark a sort of renewing of
vows, and a new beginning after the years of deception.

The father of the twin girls is hardly visible in the story; at the beginning
and the end, it is the mother whose emotions are described. The father
appears only to condemn his wife's sharp tongue at the beginning, and
(presumably) to acknowledge his daughter and arrange for the annulment
of Guroun's marriage at the end, so that he can marry Freine. At the
beginning he is described as the bosom friend of the knight whose wife
produces twin sons: one might have expected that the twin girls would
marry the twin boys, but neither the friend nor his twin sons are ever
mentioned again. At the end (if the English version followed Marie's) it is
the mother of the girls who expresses directly her joy at recovering her
long-lost daughter – and in a charming and unusual touch she identifies the
tokens, the cloak and the ring, as courtship presents from her husband.
There is no chivalric activity in this story: it is entirely concerned with more
quotidian female experience, first that of the mother, then that of the daughter. Freine is saved by the arguments and actions of her mother's maid, and
raised by an abbess; at the end, the heroine is reunited not only with her
parents, but also with her sister. Guroun speaks only to persuade Freine to

elope with him; we never hear his reactions to the marriage forced on him by his people, or to the dénouement.

In considering this story about women told by a woman, it is useful to turn to Caroline Bynum's article on Victor Turner's theory of 'liminality': she tests its value for her own work on medieval religious history by applying his arguments to medieval lives of women saints (Bynum 1984, 118–19). She characterizes his concept of 'social drama' as consisting of four stages (106), 'breach between social elements, crisis, adjustment or redress, and finally either reintegration of group or person or "element" into the social structure or recognition of irreparable breach', and then applies these to the texts she works on:

> But when I have explored more closely the relationship of Turner's models to these medieval stories and symbols, a curious fact has emerged. Turner's ideas describe the stories and symbols of men far better than those of women. Women's stories insofar as they can be discerned behind the tales told by male biographers are in fact less processual than men's; they don't have turning points. And when women recount their own lives, the themes are less climax, conversion, reintegration and triumph, the liminality of reversal or elevation, than continuity.
>
> (Bynum 1984, 108)

Bynum makes a clear distinction in her discussion between stories written by men and by women: 'Men writing about women assumed that women went through sharp crises and conversions' (111). Liminality for men may involve role reversals in which inferiority and marginalization are signalled by female symbols or images, and male writers may therefore represent liminality for women in comparable terms of gender reversal, so that a woman dresses or behaves like a man (a state of temporary superiority as well as liminality!). But women writers do not adopt such strategies: 'Only men's stories are fully social; only men's symbols are full reversals . . . What women's images and stories expressed most fundamentally was neither reversal nor elevation but continuity' (118–19). Bynum is writing about hagiography, and specifically about saints' lives written by women, but her comments seem to me very relevant to Marie's *Fresne*, and by extension to the English *Lai le Freine*. Freine's adventures, such as they are, are indeed presented as continuity rather than dramatic turns of event (and this also seems to me a useful way to look at some other lays by Marie, such as *Laüstic* and *Chevrefoil*).

The gulf that separates *Fresne/Freine* from the world of romance can be clearly seen when we compare it with a text which is evidently derived from Marie's lay, the thirteenth-century romance of *Galeran de Bretagne* sometimes attributed to Jean Renart.[17] This text gives much larger roles to men, and both protagonists, male and female, go through a series of changes and adventures which could be described in Turner's terms.

> Gente criticizes Marsile when the latter gives birth to twin boys, saying that she must have committed adultery. When Gente herself gives birth to twin daughters, she is very embarrassed. She puts one in an elaborate cradle, with a rich embroidered cloth and a pillow stuffed with phoenix feathers as tokens of noble birth, and tells a sergeant to expose her; after a long journey he leaves the cradle in an ash tree outside the convent of Beauséjour. The abbess's chaplain finds it there, and the nuns baptize and rear the little girl, naming her Fresne after the ash tree. The abbess also rears her nephew Galeran, son of her sister, the Countess of Bretagne; the two children are educated together, and fall in love.
>
> Galeran has to leave the convent when news comes that his parents are dead, but he returns as often as possible to see Fresne; this causes comment, and the abbess finds out about the very innocent love affair. She scolds her nephew, who leaves, but exchanges letters with Fresne once a month. When this correspondence is discovered, the abbess quarrels with Fresne and throws her out. Fresne takes her cloth and her harp, and supports herself by playing in inns. In Rouen she finds refuge in the house of a bourgeoise with a daughter, and does needlework.
>
> Galeran searches everywhere for Fresne, but concludes sadly that she must be dead. His knights urge him to marry. He happens to meet Fleurie, Fresne's twin sister, and arranges to marry her, although he still weeps for his lost love. News of the wedding reaches Fresne in Rouen; she arrives just before the wedding, disguised as a minstrel and wearing the cloth left in her cradle, and sings Galeran a song he had once taught her. Fresne goes to see Fleurie, and Gente recognizes the cloth. She confesses all to her husband, and Galeran is married to Fresne.

All sorts of extra details are added here to expand the story to over 7000 lines (Marie's version is 518 lines, and the English fragment with Weber's addition is 408 lines). Names, descriptions and conversations are inserted, as well as new episodes, many featuring Galeran, who gives the romance its name. After being raised with Fresne he goes off to fight in tournaments and make a name for himself, and several ladies fall in love with him apart from Fleurie. Fresne too is given a more active role, and much more dialogue; there is some charming detail about her idyllic life with Galeran as they grow up in the convent; she has a long and vitriolic quarrel with the abbess before she leaves; out in the world she has adventures reminiscent of one of the Constance group heroines (indeed the abbess seems to play the role of the jealous mother-in-law), though she also works as a minstrel, like Nicolette; and she goes to confront her lover when she hears he is marrying (this is a motif more common in *chanson de geste* than in romance). Among the characteristic aspects of the romance mode suggested by Gillian Beer, *Galeran de Bretagne* includes 'profuse sensuous detail, a serene intermingling of the unexpected and the everyday, a complex and prolonged succession of incidents usually without a single climax, amplitude of proportions, and a code of conduct to which all the characters must comply' (Beer 1970, 10). Above all, it contains an active chivalric hero often at centre stage for whom the story is named. The comparison makes *Fresne/Freine* seem even less like a romance.

Some critics of medieval literature argue for a category of homiletic or exemplary romance, in which some aspect of virtuous behaviour approved by the church brings about the happy ending (see Schelp 1967; Mehl 1968; and for a dissenting view Dannenbaum 1984). Unlike Chaucer's Clerk, Marie de France appended no moral or explanatory comment to her story, and the ending of the Middle English version is lost. Does Freine repres-ent the popular medieval figure of the Man or Woman Tried by Fate, a category which might also include Apollonius and Tarsia, Griselda and Constance (see Braswell 1965, 133; Archibald 1991, 104–5)? But her vicis-situdes seem very tame by the standards of these other literary figures: she is comfortably and lovingly raised in the convent, and then is happy with Guroun, with the brief interruption of his wedding to her sister. Her mother does certainly learn a lesson, and confesses her faults at the end of the story. Nelson suggests that the mother's prostration before her husband (in Marie's version) should be taken as indicating the proper attitude of the soul to God, just as Petrarch interpreted Griselda's submission to Walter (Nelson 1978, 154) – but there is certainly no indication of this moral in the French text. What other morals could be drawn from the story? Never slander your neighbour? Do as you would be done by? Think before you speak? Be careful to find out whether there is any blood relationship between your bride-to-be and your previous lover? Freine does indeed display 'a virtue which borders on a saintliness never explained by the poet-narrator' (Free-man 1987, 12); but as this perfect selflessness manifests itself in the context of life as a concubine, it is hard to imagine what the church-approved moral could be.[18]

Lai le Freine in its English version has attracted little critical attention, and in studies of Marie's lays *Fresne* is not particularly privileged. Interpretations of the story differ dramatically. Nelson argues, unconvincingly in my view, that *Fresne* is to be read allegorically as 'the temptation, fall and redemption of man, the theme most commonly found as the basis of medieval drama' (Nelson 1978, 155); she discusses it together with *Eliduc*, the only one of Marie's lays to have a religious ending. Spearing remarks that the Middle English version is more pious than the French source, though he attributes this to 'a stronger sense of religious propriety' rather than some explicit moral purpose (Spearing 1990, 130). Hirsh detects a more explicit religious purpose, and an emphasis on the workings of Providence (Hirsh 1969, 85–6). Freeman, on the other hand, sees Marie's *Fresne* as a 'deliberate feminization of (largely male) clerkly concerns and procedures . . . Marie has appropriated the materials of clerkly vernacular narrative (used primarily to shore up the mythic values of chivalry) and she has made of them the tools of expression for women's *aventures* and their voices' (Freeman 1987, 16). In contrast to the story of Apollonius, which is full of fathers and daughters whose relationships symbolize the moral and political standing of each father, in *Fresne/Freine* fathers (and men in general) are marginalized in favour of mothers and surrogate mothers. Freeman contrasts Marie's *Fresne* with the Griselda story, where 'although a female protagonist is ostensibly at the heart of the story, her conflicts serve above all to ensure the legitimacy of the lord and his ordering of society' (18). In *Fresne*, according to Freeman, 'It is precisely this loving nature of hers, acting outside the confines of a legal code and the social mores of feudal society, that provides the lynchpin holding together this uniquely feminine version of the Griselda story. . . .' (19). The anonymous English translator, male or female, seems to have made no effort to alter or diminish this striking emphasis on the feminine.

Freeman seems to suggest that Marie's version is almost an anti-romance: she sees the aunt–niece relationship of the abbess and Fresne as a deliberate response to the privileged relationship of uncle and nephew in so many epics and romances. (One could presumably argue for Gurun as an anti-hero, removing Fresne from the safety of the convent to make a dishonest woman of her, and giving in to the pressure from his knights to throw her over and make a 'good' marriage.) Freeman refers rather disparagingly to 'the peripheral public world of the male characters', the world where the story begins and ends (Freeman 1987, 18). Such terms could not be used of other Breton lays: even *Emaré*, which focuses on a passive woman's ordeals, is set in a very masculine world, in no way peripheral, where the heroine is both harassed and helped by men, and the only other female character is the wicked mother-in-law. In an essay comparing Marie's Fresne and Chaucer's Griselda, Armstrong seems to agree with Freeman's argument: she comments that 'the words and deeds of men, which appear so dynamic at the beginning, fade and are subsumed in the women's story', and goes on to argue that 'comic closure in redistributed marriages cannot touch the real story which has been kept alive through the years in the text which the reader sees unfold outside the perceptive range of the story's men' (Armstrong 1990, 441). It would be hard to reconcile this description with the usual definitions of romance. Spearing tries to get around the problem by calling Marie's *Fresne* 'an *aventure*. This is to say, it is a series of events that apparently happen by chance and that have their meaning only in relation to those to whom they happen, not as part of some objective social or metaphysical structure' (Spearing 1990, 119). One might argue for 'some objective social or metaphysical structure' in terms of the ethical and legal issues: the illicit abandoning of the baby must be resolved by the mother's confession and the family reunion, the inappropriate marriage between Gurun and his lover's sister must be annulled, and Fresne's situation must be regularized – but this is not the usual subject matter of romance.[19]

In view of such comments, it is hard to see how the Middle English *Lai le Freine* can be counted as a romance and included in romance anthologies, unless the definition of romance is totally reworked, both in terms of plot and of narrative mode. Given the prologue, one might argue with Barron (1987) and others that as a Breton lay *Freine* is closely related to, though not identical with, romance; but it is very different from the other extant English examples of the genre, and in any case defining lays is no less difficult than defining romances, as the prologue itself suggests. In his useful discussion of Middle English lays, Finlayson shows that none of the supposedly characteristic motifs cited by critics, such as courtly love, the fairy world, adventure or ordeal, is in fact found universally in the French and English lays, except perhaps for brevity (Finlayson 1985, 353). He is reduced to concluding that Middle English lays are short and simple, and come in two basic types: romances with supernatural elements, and ordeal tales with improbable coincidences. *Freine* has to go in the second category, though it hardly counts as an ordeal tale. The heroism of the heroine is shown only in her patient acceptance of a real-life problem which is not at all characteristic of romance: as my students often remark, how can it be a romance when the protagonists live together for a long time without marrying? Unlike Griselda, Freine has no legal or moral claim on Guroun; she is not particularly badly treated. And we are given no insight into her thoughts and feelings – or indeed into those of the other characters, except perhaps the mother.[20]

It is pleasing to think that a patron (possibly a woman, as Riddy [see n. 2] has suggested) may have specifically asked for this enigmatic story about family separation and reunion, and above all about women, to be included in the Auchinleck manuscript, whose compiler or commissioner seems to have had a taste for pious tales as well as for romances. Perhaps the positioning of *Freine* in the manuscript, between a miracle of the Virgin and a pious story from the Charlemagne cycle, is less random than we might have thought. Like the tale of Griselda, it is poised between exemplum and romance. Like the tale of Griselda, it raises questions about the everyday experience of women and their treatment by men. Like the tale of Griselda, it suggests that for women, marriage is in fact the ultimate adventure.

Notes

1   All references are to the edition by Margaret Wattie, *The Middle English Lai le Freine* (Northampton, MA: Smith College, 1929); this, like other editions, includes the lines invented by H. Weber in *Metrical Romances*, 3 vols (Edinburgh: Constable, 1810) to fill in the missing parts of the plot. For discussion of the manuscript see Pearsall and Cunningham 1977. References to Marie de France's *Lai le Fresne* are taken from her *Lais*, ed. Jean Rychner, TLF (Geneva: Droz, 1966). I shall use French forms of the names when I refer to Marie's text, and English forms for the English text. The only other lay of Marie's which survives in Middle English is *Lanval*: see the edition by A. J. Bliss, *Sir Launfal* (London: Nelson, 1960).

2   There is a tendency to assume that anonymous authors or compilers were male, though critics are increasingly entertaining the possibility of female involvement; Felicity Riddy has suggested that the Auchinleck manuscript may in fact have been commissioned by a woman (in an unpublished paper read at the Bristol conference on Medieval Romance in England in 1992).

3   D. Sands (ed.), *Middle English Verse Romances* (New York: Holt, Rinehart and Winston, 1966).

4   The earliest known versions of this remarkable legend are in French and German, from the twelfth century: see *La Vie du Pape Grégoire: 8 versions françaises médiévales de la légende du Bon Pécheur*, ed. H. B. Sol (Amsterdam: Rodopi, 1977), and Hartmann von Aue, *Gregorius*, ed. H. Paul, rev. B. Wachinger (Tübingen: Niemeyer, 1992). It was included in the very popular *Gesta Romanorum*, ed. H. Oesterley (Berlin: Weidmann, 1872), 399–409.

5   *Sir Degaré*, ed. G. Schleich (Heidelberg: Winter, 1929), repr. and corrected in Jacobs 1995, 12–37; and see the essay by James Simpson in this volume.

6   *Sir Eglamour of Artois*, ed. Frances E. Richardson, EETS o.s. 256 (London: Oxford University Press, 1965).

7   In cautionary tales such as the legends of Gregorius and Judas, these family reunions lead to further disasters, and sometimes to renunciation of the world, rather than a secular happy ending. Gregorius lives for some years as a successful knight before the discovery of his incest leads to his rejection of secular life. Judas, exposed by his parents because of a sinister dream about his evil destiny, never becomes a knight; he is a thug working for Pilate, or in some versions Herod, when he unwittingly kills his father and marries his mother (for the development of his legend see Baum 1916).

8   Emaré, Constance and Griselda are all unjustly persecuted heroines in fourteenth-century narratives. The stories of Constance and Griselda were frequently retold in the later Middle Ages; Chaucer includes them in the *Canterbury Tales* as the *Man of Law's Tale* and the *Clerk's Tale*. See Schlauch 1927, and Ad Putter's essay on *Emaré* in this volume.

9   Jean Renart, *Galeran de Bretagne*, ed. Lucien Foulet, CFMA (Paris: Champion, 1925).

10   See Elizabeth Archibald, *Apollonius of Tyre: Medieval and Renaissance Themes and Variations* (Cambridge: Brewer, 1991); *Aucassin et Nicolette*, ed. Mario Roques, CFMA (Paris: Champion, 1955); and Schlauch 1927.

11   See *Hrólfs saga Kraka*, chs 6–12, ed. D. Slay, Editiones Arnamagnæanae Series B, I (Copenhagen: Munksgaard, 1960), 16–36, trans. Gwyn Jones, *King Hrolf and his Champions*, in *Eirik the Red and other Icelandic Sagas* (London: Oxford University Press, 1961), 234–50; and the comments of Boswell 1989, 387. The oldest manuscripts of this saga date only from the early seventeenth century, but the story was circulating much earlier.

12   In Marie's version this revelation comes just as Gurun is about to carry Fresne off to his estate, so she has even less chance to react – here, as in the Middle English text, she says nothing at all (293–306).

13   As Maréchal points out with reference to Marie's version, the affinity *ex copula illicita* would have rendered Gurun's marriage to Codre invalid (Maréchal 1992, 140). This situation crops up frequently in court records from the later Middle Ages. For an interesting discussion of more modern literary examples, see Héritier 1995; I am indebted for this reference to Jane Gilbert.

14   It might be argued that this is because the foundling protagonist is female; but mothers are strikingly absent from most medieval 'romances' about women separated from their families. Tarsia's reunion with her father Apollonius is described in detail, but very little is said about the reunion with her mother. Nicolette's mother is not mentioned. In the Incestuous Father narratives the mother is always dead – hence the father's sinful desire to marry his daughter. In romances about male foundlings, it is the meeting with the father which is the crucial turning point, as was noted above; the mother plays no significant part in the ending. In cautionary tales, the mother is marginalized at the end of the story, which focuses on the fate of her son (we never find out what happens to Judas's mother).

15   This is the argument of Maréchal 1992, who associates Marie's *Fresne* with the genre of 'cas' proposed by André Jolles, in which some aspect of canon law is presented in narrative form with exemplary intention. On the exempla about the eventual confession of a female sinner, see Tubach 1969, s.v. 'incest' and 'infanticide'.

16   In both versions the mother has far more lines of speech than the daughter, and indeed is more strongly characterized; as in the Apollonius story, one might argue that the role of female protagonist is divided between mother and daughter, and that they cannot both take centre stage at the same time.

17   See n. 9 above. Foulet accepts Renart's authorship and emends the name given at line 7798 from 'Renaus' to 'Renars', but not all critics accept this attribution.

18   Foulon suggests that the twelfth-century church tolerated concubinage, as long as no bigamy or adultery was involved (Foulon 1978, 208–9); Brundage confirms this, noting that according to some twelfth-century canonists concubinage with marital affection did not count as fornication (Brundage 1987, 297–8).

19   On the other hand, it is hard to imagine Marie writing this lay with the
      intention of illustrating a point of law, as Maréchal argues (Maréchal 1992,
      140–41). Foulon calls Marie's moral conclusion very original, since it com-
      bines 'courtly love', a freely chosen union, and the Christian idea of marriage
      (Foulon 1978, 212).

20   Freine herself never speaks in the surviving English text. When Guroun asks
      her to go and live with him (much more bluntly and arrogantly than in
      Marie's version, it must be said), we do not hear her answer: 'The maiden
      grant, & to him trist, / & stale oway that no man wist' (297–8). Fresne does
      not speak at this point in the French version either, so perhaps we may assume
      that the English author followed Marie in keeping her silent until her mother
      asks about the cloth. At this point Marie gives Fresne six simple lines explain-
      ing the cloth and the ring (436–40 and 442); she never speaks again.

CHAPTER TWO

Lanval to *Sir Launfal*:
A Story Becomes Popular

MYRA STOKES

Lanval is one of the most appealing of the twelfth-century Anglo-Norman *lais* of Marie de France. Written in octosyllabic couplets, these briefish narratives proclaim themselves to be the stories underlying songs (the *lais* proper) performed by Breton minstrels, songs which Marie's tales thus purport to contextualize. Marie's poems were widely imitated, becoming the prototype of a whole new genre now known as 'the Breton *lai*', and were thus, in that sense, demonstrably popular. The sort of popularity attested to by subsequent imitative recreations is also discernible in a more specific sense in the afterlife of the particular *lai* at issue here.

Lanval tells the story of a knight whom Arthur neglects to include in one of his periodic distributions of rewards. Knights in full-time attendance at court were normally conceived of as those who had not yet come into their inheritances. Lanval is the son of a king, but from a distant land (*luin de sun heritage*, 28), and Arthur's omission therefore leaves him in straitened circumstances. Having dismounted from his horse in the course of a ride into the countryside, his disconsolate musings are interrupted by the approach of two beautiful and expensively accoutred damsels, who invite him to the pavilion of their mistress, who is likewise of superlative pulchritude and wealth. She has come specifically to offer her love to Lanval, and further promises to fund all his expenses. He must, however, never discover his new-found *amie* to anyone, or he will instantly lose her. Lanval proceeds to live with the lavish *largesse* – in entertainment, gifts and charitable donations (205–14) – which was expected from those of *gentil* status (and which was in large part responsible for any prestige and popularity they enjoyed among the many to benefit from such big-spending habits). Guinevere one day offers Lanval her love, which he refuses on the grounds of the breach of faith with his *seigneur* that would be involved. Guinevere angrily retorts that his real reason is a preference for boys over women, a charge which Lanval heatedly rebuts by declaring that he has for *amie* a woman whose humblest attendant excels Guinevere in beauty, refinement and personal worth (298–302). Guinevere demands redress from Arthur for this insult, which she represents as having been delivered in response to her own rejection of improper advances from Lanval. The court convened by Arthur declares that Lanval should be banished if he cannot purge his slander by producing his *amie* – which he cannot do, because, now that he has broken her injunction, she no longer responds to his call. Despite this, he is at the eleventh hour delivered from his dilemma by her: the barons' deliberations are interrupted by the arrival – to the accompaniment of much eye-boggling at their beauty and splendour – first of two successive pairs of her damsels, and finally of the *amie* herself. Letting her mantle fall (to maximize visibility of her person), she offers herself in exoneration of his offending words. All agree that Lanval has been vindicated; but he leaps onto the palfrey of his departing *amie*, and it is stated that the two disappeared to Avalon (an island home of the *fée* or fairy) and that nothing more was ever known of Lanval.

If it was the appeal of a Breton song (itself presented as a response to an *aventure* that struck the imagination: Prologue 35–8) which prompted this tale from Marie, her own poem provoked similar recreations. The *lai* was Englished into a fourteenth-century *Landevale*, in which the octosyllabic couplets are preserved, but in which the often trite wording does less than justice to the spare elegance of Marie's style. Landevale's poverty is caused by his own uninhibited *largesse* – an imprudence not too discreditable to the hero, given the value attached to liberal spending habits – and there is only passing mention of his being 'in uncuth londe' (27).[1] Since this poem otherwise stays close to the sense of the Anglo-Norman one, it may be that the beginning of Marie's *lai* was defective or misunderstood by its redactor, who thus virtually omits the socio-economic explanation there given for Lanval's poverty: that he had been passed over in the 'gift economy' operative at court, and, though a king's son, was a foreigner far from home.

These last two facts – so central to the impression given by Marie of a protagonist literally and psychologically alienated from his social environment – are thus likewise absent from a second English verse redaction in turn based on *Landevale*. The author of this later fourteenth-century romance (headed 'Launfal Miles' in the manuscript, but now known as [*Sir*] *Launfal*) names himself in its final stanza as Thomas Chestre. Chestre, who evidently wanted a squeaky-clean but victimized hero, substituted for the one given in *Landevale* yet another reason for Launfal's poverty. In his version, it is occasioned by Arthur's marriage to Guinevere, who is disliked by Launfal because of her reputation for promiscuity, and who thus leaves him out of her own distribution of gifts. Chestre plays other variations on his source. Launfal's signal *largesse* has qualified him (28–33) for appointment as royal steward (the official responsible for the provisioning of inmates and guests). His subsequent poverty is underlined by extended emphasis on the tangible humiliations attendant on reduced means: he can no longer afford to stay at court and, to disguise his necessitous state, offers his father's funeral as the grounds of his plea for leave of absence (76–8); Arthur furnishes him with companions in the form of two royal nephews, who, however, later have to return to the king, because of an impoverishment Launfal cannot relieve; at Launfal's request, they conceal his difficulties from the king, and a second fiction is found to explain the poor state of their attire (166–74); on leaving the court, Launfal seeks out the mayor of Caerleon, a former dependant of his (90), who at first welcomes him on account of Launfal's connections with the court (95–6), but, on hearing from him that he is out of royal favour, suddenly recalls that he is expecting seven knights, and so cannot put Launfal up; Launfal makes a sarcastic comment on the loyalty to be expected towards a lord of no account ('lyttel pryse', 119), at which the mayor rather shamefacedly offers him makeshift accommodation; the 'lyttyll pryse' enjoyed by the no longer rich and influential is confirmed when there is a feast to which Launfal is not invited, for now 'Lyte men of hym tolde' (189); he reveals to the mayor's daughter that he has not eaten for three days, and is too ashamed even to attend church, such is the state of his clothing (194–204); he takes a ride out of the city, cutting a poor figure – unattended as he is (210–12) and 'wyth lytyll pryde' – to which the finishing touch of mud-spatter is added when his horse stumbles into 'the fen' (214); it is to escape the scornful gazes he attracts ('For to dryue away lokynge', 218) that he rides into a forest. These added details provide a sharper contrast, not only with his former *largesse*, both private and official, but also with the sumptuousness that he now encounters in the apparel and pavilion of the damsels and their mistress. The lady is here explicitly declared to be a fairy (the daughter, in fact, of the 'kyng of Fayrye') and is given the name of Tryamour (278–81). To her gifts of love and inexhaustible wealth (which here takes the form of a magic purse that never empties) are added a steed and 'knaue' of her own, named Blaunchard and Gyfre respectively, who will ensure consistent gratifications of a more macho kind – to wit, unconquerability in combat (325–33). This duo, accompanied by a baggage-train of ten pack mules laden with gold, silver, rich clothing and armour, ostentatiously make their way to Launfal's lodgings (376–99) after he has returned thither. The mayor now changes his tune, only to be met with a snub from Launfal (409–14). His *largesse* quickly leads to recovery of his public 'prys' in more ways than one: it results in the staging in his honour of a tournament in which he gains 'the prys' (478) – the 'praise' and the 'prize' due to the proclaimed man of the match. The fame of his prowess reaches Lombardy, where it comes to the ears of a fifteen-foot giant called Sir Valentine, who sends a jousting challenge which Launfal accepts; he succeeds (with a little magical and invisible aid from Gyfre) in slaying both his redoubtable opponent and all the lords who, upon seeing that, attack him (601–12). Arthur invites him, ahead of a forthcoming feast, to resume his office of steward, again because of his (now renewed) *largesse* (622–3). It is at these festivities that the fatal exchange with Guinevere takes place. She, in the subsequent proceedings, declares by way of asseveration, 'yf he brynge a fayrer thynge / Put out my eeyn gray!' (809–10) – and is taken at her word: Tryamour, after vindicating Launfal, blows into her eyes, with the result that 'neuer eft myght sche se' (1008). Gyfre brings Launfal his steed, and he rides away after his mistress; but on a specific day every year, his steed can be heard to neigh, and anyone who fancies a joust can on that day have one against Launfal.

Some of Chestre's narrative elaborations may have been suggested to him by a version of *Graelent*, an old French *lai* that is recognizably an analogue of *Lanval*.[2] But he has taken up those (sometimes distant) hints with a robust inventiveness and consistency that adapt the story into a more aggressive whole, centred on a less passive hero with more to endure, combat, and exert himself to win in the external world. A measure of sturdy initiative is also evident in Chestre's metrical choice: the couplets of his source are transposed into stanzas of tail-rhyme (that is, couplets interspersed with shorter lines in a rhyme and stress scheme of a^4 a^4 b^3 c^4 c^4 b^3, etc). *Sir Launfal* is, in short, written in the metre and style burlesqued by Chaucer in his *Tale of Sir Thopas*. A modern reader cannot, therefore, but notice in it the absurdities Chaucer exposed: the jejune rhythm, the reliance on tags and formulaic clichés, the elf-queen and the giant, and so on. No-one would be reminded by Marie's *Lanval* of *Thopas* – partly for metrical and stylistic reasons, partly for narrative ones (there is no giant, and the *amie*, though one assumes she is a *fée*, is never explicitly referred to as such).

With Chestre's version, in fact, the story has become popular in a sense other than that which would refer to the evidence of the appeal and circulation of the tale. It has become popular – in style and narrative – in the aesthetic sense that is most simply glossed by the frankly snobbish term 'low brow'. Neither sense of the word necessarily implies the other. Although *Sir Thopas* presupposes a public familiar with tail-rhyme romances, there is no evidence that *Sir Launfal* itself was any more popular in the take-up sense than was *Lanval*; the manuscript evidence (inconclusive though that is) would in fact suggest the reverse: Marie's *lais* survive in four manuscripts, *Sir Launfal* in one.[3] Nor does the aesthetic and evaluative sense of the word necessarily entail the social one, although an association of ideas in this respect formerly led to folksy speculations on the socially popular audience putatively implied by Chestre's tale ('simpler, less sensitive listeners' who heard it performed by a travelling minstrel 'in market square or innyard'[4]). Such assumptions were once current with respect to the whole group of so-called 'popular' romances to which *Sir Launfal* is usually assigned;[5] but the lack of evidence to warrant them is apparent from more recent and cautious studies of what can be concluded about the audiences of these works.[6]

That Chestre's tale represents a more 'popular' version of Marie's *lai* is thus primarily an aesthetic judgement made by those who, comparing the two texts, have found the former 'cruder' and lacking in the subtlety and nuance of the latter.[7] To the contrasts that have already been drawn between them, I wish to add some observations about each which may be relevant to the instinctive assignment of them to different categories of literary art.

The persuasiveness of Marie's story seems to be partly referable to the way in which the material plays both with and against facets of familiar and less extra-ordinary experience, resonances from which are set off by the handling of the narrative. Psychological processes are certainly one of the counterparts in mundane reality adumbrated by the pattern of events in the story as here told.[8] The so-called 'omnipotent' mental modes of wish-fulfilling daydream or make-believe – whether in the child or in the less de-ceived but still wishful adult – are in effect experiments with mental magic wands which have, interestingly, been linked specifically with 'magical think-ing' in psychoanalytic literature (as comparable attempts to 'will' desires into actuality).[9] Though it seems to be totemic or ritual magic that is referred to when the analogy is made, the association of ideas is natural, and may help to explain why one is ready, at the prompting of the narrative, to be reminded of wishful fantasies by the beneficent timeliness of the magical events in *Lanval*. For daydreams and fantasies (in which the 'ideal ego' solaces itself with imagined scenarios that supply those of its desires unmet by objective reality) are an instinctive response to disappointment or pain caused by external circumstances – which is a common trigger for a switch of cathexis from the object world to the subject world:[10] that is, when things go wrong, people often start to imagine how nice it would be if they were different.

Though wishful fantasizing is scarcely in itself evidence of psychic dis-order, a pathological version of it has been identified: a condition wherein the outer world is consistently retreated from via 'the compensatory con-struction of an alternative world' in which the self lives 'an alternative life'. There is an understandably felt ban on disclosure in these cases: the fantasies are as intimately secret as a 'lover', and revelation, as if of 'a secret affair', is as compulsively shunned as if it threatened to 'terminate the relation' between the self and the private world (Bollas 1989, 118, 130). This is another analogy from psychoanalytic literature which (like the one drawn between magic and fantasy) finds a narrative correlate in *Lanval*, where the private world centres precisely on a lover – and is lost when communication betrays it and her to the outer world.

Lanval's plight has from the first a larger psychological element than Launfal's. Lanval is literally in unfamiliar territory, and his status as a stranger (which plays no part in Chestre's version) is not lost sight of by Marie: it forms part of the later reluctance of the barons to subject him – 'humme d'autre païs' (429) – to harsh treatment, and is the reason why, 'suls et esgarez' (398), he has no-one to turn to when obliged to find persons willing to stand bail for him pending his trial (until Gawain and his friends generously step forward). Arthur's oversight is quite unlike the deliberate discrimination for disreputable motives visited upon Launfal: Lanval's alien status is thereupon compounded by the further alienation of seeing himself unregarded and unvalued in both personal and economic terms. Unregarded likewise is his poverty: there is no sense in Marie, as in Chestre, that it has become a public and therefore humiliating fact – or, indeed, a fact at all (as yet) as opposed to a grim prospect, which no-one else seems to register. It is not, therefore, to escape notice, as with Launfal, that Lanval retreats from a court in which he appears to be alone and unnoticed. On adopting the reclining posture of sleep or reflection, his mood is described (51) as *pensis* ('pensive', a word used of a worried distress helpless of remedy). This adjective (for which there is no equivalent at the relevant points in *Landevale* or *Sir Launfal*) is later used of both Lanval and the barons at the arraignment of the former (338, 428, 507). In each case, the indication of troubled interiority heralds the emergence into the narrative of an external but extra-normal event which provides the resource and recourse that is wanting in the world of everyday reality.

What Lanval then meets with presents itself narrowly and specifically in terms of his present needs: it is exactly and exclusively in terms of wealth and expensiveness that the visions of feminine charm and beauty now manifest themselves. Though Chestre has been said to be the more materialistic at this point,[11] he is so only in the sense that he provides more enumeration of jewels, fabrics, etc., with the result that his description does not markedly differ from those (not uncommon) in which feminine beauty is conveyed through a classy luxuriance of accessories. Marie, in fact, in this as in other areas of less than romantic significance, is consistently more pointed and unembarrassed than her more 'popular' English redactors. In this case, she uncharacteristically concentrates on sheer monetary value in her depiction of female attractions. The link is made at once with the two serving-women first seen –

> Unkes n'en ot veü plus beles!
> Vestues furent richement . . .
> (55–6)

(He had never seen any more beautiful. They were dressed richly . . .)

– and becomes ever more marked as the *aventure* unfolds. Of the pavilion Lanval is then led to, we are given little visual detail, but only the information that it could not have been afforded even by Semiramis or the emperor Octavian (81–6), that the golden eagle surmounting it was of price incalculable (87–8), and that the very ropes and pegs were beyond the means of any king in the world (89–92). The surpassing beauty of the lady, lying in inviting *déshabillé*, is thus firmly set in a framing tent of monetary value, and the same emphasis continues into her more immediate context: she lies on a bed of which even the sheets cost a castle ('Li drap valeient un chastel', 98), and is (half-)draped in 'Un chier mantel de blanc hermine' (101). The word *chier* here epitomizes the fusion of sexual and economic attractions that doubly 'endears' this lady to Lanval.

But economic value is coupled by Marie with the affirmation of his personal value that Lanval sadly needs, in view of the lack of recognition which his service to Arthur has met with, despite his excellent qualities (21–2). The damsels have been sent specifically for *him* (73), and the lady herself has come precisely for him. Her first words to him are:

> 'Lanval, fet ele, beus amis,
> Pur vus vinc jeo fors de ma tere:
> De luinz vus sui venue quere!'
> (110–12)

('Lanval,' said she, 'fair friend, for you came I out of my own land: from far away am I come to seek you out.')

This is calculated to be balm to the ears of one who has himself travelled far from home only to find himself slighted and unrated; it is a detail left untranslated in *Landevale* (and thus has no equivalent in Chestre either), where the lady declares herself thus:

> 'Landavale,' she seid, 'myn hert swete,
> For thy loue now I swete'
> (113–14)

– which, alas, is a not untypical example of what happens to Marie's verse at the hands of her English translator.

The closely parallelled grants by Marie's lady (133–9) of her love and of limitless underwriting of the liberal spending implied by *largesse* (Lanval is to 'give' and 'spend' henceforth without inhibition) thus only bring into climactic focus a dual emphasis throughout the 'vision' that meets Lanval's eyes when, in the real and everyday world, he sees nothing that offers him any solace ('Il ne veit chose ki li plaise', 52) – and when someone to serve who would love and value him, and so fund him in a way that demonstrated appreciation, is just what he would be wishfully dreaming of. He promises to obey all his *amie*'s commands (124–7, 151–2) and to renounce all other connections for her sake (128). This traditional romantic metaphor from feudal service stresses just that replacement of the unappreciative master Lanval had left his friends for and 'tant . . . servi' ('served so loyally', 18, 40) with the liberal and grateful mistress that is a dream come true.

The closeness of the whole episode to a dream or fantasy is felt by Lanval himself, who, as he rides back to court, often looks back doubtfully towards the place he has left:

> Suvent esgarde ariere sei . . .
> De s'aventure vait pensaunt
> E en sun curage dotaunt;
> Esbaïz est, ne seit que creire,
> Il ne la quide mie a veire.
> (195–200)

(He often looks behind him . . . He goes reflecting on what has befallen him, and doubting it in his heart; he is disconcerted, does not know what to believe, and does not at all trust it to be true.)

The passage has no equivalent in *Landevale* – or in *Sir Launfal*, in which the chivalric successes granted Launfal, having no remedial relevance to his former plight (since he had not appeared to have any problems in that area), render the hero's fortunes more generally enviable, while simultaneously diluting the precise compensation for present deficits that in Marie also suggests a dream come true.

More significantly, Marie's strict separation of the private from the public world is also lost in *Sir Launfal*. The bottomless purse (319ff, 733), the public delivery of riches (376ff), the squire Gyfre and the steed Blanchard, all carry over into the public everyday world as triumphant tangibilities that establish Launfal's fairy liaison as having a comparable ontology, as belonging to the same plane of reality. By contrast, Lanval's beloved and her favours are realities only to his own consciousness; there are no sensible objects to verify an existence measurable by the same means as that of normal 'reality'. The anonymity of the lady herself contributes to the sense of a sphere of reality different from that of the objective identities of the outer, public world. She is not 'Triamor', and she is not even rationalized into the recognizable identity of a *fée*, to which category she is never explicitly assigned (cf. Spearing 1993, 98).

This leaves her as a figure more fluidly ambiguous between normality and supranormality, more suggestive of an 'alternative world'. The meetings with Lanval she promises and the ban on disclosure she imposes are both treated so as to suggest, not magic mantras or taboos, but especially close observance of the privacy and secrecy essential to what was termed in English 'derne love'. The promise is phrased thus:

> 'Quant vus vodrez od mei parler,
> Ja ne savrez cel liu penser
> U nuls puïst aveir s'amie
> Sanz repreoce e sanz vileinie,
> Que jeo ne vus seie en present
> A fere tut vostre talent;
> Nuls hum fors vus ne me verra
> Ne ma parole nen orra.'
>
> (163–70)

('When you wish to speak with me, you will no sooner have thought of a place where any man can have his *amie* to himself without attracting blame or disgrace than I will be present with you in it to be entirely at your will; no man except you will see me or will hear my words.')

The supernatural ability to be willed into presence and to be invisible is here expressed as an observance of the 'normal' rules governing lovers' trysts in romance: the lady will come to such suitably secret places as other lovers would choose (164–6) and will ensure that her presence is known to only one pair of eyes and ears. Her ban on disclosure, too –

> 'Ne vus descovrez a nul humme!
> De ceo vus dirai ja la summe:
> A tuz jurs m'avrïez perdue,
> Si ceste amur esteit seüe.'
>
> (145–8)

('Do not disclose this to anyone. – In this matter, I will tell you the short and long of it: for ever would you have lost me, if this love were to be known.')

– simply articulates a well-known point of romantic etiquette: the lover (even where no apparent social or moral taboos were breached by the relationship) must not expose his mistress to public notice or remark. An *avauntour* or 'boaster' was abhorred and deprecated as a traitor to his beloved.[12] It is precisely as a version of the romantic ban on 'boasting' of or broadcasting the lady's favours that the ultimatum here is interpreted by *Landevale* (followed by *Sir Launfal*, 361–5): 'Ne make ye neuer bost of me!' (162). Nor would the irreparably disastrous effects of disclosure have been remarkable under 'normal' circumstances. As Spearing points out (Spearing 1993, 115), there is in fact a French poem (*La Chastelaine de Vergi*) in which the lady dies from heartbreak at the breach of faith constituted by disclosure on the part of her *ami* (even though no other ill effects, such as opposition or dishonour, follow from it), and her lover responds by killing himself.

But the romantic stipulation becomes in Marie a measure of and analogy for the conditions that govern a larger private paradise that gives no evidence of itself to the outside world. Narcissistic fantasies of love, wealth, importance, etc., must similarly never be admitted into the public arena. If they are openly spoken of as objective facts, they will require the unproducible objective evidence demanded of Lanval. Such private and public selves can cohabit only under a system of the strictest apartheid; contact embarrasses and endangers the social self, simultaneously depleting the subjective world by exposing its want of objective reality.

A certain degree of narcissistic introversion and engagement in fantasies or daydreams are otherwise said to perform, in fact, an adaptive function.[13] Furthermore, positive 'self-images' give a self-sufficiency and confidence to the outer self that often prove to be attractive and interesting to others (Freud 1957, 89). Lanval's private adventure seems to have similar effects. Though he uses his new-found wealth to behave with all the generous *largesse* becoming to his status (209–14), there is no indication that this attracts any of the remark that it does in Chestre, or that the court notice it any more than they had the poverty that obviously faced him before. All that happens is that, for the first time, Lanval is registered and remembered. When a group of knights gather to disport themselves, Gawain suddenly declares that they should have brought Lanval,

> 'Ki tant est larges e curteis
> E sis peres est riches reis.'
> (231–2)

('who is so liberal and courtly, – and his father is a wealthy king.')

These facts about Lanval were known before his *aventure* (cf. 21–2, 27), but had procured him neither attention nor regard. It is only now that the court remembers and actually seeks him out (235–6) – now that he has already been remembered and sought out in his own private world, and now that his peace of mind no longer depends on such marks of notice and regard from his peers. The point is emphasized by the immediate juxtaposition of a similar reaction in Guinevere. Chestre accounts for her behaviour by assuming an existing passion (simmering for seven years for Launfal, 678). In *Lanval*, she seems simply to display in a more pronounced form the phenomenon just witnessed in Gawain. On seeing the knights from a window, 'Lanval conut e esgarda' ('she recognized Lanval and looked at him', 241). We are told nothing more of what passes in her mind at that point; acting apparently on a sudden instinctive plan, she immediately summons her ladies and joins the knights. Lanval, now self-sufficient – in the economic and emotional terms that are throughout the story so closely interrelated – has become the valued and sought-out figure that those who need no reassurance of their worth often prove to be.

Marie's story is not, of course, actually about a fantasy, nor is it reducible to an allegory of psychological processes.[14] Such a reading would be not only anachronistic, but also counter to the narrative: daydreams do not pay the bills or deliver from the dock.[15] Marie's half-amused awareness of how *like* a wish-come-true the early events are actually serves to distinguish the idyll from sheer fantasy. There are verbal winks that serve to strengthen the link between the juxtaposed gifts by the lady (of herself and of assured wealth): 'Or est Lanval en dreite veie' ('Now Lanval is on the right path', 134), 'Mut est Lanval bien assenez' ('Lanval is very well placed', 140), 'Ore est Lanval bien herbergiez' ('Now Lanval is comfortably lodged', 154). We are invited to observe, that is, how pretty our hero is now sitting. Such features, together with Lanval's own subsequent doubts (197–200) as to whether all this has not been too good to have been really true, offer not an idealizing fantasy but, more specifically, what is quite good enough to be mistaken for one. Marie grants her hero with a knowing smile the ideal self-image wistfully pictured by most: interlinked sexual/romantic and economic success, and a 'name' to be repeated with admiration and warmth – a name bestowed by Marie herself in semi-serious applause:

> Lanval donout les riches duns,
> Lanval aquitout les prisuns,
> Lanval vesteit les jugleürs,
> Lanval feseit les granz honurs!
> (209–12)

(Lanval gave the rich gifts, Lanval redeemed the prisoners, Lanval provided robes for the minstrels, Lanval performed the great honours!)

But the realization of an ideal self – to which Chestre gives prime and prolonged narrative space – is, in effect, merely this brief in *Lanval*. Marie seems interested in larger and more complex questions concerning the relation between private and public worlds.

Lanval now enjoys an independence from the court much more potentially dangerous than the psychic self-sufficiency enjoyed by the confirmed daydreamer. He looks to his social circle for neither personal nor economic gratification or advancement. It has lost the sanctions and incentives with which it can normally command the commitment of its members. Arthur rewards his followers with 'femmes e teres' ('wives and lands', 17), and it is thus from the court that domestic and economic prosperity is normally looked for. Lanval is now not interested. Herein lies the real significance of the exchange with Guinevere.

The Guinevere of the more worldly-wise Marie is not Chestre's royal tart. She is the queen: the patroness of the court, able to dispense favours and to personify in her feminine form the romantic ideal of an *amie* so central to the Arthurian ethos. What she offers is a mark of signal favour from the top and a most prestigious *amie*. It is quite clear that both Guinevere (267–8) and Marie would expect any normal knight to jump at the chance of such glamorous career prospects. Perhaps it would be nice to turn down offers of professional distinction and promotion because one is already amply provided (from other sources) with esteem and remuneration; but it would produce an impossible situation – as it does in *Lanval*.

Lanval's insult to Guinevere constitutes a much more comprehensive rejection of all the court stands for in terms of social and personal worth and desirability than it does in Chestre. In the latter, what it leads to is merely a beauty contest to satisfy the pique of a vain woman. In *Lanval*, beauty is only one of the ways in which Guinevere is surpassed, Lanval claims, by the least of his *amie*'s attendants, who

> 'Vaut mieux de vus, dame reïne,
> De cors, de vis e de beauté,
> D'enseignement et de bunté.'
> (300–302)

('. . . is of more worth than you, my lady the queen, in body, face and beauty, in social graces and in goodness.')

In this world, beauty is a measure of status, courtliness and value (cf. 489–90, 529–33, 550–74). Guinevere's angry distress at having been *si aviliee* ('so degraded') is thus not simply feminine petulance at hearing she is not the prettiest woman alive. Lanval has, in more senses than one, found an alternative 'mistress', an alternative measure of courtly ideals. Subsequent references to his 'boast' make it clear that it is interpreted as an aspersion on Guinevere's claims to courtly refinement and nobility generally (321); and the king too sees the link between 'more beautiful' and 'of more worth' in a larger sense in that boast of a mistress so *noble* (368) that 'plus est bele sa meschine / Et plus vaillanz que la reïne' ('her serving-lady is more beautiful and of more worth than the queen'). Lanval has, in effect, withdrawn his allegiance to the court.

His leap of a choice at the dénouement, to follow his mistress rather than remain at court, is a measure of how impossible further residence at court has become – even though he has loyal friends inside it and has been publicly cleared of the charges against him (626–9). No man can serve two masters (or mistresses), and Lanval cannot truly serve the court and be funded, emotionally and monetarily, from outside it. His instinctive, impulsive and irrevocable choice is a much more satisfying and conclusive one in Marie than in Chestre, in whose version Launfal's fairy *liaison* serves to establish and maintain his public identity as an archetypal knight – a role which, indeed, he returns annually to re-enact. Marie preserves to the last the antithesis between her hero's private and his public world: when he leaps onto his mysterious mistress's horse, he is carried for ever out of public perception, to disappear even from narrative view:

> Nuls hum n'en oï plus parler
> Ne jeo n'en sai avant cunter.
> (645–6)

(No man ever heard tell any more of him, nor do I know anything more to recount of him.)

The ever-growing tension created by an objective world that is oblivious to, or denies and challenges, private realities also appeals, in a larger way, to an experience undergone, in minor or acute form, by all – and Marie's conclusion is in every sense a romantic one: Lanval is loyal to his private love, his personal reality, and rejects the outside world. His effective death to the world of everyday reality is felt as a deliverance from it. The focus during the trial has been on his psychological and emotional rather than his legal or financial need for his *amie*. The economic issue gradually ceases to be one: when he betrays his mistress, it is the loss only of her company that desolates Lanval (333ff); the loss of wealth is unmentioned, though it is presumably concomitant – and this is certainly what Chestre finds most heart-rending, since he here adds one of his most effective stanzas to picture Launfal finding all his recently acquired wealth has 'malt as snow ayens the sunne' (740). Lanval prays his beloved only for the mercy of renewed sight of her (349–50), not for financial or judicial deliverance, and when she does appear, breathes a sigh of relief, expressing restoration merely by the sight of her and consequent carelessness as to what penalty, even death, may now be imposed upon him – words changed into a triumphant cry of hope of deliverance by Chestre (970–72). Lanval desires only some assertion of his private reality in the midst of the lonely estrangement into which his initial alienation, by geography and indifference, has now intensified.

Marie's story thus suggests areas of everyday experience or speculative possibility (the related and essentially private worlds of love and of imaginative fantasy; the common psychological experience of alienation from social context and of division between social and subjective identity; the possible social consequences of simultaneous independence from and membership of a collective), whilst retaining an otherness, a non-everyday drama and singularity, which resists reduction to all or any of them.

There is in Chestre little sense of a private world of Launfal's which belongs to a different order of reality, for the hero is constantly exposed, for good or ill, to public view[16] – and the connection between public standing and economics is especially evident (Chestre plays up this element of the plot, where Marie fades it out). Launfal's renown for *largesse* results in the public office of royal steward; the social reactions to his poverty are marked in the mayor's behaviour and in public scorn; his accession to wealth is public (376ff), and is accompanied by pronounced public success in a tournament held in his honour (434–5), to celebrate which he holds a magnificent public feast (493ff). This coupling of publicly acclaimed chivalry and magnificence continues when his renown in the former area spreads to Lombardy, resulting in his defeat of the redoubtable Sir Valentine (505ff); and tidings of the latter then cause Arthur to summon him to resume his office of steward for the forthcoming public feast (613ff) – causing a reintegration into the court marked by the reconferring of a public office, for which Launfal proves himself qualified by the very spending style that had earlier won him the stewardship (28–32). The public humiliations at his arraignment are as marked as were those attendant upon his poverty: he is bound (757) by the knights (and so led away 'as theff', *Landevale* 277), and threatened with similarly shameful public execution ('He schud be hongede as a thef', 803); and Lanval's sigh of private feeling on his mistress's arrival becomes in Chestre a public cry of defiant acclamation ('To alle the folk he gon crye an hy', 968; cf. *Landevale* 456).

Chestre's tale is not without distinctive emphases of an interesting kind. Squarely facing the outer world, it conveys vividly the mortifications and exaltations attendant upon economic fortunes. It has a consistent concern with *largesse* as an economic posture proper to *gentils* and as deserving of public acclaim, recognition and office. Following *Landevale* (21ff), it from the first associates signal *largesse* with the hero (28–35), where in *Lanval* this is merely one among a list of the typical chivalric virtues he possesses (21–2). Chestre's juxtaposition of triumph in combat and conspicuous magnificence also makes an interesting association between two kinds of activity that compel public endorsement,[17] and the fusion of the two kinds of large spirit (not to be deterred by wounds or bills) lends an aggressive and defiant quality to Launfal's *largesse*, as if he were defeating both physically and economically the resistance he encounters from the world.

Launfal 'shows 'em', and the success must be public, for this is part of the logic of the sort of story Chestre has turned the *lai* into: an adventure story of the type still met with in Hollywood films – a tale of dramatic incident in which the hero gets the girl and the loot and triumphs over the opposition. The defeat of Sir Valentine by the invisible aid of Gyfre has attracted deprecating comments on its supposed crude violence and dishonourable cheating;[18] but the episode is entirely in the spirit of this sort of fiction, and the hero is no more bloodthirsty than, and enjoys roughly equivalent advantages with, his modern counterpart, James Bond, whose gruesome dispatch of opponents is often achieved with the aid of the technological wizardry that stands in for magic in the twentieth-century mix of these time-honoured ingredients.

Sir Launfal – in which elusiveness has become sensible incident, and which is so much more combative, in every sense, than *Lanval* – is in some ways quite refreshing to read after the earlier *lai*. But in the element of triumph that is virtually absent from Marie's tale there is a moral polarization typical of popular or popularized fiction – in which the triumph is given an often bogus legitimization by the grafting of received types of wickedness onto the opposition, who must be seen as morally inferior to the defeater. The moral superiority of the hero is often unconvincing, as is revealed by the old French *Graelent*. The high-minded line Graelent takes in refusing Guinevere at the start of the tale (121–8) is obviously meant to establish him as a loyal and honourable vassal – but it is made nonsense of when it is followed by the rape of the fairy mistress-to-be he encounters bathing (277–90), an act at which, since the victim is unperturbed by it, the audience is not permitted to protest. Such inconsistency in the moral seriousness with which the irregularities of the hero and of the opposition are to be taken is not uncommon in popular fiction of the present century.

In Chestre, a hypocritical and snobbish mayor and a promiscuous and unprincipled Guinevere become targeted as the focal sources of Launfal's troubles, from which his emergence thus entails a form of righteous punishment – a verbal put-down in the case of the mayor (409–14), and the blinding of Guinevere (1006–8), because, the tale insists, she really did 'ask for it' (cf. 809–10). The difference between Marie and Chestre in this respect may be seen in the gnomic comments briefly interposed by each to point to a generally applicable truth emerging from the plight of the hero. Marie's occurs at the close of her scene-setting introduction, and draws attention to a *situation* (of social and psychological isolation):

> Hum estrange descunseillez,
> Mut est dolenz en autre tere,
> Quant il ne seit u sucurs quere!
> (36–8)

(A foreigner without recourse to assistance is much distressed in another land, when he does not know where to turn for help.)

Chestre's is uttered by the hero himself, to the internal audience of his companions, to point up the moral of the mayor's sudden recollection of seven imminent guests; and it takes the form of social satire:

> Launfal turnede hymself & low,
> Therof he hadde scorn ynow,
>   And seyde to hys knyghtes tweyne:
> 'Now may ye se – swych ys seruice
> Vnther a lord of lytyll pryse! –
>   How he may therof be fayn.'
> (115–20)

As to Guinevere, Chestre follows *Graelent* (rather than *Landevale*) in attributing the hero's decline in fortunes to the immorality and malice of the queen. Launfal is one of those right-minded and 'hende' members of the court who cannot approve of their master's new wife – who is credited with a promiscuity the inveterateness of which is established by a typical tail-rhyme hyperbole:

> But Syr Launfal lykede her noght,
>   Ne other knyghtes that wer hende,
> For the lady bar los of swych word
> That sche hadde lemmanys vnther her lord,
>   So fele ther nas noon ende.
> (44–8)

So when Guinevere consequently leaves him out of her gift-distribution, Launfal figures as the innocent persecuted for his uprightness. He figures in a similar victimized role at his trial, in which Chestre depicts a more vengeably choleric king (835–7) and queen (706, 713) – who in Marie takes no further part in the proceedings after her initial complaint to Arthur – than is found in either *Lanval* or *Landevale*. Guinevere's promiscuity is recalled to blacken her further at this point: whereas in *Lanval* the charge of improper advances (as opposed to the insult Lanval admits to) is simply ignored by the court, in both *Landevale* (295–302) and *Sir Launfal* (787–95) it is dismissed because, due to the queen's reputation with regard to *lemmanes* (791), all are immediately convinced that the advances were hers rather than Launfal's.

The tabloid enjoyment of detecting sexual misdemeanours in the royal family and corruption in high places thus provides a moral justification for triumph over the 'other', and the grim satisfaction afforded by the blinding of Guinevere (1006–8) is a more pronounced version of the come-uppance received by the mayor (409–14). In this sort of story, troubles are seldom viewed simply as what life can and does throw up, but traced to a 'guilty' party.

Marie, by contrast, achieves a socially and psychologically more complex picture by consistently discouraging any 'sin-spotting'. The king's initial failure to include Lanval in the gift-dividends is simply an oversight (19–20), a sin of omission too unheinous to elicit much indignation.[19] The explanation for why no-one reminds Arthur of Lanval's claims to recognition – that many knights were envious of his many excellencies (21–6) – is the closest Marie gets to any criticism of anybody; but the tale certainly does not suggest (as it could do) a court manned by mean-minded and self-serving careerists, since Lanval later meets with much generosity and consideration from a fellowship quite capable of giving both – and of conducting a hearing with unintimidated fairness and humanity.

Nor is there any disapproval implied with regard to the advances made by Guinevere to Lanval. In the world of Arthurian literature, married men or women may often take *ami(e)s* without narrative censure.[20] This presumably explains why Chestre cannot get enough moral mileage out of Guinevere's well-known possession of one particular *ami* (Lancelot), and has therefore to represent her as promiscuous to a nymphomaniac degree. The contretemps between the queen and Lanval is also intelligently handled by Marie to suggest, not clear innocence and guilt as between the parties, but something much more recognizable: a situation in which each person is surprised into an overhasty reaction.

Lanval's rejection of Guinevere is on the same grounds as those attributed to Graelent (121–8) and Guingamor (95ff):[21] it would be a breach of faith to the *seigneur* he serves (269–74). But at this point in the narrative (when Lanval is already possessed of an *amie* of such exceptional and various charms), the rectitude of his response is a little more suspect than it is in

the analogues, in which the exchange takes place at the beginning of the
tales. Lanval can well afford his moral scruples, which are at least partially
a screen for the more pressing influence of an existing *amie* he cannot
reveal. Guinevere's response is perfectly understandable: rejection is morti-
fying enough, but rejection on grounds that imply impropriety in the offer
adds insult to injury. And it is the implicit charge of misservice to Arthur
that she hotly turns back on Lanval. The charge (277–82) of homosexuality
(which is more explicit than in the English versions – another example of
Marie's more 'courtly' romance being, in fact, on certain subjects, blunter
and plainer in expression than are its more 'popular' descendants[22]) is made
chiefly to challenge Lanval's assumption of the moral high ground, by
presenting it as a cover for more sordid facts, and, by discrediting any
honour redounding to Arthur from Lanval's service, to retort on the knight
his claim that Arthur's honour is safer in his hands than in hers:

> 'Mut est mis sires maubailliz
> Ki pres de lui vus ad suffert.'
> (284–5)

('My lord is much ill-served in suffering you in his vicinity.')

Guinevere speaks, with a nice piece of psychology absent from the English
versions, not simply out of wounded vanity, but in anger at being morally
sniffed at. Moreover, her speech is prefaced by a characterization of it
entirely absent from the English redactions:

> La reïne s'en curuça;
> Iriee fu, si mesparla.
> (275–6)

(The queen was enraged at this; she was angered, and so spoke amiss.)

An equivalent introduction is provided for Lanval's reply, which refutes the
charge with angry impulsiveness:

> Quant il l'oï, mut fu dolenz;
> Del respundre ne fu pas lenz.
> Teu chose dist par maltalent
> Dunt il se repenti sovent.
> (287–90)

(When he heard her, he was most upset; to reply he was not slow. Such a
thing did he say in his ill-will which he often repented of [afterwards].)

That Lanval did not pause before speaking (288), and that he said in passion what he would not have done had he taken time to reflect, are similarly details not found in the English versions. The original not only gives more texture to this exchange, but also discourages any moral opposition between the speakers: the insult each gives the other is spoken in haste and in passion, and each says what neither would say when more themselves. Marie is more concerned to evoke a psychologically and socially familar experience in a situation that is atypical than to take up moral positions.

During the trial, attention is similarly deflected away from the fact that the propositioning actually came from Guinevere (not, as she claims, from Lanval) and away from any moral implications that might be drawn from this. Guinevere's version is offered primarily only as an explanation of how the slur (which is the substance of her complaint) came to be cast on her (317–24), and it is the latter to which Arthur gives more emphasis in his confrontation of Lanval (363–70). The charge of attempted adultery is in the event not considered at all by the court, and there are no speculations within it on this matter. Lanval, after his initial denial that he was guilty of any such *deshonur* to his lord (371–4), is required to defend himself only on the charge (the insult to the queen) that he does admit to (375–7). Marie, Arthur and the barons, it appears, consider that precisely what happened on this score is an unprovable and private matter unsuitable for public investigation or conjecture – where, in the English versions, it is of material interest to both the narrative and the court.

Even the slander on the queen is declared by the court to be an offence which would not normally require a legal defence, were it not for the fact that it might involve a breach of the duty always to 'faire honur' to one's *seigneur* (447–8). If, therefore, Lanval can show he spoke the truth, he will be cleared of any intended *vilté* (456) or cheapening of the king. This court, in other words, understands the real issue – which is here not sexual mores, but the implication that the insult to the king's consort entails (in its suggestion that the courtly ideal is better represented elsewhere) a want of respect for Arthur.

Nor is there in the *lai* any self-righteous exposure of the lie Guinevere (who could scarcely tell the whole truth to Arthur) was forced into. In his denial of the charge of improper advances, Lanval does not say that the boot was on the other foot. He, indeed, probably could not. But Marie and his *amie* observe the same decorum when vindicating him. With regard to this charge, Lanval's redemptress simply declares that 'Unkes nul jur ne la requist' ('never on any day did he request love of her', 621). She does not add that it was the other way round, as Chestre, following *Landevale* (484), takes satisfaction in publicizing through Triamour:

> He bad naght her, but sche bad hym
> Here lemman for to be.
>
> (998–9)

Marie's version of the tale thus consistently resists any focus on 'guilty parties' in its account of Lanval's dilemmas. The persons inhabiting the world around him behave understandably, and no need is felt for punishment or exposure of them. It is not uncharacteristic of memorable fictions to be more interested in the fact that people *do* feel, speak and act in such or such a way than in whether they *should* – or in whose 'fault' it is that painful or tragic things occur. It is also characteristic of interpretative processes to impose more moral categorization than appears to be there. Experiment has established that, in the course of successive retellings of a brief fictional sequence, the episode tends to acquire a conventional 'moral' at some point in its serial reproduction (Bartlett 1970, 145, 173).[23] As a story becomes popular (in the sense of 'disseminated'), it tends to take on the moral polarity typical of fiction that is popular in the aesthetic sense. By this process, perhaps, did Chaucer's Pandarus come to be transformed (as *pander*) into a synonym for a bawd. The affair between Lancelot and Guinevere came to be subjected to bourgeois readings which saw in it primarily a moral problem, whereas no moral perspective upon it is offered in the earliest versions.[24] Professional interpretation, or literary criticism, shows the same bias towards eliciting coherence by recourse to moral map-drawing. The dragon in *Beowulf* is discerned as representing 'evil' of a general or specific kind, or the protagonist detected in flaws that morally 'explain' his death in that last duel – though the poem itself seems to see each as acting according to priorities and instincts arising inevitably from their respective natures, situations and status, and certainly expresses no overt concern as to whether either or both 'ought' to die. The transformation of *Lanval* into *Sir Launfal* in that respect illustrates a minor law that seems to operate in the interpretation and retelling of fictions that – though, or because, irreducible to some existing cognitive category – catch the imagination.

Notes

1   Quotations from *Landevale* and from *Sir Launfal* are from *Sir Launfal*, ed. A. J. Bliss (London: Nelson, 1960).

2   Those departures from *Landevale* that indicate familiarity with the *Graelent* story are pointed out by Bliss (1960), 24. For the text of *Graelent*, see Alexandre Micha (ed.), *Lais féeriques des XIIe et XIIIe siècles* (Paris: Flammarion, 1992).

3   *Landevale* (surviving in three manuscripts and two fragments of early printed books) outscores both on this count; on the manuscripts of both the English poems, see Bliss 1960, 3–5.

4   Bliss 1960, 1, 31. More recently, Spearing – in his chapter on 'The Lanval Story' in Spearing 1993, 97–119 – also assumes 'social insecurity' in Chestre and a probably 'non-aristocratic public' (97, 139)

5   See, for instance, Bliss 1960, 31–3, and Brunner 1961, 223.

6   Putter 1995, 62; see further Pearsall 1985 and Meale 1994, who concludes that the audiences 'resist generalization and easy classification' (225). On the question of audience, see also the Introduction to this collection.

7   See Bliss 1960, 42ff, and Spearing 1993, 97–119.

8   Wish-fulfilment or fantasy is sometimes argued to be what the story actually represents or is about: see Spearing 1993, 98–103.

9   See Freud's essay 'On Narcissism: An Introduction' (1957) and the chapter entitled 'Magic, Omnipotence and Anxiety' in Modell 1968, 10–27.

10 Freud 1957, 74; Modell 1968, 105, 111ff.

11 Bliss 1960, 44; Spearing 1993, 109.

12 See, for instance, Chaucer's *Parliament of Fowls*, 430, 457, and *Troilus* III, 264–329.

13 See Bollas 1989, 139; Modell 1968, 59–60, 105.

14 Spearing 1993, 102–5, takes the analogy with subjective fantasy further than I would in this respect.

15 Cf. Modell 1968, 107: 'An infant may hallucinate the breast, but hallucinations do not provide nourishment.'

16 This feature of Chestre's tale is emphasized by Spearing 1993, 112–13.

17 A similar link between bravery and *largesse* is discernible in another tail-rhyme romance, *The Avowing of Arthur*, ed. Roger Dahood (New York: Garland, 1984). In this romance Baldwin is required to entertain the whole court and to defy a planted ambush in tests devised (by Arthur) of three interlinked vows he had made, in which physical fortitude is joined with economic and domestic versions of the same virtue: never to be deflected from his road, never to deny any man hospitality, never to be jealous of his wife. See Burrow 1987 for a discussion of the connections between Baldwin's three vows.

18 See Bliss 1960, 43; Spearing 1993, 143.

19 If Marie's source resembled *Graelent*, a close analogue to *Lanval*, this would represent a deliberate screening out by her of royal misconduct as the primary cause of Lanval's plight at court.

20 Cf. Marie's own tale of *Laustic*; in the prose *Lancelot do Lac* – ed. Elspeth Kennedy, 2 vols (Oxford: Oxford University Press, 1980) – neither Guinevere's acceptance of Lancelot as her *ami* nor Arthur's own extramarital courting (II, 541–6) occasions any moral comment.

21 For the text of *Guingamor*, see Micha (ed.), *Lais féeriques* (n. 1 above).

22 See *Landevale*, 226; *Sir Launfal*, 689; cf. pp. 61–2 above.

23 The experiment conducted by the psychologist F. C. Bartlett went as follows: volunteers were given a short story to remember; they might also be asked to

pass the story on to others; at regular intervals Bartlett would ask his subjects to retell the story from memory. In the process of transmission and reproduction, the story usually acquired some predictable moral.

24 E.g. *Lancelot do Lac* or Chrétien's *Le Chevalier de la charrete*, ed. Mario Roques, CFMA (Paris: Champion, 1983). Disapproval of Lancelot and Guinevere's adulterous affair in the interest of 'family values' became especially widespread in the Renaissance (Adams 1959), though some early instances of moral attitudes towards Isolde and Guinevere occur in Dante, *Purgatorio*, XVI.15, and Chrétien's *Cligés*, ed. Alexandra Micha, CFMA (Paris: Champion, 1982), 3105–24.

CHAPTER THREE

The Tale of Gamelyn: Class Warfare and the Embarrassments of Genre

T. A. SHIPPEY

Two contradictions strike one immediately on considering reactions to the *Tale of Gamelyn*. The first is that while *Gamelyn* is by one obvious measure the most popular of all the anonymous Middle English metrical romances – it exists in twenty-five manuscripts, plus a further late transcript of a printed work, and is furthermore at one remove the source for Shakespeare's *As You Like It* – it has aroused little if any enthusiasm among modern literary critics. Its normal diet in standard surveys of romance is faint praise, with such phrases used as 'honest artlessness' or 'popular yet efficient'; there is a certain suggestion that it hardly counts as a romance at all, 'nothing romantic about its tone or style', 'almost uncomfortably close [to contemporary reality] for the romance mode'; although the poem has no known source, and in spite of the relationship to contemporary reality often put forward, it is felt to have 'archaic' or 'marginal' elements. When the historian Richard Kaeuper asked for an opinion on it from a modern editor of romance, the reply he got (from A. V. C. Schmidt) was 'unclassifiable'.[1] Nearly all the studies of the poem listed in the *Manual of the Writings in Middle English* are linguistic or textual (Severs 1967).

The second contradiction is that in spite of this general lack of interest from literary scholars, historians have continued to find *Gamelyn* a major source and object of study. Two extensive articles have set it in realistic legal and social contexts (Shannon 1951 and Kaeuper 1983 – one might note the title of the latter, 'An Historian's Reading of the *Tale of Gamelyn*') – while it is also consistently drawn on or appealed to by major historical works (e.g. Bellamy 1973 and 1989, Powell 1989). This second contradiction is even more marked if one considers *Gamelyn*'s close analogues in the Robin Hood cycle, especially the long ballad-romance *A Gest of Robyn Hode*. The question of the origins and historical significance of Robin Hood has in recent years generated one genuine scholarly *querelle* in the form of a five-article sequence in *Past and Present* (Hilton 1976), a re-edition of all the early Robin Hood poems by two historians,[2] and two more full-length historical studies (Bellamy 1985 and Holt 1989, the latter by the Professor of Medieval History at Cambridge). Furthermore, the one extensive work on Robin Hood by a literary critic (Knight 1994) continues to treat the subject for the most part historically, at least in its medieval manifestations. To complete the pattern, while there has indeed been a recent extensive treatment of *Gamelyn* by a literary critic (Scattergood 1994), more than half of this is devoted to showing its close connection with 'social and political problems endemic in England in the earlier part of the fourteenth century' (163). One may sum up the contradictions in reader-reaction by saying that, for all its many manuscripts, *Gamelyn* is felt to be not literary, while, although it is regularly classified as a romance, it is more often treated as a historical document.

The first of these two contradictions is easy to explain, though it does raise further intriguing questions. All twenty-five of the *Gamelyn* manuscripts are manuscripts of the *Canterbury Tales*. The poem's apparent medieval popularity is accordingly borrowed from Chaucer; and the simplest explanation for its repeated appearance in 'the Chaucer tradition' is that a copy of *Gamelyn* was among Chaucer's papers when he died, presumably waiting to be rewritten into the form of one more 'Canterbury Tale' (see Skeat 1884, xiv). Several Chaucer scribes indeed label it as 'the Cook's Tale of Gamelyn', but this ascription has not found favour. There is a *Cook's Tale* already, if incomplete. It would have made more sense for Chaucer to assign *Gamelyn* to one of the seven pilgrims out of the *General Prologue*'s initial twenty-nine (counting the three nun's priests of line 164 as one) who do not have a tale: i.e., to one of the five Guildsmen, the Plowman, or the Knight's Yeoman. Skeat opted for the last alternative in 1884, for obvious reasons. *Gamelyn* (its rather simple plot is summarized on p. 83 below) eventually becomes a tale of outlaws in the greenwood, which involves deer-hunting with bows and arrows, if to a lesser extent than the Robin Hood cycle. The Knight's Yeoman, a 'forster' dressed in green with 'myghty bowe' and peacock-feathered arrows, therefore seems ideally suited to it. But though there has been no significant dissent from this proposal, it has also not seemed of any great significance to Chaucer scholars. Scattergood indeed suggests that the poem could as easily have been part of Chaucer's raw material for the *Tale of Sir Thopas* (Scattergood 1994).

There are, however, further and subtler indications to support the connection of *Gamelyn* with the Knight's Yeoman. Chaucerian scholarship has remained a little uncertain about what to do with the twenty-eight lines known as 'The Man of Law's Epilogue', in which the Host blasphemously compliments the Man of Law on his tale and calls on the Parson to follow it, only for the Parson to reprove him for swearing and for the Host to call him a Lollard by way of retaliation. A fourth pilgrim then joins in, and refuses to allow the Parson to speak, preach or teach, as a trouble-maker; he will tell a tale instead, he says:

> 'But it shal nat ben of philosophie,
> Ne phislyas, ne termes queinte of lawe,
> Ther is but litel Latyn in my mawe!'
> (II, 1188–90)[3]

Different manuscripts assign this thirteen-line speech to the Squire or the Summoner, but the former seems definitely ruled out by the speaker's discourteous aggression and by his swearing 'by my fader soule', for the Squire's father is alive and present; while the last line quoted above rules out the Summoner, who uses Latin continually (when drunk) (see *General Prologue*, 636–46). The *Riverside Chaucer* accordingly gives the speech to the Shipman on the evidence of one manuscript. Aage Brusendorff suggested however that the speech ought to go to the Yeoman, confused in the manuscripts with the Squire because he was in fact the Squire's Yeoman, not the Knight's (the referent of 'he' in *General Prologue*, 101 is not clear), and Chaucer might have written 'Squire' in over initial 'Yeoman' to distinguish him from a late arrival on the pilgrimage, the Canon's Yeoman (Brusendorff 1925, 70–73).

The *Riverside* editors reject Brusendorff's opinion (which has no manuscript support, as opposed to the Shipman's one-manuscript support), but the idea fits well both with Chaucer's image of yeomen and with *Gamelyn*. The last speaker in the 'Epilogue' is aggressive, and stupidly aggressive, with his ready support for the Host's accusation of heresy (which takes the Second Commandment to be heretical), his insistence that teaching the gospel detracts from belief in God, and his vigorously expressed set of all-round anti-clerical and anti-learned prejudices. But he is also perfectly self-confident, for he is sure he is defending established religion and social structure. This loyal, overbearing, scornful, potentially dangerous fool could function as an unsympathetic portrait of the yeoman class in general, or of the prejudices revealed in *Gamelyn* or the *Gest of Robyn Hode* in particular. A particularly attractive point in support of Brusendorff's speculation is that if the 'Man of Law's Epilogue' *had* been followed by a version of *Gamelyn* from the Knight's (or Squire's) Yeoman, we would gain yet one more 'cat and dog' pairing for the *Canterbury Tales*: as this discussion will show, the pairs of miller and reeve, wife and clerk, friar and summoner, were no more conventionally hostile to each other in the fourteenth century than lawyer and yeoman.

Chaucer, one can soon deduce, did not like yeomen much. He uses the word only in the *Canterbury Tales*, where it appears twenty-three times, with one further use each of the adverb 'yemanly' and the abstract noun 'yomanrye' (see Benson 1993). It identifies the Knight's (or Squire's) Yeoman once, the Canon's Yeoman twelve times. It is used twice in the *Knight's Tale* as a synonym for 'footman', and once with apparent if particularized positive meaning, when the Narrator of the *General Prologue* says of the Knight's Yeoman, 'Wel koude he dresse his takel yemanly' – he could fix his (shooting) tackle in good yeomanly fashion. All the other Chaucerian uses, however, are negative, and add up to a consistent unflattering satire on class pretension, very much *de haut en bas*.

The most obvious case is Simkin, the aggressive, socially climbing Miller who receives multiple degradation (indeed 'disparagement') in the *Reeve's Tale*. He is rich, we are told, as a result of his thefts, themselves grounded on physical intimidation, and therefore though completely uneducated himself insists on marrying a convent-bred virgin 'To saven his astaat of yomanrye', i.e. to keep up his yeomanly rank. Simkin has not in fact risen very far in society, for his virgin bride is the illegitimate daughter of a priest. There is an analogous sexual sneer in the *Miller's Tale*, where another lower-class wife is described as extremely sexually attractive, a delight 'For any lord to leggen in his bedde, / Or yet for any good yeman to wedde'. A yeoman's wife, in other words, is the equivalent of a lord's mistress; this is an insult which would not be relished by the likes of Simkin. Finally, there is consistent if complex play on the idea of yeoman status throughout the *Friar's Tale*, in which the utterly dishonest summoner in the end loses his soul and is carried off to Hell by a devil in part because he will not give up the claim he has made of being a yeoman. His worse-than-death sentence is triggered by a proud if false and stupid insistence on the sacredness of a yeoman's oath, even to a devil:

> 'I am a yeman, knowen is ful wyde;
> My trouthe wol I holde, as in this cas.
> For though thou were the devil Sathanas,
> My trouthe wol I holde to my brother,
> As I am sworn, and ech of us til oother.'
>
> (III, 1524–8)

Chaucer's opinion throughout the *Canterbury Tales* is then perfectly clear: he regards yeoman status as a goal for the socially striving lower classes, but a ludicrous one. People who want to be yeomen are aping their betters through such things as insistence on female chastity or the value of their own oaths; but their wives may be lords' cast-offs, and they do not have the sense to understand when and where to apply concepts like brotherhood or 'trouthe'. In any case some people who claim to be yeomen are not yeomen at all. As a social ambition it is merely pathetic.

One may, however, detect a challenged note in this Chaucerian scorn. Chaucer does not, for instance, satirize the Franklin's insistence on 'trouthe' in his tale, though the Franklin also appears to be a social climber, possibly (as one might conclude from Nigel Saul's close analysis) because the Franklin represents a form of *arrivisme* not directly threatening to Chaucer's class (Saul 1983). But yeomen, though further down the social scale, seemed more dangerous, needed to be put more firmly in their place. Two questions can accordingly now be framed, one historical, the other literary: what is a yeoman, and what have yeomen got to do with *Gamelyn*, whatever the latter may or may not have to do with the *Canterbury Tales*?

Historians have applied themselves at length to the first question, if with still-ambiguous results. Briefly (I now largely follow Holt 1989, 117–24), it seems that after the Statute of Additions of 1413, which ordered plaintiffs to declare the social status of their opponents, a ranking order became current which went down the scale from knights, squires and gentlemen to yeomen and husbandmen. Yeomen were then definitely not gentlemen (this agrees with Chaucer) but were treading on their heels. A yeoman might be a prosperous freeholder, or, if one defined the term purely economically, a prosperous craftsman, skilled worker, or minor capitalist like Simkin the Miller. However, the word had another original sense which was still familiar and normal, that of a retainer or servant in a lord's household, in particular (this is the phrase of Hilton 1975) an 'armed attendant' – just like the Knight's, but not the Canon's, Yeoman. To turn to philology, which Holt does not cover, the word 'yeoman' is in fact simply an abbreviated form of 'young man', Middle English 'yonge man' (see *OED*). Its semantic development is parallel to that of 'knight', from Old English *cniht*, or 'baron', from Vulgar Latin *baro(nem)*, or 'vassal, vavasour', from some Celtic root cognate with Welsh *gwas*, all of which meant originally no more than 'young man, boy'. It is all too clear how the words developed.[4] In a society where rank depended on physical force, all lords needed an entourage of strong young men in their prime, their 'boys' or 'lads'. The rewards these might expect for service are shown by their promotion over the centuries to being 'knights', 'barons', or 'vassals'.[5] In the fourteenth and fifteenth centuries, one may say, yeomen were showing signs of moving up from being 'young-men' retainers towards being 'knightly' competitors. Being a yeoman, says Professor Holt, here definitely confirmed by Chaucer's satire, had 'a certain social cachet ... A yeoman had standing' (Holt 1989, 120). Meanwhile this upward mobility may very likely have been accelerated by the special military conditions of England in the Hundred Years' War, in which the skilled and uniquely specialized bow-using English peasantry were for a while decisive battle-winners, to their own enrichment and that of their betters.[6] But could they be relied on to stay loyal to their betters? This is a question answered (among much else) by the *Gest of Robyn Hode* and by *Gamelyn*.

Both these works contain an extraordinarily obvious contradiction in themselves. Robin Hood, as everyone knows, makes it his business to poach the king's deer and kill his servants, especially the Sheriff of Nottingham. Gamelyn, meanwhile, robbed of his inheritance by his elder brother, first asserts himself against his brother and is then goaded into increasing defiance of the law. He beats up his brother's servants; goes off to win the local wrestling tournament, and brings the spectators back to his brother's hall for a riotous party; is tricked into allowing himself to be bound, when he is mocked by his brother and his brother's clerical friends; is freed by a loyal servant, to beat up the clerics and break his brother's back; then beats up one sheriff's posse, only to flee before another; retires to the greenwood, where he succeeds to the mastery of the outlaws; appears at one shire court to protest at having been outlawed by his crippled brother (now the sheriff), only to be arrested and then released on the recognizance of a third brother, Sir Ote, who himself stands in danger of punishment by proxy when Gamelyn fails to meet his bail. But all ends happily, for Gamelyn turns up to a second court hearing, to hang the sheriff his brother, and all the jurors who condemned him, and the king's justice too. And then, just like Robin Hood, he goes to the king, is forgiven, and (in a classic case of the 'poacher turned gamekeeper', to use Scattergood's phrase) is made 'Chef Iustice of al [the king's] fre forest'.

There is no doubt that this is romance in a very basic sense of wish-fulfilment fantasy. However, many of the features traditionally associated with the medieval romance genre are completely missing. There is no use or mention of the supernatural. There is no love-interest whatsoever. There is no cultivation of sentiment; *gentilesse* as a moral quality does not exist; chivalry is not recognized in any way. It is perhaps not surprising that a recurrent critical strategy is to 'archaize' the poem. As mentioned above, Barron actually calls it 'archaic' (Barron 1987, 84), while Keen suggests that it may be 'based on an older, alliterative poem' in the poetic style descended from Anglo-Saxon (Keen 1961, 80). Knight applies his remark about 'elements older than and marginal to the main romance pattern' to *Havelok*, but then immediately cites *Gamelyn* as 'A similar example of uneven development' (Knight 1986b, 110). Yet there is no evidence at all for *Gamelyn* as a poem of great age, while it has also come under fire, on much stronger grounds, for being too closely related to contemporary reality (see again Barron 1987, 83). In any case the whole 'developmental' or evolutionary model by which the romance genre – literary, sophisticated, ironic, dialogic

– is seen as arising out of some older and more primitive mode has been recently exposed as a convenient fallacy by Sarah Kay (Kay 1995, 1–11). Kay discusses only literature in Old French, but her point that the *chansons de geste*, far from predating the romances of the Chrétien tradition, are actually in most cases contemporary with them, could readily be applied to *Gamelyn* and (for instance) Chaucer's *Knight's Tale* or *Sir Gawain and the Green Knight*. The only reason for 'archaizing' *Gamelyn* is to make it fit a pre-established model of literary history. One may add that its incompatibility with that model accounts for its relative literary neglect, just as its ready fit with historical data accounts for its popularity with historians.

If, however, one abandons the 'developmental' explanation which treats *Gamelyn* as a left-over, and attempts an explanation in terms of contemporary society, there is a possibility of rescuing *Gamelyn* for the romance genre, or at least from its 'unclassifiable' status within that genre. To put it bluntly, if (as is often stated, for instance by Jameson 1981 and Knight 1986b) medieval romance as traditionally defined arises out of the social structures of Francophone feudalism in the twelfth and thirteenth centuries, could *Gamelyn* not have something to do with 'bastard feudalism' – the historians' unflattering term for the structures of Anglophone society in the fourteenth and fifteenth centuries – and the class tensions within it? Relating social structure directly to narrative structure is of course a risky enterprise. However, three general points may be made before turning to the specifically literary problems of this particular poem.

The first is that historians are unanimous in seeing *Gamelyn* as unusually and unexpectedly realistic. Shannon (1951) shows how familiar the poem is with the processes of medieval law, outlawry as a means of compelling court attendance, 'bidding to mainprise' as a form of bail, the empanelling of jurors by the sheriff, etc. Even the fantastic elements are not utterly fantastic. Kaeuper (1983) cites no less than twelve cases of sheriffs and justices being attacked or killed, even in their own courts, very much in *Gamelyn* style, while the king's readiness to forgive leaders of armed bandit gangs (in return for military service) is exemplified by the case of Eustace de Folville (see Stones 1957).[7]

UnChaucerianly sympathetic treatment of the ambitions and habits of the yeoman class is furthermore unmistakable in several places in the specifically Middle English romance tradition, though apparently at different stages in that class's development or coalescence. The Anglo-Norman *Lai d'Havelok*, for instance, composed 1190–1220, mentions Havelok's strength and wrestling prowess, which is an essential part of his story. In the Middle English *Havelok*, however, written *c*.1300, this necessary motif is expanded into a vividly realized scene where 'Mani erl and mani barun' come to the parliament, and with them, of course, their followers:

> With hem com mani chambioun,
> Mani with ladde, blac and brown,
> And fel it so that yungemen,
> Wel abouten nine or ten,
> Bigunnen there for to layke.
>
> $(1008–12)^8$

Young men, champions, 'wight lads' (the first word means 'brisk' or 'strong', the second originally probably 'those who are led', see *OED*): these are the lords' muscle, the 'armed attendants' who will eventually be called yeomen. When they begin to 'layke', or play, the sport they compete at is stone-casting or putting the shot, a raw trial of strength, and in this Havelok beats all comers with unmatchable ease, urged on by his master the cook. But when they see themselves beaten by the kitchen knave the champions take it in good part, as is very much the yeomanly ethos in the Robin Hood ballads:

> The chaunpiouns that put sowen:
> Shuldreden hi ilc other and lowen.
> Wolden hi namore to putting gange,
> But seyde 'We dwellen her to longe!'
>
> (1056–9)

Their camaraderie as they shoulder each other, laugh, and say in effect 'We're wasting our time here!' finds more than one echo in *Gamelyn*.

A deliberate ethos of 'yeomanry' is finally much more developed in the *Gest of Robyn Hode*, where it seems to have spread out from lords' attendants into the countryside as a whole. On his way to repay Robin, Sir Richard atte Lee stops to rescue a yeoman who is not being given fair play in a wrestling match, but there is no sign there that the yeoman is anyone's attendant. Meanwhile Robin himself lays stress on the thesis that a yeoman can be just as courteous as anyone, ceremoniously kneeling or doffing his hood to those his men ambush, and robbing or rewarding them very much in accordance with whether they respond politely, like the knight, or churl-ishly, like the monk. Gamelyn's own loyal bondmen, who come to the greenwood in defiance of his brother to tell him he has been 'cried wolf's head', go through the same ritual. The social prejudices of the *Gest* in fact agree exactly with those of *Gamelyn*: husbandmen and ploughmen are all right, as is any knight or squire 'That wol be a good felawe' (significant reservation). Officials of the law and clerics of all kinds are fair game. These literary images were once again mirrored, this time in macabre fashion, in reality (Maddicott 1978b). The *Gest* has two legally plausible scenes in which the abbot of St Mary's York is revealed unmistakably to have been retaining a royal justice, a practice continually complained about by one fourteenth-century parliament after another, and in the end put down

(Maddicott believes) as a result of social pressure after the 1381 revolt. In that revolt, though, the rebels caught and killed the prior of Bury St Edmunds and Sir John Cavendish the Chief Justice, cut their heads off, and then enacted a grisly puppet-play in which prior and justice whispered and kissed as they were alleged to have done in reality. The rebels are not said to have been yeomen, but it cannot have been easy to tell which way yeomen were going to side in 1381: with their upper-class employers, or against the clerisy whom many of their upper-class employers clearly disliked as much as they did, and who – on the evidence of the royal official Chaucer – clearly disliked them right back: Chaucer would not have escaped scot-free from the likes of Robin Hood, and on two or three occasions in his life apparently did not (Pearsall 1992, 213).

The world of *Gamelyn* and the *Gest* in short reflects several aspects of 'bastard feudalism', in which lords maintain retainers by pay, livery, and promises of mutual support; royal justice is largely discredited; and one's strike-force depends on small numbers of strong 'young men', rather crudely armed not with horse, lance, sword and armour (as in the French romance and its derivatives), but with bows, clubs, and bare hands. Historians insist that their term 'bastard' carries no pejorative meaning, but indicates only the change from an earlier fully feudal system based on land-ownership and the jurisdiction of the 'honour' to a more casual and commercial one based on money.[9] Whether this is invariably true or not, the semantics of *Gamelyn* fit the situation rather closely. More like *Havelok* than Chaucer or the *Gest of Robyn Hode* in its semantic development, it never uses the forms 'yeman' or 'yoman'. It does, however, use the ancestral phrase 'yonge men' some eighteen times, usually (fourteen times) to refer to the outlaw band which Gamelyn takes over after he has fled from his brother and the sheriff, but once for the first sheriff's posse, and three times to indicate Gamelyn and his henchman Adam the spencer (the latter made into an old man by Shakespeare). When Scattergood says that Gamelyn, unlike Robin Hood, is 'not a yeoman' (Scattergood 1994, 177), one can see that this is true as regards origins; but he is both closely identified with his band of 'yonge men', and made himself to look and act like a yeoman, in line, one may think, with the flattering gentry/yeomanry equations of the *Gest*. His 'yonge men' furthermore at one point show their allegiance to the conventions of 'bastard feudalism', rather than feudalism proper, in an unmistakable manner. When Gamelyn calls on them to come with him and break up the court, they reply cheerfully:

> 'We wiln stand with the whil that we may dure,
> And but we werke manly, pay vs non hure.'
>
> (831–2)

'If we do not do the job, you need not pay us.' This is very much the 'bastard feudal' spirit: very much not the spirit of *Sir Gawain*, say, where pay is never mentioned.

It may be no more than coincidence, but there are at least some indications that Gamelyn himself may be a bastard: at which point one may turn from the poem's intensely realized and strongly corroborated social context to its barely less obvious inner contradictions. The hero's name may be relevant. Skeat, preferring characteristically to look for an Old English or Old Norse derivation, divided it as *gamel-ing*, 'son of the old man' (Skeat 1884). Line 4 of the poem, however, introduces the father as Sir John of Boundys, 'He cowde of norture ynough and mochil of game'. The Middle English meanings of 'game' include 'sexual intercourse' (*MED* 2d); *game* + diminutive *-lyn* could accordingly be translated as 'love-child, bastard'. Such an explanation might account for the peculiar non sequiturs of the start. Sir John, dying, expresses his wishes clearly. He calls his neighbours and asks them to divide his lands among his three sons, not forgetting Gamelyn. They appear to take no notice, and decide 'to delen hem alle to oon, that was her thought' (43). Two lines later, however:

> Al the lond that ther was they dalten it in two,
> And leten Gamelyn the yonge withoute londe go.

The knight then tries again to assert his will, proposing to divide his land three ways, with five ploughlands which he inherited from his father going to his eldest son; five more which he won in war going to his second son; and his remaining property, which he did not inherit but earned for himself, going to his youngest son, Gamelyn. Sir John's principle of division may well have archaic roots, but was not unknown in medieval England;[10] it is hard now to see quite how realistic the scene may have been. But in any case his neighbours, 'that lawe conne of londe', ignore his second appeal as they ignored his first. It is not clear what happens to the second son, but there is no doubt that the eldest inherits and that Gamelyn is left out.

One might then expect the eldest brother simply to take Gamelyn's lands and exploit them himself, but he seems just to neglect them, while treating Gamelyn as a servant, a male Cinderella. This goes on till one day Gamelyn puts hand to chin and feels his beard, sixteen years after his father's death according to line 361 – he must have been not just a minor but very nearly a posthumous child. Immediately he challenges his brother, giving him 'goddes curs'. His brother replies by calling him a 'gadelyng'. What this word means is also not always clear,[11] but Gamelyn appears to take it to mean 'bastard'. He replies furiously:

'Cristes curs mot he haue that clepeth me gadelyng!
I am no worse gadelyng ne no worse wight,
But born of a lady and geten of a knight.'

(106–8)

This is not quite a denial.[12] Since it seems to be accepted that the two are brothers – another strange feature is that the wicked brother seems to have made no attempt to deny Gamelyn's birth or to conceal his inheritance – one might have expected Gamelyn to say 'you cannot call me "gadelyng"', for I have the same ancestry as you'. Instead he says in effect, 'you cannot call me "gadelyng", because I have as good ancestry as you'. 'Born of a lady and begotten by a knight' does not after all rule out the possibility that the knight and the lady were not married. *Gamelyn* could then be re-read as a story of the deadly enmity of half-brothers, which would once again have 'archaic' Old Norse analogues – the *Hamðismál*, the *Hlöðskviða* – rather than 'romantic' Old French ones. But these doubts, queries, anachronisms and failures in logic are all ignored by the tale, which presses rapidly on to the first of many scenes of open physical violence, with Gamelyn scattering his brother's staff-armed servants with a handy pestle.

The way is then clear for a scenario several times repeated: Gamelyn is deceived or threatened by words (his brother's promise of fair treatment, his brother's request to be allowed to fulfil a 'Rash Promise' to tie Gamelyn up, outlawry pronounced upon Gamelyn by the sheriff, judgment against him and his loyal brother in the shire court), is undeceived by deeds, and retaliates with increasing violence (breaking the champion wrestler's ribs and arm, throwing his brother's porter down the well, drubbing the assembled churchmen who refused to help him when he was bound, and so on to the final mass hanging). If there is one consistent factor in all this, it is humour. Most of the scenes in the poem seem designed to lead up to some verbal witticism or one-liner, of which I count some twenty, often coming in strings. When Gamelyn is told by the 'gentil-men' who umpire the wrestling to put his hose and shoes back on as there are no more contenders, he replies, 'I haue nought yet haluendel sold vp my ware'. The defeated champion with his broken ribs and arm says, 'He is a fool that therof byeth, thou sellest it so deere'. The franklin whose sons have been half-killed by the champion takes the image on with, 'Yet it is to good cheep that thou hast it i-bought'. In the same way when Gamelyn gets loose to take his revenge on the assembled abbots, monks and priors, there is a running joke on their clerical status. Gamelyn 'sprengeth holy water [on them] with an oken spire'. Adam the spencer says he will hold the door so none pass till they have been 'assoyled'. He tells Gamelyn:

'They ben men of holy chirche draw of hem no blood,
Saue wel the croune and do hem non harmes,
But brek bothe her legges and siththen her armes.'

(522–4)

And so on. The poem's literally battering humour seems to go together with its frequent lack of narrative logic, contributing to the evaluations of 'honest artlessness' and 'uneven development' with which it has been saddled.[13] But this may be to read a 'bastard feudal' poem against the expectations of chivalric romance. If the comparison were with *chanson de geste*, *Gamelyn* would seem much less eccentric.[14]

If one does nevertheless set *Gamelyn* up against standard accounts of the ideology or inner structure of medieval romance, it is interesting to see its partial fit – not a complete incompatibility, but a sense that it has been rotated a quarter-turn, so to speak, from some underlying pattern. To recapitulate, Stephen Knight begins his 'The Social Function of Middle English Romance' by stating that all romances share 'the figure of the knight and the ethic of chivalry', both figure and knight belonging to the 'social and economic formation . . . of feudalism' (Knight 1986b, 99). *Gamelyn* does have knights in it – Sir John, Sir Ote – but Gamelyn is not one, is never called 'Sir', and shows no sign of wanting to be. It contains no trace of chivalry that I can see (as Knight indeed notes), and its socio-economic world is that of bastard feudalism. Knight also sees courtesy and Christianity as part of the romance ideology; but while *Gamelyn* does have a rudimentary idea of courtesy (stronger in the *Gest of Robyn Hode*, as has been said), its attitude to Christianity is at best mixed, combining firm belief, or appeals to belief – the characters continually shower 'Cristes curs' and 'goddes curs' on each other – with absolute hatred of anyone who might teach that belief: very much like the last speaker of the 'Man of Law's Epilogue', indeed.

This last point leads forward, however, to aspects of the 'inherent and centrally ideological structure of the romances' with which *Gamelyn* seems at least to be in negotiation. Knight sees romance as essentially an 'imaginary' for landlords, putting forward, in the guise of narrative, attitudes which a ruling class wished to encourage with the aim of creating consent to dominance, or, to take a phrase from Jameson (1981), 'legitimation of concrete structures of power and domination'. All this in both Knight's and Jameson's view is a sort of trick, a 'false consciousness' which persuades a broader, non-landowning audience not to perceive its own interests, not to penetrate through the 'euphemistic values of chivalry' to 'the realistic values of cavalry', or to grasp the truth that feudalism 'is based on violence and self-interest' (Knight 1986b, 101, 107). One can see straight away (and Knight again concedes) that *Gamelyn* and its rough-justice analogues have no more idea of cavalry than of chivalry. They are, however, quite clear about the realistic values of archery (or in Gamelyn's case more often battery); and in them the idea that bastard feudalism is based on violence and self-interest appears self-evident. And yet these failures to match the alleged romance pattern could be seen as a narrative response to a changed socio-economic structure, in which the gentry and yeomanry classes were engaged in complex negotiation. It is very tempting in fact to see the 'yeoman ethic' as precisely a new kind of 'false consciousness', in which a dangerous, armed, servant class was encouraged to identify with its masters, not its origins, and offered not the bait of social mobility but the relatively cheaper baits of ancestral community (Sir John of Boundys and Sir Richard atte Lee are both real knights by blood, not *arrivistes*), manly camaraderie (wrestling, stone-casting, archery), and – not an insignificant factor – better diet: in a protein-starved world the attractions of legal or illegal access to the lord's deer or later on the squire's rabbit warren may have been much stronger than our overfed culture can readily realize.[15] They were also provided with a necessary 'Other' in the shape of the most dangerous (if internal) enemies of the hereditary landowning classes: lawyers, royal officials, urban *arrivistes*, members of predatory clerical corporations, in particular Benedictine monasteries like St Mary's of York. In a word, literates.

Such a view may furthermore account for some of the features of the *Gamelyn* story which appear most alien to, or most skewed from, romance tradition. *Gamelyn* does have several rather traditional romance scenes, for instance the one where Gamelyn turns up to the wrestling tournament apparently on his own, to meet the franklin bewailing the crippling of his two sons. Gamelyn tells the franklin to help 'my man' (who never appears) to take off his shoes and look after his horse, and he will see what he can do to revenge him. The franklin replies:

> 'I wil my-self be thy man and drawen of thi schoon
> And wende thou into place Iesu Crist the speede,
> And drede not of thy clothes nor of thy goode steede.'
> (212–14)

The scene is vestigially similar to Erec meeting the poor vavasour in Chrétien de Troyes's *Erec et Enide*, or Sir Lancelot in Malory borrowing the armour of Sir Barnard's crippled son Sir Tirry; but it has been transposed down at least two social notches. Similarly, scenes with porters figure prominently in romance all the way from Wulfgar in *Beowulf* to Arthur's Glewlwyd Mighty-Grasp in *Culhwch and Olwen* or the polite porter of Sir Bertilak's Hautdesert.

But though the problem of proving one's status to a doorkeeper is solved in different ways in different texts, it is characteristic of Gamelyn to solve it by kicking the door down (298), breaking the porter's neck (304) and throwing him down a well seven fathoms deep (306). One may see this as a satisfying solution mainly for those who are normally on the wrong side of the porter's rudeness. In the same way the scenes in which Gamelyn is made to show or to receive pure good fellowship (socially downscale with the franklin at the wrestling tournament, but upscale with the gentlemen-umpires) act to remove any suggestions of patronage – something especially appealing to those classes who depend on a patron. Knight rejects scornfully the idea of *gesunkenes Kulturgut* in his article, but if the 'sinking' is social rather than chronological, these scenes appear to be examples of it.

The same transposition to an altered social context may account for some of the least romantic features of *Gamelyn*. Of these the most obvious must be the total absence of any female character till five lines from the end, when Gamelyn perfunctorily weds 'a wyf bothe good and feyr' and dies two lines later. Knight stresses the importance of founding a family in romance ideology, with the most basic narrative pattern consisting of gaining title to a landholding and a wife with it, excluding challengers from it and her, and establishing autonomy over both: the wish-fulfilment fantasy of the mob of younger sons disinherited by primogeniture seen by Duby as the strike-force of the chivalric era (Duby 1964). Gamelyn ought in a way to be one of these (he is a younger son all but disinherited by primogeniture), but though his interest in title is very marked, the rest of the pattern fails to develop. As far as love-interest goes, his romance is much more like the Oxford *Chanson de Roland*, in which Roland's fiancée Aude appears only in *laisse* 274 (out of 298) and dies of grief immediately. Turning back to Sarah Kay's point mentioned above about the contemporaneity of romance and *chanson de geste*, one might note Jameson's thesis that romance emerges in the twelfth century, along with feelings of class solidarity, after a 'time of troubles' (reflected in the *chansons*) 'in which central authority disappears' (Jameson 1981). In the relatively settled world of romance, Jameson argues, unlike the *chansons*, one's enemy is very much the same as oneself (as may be revealed once he yields and removes his helmet, as happens with Maboagrain in the 'Joie de la Cort' episode in Chrétien's *Erec*, 5932–96); while true evil is displaced into an unreal world of sorcery. In *Gamelyn*, however, there is no trace of the 'Beautiful Unknown', and little of class solidarity among the landowning classes. Instead there is a striking denial of both elements when Gamelyn, having been outlawed in order to force his attendance at court, turns up without any attempt at disguise, but with a strong sense of challenge:

> Gamelyn com boldelych in-to the moot-halle,
> And put adoun his hood among the lordes alle;
> 'God saue you alle, lordynges that now here be!
> But broke-bak scherreue euel mot thou the!'
>
> (717–20)

Gamelyn's enemy of course is his brother, doubling as both disinheritor and sheriff, but he neither yields nor is forgiven; and evil is located in the machinery of the law, at once realistic and familiar. These, however, are clearly contemporary features, while the allegedly 'archaic' elements of *Gamelyn*, such as the neglect of sex and the lack of interest in the romance world of the greenwood, resemble the *chansons de geste* not because of their age but because similar social circumstances create similar social myths.

The fourteenth-century 'time of troubles' in England, in other words, created unromantic narrative features parallel to those of the *chansons* just as it created a youngman/yeoman class parallel to the earlier feudal *barones/* barons. *Gamelyn* expresses the ethos of an unmarried group which may not expect ever to own land and does not see landholding as a precondition for starting a family. Yet it functions as an 'ideological . . . response to a historical dilemma' just as much as traditional romances (Jameson 1981, 139), and preserves in its narrative a class negotiation with a 'transitional moment'. The transition from feudalism to capitalism so beloved of Marxist theorists is, however, not the only transition that ever took place, there being at least one extensive medial stage in 'bastard feudalism'. Seeing this may help us to broaden the notion of romance so as to include *Gamelyn*, Robin Hood, *Havelok*, and much of the rest of the 'matter of England', instead of excluding them as 'archaic', 'marginal', 'unclassifiable', unevenly developed, or simply non-literary – the classic signs of critical embarrassment in front of a problem of genre.

There are several minor points and one major one to make by way of conclusion. In previous articles I have tried to see 'syntactic' rather than 'semantic' patterns in romance-related narratives as distinct as *Beowulf*, the *Lais* of Marie de France, modern Robin Hood films and modern 'window' fantasies (Shippey 1969, 1988, 1996): it is a relief to record that this time neither Propp's folk-tale morphology nor Derek Brewer's 'family drama' (1980) seems to me to have anything to do with *Gamelyn* and its like. If *Gamelyn* is a 'family drama', it stops just after puberty, when the boy fingers his beard, knows he is a young man, and throws off authority.[16] Meanwhile it is remarkable, in view of what Jameson says about the importance of setting or 'worldness' to romance, that Thomas Lodge and Shakespeare between them reintroduced both the subplot based on love, and the fascination of the forest, to *Rosalynde* and *As You Like It* respectively. The latter is

almost denied by Gamelyn, with his strongly marked gnomic taciturnities in
the forest scenes:

'Many good mannes child in care is i-broght . . .'
(624)

'After bale cometh boote thurgh grace of god almight . . .'
(631)

'He moste needes walke in woode that may not walke in towne . . .'
(672)

But it is as if the yeoman narrative had always had a space reserved for the
reintroduction of more purely romantic motifs, analogous to the structural
repression of the aristocratic main plot (in Jameson's view) in *Aus dem Leben
eines Taugenichts*. And to round off the theme of literary manipulation, the
discussion above may have opened up the speculative question of what
Chaucer would have done in making *Gamelyn* into *the *Knight's Yeoman's
Tale*. He would have had every opportunity, surely, both to use the conventions of a particular genre to expose the harsh assumptions of that genre (as
with the *Reeve's Tale* for *fabliau* and the *Prioress's Tale* for saint's legend), and
to continue the sportive self-reflections of the sub-genres of romance seen in
the *Knight's Tale*, the *Franklin's Tale*, the *Wife of Bath's Tale* and *Sir Thopas*.
One can imagine, though, that the Knight's Yeoman would have received
the hostile treatment accorded to Friar or Summoner rather than the benevolence shown to Squire or Franklin. Yeomen were Chaucer's class enemies,
as his references consistently show.

Not just Chaucer's. Stephen Knight, in the piece mentioned many times
already, cites with great benevolence the 'refreshingly political comment'
made by Arnold Kettle about romance a long time ago:

> Romance was the non-realistic aristocratic literature of feudalism . . . It
> was aristocratic because the attitudes it expressed and recommended were
> precisely the attitudes the ruling class wished (no doubt unconsciously) to
> encourage in order that their privileged position might be perpetuated.[17]

We should, Knight says, hold on to the 'sharply political sense of the role of
culture in class conflict', and so perhaps we should. An evident point, however, is this. Modern critics very much enjoy the sense of superiority given
by observing *de haut en bas* the unconscious bias of defeated ruling classes (as
in Kettle above or Crane 1986, 45, commenting on *Havelok*). They are also
happy to celebrate (Jameson 1981, 105) 'the irrepressible voice and expression of the underclasses of the great systems of domination'. They do,

however, have their own biases and their own class interests, more visible from outside than inside the profession. One may note the ready sympathy with literary bureaucrats (like Chaucer), and the Whiggish tendency to equate the 'rise of Standard English' and the development of literature with such bureaucracies. Apparently provincial but aristocratic works such as *Sir Gawain and the Green Knight* are also liable to meet a kind of incredulity, which leads either to a search for a suitably metropolitan milieu (Putter 1996, 23, 'For a courtly audience . . . it is necessary to look elsewhere'), or to reclassification as essentially non-aristocratic, because (surely) there cannot have been independent baronial cultural centres out there in the – Knight writes 'North-West Midlands', but I fear he means the sticks, the boondocks.[18] A class which meanwhile receives no sympathy from bureaucrats, metropolitans, Marxists, or *Marxisants*, is of course the rural yeomanry, whether these take the shape of Russian Cossacks, American Confederate soldiers, or the English yeomanry which in later years would be called out to put down urban riots.[19] If such people have a consciousness it must be a false one, and if they have a literature it must be marginal. Literary criticism, one may reflect, has a 'political unconscious' just as much as do the objects of its scrutiny. The ironies of this more-than-marginalization need not be laboured. It does, however, lead to a significant narrowing of literary canons, at least in the field of English literature: students of other literatures, and historians, are once more showing us the way.[20]

Notes

1   The words and phrases cited in the two sentences above come respectively from Kane 1951, 48; Barron 1987, 84; Keen 1961, 79; Barron 1987, 83; Barron 1987, 84; Knight 1986b, 110; and finally n. 4 to Kaeuper 1983.

2   *The Tale of Gamelyn* is cited here from the edition by Walter W. Skeat (Oxford: Oxford University Press, 1884), the only full annotated edition. The *Gest* is cited from *Rymes of Robyn Hood: An Introduction to the English Outlaw*, ed. R. B. Dobson and J. Taylor (Gloucester: Alan Sutton, 1989). It is not clear whether there is a direct connection between the two, the latter not being recorded till the sixteenth century, though Robin Hood poems were in circulation by the 1370s: see *Piers Plowman* B.5.395ff, and an origin for the *Gest* in the 1330s is argued by Maddicott 1978a. There is a fifteenth-century ballad of 'Robyn and Gandeleyn', reprinted by Dobson and Taylor, which however offers no narrative link, and 'Gamwell' appears as a name in later Robin Hood ballads: see for both Knight 1994, 42, 87, and Scattergood 1994, n. 7.

3   The *Riverside Chaucer* explains the word 'phislyas' as 'an uneducated speaker's attempt to use the legal term *filace*, "files" or "cases"' (p. 863). It may well be contemptuous.

4   The classic account of the development of feudal vocabulary remains Bloch 1961, chs. 11, 13.

5   Though it should be noted that the semantic developments were not of consistent rise: Saul 1981, 14–18 shows that *vallettus* or *vadlet* sagged during the fourteenth century from meaning 'knight-in-waiting' to being (not inappropriately) a variant for 'yeoman'.

6   It is of course an old view to equate the yeomen of England with the bowmen of England, and to locate ancient military prowess in them. It has, however, been rather strengthened than weakened in recent years by the *Mary Rose* excavations, with their professionally deformed archer-skeletons: see further Hall 1997. Hall notes the high individual and cultural cost of training professional archers.

7   This point is also made at length by Scattergood 1994.

8   Citations here are from *Havelok*, ed. G. V. Smithers (Oxford: Oxford University Press, 1987), as are the dates given just above. Smithers's editorial diacritics have been omitted.

9   The term dates back to 1885, but was revived by K. B. McFarlane in 1945. For a recent discussion of its professional use see Hicks 1995, 12–19. I am especially grateful to Professors David Crouch, of University College, Scarborough, and Chris Dyer, of Birmingham, for considerable guidance in this area.

10 It has a faint analogue in *Vatnsdæla saga*, ch. 2, where Ketil tells his son Thorstein that according to the old 'warriors' law' what one inherited had to be passed on, but what a warrior like Sir John won 'with my righte hond' did not. For discussion of the tangled historical evidence, see Shannon 1951 and Holt 1972.

11 According to the *MED* it shifts from the meaning 'companion in arms' to that of 'base fellow . . . ?bastard', with the *Gamelyn* passage exemplifying the latter.

12 Scattergood 1994, 164 and n. 13 insists on these lines as proof of 'knightly status', rejecting the attempt of Barron 1987, 84 to see Gamelyn as a 'yeoman hero' and 'strong-arm champion of bourgeois values'. One certain thing is that Barron's equation 'yeoman = bourgeois = middle class' does not fit medieval conditions at all; but, against Scattergood, pride of birth is notoriously subjective.

13 By Kane 1951, 48 and Knight 1986b, 110 respectively.

14 The verbal and physical humour of *Gamelyn* is paralleled by, for instance, the section about Rainouart the scullion, and his cook, and his cudgel, in *La Chanson de Guillaume*, ed. D. McMillan, 2 vols, SATF (Paris: Picard, 1949–50). I owe this reference to the editors of this volume.

15 Ladurie 1987 gives a striking account of protein deficiency in France in the fifteenth century; see further Dyer 1989 and for a later period Hay 1975.

16 It is true that Gamelyn's dead father, wicked brother, and good brother parallel the parental substitute split of Cinderella's dead mother, wicked (step)mother and fairy (god)mother, with the master outlaw and the king's justice also functioning neatly as reserve positive and negative father-images respectively.

17   Kettle 1951, 29, cited in Knight 1986b, 100.
18   Knight 1986b, 116. I think that both he and Putter 1996 have been over-persuaded by Bennett 1979. Bennett gave an excellent account of that anomalous county Cheshire, but the poem's dialect area, narrow though it is, straddles the Cheshire–Staffordshire boundary, a highly significant one in local and national politics at the end of the fourteenth century. I hope to treat this topic at length elsewhere. Scattergood meanwhile does actually use the word 'backwoods' (1994, 178), though with the laudable aim of arguing for a distinctively provincial and anti-centralist voice.
19   Knight 1994, 51–2, while very ready to see yeomen as labourers, proprietors, urban craftsmen, or 'sturdy dissenting peasant[s]', ignores the (presumably equally sturdy) 'armed attendant' class completely.
20   As one can see from Kay 1995. In very different but complementary ways I feel that Ross 1997 and Hall 1997 are also crumbling away the traditional literary 'Indian summer of chivalry' model associated with late romance.

CHAPTER FOUR

The Romance Hypothetical: Lordship and the Saracens in *Sir Isumbras*

ELIZABETH FOWLER

The Middle English *Sir Isumbras* tells, hauntingly, of a wealthy knight's fall and struggle back to a state of grace, property, and power that far exceeds his original elevation.[1] Stripped of everything he owns in punishment for his neglect of the Christian God, Isumbras journeys with his wife and three boys to the Greek sea. There the three children are taken from him by fantastic heraldic beasts, and the wife is captured by an invading Saracen king who sends her off to be the queen of his nation. Before parting, Isumbras and his wife break a ring, each keeping one half. After toiling as a blacksmith, a warrior knight, and a pilgrim, Isumbras manages to regain God's favour, and – the ring proving his identity – to be reunited with his wife. She dons armour and the children appear riding their captor beasts; they join Isumbras to conquer and forcibly convert many Saracen kingdoms. The issues that animate the poem are as urgent today as they were in the late Middle Ages: the proper basis of wealth and political power, the status of sexual custom in political society, the political form of religious devotion, the conditions of religious conversion, the friction between Islamic and Christian law, and the justification of war.

Sir Isumbras was composed in the dialect of the East Midlands in the early 1330s and survives in a relatively large number of manuscripts and early prints for a Middle English romance in rhyme (Severs 1967, 122–3).[2] Its popularity also occasioned scorn: William of Nassyngton refers to it as 'veyn spekyng' in his *Speculum vitae* (c.1370).[3] The earliest manuscript is dated around 1350; the others are thought to have been made between the mid-fifteenth and the mid-sixteenth centuries (Severs 1967, 112). At least six editions of the text have been prepared in the last two centuries. Written in some 800 short lines, gathered into tail-rhyme stanzas (aab, ccb, ddb, etc., in groups of three to six tercets and rare four-line groups), and expressed in a controlled, simple diction, *Sir Isumbras* can be read in one sitting. Its availability and tight composition make the poem a pleasure to study in class; its careful composition repays close reading for both structure and poetic idiom.

Critics have often described the romance mode as fantastic, escapist, mythic, idealist, or transcendent. All of these epithets stem, I think, from the abstract nature of romances, a formal quality that pervades their stark, simplified landscapes, broad-brushed characters, logically and temporally abrupt events, and severe social conditions. Abstraction results in a simplicity that can be, and has been, misunderstood as lack of intellectual complexity and learning, yet romance is like learned philosophy and certain modes of legal writing in its combination of the abstract, the general, and the hypothetical. The similarity of these forms can be illustrated by recalling the interpretive strategies of canon lawyers such as Johannes Teutonicus and Bernard of Parma, and masters of Roman law ('civilians') such as Accursius, who wrote that judges should come to understand the abstract language of legal texts by adhering to the following hermeneutic rules: general terms should be construed as applying to every member of the class, indefinite expressions as indicating universality, and individual words as being controlled by the meaning of whole texts (Brundage 1995, 169). These sources of difficulty – generality, indefiniteness, and the relation of individual oddities to the whole – are features that, when we encounter them in romances, often plague our sensibilities.

Generality and indefiniteness, for example, might well be called a principle of romance characterization. Only one person in *Sir Isumbras* has a proper name, and even the heathen enemy is abstract: the word 'Saracen' – which could mean Arab, Turk, Muslim, or simply non-Christian, heathen, or pagan, unbeliever or infidel – was inherited by medieval Europe from the Roman Empire's designation for the nomadic Arab peoples that troubled its Middle Eastern boundaries (*OED*). Similarly, there are few geographical landmarks in *Sir Isumbras*. It is a bleak landscape made up entirely of kingdoms, which divide into the Christian and the Saracen. It is punctuated rather monumentally by the 'Grekys see', by the 'borow' of Jerusalem, and, in some manuscripts, by the port of Acre, some 70 miles north of Jerusalem on the trade routes to Asia, Byzantium, and Europe.[4] The poem's places clearly stand for Christian political claims rather than for any natural topography. Narrative events too are abstract and typified, drawn in the case-study fashion that prevails in the philosophy of logic and legal scholarship. The affinity of romance with philosophy and law is in part aesthetic, residing in the qualities of generality and indefiniteness and in the emphasis given to matter and context rather than to particular wordings or ornaments of style. These shared aesthetic qualities help to consolidate the more consequential affinity that lies in their shared topics.

In my view, romances are hypothetically posed stories that lead us to investigate the conditions of crucial social formations such as lordship, marriage, and governance by setting such formations moving in a stark landscape of 'suppose'. In the case of *Sir Isumbras*, we are asked to imagine that a prosperous knight, head of a thriving household, is suddenly stripped of everything that has given him his social status and then placed on the border of Christianity and Islam. What would it take to requalify him? What lies underneath his rights, capacities, familial status, property, and power? These are all aspects of the medieval political and legal concept of *dominion* and the central medieval institution of *lordship*. My treatment of *Sir Isumbras* demonstrates a method of recovering the philosophical and jurisprudential ambitions of romances: I shall argue that romances are complex thought experiments that lead the reader through a process of thinking about the deepest issues of political philosophy and jurisprudence.

Romances echo saints' lives when they re-imagine the plot of divestment and reinvestment that is the basis of hagiography: rather than investigating what makes a person holy, they ponder what makes a person rich, or virtuous, or triumphant, or a king.[5] Rather than pursuing these questions of achievement in a treatise, romances incorporate in their stories conventional images, formulae, characters, plot events, and scenes that we also find in other media (scholastic disputation, stained-glass windows, sermons, civic ceremonies, etc.). These I shall call *topoi*, using a technical term of ancient and medieval rhetoric that was popularized for medieval literary criticism by Ernst Curtius in *European Literature and the Latin Middle Ages* (Curtius 1953, 70) and described as part of the well-theorized medieval practice of thinking, writing, and reading by Mary Carruthers in *The Book of Memory* (Carruthers 1990, 16–45).[6]

The term *topos* ('commonplace' in Greek) means 'topic' and 'topography' at once: it is a pattern of language (often including a familiar scene or setting and its attendant set of values) that recalls us to a tradition of images, arguments, and feelings rather as if they were stored in a particular location. For example, the romance topos of the tournament appears in many forms: manuscript illuminations, civic rituals, castle architecture, military training, metaphorical accounts of the crucifixion of Christ from patristic writings to *Piers Plowman*, moral allegories of the vices and virtues, the version of ancient Athenian justice in Chaucer's *Knight's Tale*, and the trial by combat that was a special medieval juridical process. The topos of the tournament, then, is a cultural 'location' for the topics of military discipline, Christian views of Jesus' divinity, moral training of the soul, civic pageantry, questions of law, and all the familiar trains of thought and emotion that go with these topics.

Each example of a topos reminds us of other examples we have experienced, invites us to compare them, and initiates a process of thinking and feeling that is shaped by the topos. Without needing to be elaborated in abstract philosophical formulae, then, a topos initiates complex philosophical reasoning. Scholastic philosophy inserts topoi in the midst of axioms and logical propositions; romance, on the other hand, tends to string topoi together into plots. Three topoi are crucial to *Sir Isumbras* and will structure my discussion of the poem's particular treatment of lordship and dominion: the topos of investiture, the topos of the vow, and the topos of penance. These topoi serve to unify the ambitious scope of the poem, which treats political, sexual, and religious aspects of lordship on a global landscape where Christian kings oppose Saracen kings without the recognition of any institutional church or state.

I: Divestment and Investiture

Throughout the story, the hero Sir Isumbras's predicament is memorialized for us by images of clothing and nakedness. As these features of the narrative recur, they accumulate into the topos of investiture. Clothing first appears as a key signifier in the opening stanzas, where Isumbras is established as a paragon of wealth and 'gentylnesse', in part by his habit of giving clothing to his followers:

> Menstralles he hadde in his halle,
> And yafe hem robes of ryche palle,
>   Sylver, golde and fee.
>   (25–7)

Jesus will not tolerate Isumbras's pride and sends a bird to tell him, 'Thow haste foryete what thou was' (50). Job-like, Isumbras suffers the loss of his animals, retainers, buildings, and riches. His devastation is visually expressed by 'a dolfull syghte' (103) that is as central to the reader's understanding of the tale as it is traumatic for the hero:

> His wyfe and his chylderen thre
>   Owte of the fyre were fledde,
> As naked as they were borne
> There they stode hym byforne.
>   (104–7)

Stripped of their social status, the members of his family stand before him in their original animal bodies. The phrase 'naked as they were borne' alludes to Job 1.21, where Job patiently compares his loss of his children to his state of nakedness at birth and death. This image of lack of clothing resonates as a kind of limit case, a bottom line of human existence. It figures the human body without its social inflections, without dominion of any kind.

Isumbras sadly covers his wife with his own 'mantell of ryche pall' (127) and his children with 'his ryche sirkote' (130), cuts a cross into his own bare shoulder, and decides to seek God in the land where Jesus lived and died. The tattoo, an extreme kind of clothing, expresses Isumbras's vow to ground his identity as a penitent Christian in his body and to make it the least removable of all his social personae. Medieval crusaders were said to 'take the cross' in ceremonies of vows that often involved sewing a cross onto their clothing; the serious consequences of such a commitment are apparent from Matthew Paris's description of Henry III and a number of nobles taking the cross in 1250.[7]

Like the stripping of Chaucer's Griselda and Shakespeare's Lear, the stripping of Sir Isumbras represents his social devastation and his translation into an utterly different category of person. Isumbras's loss of property goes together with a loss of the social ties that had bound his family into their community. Borrowing a term from medieval legal thinkers, I shall say that he suffers *civil death* – the end of his former lordship with all its economic, political, and social distinction: the end, the bird tells him, of 'what thou was' (50).[8]

Isumbras responds to civil death by committing himself to be a pilgrim. This begins the chain of *social persons* through which Isumbras moves in the course of the plot. The social person is a representation of the human figure that we recognize as conventional, as carrying with it a set of values and possibilities that are distinct, and as belonging to a topos, discourse, or institution.[9] The scant clothing and the self-scourging of his dedicatory tattoo tell us that, after his civil death, Isumbras has taken upon himself the social person of the penitential pilgrim. From there, he moves through many different social persons in a process of reinvestment, until, at the end of the story, he becomes the richly robed imperial king of many conquered Saracen lands.

Clothing is instrumental throughout this process of divestment and reinvestiture. The heathen king takes pity at the sight of Isumbras and his wife because they lack proper clothing ('So feyre as they bothe wore, / If they were cladde aryghte', 157–8), and offers to buy the wife for 'golde and fe, / And ryche robes sevenne' (278–9) in order to crown her queen of his country. Despite his objections, Isumbras is given 'reed gold in a mantell'

(289) 'of skarlette rede' (358), bereft of his wife, and beaten. The appeal to the reader's visual sense recalls the earlier divestments and invites us to see the wife's accession to queenship as part of the chain of social persons through which Isumbras is moving. Her queenship earns him treasure and regal dress that seem to corroborate her prediction of his later triumphant revenge, though they cannot yet be enjoyed (and in fact are carried off by a griffin, not to be recovered until the spouses are reunited). The connection between apparel and social identity is also borne out by the ring, which symbolizes Isumbras and his wife's 'unity of person' – a legal and theological term used to express the 'one flesh' that marriage creates out of two bodies. In the poem the ring is a material sign of this corporate social person. Isumbras and his wife suffer a severing of their unity of person, and the ring is split between them; both ring and unity of person are restored simultaneously in their happy reunion.[10]

Perhaps the poem's most interesting use of the topos of investiture is during the episode in which Isumbras becomes an ironworker. Isumbras accedes to this social person after he loses his wife to the heathen king and loses his three sons to a series of kidnapping heraldic beasts: a lion (170), a leopard (184), and a unicorn (370). He joins a smithy and progresses by means of bodily toil and skill through the positions of labourer and apprentice, until he becomes a 'smythes man' (404) who earns 'mannes hyre' (401). The former knight learns to manufacture knightly armour:

> Sevenn yer he was smythes man ther,
>   And monethes mo also.
> By thenne he cowthe armour dyghte,
> All that fell for a knyghte,
>   To batell whenn he sholde go.
>   (404–8)

Having reached rock bottom with the loss of his family, Isumbras works his way back. His role as a smith is instrumental in his reacquisition of the martial abilities of his knighthood. He forges armour as if he were reconstituting the social person of the knight he once was: he rebuilds his social body as he builds the armour. He begins to 'own' the social person of the knight by virtue of his labour. This form of dominion, created by labour, adds another link in the chain of forms of dominion that are dramatized by the poem.

Labour hones him for the battle in which he takes up arms against the heathen king who, after crowning Isumbras's wife, has been despoiling the kingdoms of Christendom. In the battle, an earl recognizes the humble fighter's prowess:

> An erle out of the batell hym sowghte,
>   And ledde hym to an hygh mownteyne;
> And all changed the knyghtes wede;
> He horsedde hym on a full good stede,
>   And sone he went ayeyne.
>
> (440–44)

This advancement to the 'wede' of knighthood, earned by action and conveyed by political authority, equips Isumbras to slay the heathen king and win the battle. When he is brought before the grateful Christian king, he does not announce his noble roots but insists modestly on being recognized as an ironworker:

> The kynge asked what was his name:
> 'Syr', he seyd, 'I am a smythes manne;
>   Byholde and thou may se with syghthe.'
> The kynge answered ayen thanne:
> 'I trowe nevur smythes manne
>   In werre were so wyghte.'
>
> (466–71)

> Then sware the kyng that was so fre,
> If that he myghte kevered be,
>   He shulde be dubbed knyghte.
>
> (478–80)

If he can be healed of his wounds, the king vows, Isumbras shall be knighted. His social and bodily injuries seem to coincide.

It is clear, however, that reaccession to knighthood is not sufficiently merited by the combination of work, skill, equipment, achievement, and recognition. When he is cured of his bodily wounds by nuns, Isumbras does not stay to be dubbed but rather leaves to take on yet another social person, again memorialized for us in an image:

> He hym purveyde scryppe and pyke
> And dyghte hym a palmere lyke,
>   Ageyn that he wolde wende.
>
> (493–5)

Much emphasis is placed not only on the dressing – the accession to social person – but also upon his endurance in that palmer's clothing for another, presumably smelly, seven years:

> In that clothynge he wente all day,
> In that same all nyghte he lay,
>   Ryghte in his pore wedes.
> Of that penaunce wolde he not yrke,
> Forto fulfylle Goddes werke,
>   And lette all his evell dedys.
>
> (511–16)

Isumbras perseveres in his penitential habit, and, by now, the image of clothing clearly conveys not only his social person, but also the associated habitual practices that produce its *habitus*, the trained disposition or orientation of the body that suits the human animal for social persons.[11] The habit gives Isumbras the credential he lacked: it represents the *satisfaction* or penalty that is required by the medieval sacrament of penance. After seven years, his ordeal is relieved by an angel who brings forgiveness from 'hevenne kynge', the top feudal overlord.

   Not sure what will become of him now that he has been absolved, Isumbras retains his palmer's habit and seeks charity at the castle of an almsgiving queen who 'wolde hym help to clode and fede' (548). She is served by men 'in ryche robes of palle' (564), as Isumbras was served in his prime, and she is said to have 'rewed hym most of all' (561), laying a cloth upon the floor and seating Isumbras above all the others. She pledges to give him 'Evurmore cloth and mete' (591) and allows him to joust in her tournaments, where he mutilates many a Saracen and one day finds the scarlet mantle and gold he had lost to a marauding griffin.[12] This sign alerts the queen to the possibility that he may be her lost lord; she inquires after the scarlet mantle and then the broken ring. When they are accounted for, these signs become the conditions of the mutual recognition and reunion of Isumbras and his wife, imaged in the mysterious fusion of the separated halves of the ring:

> She layde togydur the partyes tweyne,
> Hole it wax, the sothe to seyne,
>   Ryghte amonge hem alle.
>
> (697–9)

The recognition scene embodies the triumph of unity of person and the long-awaited final accession of Isumbras to lordship: he is at that moment simultaneously and suddenly a knight, a husband, and a king:

> Now is syr Isumbras ryghte
> Crowned kynge, that hardy knyghte,
>   Of many ryche londes thare.

> Now is this kynge syr Isumbras
> In more welthe then evur he was,
>   And rekovereth hath all his care.
>   (715–20)

Representing the climax of Isumbras's many accessions, the crown is the most elevated in the parade of metonymies that link clothes and social persons.

After the coronation, the topos of investiture that has marked Isumbras's progress through the plot still has two further tasks to perform. The queen and the sons must be dressed in the habits that qualify and reward their new offices. The queen arms herself to join in Isumbras's battle to convert the recalcitrant Saracens to the Christianity their new king has proclaimed:

> She seyde, 'Lord God that I ne were dyghte
> In armour as I were a knyhte,
>   For with you wyll I fare.
> If Jesu wolde us grace sende
> That we myghte togydur ende,
>   Lyve wolde I no more.'
>
> He halpe his lady that she was dyghte
> In armour as she were a knyghte,
>   And forth wente with spere and shelde.
>   (739–47)

They ride out against more than 30,000, are miraculously joined by the three sons riding their heraldic beasts, and kill 30,003 Saracens, including two kings. The victory prompts Isumbras to reward his sons with yet another ceremony of investiture:

> And in a chambur fayre and bryghte,
> Ther he dede hem newe dyghte,
>   And chaunged all here wede.
>   (778–80)

This clothing prepares them to conquer three more kings, for which they are given the three seized kingdoms and crowned by Isumbras in the poem's last ceremony of investiture.

These scenes of investiture consistently describe accession to social persons as a process of performance, piety, and recognition by authority. The 'creation' of a king involves his endowment with material prosperity and power that, for this poem, must also be earned by an arduous process of labour and penance. The humans who are deposed from their social persons near the opening of the story appear 'as naked as they were borne' (106) before us: there is a great difference between those naked animals and the social persons to which they accede at the end of the tale. Ultimately, they accede by the authority of the poem's God, who, like a feudal overlord, recognizes and rewards their labours and sufferings.

All of these mentions of clothing, jewellery and equipment urge the reader to understand, through the image of investiture, how power is not inherent (we are 'borne naked'), and how human beings are endowed with their property, capacities, and offices according to a combination of virtue, works, and grace. In *Sir Isumbras*, the topos of investiture takes a trope from the medieval ceremony of coronation and applies it to all the social persons of the polity. According to the coronation ritual, dominion is not innate but laid upon the shoulders, like a mantle. *Sir Isumbras* extends these ritual meanings to rags, rings, red cloth, armour, and staffs. When the three sons appear, having mastered their heraldic beasts rather than inherited them, even heraldry is seen more as earned equipment than as the natural sign of knighthood. Accession to dominion is presented as a strenuous process rather than an inherent right for all social persons, from palmers to kings.

II: The Vow, *Raptus*, and Just War

As we have seen, in *Sir Isumbras* clothing is the sign of investiture and makes memorable the qualifications for and conditions of deposition and accession. But the story is not just about Isumbras's fall and rise; it is about his actions and about a conflict between cultures that takes place in what we would now call an international landscape. How does the romance use the topos of investiture to move us, emotionally and cognitively, towards questions about conflicts between cultures? In order to understand the workings of investiture in the story, we must notice the appearance of another motif familiar to romance readers: the vow. Vows – including pledges, oaths, promises, contracts, and professions of faith and fealty – are perhaps the dominant speech act of the romance form: for example, episodic vows play a pervasive and central role in *King Horn*, the earliest known romance in English, which also tells of the divestment and investiture of a king. Since a vow is the explicit commitment of the will to take up a social person and its practices, the topos of the vow is closely linked to the topos of investiture.

The central place of both investiture and the vow in *Sir Isumbras* corresponds with their centrality in political thought and jurisprudence. Like the donning of the robes of state, the coronation oath is a part of the ceremony of kingship and features largely in discussions of right rule; vows of religious profession are central in the ceremonies of monasticism and a topic of medieval theories of consent; marital vows are the speech acts that create husbands and wives and are much anatomized by canon lawyers and theologians; and the language that establishes oral contracts is a preoccupation of early economic thought as it develops in the canon law. In all these areas of jurisprudence, there are frequent questions about the revocability of vows, impediments to them, qualifications for making them, their proper forms, and their consequences.[13] Romances raise all these topics by means of the topos of the vow.[14]

The plot of *Sir Isumbras* is launched by Isumbras's first reported speech:

> 'Worldes welthe I woll forsake;
> To Jesu Criste I wyll me take,
>   To hym my sowle I yelde.'
>   (58–60)

This vow of submission is expanded as he commits his family and himself to pilgrimage and 'takes the cross' (140). The medieval ceremony of taking the cross initiates legal, spiritual, and financial responsibilities that were well elaborated by the fourteenth century in canon law, visual art, and poetry (Brundage 1969, 30–114). Isumbras's initiating vows are echoed and matched by a knot of vows at the centre of the poem, during the episode that results in the knight's final losses as well as in the means of his eventual triumph. At the nadir of Isumbras's fortunes he is starving on the shore of the Greek sea, the part of the Mediterranean that stands, in the late Middle Ages, as a boundary between Christendom and Islam, Europe and the Eastern empires. In this liminal space Isumbras, his wife, and last remaining child beg an invading heathen king for food. The complex conversation that follows alludes to a number of kinds of vows and deserves treatment at length. As we have seen, the king takes pity upon the couple's beauty and lack of clothing. He offers them a deal:

> He seyde to hem, 'Leveth on my laye
> And lete your fals goddes awaye,
>   And be with me in fyghte;
> Of golde schalt thou nevur have nede:
> If thou be dowghty manne in dede,
>   Thow shalt be doobbed knyghte.'
>   (259–64)

The king promises Isumbras riches and accession to the social person he has lost, but only on condition that he give up Christianity and join the heathen forces in a feudal arrangement called knight-service. The king proposes, in short, that Isumbras make a series of vows of fealty which would establish him in three new social persons: he is urged to become a Muslim, a legal subject (of the sultan-king), and a knight (in the king's retinue). The speech brings together this trio of social persons and establishes the attestation or avowal of belief as a model for accession to social status.

In response to the king's proposal, Isumbras refuses to fight Christians and to forsake his 'laye' (a word we shall return to later), but asks again – appealing rather provocatively to the love of Jesus – for 'som lyves fode' (271). The king then thinks to himself that Isumbras's wife is an angel and offers him another deal:

> He seyde, 'Wylt thou thy wyfe sell me?
> I wyll yefe for here golde and fe,
>   And ryche robes sevenne;
> She shall be crowned qwene of my lond,
> And every man bowe to her hond,
>   Shall no man bysette here steven.'
>   (277–82)

This deal promises riches to Isumbras and a new social person for the wife – one that exceeds in status those to which Isumbras had access in his previous wealth. Religion is not mentioned, and the vows of fealty that condition this second proposal are all made by hypothetical Saracens submitting to the wife's queenship. Isumbras refuses again, this time with a complex vow:

> The knyghte answered and seyde, 'Nay,
> My wyfe I wyll not selle away,
>   But thou me for here wyll sloo.
> I wedded her with Goddes laye
> To kepe here to my endynge daye,
>   For wele or for woo.'
>   (283–8)

The vow is ignored by the king, who takes the wife anyway, beating Isumbras 'full blo', but declining to fulfil the condition that he be slain.

In the abduction of the wife, we are invited to recognize the topos of *raptus*, a criminal act that, according to medieval lawyers, covers actions we would now describe as ranging from abduction to rape.[15] Raptus is the mirror-opposite of lawful marriage, because, in canon law if not always in practice, marriage consists of an exchange of vows that performs the consent of two qualified persons; raptus, of course, is defined as proceeding by force rather than by consent. The topos of raptus is an important artistic convention for depicting both historical and mythological subjects. As the defining plot motif of Ovid's much-imitated *Metamorphoses*, raptus pervades medieval and Renaissance writing of many genres. Chaucer begins his first and most ambitious Canterbury tale with the raptus of Ypolita, which epitomizes the acts of imperial conquest made by Theseus, the greatest 'conquerour . . . under the sonne' (I, 863–4).[16] A familiar topos in the chronicles, raptus instigates many events, including the Trojan war, that attract the attention of medieval historians and theorists of empire alike. Throughout the work of medieval and early modern English writers, raptus acts as an emblem for dominion established by conquest; when dominion is established by consent, its emblem is the marital vow.

In *Sir Isumbras*, the raptus of the wife by the heathen king is just such an act of conquest. Our attention is kept upon the issue of dominion throughout: notice that, when she refers to Isumbras, the wife always uses the Middle English word 'lord', equivalent to Latin *dominus*. On only one occasion (when, as queen, she longs to find him) does she supplement 'lord' with 'fere' (657).[17] The poem uses the marital vow to cast its use of the topos of raptus into stark relief: the king's actions are against the wife's will, as we see when she protests, but what is more important to the story is that the king contravenes the original wedding vows that established Isumbras in his sexual dominion. The king thus flouts the rights and responsibilities of the knight's social person as well as the institution of Christian marriage. Isumbras's reiteration of his vow conveys all these aspects of the raptus at once.

By invoking Isumbras's wedding vow, the poem stresses the contrast between the ceremonial purpose of such language (marital vows normally link people together) and the performative force of his speech act, which is emphatically to reject the king's proposals of affiliation. Isumbras's refusal is presented as a kind of chastity – it does not allow him to 'kepe' his wife, but it does allow him to confirm his right to dominion in the face of its practical loss. He holds up one of his last shreds of clothing, his status as a husband, in an attempt to shield himself from all the social persons offered by the king. Many years later, the king's abduction of the wife ironically turns out to be the means for Isumbras's accession to imperial dominion: once he has fulfilled the penance for his crime of pride, his fealty to his marriage in itself qualifies him for kingship.[18] Isumbras's marital vow, voiced to the Saracen king, thus takes on an especially heavy burden in the plot. The conjunction of kinds of vows, kinds of social persons, and kinds of social bonds implicitly invites us to compare their conditions and consequences and to transfer the standards of each one to the others. The theme of marriage and the recitation of the vow combine to push the criterion of consent to the forefront of our attention as the single most crucial aspect of just dominion.

How is the reader invited to respond to this episode? Employing a mode of proof much recommended by ancient and medieval rhetorical theorists discussing political argument, romance writers often emphasize vows by accompanying them with outbursts of intense emotion. In the scene at the Greek sea, Isumbras's wife swoons three times after she gives her parting instructions to Isumbras (342). She again swoons three times at their later reunion (704). Her swoons give us no psychological insight into her character; rather, as rhetoricians would say, they appeal to the passions, summoning the reader's pity for her. Like the persons who appear in political and legal thought, romance characters are extraordinarily devoid of inner life and what we would call individuality. This abstract characterization is instrumental: it directs the reader to the ethical, political, and jurisprudential questions raised by the plot. The wife's swoons are a mode of memorial rubrication, as if the poet had marked these especially important passages in red. In the Caius MS, 'joye' marks the two passages and urges the reader to collate them:

> There was joye to sen hem mete
> With clyppyng and with kyssyng swete
> Whenne he to the schyp scholde goo.
> (316–18)

> There was joye to sen hem mete
> With laykyng and with kyssyng swete
> In armes for to folde.
> (676–8)

These representations of passion appeal to both the emotions and the intellects of readers: the violation of the marriage by raptus is outrageous and designed to be easily understood as criminal.

We are also invited to respond with emotion to Isumbras's reiteration of his wedding vow just at the moment of the raptus of his wife. The pathos of the scene would have been considerably increased if the vow had been fervently addressed to the wife, but it is not. Instead, the vow is thrown in the face of the heathen king in a speech act of refusal. With this refusal, the narrative emphasizes the violation of Isumbras's sexual dominion rather than the violation of his wife's body or will. The poem further characterizes the raptus as a kind of theft when it stresses his property rights in his wife (277, 284, 674). The dominant pathetic appeal of this raptus is thus to anger, and outrage directs our moral evaluation of the action.

Both pity and anger help to underwrite a political argument in the poem. In the logic of the poem, the fervent and pious assertion of will expressed in Isumbras's use of the wedding vow justifies the form of his eventual revenge and seizure of Saracen territories. The vow contrasts a Christian ideal of consent with the heathen king's wicked violation of that ideal in three spheres: the political (expressed by his plan to conquer unconsenting Christian territories), the religious (expressed by his attempt to force Isumbras to convert), and the sexual (expressed by the raptus). Now we are in a position to understand the importance of the wedding vow's appearance at this crux of the plot: the contravention of Isumbras's vow by the king is designed to underwrite the later war that will be waged by Isumbras for the heathen culture's dispossession and forcible conversion. The vow is designed to extinguish any right to consent to rule or religion that we might accord the Saracens.

In staging the injury to Isumbras as a raptus that contravenes an idealized marriage, the poem keeps the criterion of consent ever before us.[19] The plot transfers the criterion of consent from the marital to the political sphere in order to justify Isumbras's eventual massacre of Saracens and establishment of Christian empire in his new lands. And once we are encouraged to see consent as a political criterion, as a means not only of establishing marriage but of diagnosing an injury that can serve as a cause for a just war, we are also in a position to apply the criterion of consent to Isumbras's forcible conversion of Saracens. When at the end of the romance Isumbras proclaims Christianity in his new kingdom, he does not concern himself with whether or not there is any semblance of consent or even understanding in the subjects' conversion to Christianity, or in their acceptance of new rulers. In one of its gestures towards closure, the romance makes a joke at the Saracens' expense about the matter of consent:

> Now is this kynge syr Isumbras
> In more welthe then evur he was,
>   And rekovereth hath all his care.
>
> Cristendome he lette crye;
> He sende abowte ferre and nye
>   To hem that hethen were.
> All the Sarezens were of on assente
> Syr Isumbras forto have shente,
>   And all that with hym were.
>   (718–26)

The line break after 'were of on assente' ('were all agreed') might for a moment suggest that the Saracens have been spontaneously converted, but the enjambment's chillingly witty turn 'Syr Isumbras forto have shente' ('to kill Sir Isumbras') reveals the agreement to be against rather than with Isumbras. And because the withholding of agreement justifies their murder, the lines form the prelude to the slaughter of 30,003 Saracens that will soon crown the accession of the hero.

111

Sir Isumbras is not unique among romances in denying any need to procure consent for Saracen conversion. Some canon lawyers argued that heathens should be grouped under the Roman law category of *hostes* or public enemies; Saracens then deserved punishment by war on account of their beliefs alone (Russell 1975, 50). Yet this bloody-mindedness differs sharply from some other well-known treatments of conversion. For example, in the fourth part of the philosophical treatise *Opus maius*, written for Pope Clement IV in the 1260s, Roger Bacon stresses the difference between two strategies of conversion: oppression by force and argument for the Christian religion. In his opinion, Saracens and Tartars yield to argument but forcibly resist servitude and the confiscation of their property. *The King of Tars*, a romance written in Middle English and dated 1300–30, grants consent such spiritual power that voluntary baptism transforms a dark-skinned sultan to whiteness. In the *Anglo-Norman Chronicle*, written for Edward I's daughter Mary in the 1330s, Nicholas Trevet similarly stresses voluntarism in his life of Constance: when Constance finds herself among heathens, she preaches the Christian faith to them, and only after they explicitly assent to the faith does she arrange for their baptism. Pope Nicholas I prohibited conversion of non-Christians by force, though others allowed it (Russell 1975, 33). Under Isumbras, Christianity must be accepted at sword-point as a consequence of political dominion, and the faith appears to have no special affective, moral or didactic content other than feudal submission and obedience. *Sir Isumbras* thus engages its readers in the larger deliberations of philosophers and theologians on the relations of Christendom to the rest of the world. Are we to add the criterion of consent to the list of justifications for war? If we do, is its effect to expand or restrict Christian aggression? Are Christians limited to argumentation in their attempts to convert other peoples, or can they legitimately flout their own ideals when others do?

The final issue we must take up is thus that of the religious practice of war and its conformity to Christian ideals. As we have seen, the hero's first vow, out of which the entire plot unfolds, is not a sexual vow, but a vow of religious submission. The analogies among the political, sexual, and religious vows that occur on the Greek shore cannot be explained by their sexual side alone. In order to understand how the poem structures the relation between religion and dominion, we must look more closely at the religious plot and at a third topos, the topos of penance.

III: Penance and the Criterion of Courtesy

The action of *Sir Isumbras* begins in the woods with the bird's annunciation of the knight Isumbras's deposition and civil death; it ends near Jerusalem with the angel's annunciation that the palmer Isumbras's penitence has been rewarded with absolution, an absolution that clears the way for his accession to empire. Penance makes up one of the important motives of the poem (Hopkins 1990). But what exactly is Isumbras's sin? It is not wealth. The poem puts it this way:

> Into his herte a pryde was browghte
> That of God yafe he ryghte nowghte,
>   His mercy ones to nevenne;
> So longe he regned in that pryde
> That Jesu wolde no lengur abyde:
>   To hym he sente a stevenne.
>
>   (37–42)

Pride is one of the seven deadly sins, of course, and Isumbras's crime is said to be a pride of the heart. But the stanza's idiomatic exposition of his pride is careful. The lines mean that Isumbras is heedless of God, but they hint at something more than a psychological state. That he should by right be giving something in acknowledgement of God's mercy suggests a feudal property arrangement where tribute is required in exchange for mercy given. Isumbras's existence seems shaped by a feudal legal custom; his rights to his social person seem to be held in tenure from the 'kynge of hevenn' (52). He has forgotten what he was (to use the expression of the bird), insofar as he has neglected to acknowledge God's mercy as the source of that status. The sin of pride suggests that he imagines himself, rather than his divine overlord, to be the source of his right to dominion.

As Isumbras's moral progress unfolds, it is worth returning to an ambiguity in the poem's beginning. What looks at first like pure praise becomes more complicated as we are led to consider the complexities of dominion:

> A curteys man and hende he was;
> His name was kalled syr Isumbras,
>   Bothe curteys and fre.
> His gentylnesse nor his curtesye
> There kowthe no man hit discrye:
>   A ffull good man was he.
> Menstralles he hadde in his halle,
> And yafe hem robes of ryche palle,
>   Sylver, golde and fee.
> Of curtesye he was kynge;
> His gentylnesse hadde non endyng,
>   In worlde was none so fre.
>
>   (19–30)

This important early stanza lays out the premises of the case, facts that are given their special emotional and moral colouring only by the actions that ensue. The insistent repetition of 'curteys' and 'curtesye' is carefully gauged to open up a wide register of meaning. First, courtesy is an ethical trait, like that of being 'hende'; then it is a description of class status, like the knightly title 'syr' and Isumbras's free, as opposed to bound, legal standing. No man can describe the knight's courtesy (an example of the inexpressibility topos), though courtesy is implicit in his humanity: he is a 'ffull good man'. 'Good' opens up into the meanings 'wealth' and 'generosity' in the following line, where Isumbras is described as a knight who supports a retinue. Finally, his political status culminates the catalogue. 'Of curtesye he was kynge' argues that his social person is maintained by his courtesy, which now means something in terms of ethics, law, household, property, and polity.[20] Yet the phrase itself is ambiguous.[21] Does it mean that he was the best among all courteous people – is 'kynge' here used in the figurative sense (*OED* 6) to suggest Isumbras's pre-eminence in good manners? Does it mean that his kingship derives *from* his courtesy – that he gained the office by his accumulated aristocratic merit? Or does it mean that he was king by leave of the courtesy of someone else? What, in sum, makes a king? The plot goes on to suggest that Isumbras is king by God's courtesy, and that this dependence on divine favour should have been acknowledged by Isumbras.

Isumbras's response to the accusation of the bird portrays a feudal understanding of the proper relation of the lord Isumbras to his overlord, heaven's king:

> With carefull herte and sykynge sore,
> He fell upon his knees thore;
>   His hondes up he helde.
> 'Worldes welthe I woll forsake;
> To Jesu Criste I wyll me take,
>   To hym my sowle I yelde.'
>
>   (55–60)

In the posture of political as well as religious submission, Isumbras yields his soul together with his wealth. The verb 'yelde' portrays the appropriate feudal action – tribute in acknowledgement of God's sovereignty – taken too late. The reader is led to see the dispossession of Isumbras as a punishment within the rights of a monarch who has been failed by one of his baronial tenants-in-chief.[22]

The religious plot is most precisely understood, then, as penitential action taken by a man who regains his lord's former grace by extending his domain. Penance has a special connection with wars against Saracens in this period because the Latin church preached that indulgence for the remission of the penalties of confessed sin (such as shortening the time and miseries the soul suffered in purgatory) could be gained by participating in the crusades. The theological fine print of this indulgence was extensive, but chroniclers and knights tended to understand it as a full remission of sins (see Brundage 1969, 144–55; Brundage 1995, 22; and Russell 1975, 33). Augustine warned in *Contra Faustum Manichaeum* that a just war was not to be undertaken out of a sinful *libido dominandi*, or lust for dominion (Russell 1975, 16). (Proper intention was one of the criteria for justifying war.)[23] Instead, the enterprise of taking Saracen lands was imagined as *peregrinatio* or pilgrimage, in what Russell suggestively understands as a legal fiction that indicates a persistent moral reservation in Christian thought about killing and warfare (Russell 1975, 294–5); this reservation prevented scholastic philosophers from easily incorporating the crusades into theories of the just war. The close association between penance and crusade allows us to see the sufferings, pilgrimage, and military acts of Isumbras as one continuous penitential action. The king of heaven rewards Isumbras with 'mercy' (39) and dominion that partakes equally of political, sexual, and religious power; at the end of the poem, the souls of Isumbras and his family do indeed go straight to heaven, bypassing purgatory.

IV: Lordship, *Laye*, and Dominion

The unity of the different topoi of *Sir Isumbras* – political investiture, sexual vow, and religious penance – lies in the social institution called *lordship*, which is the political form of a people's obligation to their lord king, a wife's obligation to her lord husband, and a Christian's obligation to the lord 'kynge of heven'. Lordship is a form of dominion that includes all three realms (the political, the sexual, and the religious) within its lexical scope. Isumbras is a lord at the beginning of the poem, but we see his lordship in a surreal isolation: no geographical identification other than 'Christian' is given about his realm, and, though he passes through the 'border' polities of the Greek shore and Jerusalem (and, in some manuscripts, Acre), we know nothing about the lands he comes to rule other than that they are 'Saracen'. Lordship is considered in the abstract, then, together with the condition of devotion. The tight interweaving of the three plots is partly accomplished, as we have seen, by means of lexical overlap. Metaphors like 'kynge of hevenn' and 'yelde' in the passage quoted above are important cues to help the reader connect religious and political interpretations. Single words that can go between the three cultural realms of the romance are important unifying devices. Perhaps the most important word belonging to all three realms of the poem is *laye*.

Middle English *laye* is lexically polyvalent: it can mean law, principle, religion, faith, belief, system of government, system of law enforcement, justice, kingdom, practice, way of life, custom (see *MED* 'laue', also attested in the spellings 'laye', lawe', etc.). During the pivotal scene on the shore of the Greek sea, the word *laye*, emphasized by both syntax and rhyme, appears four times in a short space. The heathen king repulses Isumbras's request for sustenance:

> He commanded to bete hym aweye;
> For they leved not on his laye,
>   Of hym they schulde have noghte.
>   (238–40)

The collocation of *leve* and *laye* is frequent in Middle English and can express adherence to codes of faith, law, or custom: the king's first mention of his *laye* does not specify which code, but seems to refer generally to his culture. His second use of the word targets both religion and military alliance:

> Leveth on my laye
> And lete your fals goddes awaye,
>   And be with me in fyghte . . .
>   (259–61)

The choice is between Christianity on the one hand and a new allegiance to the heathen king on the other: the parallel between religion and politics makes an alliance with the Saracen king seem idolatrous. Viewed conversely, the comparison presents Christianity as itself a version of feudal loyalty, reinforcing the feudal overtones of the bird's initial accusations. If Isumbras's relation to heaven's king is feudal, what the heathen king proposes is nothing short of treason:

> 'Syr', he seyde, 'nay.
> Schall I nevur more
> Ayeyns Cristen werre,
>   Nor forsake my laye.'
>   (267–70)

Isumbras's political obligation to God prevents him from offering fealty to the *laye* of another king. In short, political dominion and religion are equivalent in this exchange.

The negotiation then moves swiftly away from the question of faith and towards sexual arrangements when the Saracen king offers to buy Isumbras's wife and make her a queen. First, the word *laye* linked religious and political obligations; next, as we have seen, it links religious and sexual bonds:

> I wedded her with Goddes laye
> To kepe here to my eyndynge daye,
>   For wele or for woo.
>
> (286–8)

'Goddes laye' here means a Christian custom, a traditional way to marry. Isumbras clearly quotes his wedding vow in lines 287–8, a vow that the syntax presents in apposition to 'Goddes laye'.

The final appearance of the word *laye* in the poem is an early part of the process of reviving the marital bond between Isumbras and his wife. Brought into the queen's hall as a 'pore palmere' (565), Isumbras is given chair and cushion and then asked by his unrecognized wife to speak:

> 'Fech me a schayer and a coyschenn
> And make this palmere to sytte therin
>   That he me telle may
> What maner aventours he hath seyn
> In dyvers londes ther he has bene,
>   By many dyvers way.'
> Ryghte soone a cheyere was forth fette;
> The pore palmere therin was sette:
>   He tolde here of his leye.
> Goode tales he her tolde;
> The lady asked what she wolde,
>   In longynge as they satte aye.
>
> (577–88)

Students of medieval romance will recognize that the word 'leye' or 'lay' also designates a short romance, and indeed an 'Ysanbras len veyse' is listed in a thirteenth-century list of French lays, which suggests that *Sir Isumbras* may be a version of an earlier French lay (Brereton 1950). 'He tolde here of his leye' means that he told her the story that is *Sir Isumbras*, that he told her of his religious faith, and that he told her of his marital devotion. The queen rewards him with a grant of perpetual 'cloth and mete', a room, and a serving page. *Laye* here becomes intertwined in the chain of social persons occupied by Isumbras and marked by clothing: his ability to tell stories transforms the palmer into a knight of the queen's court. The erotic 'longynge as they satte aye', induced by her questions and his storytelling, is a desire each feels for the lost unity of person that will be restored when Isumbras, proven by tournament and token, is finally recognized by the queen as her lord.

What then is the *laye* of Isumbras? It is, all at once, his marriage, his belief and faith, the 'aventours' he has seen, the penitential rule under which he has lived as a palmer, his once and future dominion, and the story of his life – the romance of *Sir Isumbras* itself. This moment of reference by the story to itself sums up the meanings of the word *laye* and clarifies the purpose of the poem. The longing the poem describes is one its audience is invited to share – a longing to find a place for one's body within the three forms of dominion: the political, the sexual, and the religious. As it instructs its adherents by law, sexual custom and faith, any *laye* helps to fit – habitu- ates – their bodies to social persons. Through a proper evocation and direction of the passions, the penitent Isumbras is redressed in his faith, his knighthood, his husbandhood, his lordship, and then promoted to dynastic, imperial kingship. His *laye*, in all its meanings, propels him to empire.

Middle English *laye* describes the narrative qualities of such codes as law, faith, sexual custom, and medieval romance itself. Social structures manage to reproduce themselves because the ideological values they embody are instructions to the bodies of the people to whom those structures appeal. By explaining the body's experiences of anger, joy, and pity as motives for the actions and alliances that cement social structures together, people are re- cognized by others – just as the recognition scenes of the Middle English romance imagine – to merit accession to social persons. Recognition scenes are as performative as vows are: they bring into being states of affairs – accessions that are new despite being reinstatements of previous or seem- ingly inherent states. Recognition creates social persons in accordance with *laye*: accession to social person is impossible to accomplish without the collaboration of supporting persons and bonds; it is equally impossible with- out the ideological support of some kind of *laye*, be it political, sexual, religious, or all three.

Sir Isumbras analyses dominion by stripping it from the protagonists and then restoring it to them bit by bit. The poem invites us to consider at some length the problems of accession to social person through the imagery of clothing. At the same time, through the topos of the vow, the poem gives us a means of assessing the formation of social bonds. That assessment is quickly transferred to the larger relations of global politics when, during the scene at the Greek sea, the poem elevates consent to a political criterion. With such topoi, the poem provides an excellent means of testing political, sexual, and religious ideals against each other. It draws both learned and unlearned audiences into surprisingly complex conceptual assessments of difficult problems.

If we were to take up the invitation of *Sir Isumbras* to moral deliberation, we might argue that dominion at its greatest scale (international empire) should be subject to the same criteria of justice that govern other kinds of dominion (especially, here, those embodied in marriage and religious practices). Paradoxically, the argument of *Sir Isumbras* fails by its own criterion: the poem loses moral cogency when the raptus committed by the heathen king justifies the deaths of 30,003 Saracens and the forcible conversion and subjugation of many more. Raptus certainly deserves censure, but in the conclusion of the tale it is deplorably used to justify, on a yet larger scale, precisely the same conquest and disdain for consent which caused the reader to abhor the heathen king's action. The poem, however, seems not to expect a reader who would credit non-Christians with the capacity for consent.[24] As its topoi engage us in the problems of a divided world, *Sir Isumbras* seems unable to anticipate the full consequences of its intellectual and affective power; its grasp exceeds its reach. Perhaps that is one measure of a successful thought experiment.

Notes

1   I rely mainly on the edition of British Library, MS Cotton Caligula A.ii by Maldwyn Mills, *Six Middle English Romances*, Everyman (London: Dent, 1973). All references to the poem are to this edition, noted by line number, unless otherwise indicated. Occasional references are made to the edition of Cambridge, Gonville and Caius College 175, by Harriet Hudson, *Four Middle English Romances*, TEAMS (Kalamazoo, MI: Medieval Institute Publications, 1996).

2   Hudson, H. 1996 lists nine manuscripts or fragments and five prints; Mills 1994 counts fewer. See Mills 1994 for a discussion of the manuscripts and prints of *Sir Isumbras*, the relations between them, and revealing problems faced by editors.

3   For the passage and discussion, see Thompson 1994, 115–16, and Crane 1986, 94–6.

4   Until the fall of Acre in 1291, the kingdoms of Jerusalem and Acre were among a handful of Christian colonies in the Middle East – something like frontier outposts in a sea of Islam.

5   See Crane 1986, especially 115–17, 220. Mehl 1968 calls such romances 'secular hagiography'. Their status is a lively critical issue. The closest hagiographic analogues of *Sir Isumbras* are adduced in Gerould 1904 and Braswell 1965.

6   Wittig 1978 analyses a large group of romances for 'type-episode' and 'type-scene'. This yields useful structural results that help us to collate similar plot events, but such abstraction can lead the reader away from recognizing the cognitive and affective provocation embedded in such scenes.

7   *The Illustrated Chronicles of Matthew Paris: Observations of Thirteenth-Century Life*, ed. and trans. Richard Vaughan (Cambridge: Corpus Christi College, 1993), 128–32.

8   For example, the thirteenth-century English legal text we call Bracton uses *mors civilis* to refer to the legal status of slaves and monks because they are entirely subject to their lords and have no legal capacities before the common law: 'Est etiam mors civilis in servo in servitute sub potestate domini constituto' ('the villein being under the power of his lord may . . . be considered as "civilly dead"'). Quotation and translation from Pollock and Maitland 1959, I, 28.

9   For more on the concept of the social person and on the topos of investiture in early modern colonial law, Shakespeare's *Macbeth*, and Jonson's *The Irish Masqve at Covrt*, see Fowler 1999.

10   On the relation between civil death and unity of person, see Fowler 1995.

11   *Habitus* is a term used by medieval philosophers such as Albertus Magnus and his student Thomas Aquinas; it derives from the notion of *ethos* in Aristotle's *Nichomachean Ethics* and has been revived by twentieth-century sociologists such as Marcel Mauss and Pierre Bourdieu.

12   In some other manuscripts it is an eagle or an angel. The griffin was one of Edward III's 'favoured emblems' (Mitchiner 1986, 119), and it may be that the heraldic beasts of *Sir Isumbras* are specific political allusions. There are English illustrations of Saracen warriors in medieval manuscripts such as the Luttrell Psalter and the chronicle of Matthew Paris.

13   The topic of consent played a large role in the constitutional developments of the period: 'The conceptual framework that made possible the development of legislative assemblies, such as the English Parliament, the Spanish Cortes, and the French Estates-General, among others, emerged gradually out of specu- lative arguments among academic lawyers in the thirteenth and fourteenth centuries about [the nature of representation and consent] and related matters of legal principle' (Brundage 1995, 110–11).

14   For more on vows and medieval poetry, see Green 1998.

15   On definitions of raptus with reference to medieval literature, see Gravdal 1991, Dinshaw 1992 and Cannon 1993.

16   On raptus and political thought in the *Knight's Tale*, see Fowler 1998.

17   The *MED* cites 'spouse' as only the third meaning of 'fere', whose usual senses range from 'companion' and 'armed supporter' to 'equal' and 'peer'. The wife does not use words such as 'make' or 'spouse' that refer primarily to sexual affiliation.

18   Isumbras's claim to his wife procures him a kingship because she has become a Saracen queen; he proclaims Christianity and the family then conquers further Saracen kingdoms. The poem carefully skirts the legal bigamy that threatens by suggesting that the raptus is a forced sale (277, 284, 674) and that the sultan does not marry (or sexually violate) the wife but immediately crowns her and ships her to his castle. Thus she accedes to the monarchy not as his consort but by his delegation of his office as monarch (in the Caius and Thornton MSS the sultan pointedly executes a legal charter appointing her queen).

19 By making raptus the injury, the poem also invokes Augustine's primary re-
    quirement for the just war, repeated by Thomas Aquinas in his *Summa Theologiae*,
    qu. 40, art. 1, and canonized in Gratian's legal compilation, the Decretum,
    c. 23, qu. 2, c. 2. 'Justa bella ulciscuntur iniurias', writes Augustine: 'just wars
    avenge injuries', such as securing the return of what has been taken away
    unjustly: *Quaestiones in heptateuchum* VI, 10, ed. J. Zycha, Corpus Scriptorum
    Ecclesiasticorum Latinorum 28 (Vienna, 1895), p. 428. The legal tradition
    usually specified six main criteria for the just war: that it have a just cause and
    a right intention (such as recovery of property); that war be declared by a
    proper authority; that the force used be proportional to the occasion; that war
    be an action of last resort; and that the goal of war be peace (Johnson 1981,
    xxix; Brundage 1969 and 1976 and Russell 1975). Isumbras respects only the
    first of these six, and even that incompletely. For though just wars may be
    waged to secure the return of property taken away unjustly, further takings of
    property and dominion require further justification. If the wife is what was
    taken away, there is no doubt that Isumbras goes on to take more than he lost
    when he sacks numerous Saracen kingdoms and installs his family as rulers
    over them.

20 The special meaning of 'courtesy' in jurisprudence adds a further dimension:
    'courtesy' is a synonym of 'comity', Latin *comitas*. *Black's Law Dictionary* defines
    'comity' as 'courtesy, respect, a willingness to grant a privilege . . . In general,
    principle of comity is that courts or jurisdiction will give effect to laws and
    judicial decisions of another state of jurisdiction.' Cf. Joseph Story, *Conflict of
    Laws* (1834), who defined the concept as 'the obligation of nations to give
    effect to foreign laws when they are not prejudical to their own rights and
    interests' (*OED* 'comity' 2). The association of courtesy with Isumbras's story,
    which takes place 'between' Saracen and Christian realms and 'layes', invites
    us to bring to the story the principle of reciprocity that nourishes international
    law. On the other hand, since the proper reading of the phrase 'Of curtesye
    he was kynge' turns out to be 'by the grace of the Christian God he was king',
    we might reason that all the world is under a single jurisdiction, and that no
    comity need be extended to Saracen law. Conflict of laws is one of the topics
    that the poem invites its audience to deliberate.

21 See Putter 1996, 162–8 for an analysis of similar ambiguities in *Pearl* (invol-
    ving the words 'asente', 'deme', 'grounde' and especially 'quene of cortaysye').
    Such wordplay upon common idioms often concerns grey areas in the attribu-
    tion of action or authority.

22 See Crane 1986 for the important argument that the religious feeling of this
    and other romances is entirely assimilated to secular achievement.

23 On the criteria justifying war, see n. 19 above.

24 See Tierney 1997 and Tuck 1979 for topics in the development of rights
    theories. This area of medieval political philosophy (one background of mod-
    ern international law) often concerned itself with wars for pagan lands in both
    the Middle East and, later, the Americas.

CHAPTER FIVE

Violence, Narrative and Proper Name: *Sir Degaré*, 'The Tale of Sir Gareth of Orkney', and the *Folie Tristan d'Oxford**

JAMES SIMPSON

Scholarly study of Middle English romance begins in the latter half of the eighteenth century. Whereas sixteenth-century antiquarian study of earlier literature had been resolutely author-based,[1] eighteenth-century scholars were more receptive to the simplicities of anonymous romance precisely because it was simplicity that offered access to the 'manners and customs of the time in which they [the romances] were composed'.[2] This view is pre-mised, of course, on a condescension towards the entire civilization that romances were taken to reflect. In the greatest of the eighteenth-century literary antiquarians, however, this condescension stands unresolved with an acute nostalgia for the age of romance. Thomas Warton begins his extraordinary *History of English Poetry* (1774–81) with apparently serene con-fidence in the superiority of his own age, an 'age advanced to the highest degree of refinement', in which 'that species of curiosity commences, which is busied in contemplating the progress of social life, in displaying the grada-tions of science, and in tracing the transitions from barbarism to civility' (Warton 1774–81, I, A.i.r). Even before he has finished his introduction, however, Warton's confidence in the superiority of his own age is searching for ways of discreetly articulating its own poverty of spirit. The solution is to affirm that the Catholic centuries were indeed beset with 'the gloom of ignorance and superstition', but at the same time to argue that gloom and superstition are exactly the conditions in which the imagination flourishes best (Warton 1774–81, I, K.iv.r). By the time Warton comes to the recovery of classical literature in the sixteenth century, he both praises and attacks it, progressively sustaining and undermining the standards of taste he ostens-ibly admires. After recognizing all the benefits that the 'revolution' of the

* I am grateful to Ad Putter and Christopher Cannon for learned and penetrating readings of this article.

classical revival had brought (good sense, taste, criticism), he goes on to end his second volume in this remarkable way:

> But, in the mean time, we have lost a set of manners, and a system of machinery, more suitable to the purposes of poetry, than those which have been adopted in their place. We have parted with extravagancies that are above propriety, with incredibilities that are more acceptable than truth, and with fictions that are more valuable than reality.
>
> (Warton 1774–81, II, 463)

Warton here presages the Romantic reappraisal of romance's irrational truths, and in so doing he expresses not curiosity so much as longing for all that taste and reason have repressed.

One of the romances that Warton discusses with admiration is *Sir Degaré*, to which he had access through the late fifteenth-century manuscript Cambridge, CUL Ff.2.38 (which preserves lines 1–615), as well as two sixteenth-century prints.[3] He deploys *Degaré* to exemplify his point that romances are not 'incoherent rhapsodies', but that they are possessed of a 'regular integrity, in which every part contributes to produce an intended end' (Warton 1774–81, I, 182). After this introduction, however, Warton can do no more than recount the plot in (accurate) detail; he lacks the vocabulary to link specific romances to his general, and very enthusiastic, ideas about the value of these works as expressions of an imagination at once 'superstitious' and powerful. I sympathize with Warton's incapacity, since for romance, more than for any other genre of medieval writing, understanding of the general must inform understanding of the particular; one can, however, move to the general only from the particulars, and the particulars often fail to manifest what were until recently the standard characteristics that mark literary works out as worthy of critical attention. Individual romances, that is, often lack (for example) stylistic density; an implied yet elusive authorial perspective; explicit ethical complexity; resistance to narrative closure; historical specificity. The fact that a sophisticated romance like *Sir Gawain and the Green Knight*, consistently a darling of Anglo-American critics since the mid-twentieth century, has all these qualities in abundance (even, possibly, the last) merely proves the rule by exception.[4] In this article I want to move between the particular and the general, by way of confirming Warton's sense that something powerful lurks within these deceptively simple stories. By reference to particular works, I intend especially to investigate his general point that romances manifest 'extravagancies . . . above propriety'. The propriety I am concerned with is that of name, and the extravagancies (or wanderings) I investigate are those violent and/or transgressive actions that establish propriety over name. My control works span the twelfth to the late fifteenth centuries: Malory's 'Tale of Sir Gareth of Orkney' (finished by 1470, in prose) and the Anglo-Norman *Folie Tristan d'Oxford* (late twelfth century, 998 lines of octosyllabic couplets).

In *Sir Degaré* the hero is named by the hermit in whose keeping the abandoned child has been placed. The name given is, clearly enough, thematic, based as it is on the French word *égaré* (which has the literal sense of English 'lost', and the figural sense of English 'errant'):[5]

> He hit nemnede Degarre:
> Degarre nowt elles nis
> But thing, that not neuer, whar it is,
> Or thing, that is negh forlorn, also;
> Forthi the child he nemnede thous tho.
> (254–8)[6]

This short passage is almost the only moment in an otherwise wholly streamlined narrative where the narrator breaks the story to explain something to his audience. Why should he pause in this way? What's in a name? I shall argue that the thematic content of this name drives the entire narrative (even the sequence prior to the hero's birth). The narrative of this little work continues only so long as the hero's identity remains unknown, and draws to a close as soon as he is recognized by all who must know him (grandfather, mother, fiancée, father). This is an observation to do with the purely formal, structural shape of the work, but it has thematic and ideological implications, which I shall develop in Sections II and III. Before I look to particular narratives, however, I should like to dwell for a moment on the relationship between names and narrative. How, my reader may be objecting, can a name drive a narrative? Isn't it the other way round?

I

The trope of personification is, of course, an extreme example of a figure whereby names quite obviously generate narratives. *Piers Plowman* provides countless examples, of which this is one:

> Now bigynneth Gloton for to go to shrifte,
> And kaireth hym to kirkewarde his coupe to shewe.
> Ac Beton the Brewestere bad hym good morwe
> And with that asked of hym, whiderward he wolde,
> 'To holy chirche,' quod he, 'for to here masse,

And sithen I wole be shryven, and synne na moore.'
I have good ale, gossib,' quod she, 'Gloton, woltow assay?'
'Hastow,' quod he, 'any hote spices?'

(B.5.297–304)

The narrative structure of this passage is established by its main actant, whose name activates two competing narratives, of penitence and debauchery (both contained in the pun on the word 'coupe', English 'cup' and Latin *culpa*, 'guilt'). In the context of the confession of the other sins, the narrative is initially pointed towards church, but is derailed by the competing narrative of the pub. The sequence as a whole develops predictably within the space determined by the possibilities of Glutton's name – Glutton joins his drinking-partners in the pub, eats and drinks too much (as he must), vomits, and is carried to bed. As he wakes up, the penitential discourse implicit in his name is activated: he is rebuked by Repentance, at which point he confesses his sin. The syntagmatic set to which the name belongs determines that he must confess, just as, of course, the name itself prohibits any real change of person through penitence (in contrast to Haukyn's penitence in Passus B.14, where the proper or personal name allows for change in a way that the personification does not).

Here, then, we have a narrative structure that is formed by a name, and is held tightly within the constraints imposed by that name. Even the action of the properly named figures in the pub ('Beton the Brewestere', and so on) must be held within the conceptual frame determined by Glutton: he is the leitmotif of the action, and no-one in this narrative can move outside the semantic limits and institutional affiliations determined by his name. The action that results from this naming premise is both iterative (repeating, elaborating 'gluttony'), and foreclosed (it cannot escape repeating 'gluttony'). The narrative presents itself as sequential, as a progressive story of psychological temptation, but its shape (even for the properly named figures it includes) is determined by possibilities present in its governing word from the beginning. Once Gluttony confesses, the scene must come to an end, since Gluttony can do nothing else in this narrative frame: he has been absorbed back into the institutional discourse that produces the concept.[7]

On the face of it, this example of naming generating narrative is irrelevant to romance: the foreclosing of narrative by personification differs ostensibly from those romances where the meaning of the protagonist's name accrues by the action of the narrative itself. In *Sir Gawain and the Green Knight*, for example, personifications hover at the edge of the narrative, framing but not foreclosing Gawain's action. Take this passage, for example (Gawain thematizing his own action, as he casts aside the belt):

> For care of thy knokke cowardyse me taght
> To acorde me with couetyse, my kynde to forsake,
> That is larges and lewté that longez to knyghtez.
>
> (2743–5)

The third line here almost certainly neutralizes the mini-personification in the first two, as the verb 'longez' (meaning 'pertains to') can have, in this context, only an abstract sense. The *Gawain*-poet reverses the disposition of proper to personified names found in the Gluttony passage from *Piers Plowman*: a proper name ('Gawain') governs the centre of the action, whereas personifications stand on the margins, subject to the decisions and judgements of the properly named figure. Of course the actions of the properly named protagonist can themselves be conceptualized only by reference to abstract qualities, but no abstract quality can claim possession of the narrative in the way 'Gluttony' does in the passage discussed above.

In some romance narratives, then, names do not determine narrative. In many, however, they do, and I am not immediately thinking of the romances whose main figure is given a thematized name, like Degaré, Egaré, Constance, Amans, Amis, Amiloun, Gudmod, or even Tristan.[8] My point derives rather from the fact that in some ideologies names are considered to be revealing of innate selfhood. The liberal ideology of our own society (as distinct, possibly, from our practice) has it that names bear an entirely arbitrary relationship to self (even names like 'Justice', or 'Scattergood').[9] We designate one aspect of our lineage with our surname, but we expect others not to 'thematize' us in any way by decoding that surname into any moral, familial or especially ethnic stereotype. We like to think of names as initially open ciphers, waiting to be filled, *a posteriori*, by our experiences of individuals. The ideology of a very strong kinship system, by contrast, will attribute thematized qualities to the name, since the name is felt to lead directly to the innermost, genetic recesses of the self. Names, according to such ideologies, are not empty ciphers, but are already thematic, or coded; they will, accordingly, operate much more in the manner of personification narrative, since the name's relationship with self is not at all arbitrary, and the self can be thematized. As Perceval's mother instructs her son in Chrétien de Troyes's *Perceval*:

> '... le non sachiez a la parsome,
> car par le non conuist an l'ome'
>
> (559–60).[10]

('Learn the person's name, for by the name one knows the man.')

126

In this article I propose that many romances operate in the manner of personification narrative, given their aristocratic ideology of name. In these narratives reclamation of a 'proper' name equally predicates a world in which everything else sits in its proper place. The recovery of proper name represents, that is, the restoration of propriety both in the order of language and in the social order. Reclamation of semantic and social propriety is only possible, however, by significant violence.

II

The story of *Sir Degaré* runs as follows: on the anniversary of the death of a queen, the widower king of Brittany and his beloved daughter ride through a forest to the abbey where his wife is buried; the daughter's retinue is detached from the king's, and the daughter from her retinue. She is raped by a 'fairi-knyghte', who gives the girl a broken-tipped sword, asking that it be given to the son who, he is certain, will be born from their union. The child is born in secret, and discreetly taken to be left at a nearby hermitage, with treasure, gloves and a letter instructing that the foundling should be given the pair of gloves when he is ten years old, and that he should love no woman unless he should first try the gloves on her, since the gloves will fit only his mother. The child is named 'Degarre' by the hermit, and given into the hands of a rich merchant's family until he is ten, when he returns to the hermit until he is twenty. At this age the hermit gives him the treasure and the gloves, with which Degaré goes in search of his kin, refusing to take any armour or weapon except a sapling. He kills a dragon besieging an earl, and will accept the earl's offer of lands as a reward only if the gloves fit one of the women in the earl's retinue. They do not; the earl knights Degaré and arms him. Degaré leaves, and hears of a tournament where challengers must fight with a king for the hand of his daughter. Many challengers are maimed, but Degaré finally wins, after a violent encounter with the king, using lances. Degaré is married to the daughter. Before consummating their marriage, however, Degaré insists that his bride tries the gloves; when they fit, a recognition scene between mother and son and a confession scene between daughter and father are the prelude to Degaré setting out again in search of his father, this time armed with the broken-tipped sword. He arrives at a castle, inhabited only by women; although they are hospitable, they will not talk with him. Degaré carves the food before sleeping to the sound of the harp. In the morning the lady of the castle explains to him that she is under siege by a local knight, who has killed all the men in her retinue. She offers Degaré her lands and body if he can kill the knight; a violent fight ensues, in which Degaré kills the knight with his sword. The lady offers her lands and herself; Degaré says that he will seek further adventures, and return within a year. He enters a forest and is challenged by a knight who accuses him of trespass; Degaré, armed with a lance and a helmet encrusted with precious stones (given him by his fiancée), violently encounters his father (as yet unknown). They both break a lance before fighting with swords; the father recognizes the broken-tipped sword, at which point he asks his birth and name. Hearing it, the father puts the point back on the sword, and they are reconciled. They return to Degaré's mother and grandfather, who welcome the knight, whereupon Degaré's parents marry. Degaré returns to the castle of his lady, accompanied by his reunited family, where he and his lady marry.

This narrative is well chosen by Warton to exemplify his larger point that romances have a coherent structure, whereby 'through various obstacles and difficulties one point is kept in view, till the final and general catastrophe is brought about by a pleasing and unexpected surprise' (Warton 1774–81, I, 182). One might only take exception to the unexpectedness of the final surprise: the logic of encounters is so rigorous that the final fight must surely be with Degaré's father, since the narrative clearly moves back to its point of origin, preparing for the future by way of reconstructing the past. Each of Degaré's encounters contributes to this double movement, whereby debts incurred by two past generations are repaid in the hero's forward movement: he is knighted first, replacing his sapling with a sword and armour; from his mother he receives another sword, the broken-tipped sword of his father; and from his future wife he receives a helmet, encrusted with 'stones' (1018). This sequence, whereby the hero is literally armed, is also, quite obviously, a sequence whereby he is sexually armed (were it not for the date of the texts, one would have sworn that this was written by Freud):[11] if the initial sword and the gloves need no glossing as metaphors, neither (in my view) do the 'stones' given by his future wife, nor the broken-tipped sword made whole by his father. The sequence of gifts is subject to an obvious logic of sexual maturation: the two moments when Degaré is offered a wife are controlled by the more immediate necessity of transactions with parents; thus Degaré cannot marry the first bride offered him because he has not found his mother, just as he cannot marry his future wife until he has sought out his father. If, however, both encounters with potential wives are governed by the exigencies of parental demand, so too, by the same token, do the encounters with potential wives prepare the hero to face and meet parental demands, by supplying him with weapons.

Just as *Sir Orfeo* (also in the Auchinleck manuscript) recasts a classical myth, so *Sir Degaré* rewrites the catastrophic disruptions and miscegenation of the Oedipus myth as a constructive narrative of past disasters rescued by the new generation. This positive recasting cannot, however, disguise the violence of this story. Although it is true that the final moment has each of the three generations harmoniously in consort with the other two, this image of familial integration is premised on the near-infringement of incest- and parricide-taboo. Civilized order, in the world of this romance, is only achievable by entering into (rather than repressing) all that threatens that order. A father's incestuous and violent possessiveness of his daughter is the transgression that drives this narrative; in the logic of romance this pro- vokes the rape of his only daughter (on the anniversary of his wife's death). We can see this logic only in retrospect, since from that vantage-point the rape turns out to be a marriage in disguise, dislodged from its proper place by the father's improper possessiveness of his daughter. Incestuous desire provokes the counter-impulse of restorative activity. Restoration only begins in response to violent transgression.

More revealingly, the restorative impulse must itself operate by violent near-transgression. Degaré must nearly kill his grandfather, must nearly sleep with his mother, and must nearly kill his father before proper relations can be established between and within generations. This can be seen most clearly in the strange way in which the romance blurs the logic behind Degaré's search for his mother. On the face of it, the narrative logic is straightforward: before Degaré can marry, he must first find his mother. The initial statement of this logic, however, takes us just a little further than we had bargained for: the letter left with the hermit stipulates that Degaré must love no woman 'But this gloues willen on hire honde' (215–16). In the first encounter with a potential bride, the strict logic apparently holds: Degaré agrees to the earl's offer of territory only on condition that the gloves he bears fit the hands of one of the women in the earl's retinue (394– 402) (marriage is not mentioned). In the next glove episode, however (when the woman involved is his mother), the logic blurs again. About to consum- mate his marriage, Degaré remembers the hermit's words that he should love no woman unless the gloves fit. Deeply troubled by this thought, and asked what disturbs him, he replies thus:

> I chal neuer for no spousing,
> Therwhiles I liue, with wimmen dele,
> Widue, wif ne dammeisele,
> But she this gloues mai take and fonde
> And lightlich drawen up on hire honde.
>
> (654–8)

The strict necessities of the plot (that Degaré should find his mother first, and then seek a wife) give way to what such a plot might really mean (i.e. that seeking mother and wife amount provisionally to the same thing). Restoration, then, is not only provoked by transgression, but also, more revealingly, must itself deploy transgression. Order and chaos stand in obverse rather than oppositional relationship in this story, since movement towards order necessitates negotiation with, rather than simple repression of, all that threatens it.

This narrative clearly traces a *rite de passage*, but it is by no means exclusively about an individual.[12] The wholeness of the individual hero is impossible without the correlative wholeness of the kinship group to which he belongs; his own maturation is identical with the job of restoring the proper cohesion of the previous two generations. If this story contains Freudian insights about the necessity of filial transgression against parents, it does so in order to incorporate them within a larger structure, whereby filial violence is restorative for the parental generation. The further reason why *Degaré* is not about an 'individual' is because the work operates as a personification narrative.[13] The hero's name determines the trajectory of the story, since it sets up an expectation of identity restored. The name, it will be recalled, means 'thing, that not neuer, whar it is, / Or thing, that is negh forlorn also' (256–7). This name is clearly not arbitrary to self in the story, since the name is given to a foundling, in a story of several near-misses that traces the return to self-knowledge from being 'near-forlorn'. The hero has no choice but to trace that path, given his precisely defined name: not 'forlorn', but only nearly so.

If the name is a personification, then one might argue that a new name should be given at the end of the story, since Degaré is no longer lost. The anagnorisis of the closing moment, when father recognizes son, suggests why this is unnecessary. Once he has remarked on the fact that his opponent's sword has no tip, the father first asks where Degaré was born, to which Degaré replies:

> In litel Bretaigne, ich understond,
> Kingges doughter sone, withouten les;
> Ac I not, wo mi fader wes.
>
> (1054–6)

The hero's identity is recoded here with place and lineage, in the beautifully crisp formulation (that encapsulates almost the entire plot so far), 'kingges doughter sone'. The father goes on to ask the name:

> 'What is thi name?' than saide he.
> 'Certes, men clepeth me Degarre.'
> 'O, Degarre, sone mine,
> Certes, ich am fader thine.'
>
> (1057–60)

Until the very moment that the son is recognized by the father, the name Degaré (as a personification) retains its power to generate the story. Once the father recognizes the son, the story must come to an end, because the semantic force of the name is spent. This is equally to say that the name has become a proper name.[14] As a proper name, it has no power to generate narrative, precisely because the recovery of proper name, in the world of this story, implies a world where everything is exactly where it should be.

If, however, the recovery of proper name does entail the confirmation of 'propriety' in the world of the story more generally, then the proper name is itself coded, as 'nobly born'. It is no accident that Degaré should be the grandson of a king; in this story all the figures related or relatable by family must return to their 'proper' place in a pre-given scheme of things, before any single figure can regain identity. There are, indeed, no accidents in this story at all. Like all romances, the narrative gives very high profile to *aventures*, or apparently chance happenings. When the king (Degaré's grand-father) hears that he has a challenger, he welcomes the news as if he lived in a world where people made themselves by virtue of individual initiative:

> De par deus! he is welcome!
> Be he baroun, be he erl,
> Be he burgeis, be he cherl,
> No man wille I forsake:
> He, that winneth, al sschal take.
> (478–82)

The challenger, however, does not at all present himself on a randomly meritocratic basis. He turns out to be the king's own grandson, who acts according to the ineluctable demands of the identity he possesses by virtue of birth, just as a personification acts according to the demands of its meaning. *Aventures*, in this and other romances, are given such high profile precisely because they disguise the entirely providential nature of the romance world; in such a world accidents are programmed to reaffirm a genetically pre-given order of things.

The premise of the story (impossible in bourgeois fiction) is, then, that the world does indeed have a place ready for the hero, to which he will return – a terminus, or *gare*, at which the *égaré* figure is destined to arrive. The bestowal of the name 'Degaré' itself implies that retrieval of identity is not only possible, but also prepared. The world before or after narrative has everything where it should be, whereas narrative marks the space of transgressive movement from and to propriety, the space, in Warton's words, of 'extravagancies . . . above propriety'. In the terms of medieval rhetorical theory, romance narrative is the space of rhetoricity itself, since tropes are defined as that area of verbal extravagance in which words are licensed to wander from and transgress their 'proper', originary place and limits.[15] If it is the function of exegesis to return words to that proper, originary space, then romance itself does the work of exegesis, since personification (the trope governing romance) is the trope that sets the most definite limits on its own licence to wander.

III

So the establishment of the 'proper' name is in all senses the end of this narrative. Propriety of name itself, however, simply recovers a deeper coding to name that existed prior to the narrative. For now the name means 'noble', 'having a natural place in the world by virtue of birth'. 'Degaré', in its meaning of 'lost', is indeed a thematic name that drives narrative in the manner of personification, but the *égaré* figure can be found because he encodes a more powerful meaning. As in the case of narrative driven by personification, narratives must come to an end both when the full senses of the word are exhausted, and when the full pattern of ideas to which a word belongs has been traversed.

If 'proper' name in this romance encodes a single meaning (that of 'noble'), is the same true of other romances? In this section I want briefly to consider another romance narrative where naming is especially important, but where the name is, on the face of it, wholly without thematic significance, Malory's 'Tale of Sir Gareth of Orkney'. I want to argue that here, too, naming and violence stand in obverse relationship (no naming produces maximal violence, and vice versa), and that Gareth's name is effectively coded in such a way as to determine the shape of the story. He takes possession of his proper name 'Gareth' only by manifesting its collective force. Gareth can only become 'himself' by declaring that he is a member of his noble family.

Malory's 'Tale of Sir Gareth' is exceptional in Malory's known *oeuvre*, not only because we have no known source for it, but also because it is the single narrative where people do end up where they 'should' be.[16] The fact that it is placed between 'The Tale of Sir Lancelot du Lake' and 'The Tale of Sir Tristrem' only sets its integrated quality into sharper relief, since 'Lancelot' and 'Tristrem' are both unfinishable romances, whose central relationship is adulterous. The integrated story of Gareth begins with, and is generated by, Gareth's refusal to declare his name.

'"But what is thy name, I wolde wete?"', asks Arthur when Gareth enters supported by two helpers; '"Sir I can nat tell you"', replies Gareth.[17]

At this point a scoffing Kay nicknames Gareth 'Beawmaynes', ironically pointing to the fact that Gareth must be a 'vylayne borne', since he has asked for nothing more than food from Arthur. Apart from his bad French, Kay seems not to have noticed that Gareth does have 'the largyste and the fayreste handis' (I, 293.31). This initial moment of naming both generates the story by depriving us of Gareth's name, and encodes what his name might mean, since powerful hands, throughout Malory's works, are a sign of noble birth and fighting power.[18] In the first physical encounter of the story Kay's irony is undone, since Gareth proves that he does indeed have 'fair' hands. Kay follows Beawmaynes – Malory's narratorial naming colludes scrupulously with Gareth's desire for anonymity (Mahoney 1980) – as he goes out on a quest to help the Lady who is besieged by the Knight of the Red Lands. ' "Beawmaynes! What, sir, know ye nat me?" ', Kay accosts Beawmaynes; ' "Yee, I know you well for an unjantyll knyght of the courte, and therefore beware of me!" ' (I, 298.10–15). Kay's known identity seems to render him vulnerable, as the anonymous knight, in possession of the name of his enemy, wins easily.[19] Beawmaynes is, however, not strictly anonymous so much as coded: he calls his enemy 'unjantyll', and the nickname that Kay gives him ironically proves to be literally accurate, as a sure sign of Gareth's superior birth. His mother makes the point later in the story, to Arthur: 'yet Sir Kaye . . . named hym more ryghteously than he wende, for I dare sey he is as fayre an handid man and wel disposed . . . as ony lyvynge' (I, 340.19–21). Gareth is barely able to disguise his nobility, since even ironic names mockingly attributed to him turn out to manifest his innate quality.

The entire story of 'Sir Gareth' is marked by moments of hiding or disclosing the name (Benson 1976, 101–2). Gareth reveals his name only to those whom he cannot defeat (i.e. Lancelot) or to those whom he has already defeated. Refusal to disclose the name leads invariably to violence, a violence that issues in Gareth's victory and the disclosure of his name and lineage. Disclosure of name produces, correlatively, reconciliation and the winding down of narrative. This is true of Gareth's encounter with Sir Persaunte of Inde (I, 317.6–11) and with Sir Gryngamour (I, 329–31). At this point the main quest seems to have been achieved, and Gareth's mother enters the court (which has been wondering about the identity of Beawmaynes), to disclose the name as if by accident: ' "Where have ye done my yonge son, sir Gareth?" ' (I, 339.6). Everyone now knows Gareth's name, and the story would seem to have nowhere further to go. Gareth has matched himself only against knights external to the Round Table, however; in order to generate violence against knights of the Round Table (in the tournament called by Arthur), he insists on further repression of his name: 'I woll nat be knowyn of neythir more ne lesse, nothir at the begynnynge nother at the endyng' (I, 345.11–13). As long as anonymity is preserved, significant violence remains possible, and the narrative remains unclosed.

In the tournament itself, Gareth changes colour by virtue of the ring given him by Lyonesse, such 'that there myght neyther kynge nother knyght have no redy cognyssauns of hym' (I, 348.8–10). Forgetting his magic ring after his final victory (to the relief of his dwarf, who has no patience with disguise), Gareth is discovered; his name is publicized as widely as possible, with the herald now shouting '"This is sir Gareth of Orkenay in the yealow armys!"' (I, 351.16), thus bringing the tournament to an end (from this moment on he is called 'Gareth' by Malory). With this resolution of publicity, we expect the story to end, with nowhere else to go. As in *Sir Degaré*, however, the narrative seeks one further step, since it cannot end before Gareth violently and anonymously encounters his own kin in individual combat, in the person of Gawain. The carefully graded pattern of violence begins with common thieves, moves to knights exterior to the Round Table, almost culminates with knights of the Round Table, but can only end as Gareth moves as close to himself as possible, in a fight with his own brother. Once this has happened, the story can come to an end, with Gareth's marriage to Lyonesse, and the establishment of their household (made up of all the knights he has defeated). The story that began with an orchestrated display of feebleness by the younger generation (Gareth enters apparently unable to walk unaided) ends with the parental generation sinking: Arthur, on recognizing Gareth, 'wepte as he had bene a chylde', while Gareth's mother 'sodeynly felle downe in a swone' (I, 358.23–4).

This account of 'The Tale of Sir Gareth' puts us in a position to understand the ideological premises of this narrative. Not only does anonymity generate the significant violence of the narrative, but Gareth cannot be named initially, since that would have exhausted the narrative of any energy before it had begun. This can only be the case if Gareth's name already possesses its noble coding. Each fight is consistently resolved by manifesting Gareth's superior birth, whereby levels of physical power and birth are identified: '"Thow lyest!"', Gareth says to one of his adversaries, '"I am a jantyllman borne, and of more hyghe lynage than thou, and that I woll preve on thy body"' (I, 304.10–12). Almost whenever Gareth is named, his kin is identified at the same time – his proper name is inseparable from the collectivity to which he belongs, a collectivity that is defined by its royal blood: '"Wete you well, he is a kynges son and a quenys, and his fadir hyght kynge Lot of Orkeney, and his modir is sistir to kyng Arthure, and he is brother to sir Gawayne, and his name is sir Gareth of Orkenay"' (I, 329.24–8).[20] If power and birth are coterminous, then this narrative does not trace any moral trajectory, and cannot be described, despite appearances, as a story of becoming. Instead, Gareth manifests what he already is.

For this reason (again despite appearances) there are no chances, or *aventures*, in this story, since Gareth's progress is genetically determined. This point is made from within the story when Gareth defeats the Black Knight. The scoffing Lyonet accompanying him dismisses the victory as 'myssehappe'; Gareth replies by courteously using Lyonet's word 'hap' in such a way as to point to its irrelevance: '"for ever ye sey that they woll sle me othir bete me, but howsomever hit happenyth I ascape and they lye on the ground"' (I, 304.35–6). The story is designed to demonstrate and to reiterate (by way of personification) what it knows from the beginning. The only thing that changes are the power relations around Gareth, relations that are established by the noble figure simply manifesting his (disguised) innate superiority by strategic violence.[21] Precisely because the name so thoroughly encodes innate quality, it must be disguised for the narrative to 'happen' at all.

IV

In both *Sir Degaré* and 'The Tale of Sir Gareth of Orkney', then, naming and narrative are intimately linked, because the name so thoroughly encodes the thematic idea of nobility. The obvious meaning of Degaré's name ('lost') clearly generates a narrative of being found, but a deeper coding authorizes that finding, so that the name comes to mean 'nobly born'. Gareth's name is, on the face of it, a simple proper name; coded as it is, however, the name has the power to stop narrative, since it implies prior possession of all the qualities narrative pretends to offer protagonists. It might therefore be argued that these narratives are merely shadow-boxing, pretending to trace developmental narratives when in fact they are (like most personification narratives) stories of showing, or manifesting what is wholly possessed by the protagonist before the narrative begins. Of course there is a good measure of truth in such an argument: as we have seen, romances give such high priority to chance *aventure* and anonymity precisely because such ploys disguise (in order ultimately to proclaim) the real and providential nature of the romance world, in which displaced figures will end up where they properly belong. Insofar as that is the case, romances of this kind are deeply conservative in ideology, underwritten as they are by a desire for return to a pre-given, naturally determined world. But romance narrative is not *wholly* redundant, merely reiterating what is known before the story begins. Just as personification can be exploratory by extending the 'proper' meaning of abstract concepts (Mann 1992), so too does romance have a reformative impulse towards the conservative order. It does so not only by revealing all that threatens it, but (more trenchantly) by revealing that the stability of the given order demands constant negotiation with its obverse. Challenges are defined as internal to the system itself, requiring flexible and transactional response, rather than straightforward repression.

Sir Degaré, simpler as it is, resolves back into a pre-given order, with each generation properly placed as the hero regains his name. Malory's ending is more complex, in a characteristically Malorian way. Gareth's last fight is with his brother, who, by the logic of the story as I have defined it, should be identical to Gareth (the level of either's birth being indistinguishable): this fight (along with the fight against Lancelot) is the only moment in this story for real ethical distinction, since it cannot be resolved by the genetic logic that resolves all the other fights. Significantly, it is the only fight that is not resolved: neither brother wins, and, as the story draws to its close, we are told that Gareth preferred Lancelot, and kept his distance from Gawain, 'for he [Gawain] was evir vengeable, and where he hated he wolde be avenged with murther: and that hated sir Gareth' (I,360.34–6). This little sequence has enormous implications for the collapse of the Round Table (produced as much by Gawain's vendetta with Lancelot for having accidentally killed Gareth as by Lancelot's adultery with Guinevere). So even within the one apparently perfect romance in Malory's works, there extrudes a fraternal rivalry that is necessitated by, yet unable to be accommodated within, the logic of romance.

Although there is a small but critical extrusion in Malory's romance, the narrative tends to move, like *Sir Degaré*, to a point of apparent propriety (of both name and world), in which it has no further to go. Let me end this essay with the obverse of the case I have made, drawn from the unfinishable, disintegrating narrative of Tristan and Isolde, as exemplified in the Anglo-Norman *Folie Tristan d'Oxford*. However much the name 'Tristan' is of Celtic origin (Loth 1912, 16–23), it accrues the meaning of French *triste* ('sad') in the Tristan narratives (Blakeslee 1989, 15). Precisely because the name of the protagonist can be nothing but 'sad' in his adulterous relationship with the king's wife, he can never be enfolded back into the unselfconsciousness of propriety, just as the society in which he lives cannot cohere in propriety. Instead he remains forever in the improper space of narrative, even as narrative disintegrates. Written close to the beginning of vernacular romance writing in the late twelfth century, this work exposes the shadow of unfinishable disintegration that haunts all romance writing, since it sets the mechanisms of romance into reverse.

Tristan arrives at the court of King Mark, having decided to disguise himself as a fool in order to gain entry to the court. In the presence of the court, he openly declares his love to Isolde by recounting the story of his slaying the dragon and being cured by her. The court is amused by his story, fooled as the courtiers are by his physical disfigurement, and by his calling himself 'Trantris' (Tristan can never move far from his name). The poignancy of the court scene is that Tristan now hides himself by telling the truth, which is the final ruse of deception. The poignancy is only sharpened when, in Isolde's chamber, the truth (of the many stories Tristan tells to persuade her of his identity) seems to have no purchase, since Isolde is unpersuaded by it. Whereas the other romances we have considered recuperate history and so identity, in this work history slides away from Tristan. Many of the stories Tristan tells in formal paraphrase turn on recognition of evidential signs (e.g. traces in the snow; blood on beds; shavings in water; the king's shadow), but in the narrative of the *Folie* itself, Tristan has himself become the dubious sign. The only proofs he can adduce to authenticate himself are stories from the past (stories that themselves turn, as I say, on the recognition of signs); now, however, authenticating power has drained from these stories, and Tristan seems suspended in time, unable to propel himself forward without authentication from the past. The recapitulative impulse so central to romance narratives is here rehearsed to no effect. Tristan and Isolde are condemned to retell their own story, but as they do so its evidential power wanes, and its sequence fragments. Tristan tells many episodes of their former life, each within a very short sequence, but in a significantly different narrative order from their occurrence in Thomas's narrative (to which the *Folie d'Oxford* clearly refers).[22] While in court, Tristan had maintained narrative sequence, but in the chamber the stories he tells are chronologically scrambled. All human resources of recognition and self-authentication seem to be exhausted; only the animal instinct of the dog Husdent does not hesitate to recognize Tristan, but not even this persuades Isolde, just as she remains unpersuaded by the ring Tristan produces. The only thing that persuades Isolde is what Tristan has been hiding, from us and from the queen, all the while. Although we had been told early on that Tristan was capable of changing his voice (212), the author makes no further reference to that, and we have believed all the protestations of authenticity produced by Tristan, even if Isolde cannot. Tristan even goes so far as to convict Isolde of deception: '"Or vus ai jo de feinte ateinte"' (855).[23] Suddenly, however, as Isolde weeps and Tristan takes pity on her, we realize that Tristan's display of 'truth' has itself been merely another feint:

> Puis li ad dit: 'Dame raïne,
> Belë estes e enterine.
> Des or ne m'en voil mes cuvrir,
> Cunuistre me frai e oïr.'
> Sa voiz muat, parlat a dreit.
> Isolt sempres s'en aparceit.
> (971–6)

(Then he said: 'My lady queen, now you are beautiful and true. Now I will no longer hide, but make myself heard and known.' He altered his tone and spoke in his true voice. Ysolt realized at once.)[24]

When Tristan had first decided to disguise himself the author interjects to commend discretion, practised by Tristan such that no one, not 'parent, procein, per ne ami' (45), could perceive that it was him. The moment he reveals himself to Isolde (and to us), we realize that his professions of innermost identity to his *amie* have themselves been forms of disguise.

Tristan begins the little story sad ('Dolent, murnes, tristes, pensifs', 2); he ends happy ('Tristran en est joius e lez', 997), having regained his 'propre furme' (987). The action of the story, however, points only back to its beginning, towards death, madness and *tristesse*.[25] For the reunion is premised on the recapitulation of true narrative as a lie, to the point that narrative fragments, becomes disordered and opaque, and loses its power to affirm 'proper' identity. Tristan's name generates the narrative; the only difference with the other two works considered in this essay is that what his name encodes disallows the narrative from ever ending, as Tristan himself becomes an increasingly indecipherable and opaque sign, locked into ineluctable rhetoricity. Indeed, the impossibility of 'Tristan' ever becoming a proper name threatens to destroy the possibility of narrative altogether. This astonishingly penetrating and prescient text effectively predicts that what Tristan says as a self-promoting understatement ('"Hom ki ben aime tart ublie"', 702)[26] will finally be proved true.

Notes

1 I think in particular of the sixteenth-century antiquarians John Leland and John Bale, for which see Simpson 1997.

2 G. Ellis, Preface to G. L. Way, *Fabliaux or Tales* (1796–1800), I, p. ii, cited from Johnston 1964, 26. See also Warton 1774–81, I, 209, who explicitly distinguishes his interest in 'fables of chivalry' as sources for social history from the unenlightened researches of the 'antiquaries of former times'.

3 Warton 1774–81 refers to his sources for *Sir Degaré* (I, 180, note f). The oldest version of the work is preserved in the so-called Auchinleck manuscript, National Library of Scotland, Advocates' 19.2.1, dated *c*.1330. The latest of the nine texts preserved in varying states of completeness is that in the mid-seventeenth-century Percy Folio (British Library, Add. 27879). For full information about the surviving texts, see Jacobs 1995, who comments that *Sir Degaré* has 'possibly the longest recorded textual tradition of any Middle English text' (1). For the textual environment of *Sir Degaré* in surviving manuscripts, see

Guddat-Figge 1976. Johnston 1964, 229 offers information about eighteenth-century study of *Degaré*.

4   The subtlest account of the style of romances is Spearing 1987, 24–55. Edwards 1991 exposes the irreducibly variant quality of the texts of many Middle English romances. The instability of the texts need not lead to the strong scepticism Edwards expresses about the possibility of literary interpretation of these works (e.g. 100, 102, 104). Romances create meaning much more through narrative structure than verbal particularity (the same structure survives wide verbal difference); the most rigorous book based on this perception is Wittig 1978.

5   For a concise account of the history of the word *égaré*, see Guilbert et al. 1972. Jacobs 1970 demonstrates both that the hero's name has an abstract sense, and that the name is drawn from an Old French word *desgarer*, even though no instance is recorded.

6   The text of *Sir Degaré* is drawn from the edition of G. Schleich, *Sire Degarre* (Heidelberg: Winter, 1929), repr. and corrected in Jacobs 1995, 12–37.

7   The most sophisticated account of Langland's use of prosopopeia in narrative is Griffiths 1985. The essence of her position (which I argue is also applicable to romance) is that '. . . because [a] noun is now potentially both common and proper, there is a tension between its discursive and story functions, a tension which is exploited as the personification enters the story and accumulates an imaginative being which collapses as it reverts to mere term' (10).

8   The names are drawn from the following romances respectively: *Sir Degaré*, *Emaré*, Chaucer's *Man of Law's Tale* (also in Gower's *Confessio Amantis*, II.587–1612), *Roman de la Rose*, *Amis and Amiloun*, Anglo-Norman *Horn*, Béroul's and Thomas's *Tristan*. The names 'Egaré' and 'Gudmod' are the names adopted by the protagonists of *Emaré* and Anglo-Norman *Horn* respectively, while they are incognito; in Gower's 'Tale of Constance' the heroine goes under the name 'Couste'. It is revealing for the argument of this essay that incognito names turn out to be abstract concepts: 'couste' is presumably from Old English 'cyst'; Gower explicitly mentions its 'Saxoun' derivation, and states that it has an abstract meaning, which Gower thinks is the same as the Latin-derived 'Constance' (II.1405–6).

9   It is no accident that it should be liberals who stress the entirely arbitrary relation of name to self so forcefully: 'a proper name is but an unmeaning mark which we connect in our minds with the idea of the object' (John Stuart Mill, cited in Mustanoja 1970, 51–2).

10 *Le Conte du Graal (Perceval)*, ed. Félix Lecoy, 2 vols, CFMA (Paris: Champion, 1973–5). For an account of naming in the romances of Chrétien more generally, see Schwake 1970.

11 A Freudian reading of *Sir Degaré* was first proposed by Du Bois 1937. For a conspectus of criticism on *Degaré* up to 1968, see Kozicki 1968.

12 The idea that romance serves the end of self-realization alone is most forcefully expressed by Auerbach 1953: with reference to Calogrenant's mission in Chrétien's *Yvain*, Auerbach argues that the 'feudal ethos' 'no longer has any

purpose but that of self-realization' (134). For a full account of romances as narratives of *rite de passage* within the structure of family units, see Brewer 1980.

13 I resist using the term 'personification allegory', since the whole point of personification is to delimit the obliquities of allegory. If allegory is 'to say one thing and mean another', then personification veers in the opposite direction, of exaggerated explicitness.

14 Jacobs 1995, 1, n. 1 points out examples of the name as a proper name, without pointing to its abstract sense (though see Jacobs 1970).

15 For accounts of classical and medieval rhetorical theory, and its relevance to narrative, see Bloch 1983, 40–54, 115–19, 159–60, and Zeeman 1996.

16 For a summary of the two story-types on which 'Gareth' draws (the Fair Unknown and the younger brother competing with his older brother), see Nolan 1996, 156–7, 163–4.

17 The text of 'The Tale of Sir Gareth' is cited from *The Works of Sir Thomas Malory*, ed. Eugène Vinaver, rev. P. J. C. Field, 3 vols (Oxford: Oxford University Press, 1990), I, 294.25–7. Further reference to volume, page and, if relevant, line numbers of this edition will be given in the body of the text. For a penetrating account of the function of names in Malory more generally, see Lynch 1990.

18 See, for example, I, 241.7 ('lyveth nat a bettir knight nor a noblere of his hondis'), and II, 692.28 ('a noble knight of his hondis').

19 For the same phenomenon in the works of Chrétien de Troyes, see Pellegrini 1967.

20 For other examples, see I, 299 and I, 317.

21 For the social context of Malory's stress on innate nobility, see Riddy 1987, 69–83.

22 There can be no doubt that the *Folie d'Oxford* draws its matter from the *Tristan* of Thomas (*c.*1173), for which see Hoepffner 1938, 7–8. The *Folie de Berne*, which instead is dependent on Béroul, is criticized by Hoepffner for being disordered in its renarration of events, while he praises the *Folie d'Oxford* for the care with which it follows Thomas, despite the occasional slip (2). But the *Folie d'Oxford* does not follow Thomas scrupulously. The matter is complicated by the fact that this section of Thomas's text has been lost, and its narrative sequence can be reconstructed only from other texts, principally the Old Norse *Tristrams Saga*. For Bédier's reconstruction, see *Le Roman de Tristan par Thomas, poème du XIIe siècle*, ed. Joseph Bédier, SATF, 2 vols (Paris: Firmin Didot, 1902–5), I. In the *Folie d'Oxford*, the sequence of events narrated from his own past by Tristan (after the king has left) begins with his encounter with Brengain in the hall at line 612, and continues in Isolde's chamber (from line 679). These correspond to the events narrated between Bédier's chapters 10–30. The following events (using Bédier's chapter headings) as narrated by Tristan in the *Folie d'Oxford* are discrepant with the order of Bédier's reconstruction (line numbers of the *Folie* in parentheses): 'Meriadoc' (715–26) is narrated before 'La Harpe et la Rote' (763–76), whereas in Thomas it comes

after 'La Harpe et la Rote'; the first section of 'Le Fer Rouge' (727–56) is narrated before 'Le Rendez-vous Epié' (777–816), whereas in Thomas it comes after 'Le Rendez-vous Epié'; 'Le Petit Crû' (757–62) interrupts 'Le Fer Rouge' (727–56, 817–35), whereas in Thomas it comes after 'Le Fer Rouge'.

23   *Folie Tristan d'Oxford*, ed. Ernest Hoepffner (Paris: Belles Lettres, 1943).

24   The translation of the *Folie Tristan* is drawn from *The Birth of Romance: An Anthology*, trans. Judith Weiss, Everyman (London: Dent, 1992), 121–40 (p. 139).

25   I therefore disagree with the conclusion of the otherwise persuasive discussion of Bruckner 1993, that the 'optimism of the *Folie Tristan d'Oxford* results from the transfer of closure from the domain of God into the realm of human experience: truth can put off its disguise, when it resumes its own voice to tell its own human story' (36).

26   'The man who loves well is slow to forget'; or, putting the emphasis on another sense: 'The man who loves well finally forgets'.

CHAPTER SIX

Loving Beasts: The Romance of
William of Palerne

ARLYN DIAMOND

The Middle English romance *William of Palerne* exists in a unique manuscript, King's College Cambridge 13.[1] We know that it was read in the
sixteenth century, when it was praised as a work to be read on holy days, to
drive away idle thoughts – perhaps a strange judgement for a poem about
rebellious lovers, wicked stepmothers and an extraordinarily caring werewolf.[2] We also know that it was read in the eighteenth century, when, as Sir
Frederick Madden tells us, it was pressed into service in the Chatterton
controversy.[3] Jacob Bryant, a fellow of King's, pulled it out of obscurity
because he thought its dialect would demonstrate the authenticity of the
Rowley ballads. When more knowledgeable partisans suspected it would
not, *William* was returned to the shelves.[4] And, unless it is briefly touched
upon in general surveys of alliterative poetry, or of the Middle English
romance, there it has tended to rest.[5] Such neglect is to be regretted, since
the romance, rightly read, offers a story with intrinsic charm, one which explores the connection between individual happiness and social order through
sensitive evocations of human affection and a rich descriptive vocabulary.

   It is hard to say whether the lack of critical attention reflects its anomalous nature or what have been judged to be its aesthetic failures. In fact, in
the literary history of the popular romance, critical evaluation and generic
expectations seem too frequently intertwined, and works that neither satisfy
the modern preference for irony and originality, as do the *Knight's Tale* or *Sir
Gawain and the Green Knight*, nor fit the dominant paradigms of Middle English romance – that it is indifferent or hostile to love, didactic, and written
for an unsophisticated audience – tend to be ignored, or unhelpfully described.[6] As a consequence, we have too narrow a sense of the form, and
therefore too narrow a sense of the range of ideas and emotions it could
address. Although Charles Dunn calls it 'a worthy forerunner of *Sir Gawain*

and the Green Knight' (Severs 1967, 37), others have not been so positive, and the bewildering divergence of critical responses intimates that it is time to revisit *William*. When David Lawton wonders, 'What can have provoked the poet to choose a rare metre of which, to judge from his performance, he lacked good models?', he addresses what many have thought to be the work's most interesting characteristic, its choice of verse form (Lawton 1982, 3). It would be nice to be able to answer this question, even without sharing Lawton's scorn for the poet, since *William* is one of the earliest, if not the earliest, works of the so-called alliterative revival (Lawton 1982, 2–3 and Pearsall 1981, 1–24).[7] It can be dated because the poet tells us:

> Thus passed is the first pas of this pris tale.
> And ye that loven and lyken to listen ani more,
> alle with on hol hert to the heigh King of hevene
> preieth a pater noster prively this time
> for the hend Erl of Herford, Sir Humfray de Bowne,
> the king Edwardes newe at Glouseter that ligges.
> For he of Frensche this fayre tale ferst dede translate
> in ese of Englysch men in Englysch speche.
> And God graunt hem his blis that godly so prayen!
>
> (161–9)

The Earl of Hereford, grandson of Edward I, nephew of Edward II, died in 1361. Although he probably spent most of his time on his estate in Essex, Pleshey, he also owned estates in Gloucestershire, the dialect region of the poem (Turville-Petre 1974, 250–52).[8] This appears to be a remarkably clear moment in literary history, a closely locatable instance of the dissemination of courtly French poetry into Middle English for the benefit of a new audience, 'hem that knowe no Frensche, ne neuer vnderston' (5533). The English version is replicating an earlier stage in the history of romance as a genre, for the French original, *Guillaume de Palerne*, was apparently translated from Latin into French for another patron, Countess Yolande of Hainaut (*c.*1131–*c.*1212), wife of the Count of Saint-Pol and aunt of Baldwin VI, who was briefly Emperor of Constantinople (Dunn 1960, 25–38).

> Cil qui tos jors fu et sans fin
> Sera et pardoune briement
> Il gart la contesse Yolent
> La boine dame, la loial,
> Et il destort son cors de mal.
> Cest livre fist diter et faire
> Et de latin en roumans traire.
>
> (9654–60)[9]

(May he who ever was and will be without end, and who is quick to pardon, protect the Countess Yolande, the good, true lady, and guard her person from evil. She caused this book to be composed and made, and to be translated from Latin into French.)

Without more textual evidence than we now have it seems unlikely that we can address satisfactorily the poet's choice of metre, but I think it is possible to speculate with profit on the potentially broad appeal of the story from the perspective of Duke Humphrey, if not of modern critics. An illustrative (and critically illustrious) sample of comments reveals that to redeem *William*'s literary reputation is no easy task. W. R. J. Barron calls it 'a faithful if somewhat plodding redaction' of its French original (Barron 1987, 197); Lee Ramsey finds it 'dull and conventional' (Ramsey 1983, 123); Dorothy Everett, even less generous, finds the story 'fantastic even for a romance', and the author a man 'not even skilled in his chosen style' (Everett 1955, 53–4); Derek Pearsall says, somewhat grudgingly, that 'the English poem is by no means squalid, but it aligns itself with the popular metrical romances in its uncultured reflection of courtly life' (Pearsall 1982, 47). The vocabulary of critical condescension here both contradicts itself – conventional and fantastic – and yet addresses significant obstacles to sympathetic readings of popular romances in general and this one in particular, with its long, complex plot, its extended passages of moral reflection, and its use of repetition as a structural principle.

As Derek Brewer points out in 'Escape From the Mimetic Fallacy', 'the problem of romance . . . [is that] we still find it hard to account for the acknowledged draw of self-evidently implausible, not to say improbable, sequences of events, where characters are stereotypes and where we often know as it were innately, or at least from pre-literary experience, what the outcome of the narrative will be' (Brewer 1988, 4). Where Brewer finds a solution to this dilemma in critical analyses of myth, dream and folktale, themselves elements self-consciously adapted by the French poet, Susan Wittig suggests that we can best approach such narratives by paying attention to the formulaic language and narrative patterning characteristic of medieval romance,

the semiology of social gestures, the language of social ritual: leave-takings, greetings, meals and banquets, marriages and knightings and tournaments. Each one of the highly ritualized events to which the formulas themselves refer is also a kind of formulaic language, a complex system of significations which is as thoroughly understood and articulated in its own culture as that culture's natural language and which is indeed a language even though it may not be a verbal one . . . The language of these narratives functions not only as a medium of narrative, but as a powerful social force which supports, reinforces, and perpetuates the social beliefs held by the culture, perhaps long past their normal time of decline.

(Wittig 1978, 45)

Following Wittig's suggestion, I propose to argue for *William*'s worth not by denying what critics have found so objectionable, but by reading it with and through its fantasies and conventions, finding social and psychological meaning in the formulas and motifs which constitute its symbolic discourse. Reading it in this way allows us to see how the poet creates and resolves the tensions between honour as merit and honour as birth, between court and countryside, between marriage as a social duty and marriage as personal gratification. What we can learn about *William*'s patron might then help us to see how these tensions are culturally and historically locatable. Here used without irony (which does not mean without intelligence), these conventions join the new, so-called popular audience to its patrician benefactor, for while they affirm the traditional values of hierarchy and inherited status they also naturalize these values as the source of a social harmony which enriches everyone in the narrative, from emperor to peasant. Even the deployment of apparently esoteric conventions of aristocratic young love enables the poem to speak simultaneously to an ideology of ancestral merit and a less exclusive vision of individual fulfilment.

To begin, however, I would like to borrow W. R. J. Barron's summary of the romance's complicated plot, with its multiple episodes of betrayal and rescue:

William, Prince of Apulia, is stolen in infancy by a werewolf who, to protect him from the murderous designs of his uncle, swims across the straits of Messina with the child and conceals him in a wood near Rome where he is brought up by a cowherd. As a youth, William is seen by the Emperor of Rome during a hunt and appointed page to his daughter Melior. Feeling herself attracted to William, the princess confides in her cousin Alisaundrine, who brings them together in a secret betrothal. When Rome is threatened by an invasion, the emperor knights William who is largely responsible for repulsing the enemy. Then, as Melior is about to be married to the son of the Emperor of Greece, Alisaundrine helps the lovers to escape, disguised in two white bear skins. With the aid of the werewolf they cross to Sicily where William's father is now dead and his mother besieged in Palermo by the King of Spain. The lovers enter the city disguised as hart and hind, William captures the king in battle and forces his queen to disenchant the werewolf, her stepson Alphonse, whom she had hoped to replace in the succession with her own son Braundinis. William's true parentage is revealed, he is married to Melior, his sister to Alphonse, and Alisaundrine to Braundinis. William then becomes the Emperor and Alphonse King of Spain.

(Barron 1982, 75–6)

The almost 6,000 lines of the English follow closely but not slavishly the nearly 10,000 lines of the French, given the difference between the long alliterative line and the octosyllabic couplet (Blessing 1960, 13–69). Although we tend to think of the translation from French to English romance as a process of simplification and compression, even a kind of dumbing-down for the groundlings, it is obvious from the way the poet adds as well as subtracts details, expands descriptive elements and moves sections that this view of the popular romance is in itself an oversimplification of a complex process of rewriting for a wider audience. The familiar narrative patterns of exile and return, the conventional love monologues and battle descriptions and courtly feasts, those elements which Wittig calls 'the language of social ritual', associated with the aristocratic origins and themes of the original, are retained. The elaborate rhetoric characteristic of the French courtly style is eliminated, in favour of an enhanced stylistic and thematic accessibility. The astonished reactions of ordinary people are woven into the narrative, with a kind of light-hearted realism which emphasizes what a wonderful story this is. A Greek servant, terrified by the escaping bears, describes them to his fellows, who mock his fear (1764–84). The werewolf roars at a peasant returning from market, and brings William and Melior the bread and beef he drops in his fright. Then, realizing their meal is inadequate, the werewolf goes back and bellows at a clerk who is carrying fine wine. The flask he drops completes their meal (1884–900). Quarry-workers think their fortunes are made when they spy the sleeping bears, and take heroic oaths to stand their ground (2241–69). Disguised as deer, the lovers stow away aboard a ship for Sicily, and a boy who tries to stop their escape is amazed to see the hart pick up the hind, carrying her off in his arms (2768–84). The witnesses, like the cowherd and his wife who adopt William, are an integral part of the poem's imagined social world. As the English poet adds or expands playful depictions of everyday life, familiar sentiments and scenes of affection between friends, lovers and family, patron and audience, nobles and commoners are linked in a celebration of happiness and right rule rooted in kindness and love.

None the less, while broadening its community of readers, the romance preserves some of the specifically class-based concerns of the French poem which first captured Duke Humphrey's interest. Just as William and Melior, in their courtly dress, are disguised by the skins of bears, so this celebration, with some success, disguises a representation of the struggle between nobility (as a social practice based on inherited rank and power) and chivalry (as a social ideology based on virtue and personal morality). This conflict was already old when Chaucer incorporated it in the *Wife of Bath's Tale* about a knight who is forced to marry an old hag. 'Allas', he says, 'that any of my nacioun / Sholde ever so foule disparaged be'! (1068–9). To be disparaged in the Middle Ages meant literally to be married unequally, to be shamed irrevocably through union with a social inferior. The fact that the knight is a rapist does not in his own eyes constitute a lack of nobility, which for him depends on his 'nacioun' or lineage. Her response to his assertion of superior status is a long lecture, drawing on authorities as diverse as Dante, Seneca, Juvenal and the Bible. 'Gentilesse' based on ancestral wealth or prestige is 'nat worth an hen', and 'men may wel often fynde / A lordes sone do shame and vileyneye' (1150–51). Only the 'gentilesse' of virtuous living to which all men can aspire, based on the example of Christ, is worthy of the name. None the less, the problematic happy ending has her transforming herself into a lady (at least in appearance), thus finessing away the gap between a theoretically democratic Christianity and the medieval class system. In *William*, too, the happy ending depends on reconciling allegiances to these two inextricably intertwined and competing systems, figured here as arranged marriage, the realm of governance and inheritance, versus courtly love, the realm of personal character and feeling. As Maurice Keen has amply demonstrated, all the 'chivalrous erudition' devoted to the exploration of the 'true' meaning of nobility, whether it was to be determined by blood, or wealth, or status, or military vocation, or Christian virtue, or some combination of these, testifies to the difficulty medieval thinkers perceived in adjudicating the rival claims of inherited rank and individual merit (Keen 1984, 2–3, and passim). History tells us that medieval knights could be, and often were, brutal, greedy and treacherous. Romances like *William*, on the other hand, try to convince us that, despite appearances, merit inevitably coincides with noble blood, even though noble blood does not guarantee that merit.

Ambition, inheritance, dynastic instability and aristocratic warfare, the normal practices by which a hereditary aristocracy maintained, enlarged (and lost) its power, constitute the narrative's motive power. A few scenes refer to a social context which the poet hardly need explicate – the councils where marriages are decided, Melior's father's rage at her disobedience, the relentless search for the runaway lovers, wars of ambition, treaty negotiations. Duke Humphrey knew intimately how brutal and unstable the life of his class could be. That several of his siblings died young, and that his mother died when he was only eight or ten years old (he was probably born between 1306 and 1308), could be accepted as part of the ordinary tragedies of medieval family life, and it is dangerous to speculate too deeply on his personal investment in the poem's sentimental representation of loving kin. As Kate Mertes points out, 'for the historian of the family the determination of affective bonds between individuals is fraught with difficulty. The little material that is amenable to such an analysis is generally ambiguous and complicated' (Mertes 1988, 168). Entries in his mother's household accounts suggest, however, that birth and death were not matters of indifference to medieval parents. In September 1304 the Countess Elizabeth paid for two monks to bring 'the girdle of the Blessed Mary' from Westminster to Knaresborough and back again, a considerable distance to travel, apparently to aid in the successful delivery of a child. On 11 October she paid the king's minstrel and fifteen of his companions to celebrate her purification after the birth of a son. Then, on 15 October the body of the dead infant was carried in solemn procession back to Westminster, the expenses of each step of the journey and the elaborate obsequies carefully recorded (Ward 1995, 68–9).

We cannot know what his early experiences of loss meant to Humphrey, and it is hard to know much about his character, although R. P. Davies describes him as 'a life-long invalid, a pious bachelor given to the company of priests and Augustinian canons', as well as an aggressive landlord who worked closely with his brother to make the most of his Welsh estates (Davies 1978, 92). We know that his father's death was not only traumatic but determined by his aristocratic ambitions. As part of the baronial opposition to his brother-in-law, Edward II, the elder duke was one of the ordainers who first exiled and then executed Piers Gaveston. Taken prisoner at the battle of Bannockburn, Humphrey's father was killed in 1322, while fighting the king at Boroughbridge.[10] William's uncle's desire to displace him as heir to the throne, like Alphonse's stepmother's desire to see her own son inherit, is undeniably evil, but patrician infighting is perfectly comprehensible to the poet and his audience, and in the end the Spanish queen is forgiven.[11]

Royal birth, with its concomitant obligations and insecurities, is a source of danger for William, Melior and Alphonse, as it was for Edward II and Humphrey's father. At the same time, their inherited roles are their route to power and happiness, and the idea of family as something to be feared and yearned for is a paradox at the heart of the poem. In exile, these children of privilege seem to have lost not only their public identities, but even their place in human civilization. They are not just refugees; they take the form of savage beasts, whose very appearance arouses terror and hatred. However, this is not a poem which probes what it means to be human. In Marie de France's *Bisclavret* the werewolf is a horrifying figure, through which Marie can explore the relationships expressed by the opposition of wolf/dog, outlaw/knight, naked/clothed. Not so in this poem, where even the werewolf's name, Alphonse, suggests his essentially civilized character, and where, for all his threats, he never actually harms anybody. William and Melior's ursine natures are literally skin deep. A brutish appearance only underscores the essential 'gentilesse' of the protagonists.

Throughout the period when they are arrayed in animal hides, William and Melior wear their noble garments underneath. If a hairy covering in this poem does not denote the fragile boundaries between the natural and civilized worlds, clothes do denote public status, and the poet frequently comments on the magnificent attire of the nobility. The robes he is wearing when the cowherd discovers him, 'comly clothing for any kinges sone' (294), are proof, for him, the emperor, and later Melior, that William is indeed of noble birth. In their unwitting flight back to William's home the two lovers gradually shed their disguises, first exchanging the bearskins for the gendered covering of hart and hind. We know that William is ready to claim his patrimony when he starts longing for armour, the tools and symbol of his rank. The queen herself cuts them out of their 'hidous hides', and when they are bathed and clothed 'worthli' there is no fairer couple on earth. For Alphonse, too, clothes make the man. His wicked (but reformed) stepmother, after disenchanting him, thoroughly inspects the naked and blushing Alphonse, assuring him that he is 'proper' in all respects, but William is not really convinced that he is whole until the Spanish queen tells him, 'Yis, bi Crist, . . . clothes he askes' (4483). The former beast receives his attire and his membership in the order of knighthood from William, and finally, for all of them, private and public selves no longer diverge. Who they are becomes identical with what they are and what they appear to be.

Thanks to Alisaundrine and Alphonse, the flight from Melior's father has become the route to the restoration of the legitimate line of descent of three royal houses. William is able to complete the familiar narrative pattern of exile and return, becoming the adult son who will replace his father, because he has been given the disinterested love and protection of a series of surrogate parents. The scenes depicting William's life outside the courtly world to which he naturally belongs are among the most appealing and original of the poem, expanding its social horizons in a way remarkable in the romance as a genre. The ordinary lives of 'those who know no French' are given narrative and moral significance, and William learns the lessons of noble behaviour from those he is born to command.

Because the first three folios of the manuscript are missing, we enter the story at the point where the werewolf has rescued the threatened infant, leaving him hidden in a den. The English poet has so enhanced this scene, introducing important images and themes, that it is worth citing at length:

> Hit bifel in that forest, there fast byside,
> ther woned a wel old cherl that was a couherde,
> that fele winteres in that forest fayre hade kepud
> mennes ken of the cuntre as a comen herde.
> And thus it bitide that time, as tellen oure bokes,
> . . . .

149

> The herd sat than with hound agene the hote sunne,
> nought fully a furlong fro that fayre child,
> cloughtand kyndely his schon, as to here craft falles.
> That while was the werwolf went aboute his praye,
> what behoved to the barn to bring as he might.
>
> . . . .
>
> Lovely lay it along in his lovely denne,
> and buskede him out of the buschys that were blowed grene
> and leved ful lovely, that lent grete schade;
> and briddes ful bremely on the bowes singe.
> What for melodye that thei made in the Mey sesoun,
> that litel child listely lorked out of his cave,
> faire floures forto fecche that he bifore him seye,
> and to gadere of the grases that grene were and fayre.
>
> (3–27)

William is discovered by the dog, who so frightens the child that he retreats weeping to his den. (The French poem has the baying hound but lacks the long description of the landscape.) The peasant calls him out with kind words and promises of 'appeles and alle thinges that childern after wilnen' (59). When the werewolf returns, frenzied at the loss of the child, he tracks him to the cottage where he has been taken. Peeping in at a small hole he sees him safe, cuddled in the loving arms of the cowherd's wife. There is a nostalgic charm in the ensuing scenes of William's childhood. Loved, active, the natural leader of a little band, his life is a rural idyll, richly and affectionately described by a poet with a real gift for pastoral. The passage cited above is typical of his use of the kinds of rhetorical conventions which are customarily seen as beyond the scope or interests of Middle English romance.

My use of the term 'pastoral' here is neither anachronistic, nor meant to point to mere poetic decoration. As Helen Cooper has thoroughly demonstrated, there was a rich vernacular pastoral tradition in the Middle Ages, which she describes as 'the attempt of the court or city to find an image of life outside itself, and the simple life of the pastoral world is the opposite of the society that creates it. . . . the poets of the Middle Ages withdrew [from society] in order to comment on it' (Cooper 1977, 2). In *William*, however, this commentary can be read in two ways. On the one hand there is an implicit contrast between the courtly garden where the child's life is in danger and the innocent pleasures of the cowherd's cottage. In a poem where landscape is so richly imbued with social meaning we can recognize the critique of aristocratic society these scenes offer, even though it is a critique which is ultimately repressed, in favour of an ideal of social harmony generated by hierarchical order. On the other hand, the values and activities of William's early life foreshadow his life at court, suggesting that peasant and knight are all part of the same ethical community. For example, when William goes hunting he never keeps anything for himself,

> til alle his felawes were ferst feffed to here paie.
> So kynde and so curteys comsed he there
> that alle ledes him lovede that loked on him ones,
> and blesseden that him bare and brought into this worlde,
> so moche manhed and murthe schewed that child evere.
>
> (193–7)

William's acknowledgement of the care he has received demonstrates simultaneously his innate 'gentilesse' and therefore fitness to rule, and his dependence on the social reciprocity of his ostensible inferiors.

> To this man and his meke wif most y am holde,
> for thei ful faire han me fostered and fed a long time;
> that God for his grete might al here god hem yeld!
> But not y never what to done, to wende thus hem fro,
> that han al kindenes me kyd, and y ne kan hem yelde!
>
> (317–21)

His departure is justified by the assurance that if he does well at court he can reward his foster parents. By being 'servisabul to the simple so as to the riche' (338), as the churl advises him, he will further integrate pastoral and courtly worlds.

In spite of the attractions of rural simplicity, when William is ten the werewolf must intervene to rescue him once more, this time from a loving but socially inadequate family. The pastoral world can only be an interlude, not a real alternative to William's true destiny in the world of courtly romance. When they have first fled to the woods, Melior tells William,

> We schul live bi oure love, lelli, atte best,
> and thurghth the grace of God gete us sumwat elles:
> bolaces and blake-beries that on breres growen,
> so that for hunger, I hope, harm schul we never;
> hawes, hepus and hakernes, and the hasel-notes,
> and other frut to the fulle that in forest growen.
> I seie you, sire, bi mi liif, this liif so me likes!
>
> (1807–13)

William knows that this is merely a fantasy, but Melior is not wrong to find something of value in their fugitive life. In a childish, passive and deeply dependent state, relying on the werewolf for everything, not even questioning

151

his care for them, they are, ironically, most truly intimate. Outside the court they can be constantly together, always wrapped in each other's arms, kissing and embracing and playing at love, as the poet describes them over and over again. The restoration of their fortunes means that they take on the traditional roles of their class, and in growing up they grow apart. The public world is essentially masculine, despite the prominence of William's mother in her role as queen. Melior has nothing to do in Palermo but join the other females in greeting the returning knights, and she vanishes into the queen's chamber, where she becomes a relatively minor figure, while William in his armour takes centre stage.

This process begins when the Emperor of Rome, out hunting, is lured by Alphonse to William, whose innate nobility he instantly recognizes. Forced to reveal that William is a foundling, the grieving cowherd hands him over to the emperor. The child's farewell to his foster parents is at once humorous and touching. He weeps until the emperor puts him up on his horse, and then 'bygan for to glade / that he so realy schuld ride' (351–2). William is ready to leave his foster family, and Melior is ready to love him, because he is noble by birth as well as by character. When the emperor becomes a new father to him, he enables him to learn the knightly skills he would have acquired had he never left home.[12] William is not a Cinderella figure, like Horn, as some critics have claimed (Hudson, H. 1984, 75–6; Barron 1987, 197). He is born to royalty; he does not need to achieve it through a mistress of higher rank. Although as a hero he must be shown earning the respect of his peers on the battlefield, proving his right to a throne of his own and his capacity for gratitude by defending her father against the rebellious Duke of Saxony, Melior's love for him is not dependent on prowess. She falls in love with William before the extended passages in which we see him excel in the theatre of war, and conventional lovers' encounters in the conventional courtly garden balance conventional battle scenes. This love is 'courtly' and the object of its desire is inevitably appropriate. Melior, in her long internal debate about loving William, weighs his stellar virtues against his low birth, and decides to love him precisely because her heart tells her that there is no problem – he really is of noble kin:

> And though he as fundeling where founde in the forest wilde,
> and kept with the kowherde kin, to karp the sothe,
> eche creature may know he was kome of gode.
> For first whan the fre was in the forest founde in his denne,
> in comely clothes was he clad for any kinges sone;
> whan he kom first to this kourt, bi kynde than he schewde,
> his maners were so menskful, amende hem might none.
>
> (502–8)

And yet their love makes painfully apparent the discrepancy between virtue and rank. William, dreaming of her, admonishes himself,

> For sothe, ich am a mad man, now wel ich may knowe,
> forto wene in this wise this wrong metyng sothe.
> Min hert is to hauteyn so hye to climbe,
> so to leve that ladi wold louwe hire so moche,
> that is an emperours eir and evene his pere,
> to come to swiche a caytif! Nay! Crist it forbede.
>
> (705–10)

Beloved as he is by all the court, including the emperor, he is still a foundling in their eyes, and therefore not a fit marriage prospect. Marriage, the nobility's legitimate vehicle for establishing social stability and the orderly transmission of goods and power, is a matter of policy, not personal happiness. Thus the narrative has him leave the cowherd's household before he reaches the age of marriage and the danger that he might be coupled out of his class, lowering his own status and rendering his children unworthy of inheriting his true rank. 'What? fy! Schold I a fundeling for his fairenesse tak'? asks Melior, 'desparaged were I disgisili yif I dede in this wise' (481, 485). Like the Wife of Bath's self-centred knight she knows that to be tied to a partner of a lower class is to be demeaned in the eyes of her peers, to lose the privileged position which constitutes her identity. (For us marriage is a private act, and we have lost entirely the original meaning of *disparage*. The word has come to mean 'to speak disrespectfully of something or someone'.) But because Melior's father understands that marriage is never merely an individual choice, but a way of reinforcing structures of domination, he accepts an offer for her hand which everyone agrees is a good one. Nobody need ask her what she thinks about the proposal – it is a matter for parents and royal councils. The poet, despite his conventional morality on other matters, appears to validate her refusal to accept the bridegroom chosen for her, as the plot validates William's sister's refusal to marry the younger son of the King of Spain. As Alphonse tells his father, 'folili ye wroughten / to wilne after wedlok that wold nought assente' (4596–7). On the other hand, a feudal lord's right to make marriages is too important a prerogative to abandon altogether. The poem's solution is to have it both ways. Marriage in the romance forces a narrative crisis, one in the end resolved by an apparently disruptive love, which in turn leads to a 'better' marriage. The newly transformed Alphonse falls in love with Florent, and she with him, but it is the two men who agree to the marriage, one which will make official and material the bonds of brotherhood between them, and fulfil the queen's prophetic dream, that her right arm will stretch over Rome and her left over Spain. As modern readers, we might expect Alphonse to marry

Alisaundrine, Melior's cousin and confidante, who like the werewolf guides and protects them, whose wit and devotion are essential to the happy ending, but her rank is not sufficiently high, her ties of blood too distant to establish a new dynasty or reinforce an existing one. What the narrative gives us instead is a more socially suitable union:

> Thann William and his moder and Meliors als
> and Alphouns anon right of Alisaundrine toched,
> to marie here menskfulli among hem right thanne
> and so thei touched hem betwene, to tele the sothe,
> that Braundnis, Alphouns brother, schuld be hire make.
>
> (4990–94)

In Palermo, William has returned to his original garden, and to his inheritance. His father now dead, his land devastated by war, he finally achieves his true identity. The revelation of his birth is made publicly, since unlike love, which is secret and personal, inheritance and rule are matters for the entire society. In this poem one might argue that love comes by grace, but the throne by works, and in the kind of ideological negotiations common in the popular romances, all the inherent contradictions of noble life are submerged in family reunions and the weddings of true lovers.

The ending, which is long and to modern tastes tedious, is a compulsive reiteration of scenes of celebration, demonstrations of loyalty, penitence, forgiveness, generosity, in what William Calin calls 'a slow, measured pace of solemn festivity' (Calin 1994, 483). Unlike Havelok, William does not publicly execute those who denied him his throne, although like him he remembers those who once nourished him. At the height of his power, when he has inherited the Roman throne, he

> as a curteys king on the kowherd thought,
> that him hade fostered tofore seven yere,
> and sent sone after him and his semli wive.
> And whan the kowherde kom, the king to him saide,
> 'Sire kowherde, knowestow me ought, so the Crist help?'
> The kowherd kneled sone and karped these wordes,
> 'Ya, lord, with your leve, ful litel I you knewe.
> I fostered you on mi flet, forsothe, as me thinketh,
> and seide ye were my sone seven yer and more.'
> . . . .
> William, the worthi emperour, ful wightli thus saide,
> 'Bi Crist, sire, thou hast seid al the sothe evene;
> Thou me fostredes ful faire as fel for thin astate,
> and bi our Lord, as I leve, that schaltou lese never!'
>
> (5361–77)

These scenes, played out as public spectacle, to huge crowds, are a narrative performance of the poem's ethos – a celebration of rule based on the meshing of power (more than 1,000 lines have been devoted to William's prowess as a warrior) and love. Wherever he goes, William is adored by peers and commoners alike, not just because of his beauty and skills in battle, but especially because of his kindness. What is asserted in the poem explicitly about the nature of the good ruler, in a repetitive series of speeches to and by William, Melior, the queen, and others, is replicated in the very structure of the plot.[13] The story describes a whole network of affiliations – freely chosen, based on instinctive compassion – which sometimes duplicate, sometimes counter, sometimes lie outside of feudal hierarchies and obligations, but which ultimately are knit into the social fabric. In the end William and Alphonse not only recover their own original families, they reproduce them through happy marriages. By a series of parallels and oppositions, the romance explores the nature of 'true' nobility, the nobility of a gentle heart, an ideal to which both Humphrey and his audience can subscribe, and then reconciles it with a 'conservative' social vision which reinscribes a benevolent patriarchy. The good court and a contented country are the domain of a ruler who earns the throne he is born to, and where people live in happy families.

Notes

1 *William of Palerne*, ed. G. H. V. Bunt (Groningen: Bouma's Boekhuis, 1985). All citations will be from this edition. On the text of *William of Palerne* see also Foster and Gilman 1973, 481–2. By the sixteenth century it was bound with a copy of the *South English Legendary*, but the two works are not in the same hand, although David Lawton believes that they are closely associated (Lawton 1980).

2 *William of Palerne: otherwise known as the Romance of 'William and the Werwolf'*, ed. Walter W. Skeat, EETS e.s. 1 (London: Trübner, 1867), p. xxii.

3 'Preface to the Original Edition of 1832', repr. in Skeat's edition, pp. vii–ix.

4 Madden edited it for the Roxburghe Club in 1832. After Skeat's edition (repr. in 1890), there have been no major editions published until G. H. V. Bunt's, in 1985, although it has been the subject of a number of dissertations.

5 For a summary of the romance, and brief evaluation, see Barron 1987, 195–9. This is basically an elaboration of the section on the romance in his chapter 'Alliterative Romance and the French Tradition', in Lawton 1982, 75–80. See also Turville-Petre 1977.

6 In the first volume of the *Manual of Writings in Middle English*, on romances, *William* is treated in Charles Dunn's section, 'Romances Derived From English Legend', because the editors could not figure out where else to put it

(Severs 1967, 17–18). Dieter Mehl classifies it with novels in verse, although, as he admits, even in this grouping it is unique (Mehl 1968, 209). Grouping it with Middle English alliterative romances does not work either, since it lacks their characteristic interest in chronicle and indifference to love (Field 1982, 54–69).

7   Lawton's introduction surveys the debate about the social and literary origins of fourteenth- and fifteenth-century alliterative poetry.

8   He argues that Humphrey would have had no interest in the work itself, since he would have been immersed in French culture, but Bunt disagrees (Bunt 1984, 25–36).

9   *Guillaume de Palerne: Roman du XIIe siècle*, ed. Alexandre Micha, TLF (Geneva: Droz, 1990).

10   For information on Humphrey's family, see Holmes 1957 and Denholm-Young 1978.

11   Humphrey's own life was made easier by Edward III's policy of reconciliation with the families of those who had conspired against his father (McKisack 1959, 152–4).

12   Indeed, it was quite common for noble children to be fostered at other courts, so that William and the emperor are unwittingly doing what might have happened by design (Orme 1984).

13   Calin notes a 'concern for status and power [which] will also explain a number of speeches (a thematic augmented in the English) concerning behavior at court, feudal duty, and the exercise of kingship' (Calin 1994, 482).

CHAPTER SEVEN

The Narrative Logic of *Emaré*

AD PUTTER

I: Introduction

Like most other medieval popular romances, *Emaré* is a poem without an obvious historical context.[1] The poet has remained anonymous,[2] and though the single extant manuscript, British Library, Cotton Caligula A.ii, contains the words 'Donum Jo. Rogers' in a later hand, the identity of this owner (if that is what 'Jo. Rogers' was) or that of earlier owners is unknown.[3] The company that *Emaré* keeps in the manuscript – containing Latin and English lyrics, tail-rhyme romances, alliterative romances, devotional and confessional material and several pieces by Lydgate – is so motley that it can tell us little about *Emaré*'s provenance or textual affiliations. All that can be inferred from the manuscript is a rough date for *Emaré* (no later than *c.*1460), and the likelihood that at some stage after it was written down (in a Northern dialect) the story found its way south – possibly to a London scriptorium where miscellanies like Cotton Caligula A.ii were produced to meet the demand for books of a growing circle of literate layfolk (Richardson 1965, xi).

Attempts to contextualize *Emaré* more precisely are bound to be frustrated by the large number of chronicles and romances, composed anywhere between the twelfth and sixteenth centuries, that share the following plot:

A daughter rebuffs the incestuous desires of her father. She is put to sea in a boat (or abandoned in the desert), but survives miraculously. She is eventually married to a king, despite the protests of his evil mother. During the king's absence the mother-in-law contrives to have the heroine and her newborn son cast adrift (or left in the desert) for the second time. Again she survives, and is taken in by a family in a foreign city, where she is finally reunited with her lost husband (in some versions also with her remorseful father).

157

More than twenty versions of this story survive in various European languages. The two that provide the most significant parallels with *Emaré* are in French and German.[4] The first, Philippe de Beaumanoir's *La Manekine* (*c*.1270),[5] turns the story into a long courtly romance, with elaborate descriptions of lovesickness and splendid feats of arms. In the absence of the original French lay on which *Emaré* claims to be based, Philippe de Beaumanoir's version is probably the best witness to what that lost text may have looked like. The German version is the brief but powerful prose narrative *Der König von Reussen* (The King of Russia),[6] which survives in a fifteenth-century manuscript but must have circulated in Germany well before that, since it was put into verse by Jansen Enikel in his thirteenth-century *Weltbuch* (a universal chronicle).

I shall be returning to Philippe de Beaumanoir's *Manekine* and *Der König von Reussen* later on in this essay; they are mentioned here only to substantiate the point that stories about a daughter's flight from incest enjoyed enormous popularity across different periods and countries of the Middle Ages. Paradoxically, such popularity throws up barriers to a modern appreciation of the poem, for of the many claims for cultural distinction that critics like to make (or make up) for any text they interpret – that it is original, self-conscious, ironical, historically specific – none can be made for *Emaré*. Unlike, for example, *La Manekine*, which has been especially admired for its ample descriptions of tournaments and weddings (Suchier 1884, lxxx) and its artfulness (Shepherd 1990), in short, for its digressions and artistic distance from the plot, the poet of *Emaré* seems to have been content to let the story do the work for him.

The consequent lack of distinction puts the interpreter of *Emaré* in the awkward position of having to say about the text things that might equally well be said about countless other texts; but it makes *Emaré* interesting for anyone seeking to discover how and why the conventions of this story work. Why is it that in romances such as *Emaré* the solution to the problem so clearly repeats or mirrors the events that first created this problem? Why do victimized heroines such as Emaré adopt new names and identities? And why do these romances always reconfigure the most arbitrary and intractable incidents – boats that drift out of human control; misguided decisions taken in haste; letters that never arrive at their destination, and so on – into the most purposeful and patterned design?

One obvious function of familiar storylines and motifs is the mnemonic support they offer to anyone having to recite the story from memory. There has in recent years been a powerful and largely beneficial backlash against the old view that Middle English romances are the improvisations of wandering minstrels (see especially Taylor 1991, 1992). Too many so-called minstrels' tales turn out to be translations of French originals, or survive in different manuscripts in a text so stable as to make oral transmission unlikely. *Emaré*, too, claims descent from a French source (1030–32), a fact confirmed by the French derivation of its personal names (Rickert 1908, xxix). But despite its embeddedness in a literate culture, *Emaré* did, I think, circulate orally at least at some stage in its evolution. The text retains the formulaic language, the repetitions and redundancies, and the mnemonic use of a focal image (in *Emaré* the robe) that characterize orally transmitted stories.[7] While such features help to make *Emaré* 'memorable' for a story-teller, I would also argue that its conventions, its store of recyclable patterns and motifs, make *Emaré* 'memorable' in another sense ('*worthy* of memory'), since they encode and affirm important meanings for its audience.

It is unfortunate that we tend to accept conventions without inquiring much into the meanings invested in them, and perhaps even more unfortunate that our ability to recognize conventions in medieval texts is rarely matched by an ability to recognize the operation of similar conventions in our own lives. C. S. Lewis confessed that he had always taught his students that lovesickness was a purely literary motif, until he fell in love himself and found himself, like the pining hero of *Troilus and Criseyde*, unable to eat or to sleep (Lewis 1960, 127). Responding to literary conventions is often a matter of appreciating that the 'truths' they embody are also embodied in ourselves. In this essay I want to explore the meanings of three conventions in *Emaré*: the repetitive storyline, the falsification of names, and finally the reconfiguration of coincidence as design. Because I believe that the narrative laws that shape *Emaré*'s world have not wholly ceased to operate in ours, I shall draw freely on insights from other domains – psychoanalysis, philosophy, and self-observation – in the hope that they may sharpen our responsiveness to this underrated romance.

II: Repetitions

First a fuller plot summary:

> The rich emperor Artyus has one child by his wife Erayne. When she dies, his little daughter Emaré is entrusted to a nurse (Abro). Sir Tergaunte, the King of Sicily, visits Emaré's father, and gives him a beautiful cloth. Embroidered on it are famous pairs of lovers. After Sir Tergaunte's departure, the emperor sends for his daughter and falls in love with her. On seeing her attired in a robe cut from Tergaunte's cloth, he announces his intention to marry her. Messengers are sent to Rome to get the pope's permission. Papal permission duly arrives, but Emaré denounces her father's perverse desires, upon which he casts her adrift in a boat, dressed in the robe. As the boat passes beyond the horizon, Artyus repents.

The boat lands in 'Galys',[8] where Egaré, as the heroine now calls herself, is found by Sir Kador, the steward to the local king. At a feast, the king sees Emaré in her robe and falls in love with her. He asks Kador where she has come from, and Kador replies that she is an earl's daughter, come to teach his children manners. The king marries her despite his mother's opposition. While he is away fighting Saracens, Egaré gives birth to a healthy son whom she names Segramour. A letter is sent to the king reporting the birth of an heir, but the message is intercepted by the king's mother, who substitutes a letter alleging that Egaré has given birth to a monster. The king requests that queen and baby be well looked after until his return, but again the message is intercepted by his mother, who substitutes a letter ordering that Egaré and her son be put out to sea.

In her rudderless boat Egaré drifts to Rome, where Jordan, a local merchant, finds her and takes her in. In the meanwhile, the King of Galys has come home; he discovers his mother's treachery, and exiles her. Years later he decides to go to Rome to do penance. He takes up lodging in Jordan's house; Egaré, who now regains her old name Emaré, recognizes him and sends his son Segramour to wait on him. The king, who believes his wife and child to be dead, is reminded by Segramour of the son he might have had, and offers to make him his heir. Segramour reports the king's behaviour to Emaré, and she reveals the truth.

Emaré's father also undertakes a journey to Rome to be absolved from his sin. Emaré sends her husband and child to meet him, and a joyful reunion follows.

As the summary suggests, Emaré is a fast-moving and eventful romance. With the exception of a lengthy digression about the embroidered cloth, nothing gets in the way of the rapidly unfolding plot. But the plot owes its impression of ceaseless toing and froing above all to the fact that travelling is about the only thing that happens in it. If we break the plot down into its basic activities (the narratologist Todorov calls them 'verbs'[9]) we cannot fail to be struck by the limited scope for human expression, which is virtually restricted to the following two possibilities: 'to travel' and 'to love'. Both these 'verbs' share a similar dynamic potential: in a negative modulation they set a distance between people (hate, unwanted love, travel away from, exile), while in a positive one they reduce distance (reciprocal love, travel towards, reunion).

If it is the business of storytellers to invent and then remove obstacles, to separate and unite subjects and objects of desire, then few other 'verbs' can be more useful to their craft than those which open and close physical and emotional distance. *Emaré* positively exhausts itself in the energy that it creates by combining verbs of 'love' and 'travel' in various permutations. Here is a parodic reduction of the plot:

Emaré's father *loves* his wife, but death *takes her away*. He *falls in love* with his daughter, but she *does not love* him, and so he makes sure she *goes away*.

The King of Galys *loves* Emaré; she *loves* him, and so they marry. He *goes away* on crusade. The Queen Mother *does not love* Emaré, and makes sure that she *goes away*.

The father and the husband *still love* Emaré, but she *has gone away*. They *go away* as well and, moving towards her, are reunited with Emaré who still *loves* them.

The same 'verbs' of emotional and physical displacement also dominate minor incidents in the story: Emaré is *sent away* from home to a nurse and *returns* when she has reached marriageable age; Sir Tergaunte *travels* to Artyus from Sicily with a cloth, described as a *love-token*; Emaré's husband *no longer loves* his evil mother and *exiles* her. The narrative laws which operate in *Emaré* can thus be summed up as follows: hatred or improper love is followed by movement away from (exile); love, frustrated by distance, is followed by movement towards (union).

The repetitiveness of human actions in *Emaré* is thrown into higher relief by its verbal repetitiveness. Whenever the text restates a theme, it repeats a phrase, a line, even an entire stanza. Thus the description of Artyus seeking approval for his incestuous marriage –

> And when the metewhyle was don,
> Into hys chambur he wente son
> And called hys counseyle nere.
> (229–31)

– is recycled with minimal changes to describe the King of Galys's resolve to marry Emaré:

> And when the metewhyle was don,
> Into the chambur he wente son,
> And called hys barouns bolde.
> (406–8)

Similar large-scale repetitions appear in Emaré's exile in her boat (cf. 313–36 with 349–60 and 673–84); her rescue by Kador and Jordan respectively (cf. 340–84 with 685–732); and the rejoicing that accompanies the two reunions (cf. 925–36 with 1009–20). Admittedly, repetitive language characterizes tail-rhyme romances in general, but no Middle English romance rivals *Emaré* in this respect. As Edith Rickert noted, roughly 16 per cent of this romance consists of verbatim repetition (Rickert 1908, xxvi). Using the formula rather than verbatim repetition as her unit of measurement,[10] Susan Wittig calculated the number of formulaic lines at 42 per cent, which makes *Emaré* the top-scoring Middle English romance (Wittig 1978, 18).

Taken by themselves, frequent mention of minstrels in romances (see *Emaré* 13, 132, 388, 468, 867) and avowals of oral delivery (*Emaré* 24: 'As I here synge in songe') are now considered insufficient evidence to prove oral transmission; they may be intended 'to offer the solitary reader the pleasures and consolations of an imaginary community' (Taylor 1992, 62). But can the same also be said of *Emaré*'s formulaic and repetitive style? Is this too an artful device designed to give us the illusion of a vanished world of orality? It may be simpler to admit to the likelihood that *Emaré* was at one time stored in living memory, and so developed the form of organization which the constraints of memorizing impose on narrative material.

No exploration of *Emaré*'s repetitiveness, however, should overlook its effectiveness in highlighting the surprisingly symmetrical pattern in which the plot resolves itself.[11] By the end two remarkably similar storylines have come full circle. In the first a father condemns his daughter to exile at sea, after which his conscience drives him to her abode in Rome. In the second she is again separated, now from her husband; she is cast adrift a second time; and again the separation is undone when the man involved travels to Rome to do penance. The duplication of verbal material across these two plotlines reinforces the curious correspondence between the father's and the husband's histories. Without knowledge of the other, both men are somehow bound to 'take after' each other.

The repetition, then, is not incidental or random, but involves the reproduction of an entire history. And, teased by the resemblances between the two storylines, we do notice intriguing parallels which the elaborate courtly versions of the story, such as Philippe de Beaumanoir's *Manekine*, refine out of existence:

– Emaré has only a father; her mother has died. The King of Galys lives with his mother; no father is mentioned. (*Der König von Reussen* adds he has died: 'wan sîn vater was gestorben', p. xi.) Is there a similarity between the father's incestuous love for his daughter, and the queen's possessiveness of her son? Does the queen try to prevent her son from marrying Emaré (445–53) because she sees Emaré as her rival?[12]

– Two single-parent families, a father and his daughter, a mother and her son, implode soon after the arrival of an outsider. In the first case the outsider is a man (Sir Tergaunte), in the second case a woman (Emaré). Does Sir Tergaunte, like Emaré, shadow forth the figure of the marriage partner, whom in other incest stories the father wards off?[13]

Moreover, the poem traces its symmetrical pattern not only by repeating two plotlines, but also by imposing closure in an ending that deliberately doubles up on the beginning. When Emaré's double exile has left the story in a tangle, the poet contrives a resolution by unwinding the two strands of the plot in reverse direction. Thus the same 'verb' that creates the dilemma also liquidates it. Emaré's expulsion from father and husband is redeemed only when the men voluntarily abandon home to do penance. *Emaré's exile must be repeated in order to be undone.* In sequencing, too, the plot goes into reverse: separated first from her father and then from her husband, Emaré is reunited first with her husband and then with her father.

The principle of redemption through inverted repetition is so strong that it overrides all other rules of narrative coherence. The reader may well wonder why the father decides after many years to take penance from the pope in Rome – 'He thowght that he wolde go, / For hys penance to the Pope tho' (955–6) – when the pope earlier sanctioned his incestuous marriage:

> He bad thay [messengers] shulde sone go and come,
> And gete leve of the Pope of Rome
> To wedde that mayden clere.
>
> (232–4)

How can the pope impose penance for an incestuous marriage to which he earlier gave his blessing? The thing is absurd, unless we submit ourselves blindly to the logic of inverted repetition. If Rome aids and abets the father, then it must redeem itself by becoming the scene of reconciliation. The contrasting presentations of Rome, first as a place of corruption, then as a place of atonement, are in this light not a weakness but a strength. Redemption – the word originally means 'buying back' – necessarily involves the repetition of a process in inverse form: the seller becomes the buyer; a father's perverse petition to the pope is transformed into his resolution to obtain penance from him.

In the theological sense, too, redemption (mankind's deliverance from hell) depends on inverted repetition. Satan, tricking mankind in Eden by means of a tree, is paid back by Christ, whose death, also by means of a tree, tricks Satan and redeems man. In *Piers Plowman*, Langland sums up the logic of redemption as follows:

> So shal grace that al bigan make a good ende
> And bigile the gilour – and that is good sleighte:
> *Ars ut artem falleret.*
>
> (B.18.160–1)[14]

My point in alluding to the Christian redemption is not to suggest that *Emaré's* ending is in any way dependent on it,[15] but to draw attention to the miraculous power of inverted repetition to close narratives whose troubled beginnings appear to defy 'a good ende'. Whether the narrative problem is Emaré's exile or the Fall of Man, resolutions must mirror beginnings. And the reason why non sequiturs or contradictions, such as the pope's opposing functions in *Emaré*, cannot derail redemptive endings is that the purpose of such endings is as much to confute or undo what has gone before as to follow on from it.

But if repetition may be a blessing, it is equally true that it haunts Emaré like a curse. Making fiendish enemies, being exiled in boats and adopted by strange men – this seems to be Emaré's destiny in life. It may be useful at this point to put the problem of repetition in a wider context by asking ourselves whether we do not all know people who seem, like Emaré, to be plagued by an eternal return of the same. In 'Beyond the Pleasure Principle', Freud wrote:

> Thus we have come across people all of whose human relationships have the same outcome: . . . the man whose friendships all end in betrayal by his friend; . . . lovers each of whose love affairs with a woman passes through the same phases and reaches the same conclusion. This 'perpetual recurrence of the same thing' causes us no astonishment when it relates to *active* behaviour on the part of the person concerned and when we can discern in him an essential character-trait which always remains the same and which is compelled to find expression in a repetition of the same experiences. We are much more impressed by cases where the subject appears to have a *passive* experience, over which he has no influence, but in which he meets with a repetition of the same fatality.
>
> (Freud 1955, 22)

The analogy between Freud's 'compulsive repeaters' and Emaré is obviously imperfect. For one thing, the repetitions in *Emaré* are hardly 'endless'; rather, they are organized in a threefold sequence that might be schematized as follows: home[1], exile[1]: home[2], exile[2]: home[3], exile undone. The repetitions thus provide a good example of 'trebling', a pattern commonly found in narratives for the simple reason that a threefold series is the minimum required to produce a design, an expectation, and a resolution.[16] For another, Emaré's story of passive persecution does not, in my view, benefit from an interpretation that would see it as a case of unconscious wish-fulfilment. Freud was notoriously tempted by such interpretations (note his hint: '*appears* to have a passive experience'); but, in fairness to Freud, the thrust of his essay is precisely to suggest that some phenomena cannot be explained by the 'pleasure principle', since they lie beyond it. A case in point is the 'repetition compulsion' associated with trauma (e.g. shell-shock), which constrains people to repeat in the present painful and unassimilated events from the past. Unable to bring the trauma within the agency of the self, they are dominated by it: the trauma will not get into the past. Thinking of Emaré's past as a 'trauma' is no doubt anachronistic, but it brings into focus the strange persistence of her past, the way that possibilities of incest and realities of exile continue to structure her experiences even after her first ordeal is over.

This is repetition in its tragic dimension, when the past dominates and usurps the present. But in the same essay Freud suggests that repeating the past in symbolic form may also be liberating. His example is a little boy who experienced his mother's continual comings and goings as abandonment. In response he developed a ritual. He would throw out a wooden reel over the edge of his cot, shouting 'O-o-o' (interpreted by Freud as the child's attempt at *fort*, German for 'out', 'gone'), and then he would haul it in again, exclaiming '*Da*'! ('There'). Freud observed that the child dealt with the trauma by repeating it as a game of which he was in charge: 'He compensated himself for this, as it were, by himself staging the disappearance and return of the objects within his reach' (Freud 1955, 15). Readers allergic to Freud may prefer an autobiographical example. Still smarting from my humiliation in an argument with a taxi-driver, I replay the episode in my mind again and again, but this time I supply the devastating retort that did not occur to me the first time around. Repetition and inversion (the loser becomes the winner) enable me to replace what has been by what might (and I think should) have been. Inverted repetition converts pain into pleasure, passivity into an active triumph.

Repetition, then, presents itself under a double aspect, tragic and therapeutic. Kierkegaard tried to capture this ambivalence in the intuition that – in his terms – the 'movement' of repetition can be experienced as flowing in two different 'directions': 'backwards' or 'forwards' (Kierkegaard 1983, 131). Backward repetition is the kind that impoverishes the present by reducing it to recurrence, as if it were a regression into a never-ending past. As examples of 'backward repetition', we can think of Freud's unconscious repetition or of nostalgia, the hankering after a lost era or person whose return is so intensely desired that present time is perceived as no more than a reverberating echo of time past. Forward repetition, by contrast, allows us to impose a pattern on the past and thus to assert our control over it. It is progressive, for 'that which is repeated has been – otherwise it could not be repeated – *and the very fact that it has been makes the repetition into something new*' (Kierkegaard 1983, 149; my italics). Precisely because the inevitable newness of what is repeated condemns to futility all attempts to have the past again, the repetition itself can liberate us from the past.

The theoretical distinction between 'backward reliving' and 'forward reliving' is useful for *Emaré*, where repetition is at once the problem and the solution: the problem, because 'backwards reliving', the sense of being in thrall to the past, is the curse from which its characters are to be delivered; and the solution, because its happy ending depends on projecting the past forwards, on retrieving Emaré's lost husband and father. The best way of putting these claims to the test is to re-immerse ourselves in *Emaré* at the point where it moves beyond 'repetition compulsion' – when Emaré is again washed ashore, and found by the local merchant Jordan:

> A marchaunte dwelled yn that cyté,
> A ryche mon of golde and fee,
>   Jurdan was ys name.
> Every day wolde he
> Go play hym by the see,
>   The eyer forto tane.
> He wente forth yn that tyde,
> Walkyng by the see syde,
>   All hymself alone.
> A bote he fonde by the brymme
> And a fayr lady therynne,
>   That was ryght wo-bygone.
>   (685–96)

The fact that this stanza recycles the description of Emaré's earlier rescue by Kador –' Every day wolde he go, / And take wyth thym a sqwyer or two, / And play hym by the see' (343–5) – is a reminder (if any were needed) that we have seen this all before. Emaré, the inveterate exile, is stranded yet again, and returns once more to a man's world. 'Thus we have come across people all of whose human relationships have the same outcome', Freud said gloomily; and if Emaré's relationship with Jordan were to follow suit, the story might continue like this: 'Jordan falls in love with Emaré, but, faithful to her husband, she repulses his advances and is exiled in a boat. Washed ashore . . . and so on *ad infinitum*.

Imagining alternative endings is sometimes regarded as self-indulgence in our discipline, so it needs to be said that happy endings often derive their sense of triumph from their unlikelihood, from our awareness of a probable tragic outcome which, though it fails to materialize, is always present as an unrealized possibility. Consider Shakespeare's *Winter's Tale*.[17] It is based on Thomas Greene's *Pandosto*, in which the slandered queen is *not* brought back to life, but in which the tyrannical king re-enacts his earlier cruelty to the queen by making his own daughter his mistress. While *Pandosto*'s tragic ending is deflected in Shakespeare's adaptation, it is nevertheless an absence that positively determines the upbeat finale, a possibility that sits just around the corner of the play (see e.g. V.1.224–9) like a disastrous turning not taken. And just as the euphoria of *The Winter's Tale* is coloured by the tragic ending that is averted, so *Emaré*'s happy ending is made up both of what it delivers and of what it delivers us *from*.

In *Emaré* the deliverance is from the heroine's unfinished past, which has yet to be laid to rest. We have already witnessed Emaré's initial trauma twice over. First her widowed father wants to commit incest with her, and exiles her when she objects; then her widowed mother-in-law gets jealous and exiles her. And now Emaré takes her place in a third family, headed by a third man, the merchant Jordan. His mercantile status, however, signals that Emaré's new adventure will not be the 'same old story' but a dénouement that will put an end to it. Because Jordan is a *bourgeois*, and so not in Emaré's class, a liaison with him is effectively ruled out, especially since he is also said to be older and married:

> When he come to hys byggynge,
> He welcomed fayr that lady yynge
>   That was fayr and bryght;
> And badde hys wyf yn all thynge,
> Mete and drynk forto brynge
>   To the lady ryght.
>
> (709–14)

We know that we have turned a corner when Emaré's third home is, at last, a happy two-parent family. And in this safe environment the wedded merchant bestirs himself to carry out the ungrateful narrative task for which he is ideally qualified: to be a father to the young Segramour (887–8), to stand in for Emaré's absent father and husband, but, lest he repeat their histories, to be otherwise as uninteresting to her as possible.

Jordan's disqualification from doing anything apart from keeping the seats of husband and father warm sends out loud signals that Emaré's men are about to reassemble themselves around her. Then the inverted repetitions begin in earnest. Last to be separated from Emaré, the King of Galys must be the first to be reunited with her; her exile must be matched by his self-exile; his penitential journey must retrace hers. But when chance brings him to her, Emaré does not, as we might expect, run from her cover, but sends out Segramour to wait on the king. Why?

We have been told before that the mournful king still lives in the shadow of his lost family, to the extent that he sees in the lively play of children only the ghosts of the past:

> When she was fled ovur the see fome,
> The nobull kyng dwelled at hom,
>   Wyth full hevy chere;
> Wyth karefull hert and drury mone,
> Sykynges made he many on
>   For Egarye the clere.
> And when he sawe chylderen play,
> He wepte and sayde, 'Wellawey,
>   For my sone so dere!'
> Such lyf he lyved mony a day,
> That no mon hym stynte may,
>   Fully seven yere.
>   (805–16)

Seeing the little boy in Jordan's house, the king again falls prey to the 'backwards reliving' that makes people unhappy – especially when he hears that the child has the same name as his lost son:

> The kynge sayde to hym *in game*,
> '*Swete sone*, what ys thy name?'
>   'Lorde', he seyd, 'y hyghth Segramowres.'
>
> Then that nobull kyng
> Toke up a sykynge,
>   For hys *sone* hyght so;
> Certys, wythowten lesynge,
> The teres out of hys yen gan wryng;
>   In herte he was full woo.
>   (874–82; my italics)

The use of the word 'sone' here is interesting. Its primary meaning in Middle English is 'son', but it could also be used as a familiar form of address, equivalent to our 'young man' or 'sonny' (*MED* 6b). The double meaning makes for a poignant dramatic irony: both senses of the word fit the context, since, unbeknownst to the king, the addressee *is* his son.

But in what sense does the king *intend* 'swete sone'? The addition that he says it *in game* seems to suggest that he has chosen this form of address precisely because it covers both senses. For the *game* the king is playing with the child consists of fondly pretending to himself that the boy is his lost son. The desire to transform the child into his son explains the unrefusable offer which the king later makes the burgess. He will adopt his boy and make him his heir:

The kyng called the burgeys hym tyll,
And sayde, 'Syr, yf hyt be thy wyll,
  Yyf me thys lytyll body!
I schall hym make lorde of town and towr;
Of hye halles and of bowre,
  I love hym specyally.'

(895–900)

The motivation for this gratuitous act of generosity to a stranger is never explained, but we readily understand the transference which charges it with meaning. The king's mysterious fondness for the little boy – 'I love *hym* specially' – is overdetermined by his attachment to his lost son, the unspoken antecedent of 'hym'. And so the king seizes on 'thys lytyll body', to realize in the present all the lost hopes of the past.[18] He will love this Segramour as if he were his own; but this 'swete sone' must come to the inheritance from which his own son was tragically debarred. 'When anything has not happened in the desired way', Freud wrote, 'it is undone by being repeated in a different way' (Freud 1959b, 120).

Emaré's ploy – for she has orchestrated the scene – has made the king repeat the past as he would like it to have been, and the repeat performance proves redemptive rather than regressive. When Emaré hears about the king's eccentric behaviour from her son, no further proof is needed that her husband, who for all she knows authorized her and Segramour's exile, did not really wish them dead. She now sends her son to reveal all, while the poet cranks up the tension by showing the king recoiling from his wife's name in disbelief:

The kyng yn herte was full woo
When he herd mynge tho
  Of her that was hys qwene;
And sayde, 'Sone why sayst thou so?
Wherto umbraydest thou me of my wo?
  That may never bene.'

(925–30)

'Why mock me like this?' the king answers when the boy mentions his mother's name. He has treated the boy as his would-be son, but reality seems wantonly cruel when it plays along with his private pretence. A boy called Segramour, a mother called Egaré: the cast is perfect, but rehearsals of the past cannot bring it back again. 'What is repeated has been', and trying to recollect it makes life go backwards, turning the present into a play of shadows that mimic the past – so it seems to the king – to mock his obsession with it.

Only after the king has seen Emaré in the flesh does he realize his wishes *have* come true; not, of course, because the death of his wife and son can be undone, but because they never happened in the first place. Repetition, as Kierkegaard wrote, makes us happy when we realize it is not the same thing twice. The king discovers this for himself: the boy he has just appointed heir and the woman called Egaré are not doubles, reincarnations of lost people; they are these people themselves. Repetition does not have to copy the past, but may recollect it forward to create a new beginning.

III: Names

Emaré's recovery of her husband, soon followed by that of her father, also creates the conditions for the recovery of her name. In his essay for this collection, James Simpson deals with the different cultural assumptions that underlie the motif of naming and re-naming in medieval romance. In contrast to our modern belief in the arbitrariness of names, medieval texts treat the name as a motivated sign, which implies an important truth about its bearer. Changes in self-understanding may therefore prompt characters in medieval texts to drop their names, to change them, or to re-appropriate them.

Emaré provides an excellent example of the meaningfulness of names. Derived from Old French *esmeree* ('purified', 'refined'),[19] the name Emaré is dropped when she is exiled by her father. When she is found by Kador and his companions, she identifies herself by her new name, Egaré:

> They askede her what was her name:
> She chaunged hyt ther anone,
>   And sayde she hette Egaré.
> (358–60)

The Old French verb *esgarer* meant 'lose' or 'displace', and so her new name encrypts the secret that she tells no-one: she has been cast out, exiled. But no sooner has her husband entered her dwelling in Rome than the old name returns:

> At the burgeys hous hys yn he nome,
>   Theras woned Emarye.
> (839–40)

The exile has been found and 'Egaré' can no longer name her: she becomes Emaré again.

The significance of the name is a motif found in most versions of the story. In Philippe de Beaumanoir's *Manekine*, the daughter is originally called Joie because everyone is joyful at her birth (69–71). When her father wants to marry her, she cuts off her hand to make herself repugnant, and the furious father casts her adrift at sea. Deprived of joy, her name 'Joie' becomes meaningless, and when she refuses to name herself, she is given the nickname 'Manekine', which encodes her handlessness (Latin *mancus* = cripple).[20] Only after a reunion with father and husband does her old name 'Joie' become applicable again. Her missing hand is miraculously restored: she is 'Manekine' no more.

Because, as in *La Manekine*, the name in *Emaré* expresses the heroine's inner being, changes of name stage a larger drama of identity.[21] Emaré's suppression and retrieval of her name signify her suppression and retrieval of what she is. The pseudonym 'Egaré' is therefore doubly appropriate. Since she is an outcast, it obviously denotes her physical displacement, but, since it is not her authentic name, it simultaneously connotes her *self-alienation*. Nor is it just her name that Emaré drops; with it she discards her whole past, which she carefully conceals even from her husband. Just before marrying her, the King of Galys asks Kador about her past, but his reply is a smokescreen:

> Then sayde syr Kadore, y unthurstonde
> 'Hyt ys an erles thowghtur of ferre londe,
>   That semely ys to sene.
> I sente after her certynlye
> To teche my chylderen curtesye,
>   In chambur wyth hem to bene . . .'
>   (421–6)

We are not told whether Kador is simply glossing over his own ignorance with a white lie, or whether Emaré and Kador have cooked up this alibi together. In any case, we know the truth is different: Emaré has not left home to work in Galys as an *au pair*.

'Why Kador makes up the story, I fail to see', wrote Edith Rickert in her editorial notes (Rickert 1908, 40); but, surely, the reasons for 'Egaré' and Kador's suppression of the past are obvious: Emaré's history, her father's attempt at incest and her sea exile, cannot be spoken of because they are unspeakable. And if we think it enigmatic or 'unrealistic' that Emaré falsifies her name and her biography, do we not miss the truth that we may all experience things that cannot be reconciled with our self-understanding, things so repugnant that, as the expression still goes, we *cannot put our name to them*? Such unassimilable events have happened to Emaré, and the change of name is a shorter and far better way of saying that she will not have them to her name.

Emaré therefore becomes someone else, and lives as Egaré in a perpetual present from which the past has been cut off. But without mediation between past and present, the heroine's successive selves – first Emaré, then Egaré – cannot be resolved into coherence. The solution the story provides is to retrieve the past so as to make it available, in the light of the present, for a revised interpretation that allows her to re-integrate it into her life story. The incestuous father returns, but his remorse shows that his infatuation with her was a moment of madness; the husband, too, returns but his love shows he did not really order Emaré and her son to be abandoned to the waves. But in surmounting her 'multiple personality disorder' Emaré has herself a crucial part to play. I have commented earlier on how carefully she stage-manages the reunion with her husband. Keeping herself concealed, she scripts the lines for her son and comes on stage only after the king has given a satisfactory performance. When her father arrives in Rome, Emaré again sends out her son, deliberately delaying her own entry until after the emperor has expressed his sorrow:

> The emperour wax all pale,
> And sayde, 'Sone, why umbraydest me of bale
> And thou may se no bote?'
> . . . .
>
> Neverthelesse wyth hym he wente;
> Ayeyn hym come that lady gent,
> Walkynge on her fote.
>
> (1009–17)

Reconciliation, the closing of emotional distance, is again memorably represented by the closing of physical distance, as Emaré agrees to meet her father halfway. And it makes a real difference that the heroine is not merely passively found but actively wills herself to be found. The passive victim of persecution now controls the happiness of her erstwhile oppressor. With roles reversed, the trauma of exile is replayed in Emaré's game of hide-and-seek. Like Freud's child who, by playing with a reel, turns the frustration of passive abandonment into an active triumph, Emaré makes the past right with herself by dramatizing loss and disappearance in a form that brings it under her control.

To move beyond repetition compulsion, Freud believed, it is necessary for the patient to rehearse the trauma consciously, 'remembering it as something belonging to the past' (Freud 1955, 18). Glossing this insight, D. W. Winnicott wrote that 'the original experience of primitive agony cannot get into the past unless the ego can first gather it into its own present time experience' (Winnicott 1989, 91). The return of father and husband enables Emaré to gather up the past into her present time experience so that she can reclaim it as the missing fragment of her past. For the last time repetition retrieves the past in an altered present in order to move the story beyond it.

And so Egaré, too, finally recovers her past name, though, needless to say, she is not the Emaré of old. The identity to which she returns now includes the episode of self-estrangement, and it follows that the name that stands for her new-found identity must contain the very name 'Egaré' that it supersedes. She is now 'Emaré that was Egaré'. And this is precisely how she names herself when she discloses her true identity. Instructing her son how to greet his father, she says:

> 'Byd hym com speke wyth Emaré
> That changed her name to Egaré.'
> (907–8)

And to Emaré's father, too, the little boy says:

> 'Ye shull come speke wyth Emaré
> That changede her name to Egaré.'
> (1006–7)

There may be redundancies in *Emaré* that one would wish away, but not the glorious epithet 'That changede her name to Egaré' which now graces Emaré's name (again in 922–3). The episode of estrangement from her family and herself has literally got 'into the past tense'. Her different selves in the story, Emaré and Egaré, are finally integrated and harmonized in a rhyme, the first name subsuming the second just as the main clause of the couplet subordinates the relative clause that follows.

IV: Causality

The narrative determinacy, which destines the story to resolve itself in pattern and symmetry, is all the more impressive because it operates on adventures that seem designed to resist it. Emaré cannot steer her boat; it drifts out of her father's control, too; yet the course of her boats is purposeful, for they lead her first to her husband and then to Rome, where father and husband eventually find her again, unsought. The story in this way pays tribute to a creative force more powerful than human will, to a causality that cannot be explained with reference to human agency. It portrays, as St Augustine would have put it, 'an order of causes in which the highest efficiency is attributable to the will of God'.[22]

This different model of causality and agency accounts at least in part for the far greater tolerance of medieval writers and readers for the 'irrelevant' in stories and histories, for incidents and episodes whose meaning and purpose resist explication (Brandt 1966, 47; Vitz 1989, 113). Frank Kermode describes how we moderns tend to approach a narrative:

> First we look for story – events sequentially related (possessing, shall we say, an irreducible minimum of 'connexity'). And sequence goes nowhere without his *Doppelgänger*, or shadow, causality.
>
> (Kermode 1983, 133–4)

A narrative must be a series of incidents connected by more than just temporal contiguity; we expect causal connections, sequence made intelligible. But in *Emaré* sequence goes everywhere without its *Doppelgänger*, causality. What, for example, is the relationship (other than chronological) between Sir Tergaunte's sudden arrival and departure and Artyus's equally sudden desire to see his daughter again? What is the relationship (other than iterative) between Emaré's first and second sea-exiles? Whence the sudden urge of Emaré's husband to do penance for deeds done so long ago? And what explains the coincidence that Emaré's father is overwhelmed by the same urge moments later? The unanswerableness of these questions shows up the desperate shortage of 'connexity', which makes the orderly pattern of repetitions and symmetries at once more baffling and more suggestive of a profound causality that could, if only we understood it, connect this string of coincidences into a perfectly rational whole.

No motif raises the problem of 'connexity' more acutely than the robe. For a story told as tersely as *Emaré* this object takes up a huge amount of space.[23] A hundred lines and more (79–186) are spent telling us that the robe is presented to Artyus by Tergaunte, King of Sicily, who visits him for some inscrutable reason. We are further told that this splendid cloth was made by an emir's daughter, who embellished it with precious stones and with portraits of famous lovers in each corner. Does the robe need this long digression? The only justification is the robe's recurrence at crucial moments of transition in the story. Thus Artyus announces his marriage plans after dressing Emaré in a robe cut from Tergaunte's cloth:

> And when hyt was don her upon,
> She semed non erthely wommon,
> That marked was of molde.

174

> Then seyde the emperour so fre,
> 'Dowghtyr, Y woll wedde the,
> Thow art so fresh to beholde.'
> (244–9)

A description of Emaré in her robe heralds the moment when the King of Galys falls in love with her:

> The cloth upon her shone so bryghth
> When she was theryn ydyghth,
> She semed non erdly thyng.
> (394–6)

The robe further attracts the attention of Sir Kador and Jordan, who wonder about her robe before taking pity on her (349–60; 696–708); it also captures the attention of the wicked mother who, for some reason, takes serious exception to Emaré after seeing her in the robe (439–50).

But while the recurrence of the motif, like the pattern of repetitions in *Emaré* as a whole, suggests some deep significance, the text appears clueless about what this significance might be. If the robe matters because it 'does things', then how and why does it do these things? Critics have understandably jumped into the breach of 'connexity' with interpretations that seek to restore it. Dieter Mehl argues that it symbolizes Emaré's 'inner perfections' (Mehl 1968, 139); Margaret Robson sees it as an expression of Emaré's own desire (Robson 1996), and W. A. Davenport as 'an indirect expression of Emaré's sexual allure' (Davenport 1998, 135). Common to these very different interpretations is the assumption that the robe's lack of inherent meaning must be significant; that we are invited to supply the missing causal connection. Thus all three interpretations translate meaningless sequence into meaningful causality:

> 'Seeing Emaré in her robe, the emperor/king wants to marry her' becomes 'Responding to her virtue/desire/sexual allure, the emperor/king wants to marry her'

> 'Having seen Emaré in her robe, the wicked queen dislikes her' becomes 'Recognizing her virtue/desire/sexual allure, the wicked queen dislikes her'

If stories must be internally persuasive, these readings clearly do good remedial work, but they have difficulty explaining why the poet's own work was so shoddy. For it seems to me that in his story the robe makes things happen, not because it symbolizes something (exactly what critics cannot agree on), but simply because making things happen is what it does.

175

The robe's mysterious agency can be illuminated by considering the function of similar objects in other orally transmitted stories. About one such object, a juniper tree, which is always associated in the folk tale of that name with turning points in the narrative, James Fentress and Chris Wickham write:

> The juniper tree provides a strand of connectedness that runs through
> the entire story . . . [it] is, in fact, less of a symbol than a connecting
> thread in a series of metamorphoses. It is, somehow, the 'cause' of these
> metamorphoses . . . One suspects that the significance of the juniper tree is
> (in part at least) to remind the storyteller not to tell 'Snow White'.
>
> (Fentress and Wickham 1992, 70)

The robe in *Emaré* similarly helps to individuate the heroine and her story, and to facilitate the passage from one episode to another. Like the tree in the folk tale, it does not symbolize immanent forces of causation (*Emaré*'s virtue/desire/sexual allure) but covers for their absence. In oral stories, striking images, images that stick in the mind, stop the gaps in cause and effect. For unlike causality, such objects can be visualized, and hence remembered. In Eric Havelock's words:

> What you cannot visualize is a cause, a principle, a relationship and
> the like . . . To be effectively part of the [oral] record they have to be
> represented . . . and sharply visualized.
>
> (Havelock 1963, 188)

Storytellers relying on memory typically render agency in visualizable form, for the simple reason that a concrete image is more easily remembered and represented than an abstract process of cause and effect. The beautifully symmetrical robe in *Emaré* is memorable in precisely this way: the striking image fills out the voids in the causal chain. Converting meaningless temporal sequence into meaningful spatial form, the robe is a fitting poetic emblem for the whole romance, which similarly monumentalizes the haphazard wanderings of its characters in a timeless symmetry.

But, as I suggested earlier, the reconfiguration of coincidence as design also exudes an assured belief in God's providence, within which the arbitrary must inevitably be more than a trace of orality. To be convinced of God's primary causation is to accept that in stories and histories the only way of answering the question 'why?' may be: 'God only knows'. The robe 'causes' things with the same unanswerableness. Like the theological notion of 'grace', it transforms situations by an unknowable power of determination that is *external* to them, and distinct from the forces that change a situation from within. All symbolic interpretations of the robe share a view of causality that explains change by way of *intrinsic* anterior conditions (Emaré's virtue/desire/sexual allure). The suggestiveness of the robe stems, by contrast, from the irreducible externality of its transformational power.

This same externality also characterizes the strange episode of Sir Tergaunte, who enters the story, deposits the robe, and then departs never to be heard of again. Critics have wisely responded to his interruption in the story by ignoring it altogether. In the plot summary of *Emaré* in the original *Manual of the Writings in Middle English* (Wells 1916–51), Tergaunte's troubles were still thought worth a mention, but they have disappeared from Mortimer Donovan's revised entry in the updated edition:

> As Emaré passes on from childhood her beauty so increases that the Emperor plans to marry her, his own daughter. He has a beautiful robe made for her from a richly embroidered cloth . . .
>
> (Severs 1967)

True, the robe needs some kind of introduction, but clearly it does not need Sir Tergaunte to provide it. Omission is the price that Tergaunte pays for his irrelevance.

Could the Tergaunte episode be a later interpolation in the story of *Emaré*? The robe is given a more coherent history in the fine German analogue, *Der König von Reussen*, in which the incestuous father sets his daughter to work on a costly wedding gown, without telling her who 'the lucky man' will be:

> Ouch liez er sîner tochter machen daz aller kostlîchest gewant, mit edelem gesteine und mit perlen durchleit, unde von golde und von silber. . . . Und dô diu zît kom, daz man die hôchzît wolte haben, dô legte man ir an daz kostlîche gewant. Dô sprach si 'lieber vater, zwiu sol daz kostlîch gewant. Nu weistu doch gar wol, daz ich keinen man nime, er gevalle mir dan gar wol.' Dô sprach der vater, 'ich weiz wol, daz du den gerne nimst, unde gevelt dir wol, unde bist im ouch holt.'
>
> (p. x)

> (Also he had his daughter make the most costly robe, studded with jewels and pearls, and with gold and silver. And when the time came for the wedding, she was dressed in that costly robe. Then she said: 'Beloved father, what is the purpose of this robe? Don't you know that I will have no husband unless he pleases me.' Then the father said: 'I know that you will take him gladly, and he will please you, and you are dear to him, too.')

If *Emaré* once contained a similar history of the robe, the frequent mentions of Emaré's skill in needlework would fall into place. The hypothesis that the episode of Sir Tergaunte is an interpolation, possibly induced by a redactor's memory of romances such as *Apollonius of Tyre* in which the incestuous father is also visited by a guest from abroad,[24] would also explain the fact that the text is demonstrably corrupt in the stanza that tells of Tergaunte's arrival (74–83: the tail-rhyme is defective) and the stanza that tells of his departure (188 is overlong).

However, dismissing the curiously tangential episode as textual corruption does scant justice to the way it deepens the mystery of the robe in a way that internally consistent explanations, such as that offered by *Der König von Reussen*, cannot match. Ask why Sir Tergaunte brings it, and we come up against this text's usual non-answer: God only knows! Explicable at the level of narration (the robe needs to come from somewhere, so the poet invents a stranger who brings it), but inexplicable at the level of the story (what does Tergaunte want?), the account of the robe's foreign provenance contributes to our impression that the robe's full meaning can only be comprehended by a higher-order explanation.

I end with a caveat: words like 'redemptive' or 'grace' are not intended to license interpretations of *Emaré* as a Christian allegory. As one might expect, *Emaré* invokes God at appropriate moments of crisis (for poets these are beginnings and endings), but this romance is self-evidently not *about* God, his church, or its teachings. *Emaré*'s Christianity runs deeper than this; it is, to borrow Vitz's subtle distinction, *structural* rather than *thematic* (Vitz 1989, 213), evident not so much from its *parole* (what it says) as from its *langue* (the deep structures that generate the utterance).

Criticism that turns medieval romance into allegorical stories *about* religion makes medieval literature sound suspiciously like modern Christian discourse, the spirit of which often seems, to my non-believing ears at least, the exact opposite of its medieval counterpart: it is *thematic* rather than *structural*. Criticism of this kind inevitably finds and produces Christianity, not at the heart of medieval stories, but at their surface, where it tends (as when *Emaré* actually talks *about* God) to take the form of pious platitudes. We take the full measure of *Emaré*'s piety only by realizing that its God is, in more senses than one, real rather than symbolic. (In Roland Barthes's terminology, 'reality' in literature is the *effect* produced by signs that cannot be assimilated to any symbolic code [Barthes 1968] – as a senseless detail in a description persuades us that it is 'real' because of its mute 'thereness'.) Just as in modern fiction things pass for 'real' by virtue of their resistance to symbolic elaboration, so in *Emaré* God manifests himself not in symbols or semantic plenitude but in senseless coincidences, in the inexplicable gap between cause and effect, human intentions and outcomes. Attempts to repair the gaps in *Emaré* with Christian doctrine are instructive only to the extent that they mark this fundamental difference between us and the poet:

that while to us God only comes with a good deal of 'saying', in *Emaré* he largely goes without it.

Notes

1 References will be to the recent edition by Anne Laskaya and Eve Salisbury, *The Middle English Breton Lays*, TEAMS (Kalamazoo, MI: Medieval Institute Publications, 1995). *Emaré* was earlier anthologized by A. C. Gibbs in *Middle English Romances* (London: Arnold, 1966), who chose it to illustrate 'the depths of ineptitude to which an English medieval romance could sink' (37).

2 I refer to the 'poet' of *Emaré* for the sake of brevity. As I argue later, the romance is likely to have been memorially transmitted at some point in its textual history, and may therefore be the product of collaborative recomposition.

3 For information about the manuscript see Thompson 1996.

4 Detailed discussion of the various versions can be found in Suchier 1884, xxiii–xcvi. The Incestuous Father story is also closely related to the Constance saga, retold by Chaucer in the *Man of Law's Tale* (Schlauch 1927).

5 *Oeuvres Poétiques de Philippe de Rémi*, ed. Hermann Suchier, 2 vols, SATF (Paris: Firmin Didot, 1884), I. Subsequent references and quotations are drawn from this edition. An English translation is available in *Philippe de Rémi's 'La Manekine': Text, Translation, Commentary*, ed. and trans. I. Gnarra (New York: Garland, 1988).

6 Ed. in *Mai und Beaflor* (Leipzig: Göschensche Verlagshandlung, 1848), ix–xv.

7 On the common characteristics of orally transmitted stories see Rubin 1995.

8 Editors have identified 'Galys' as Wales or Galicia. Another plausible identification is Galloway in Scotland (the daughter's destination in many of the analogues), which is not uncommonly referred to as 'Galles'. See Jean Froissart, *Chronicles*, trans. Geoffrey Brereton (Harmondsworth: Penguin, 1968), p. 355n. As George Ellis suggested, the country of 'Galias' in *Eger and Grime* (H-L, 2277–8) probably also refers to 'Galloway' (Ellis 1805).

9 Todorov 1969. I acknowledge a major debt to Vitz's narratological readings of medieval narratives, especially to her superb chapter on *La fille du comte de Pontieu*. See Vitz 1989, 96–125.

10 A formula is 'a group of words regularly employed under the same metrical conditions to express a given essential idea' (Parry 1971, 272). Thus the formula for 'beautiful' in *Emaré*, and many other romances, consists of an adjective of praise + 'under' + an alliterating word that designates a garment: 'worthy unthur wede', 'goodly unthur gore', 'comely unthur kelle', etc.

11 Suggestive comments on the structure of *Emaré* can be found in Mills 1973, xiv–xv.

12 For an attempt to pursue this line of interpretation with reference to an analogue of *Emaré*, Chaucer's *Man of Law's Tale*, see Dinshaw 1989, 88–112.

13 I am thinking of narratives like *Apollonius of Tyre* or Shakespeare's *Pericles* (on which see Archibald 1991), in which the hero discovers that the woman he wishes to marry is involved in an incestuous relationship with her father. Following the discovery the hero sets sail empty-handed, to pursue further (unrelated) adventures. *Apollonius* is the kind of story we would get if *Emaré* were told from Sir Tergaunte's perspective.

14 The Latin phrase ('trickery to foil trickery') is from Venantius Fortunatus's hymn *Pange Lingua*, the *locus classicus* for medieval reflections on the 'poetic justice' of the redemption.

15 As Helen Cooper has suggested to me, the systematic pursuit of poetic justification in medieval treatments of the redemption is as likely to be inspired by the structure of romance as the other way around.

16 Take for example the three Exchanges of Winnings in *Sir Gawain and the Green Knight*, in which the third also deliberately breaks the pattern set up by the first and the second. As noted by Davis 1985, 28–9, such trebling is often encountered in orally transmitted narratives.

17 I refer to the Arden edition by J. H. Pafford (London: Routledge, 1963), which also prints the text of Greene's *Pandosto*.

18 Editors of *Emaré* helpfully gloss this idiomatic usage of 'body' as 'person' (*MED* 6a), but the primary sense 'body, corpse' seems, again deliberately, to brood over the father's words. After all, what does the father see in the 'person' of Segramour if not the 'body' of his lost son?

19 See Rickert 1908, xxix, for a discussion of the name 'Emaré'. On the name 'Egaré' see Simpson above, p. 124.

20 This (false) etymological explanation of the name 'Manekine' is spelt out by the husband in Jean Wauquelin's fourteenth-century prose adaptation of *Manekine*, ed. Suchier, *Oeuvres Poétiques*, I, p. 300: '*mancus* c'est à dire homme qui n'a que une main et par ce je vos mech a non *Manca*, qui sera à lire en Rommant Manequine' ('*mancus* is to say a man with only one hand, and so I called you *Manca*, which in French is to be written as Manequine').

21 This is why in romances (e.g. Chrétien de Troyes's *Yvain*) the loss of the protagonist's name often coincides with madness, the loss of self.

22 I translate from Augustine, *De Civitate Dei*, ed. E. Huffman, Corpus Christianorum Series Latina 40 (Turnhout: Brepols, 1954–), V, 9.

23 Cf. Donovan 1974, 338, who writes of the robe: 'there seems to be a problem of proportion, to say the least'. Donovan briefly compares the robe with symbolic objects in other lays.

24 See n. 13.

CHAPTER EIGHT

The Seege of Troye: 'ffor wham was wakened al this wo'?

NICOLA F. MCDONALD

Critics have not been kind to *The Seege of Troye*.[1] J. S. P. Tatlock's enthusiastic review of M. E. Barnicle's 1927 parallel-text edition marks a high point in the poem's critical reception, but his assessment, echoing the sentiments of Thomas Warton,[2] could hardly have done more to deflect the attention of the serious medievalist. Tatlock brands the *Seege* 'a capital example of a minstrel romance' and judges the 'jolly good fights' which punctuate the narrative incontrovertible evidence for its popularity among 'light-thinking and heavy-hitting Englishmen' (Tatlock 1929, 74). Aside from a series of source-study articles by the Stanford scholar E. Bagby Atwood – whose opinion of the poem is best summarized by his reference to its 'simple-minded author' (Atwood 1938a, 125) – the *Seege* was ignored until 1965 when Derek Pearsall, in a landmark attempt to construct 'a historical morphology of romance' (Pearsall 1965, 95), rang its death knell. Identified as a post-1320,[3] second-phase composition, the *Seege* was doomed to inhabit a literary 'backwash' distinguished by 'third-rate fumbling in an enfeebled tradition' (Pearsall 1965, 104). Subsequent criticism has done little to enhance the poem's reputation and the dominant tone has been set by the likes of Dieter Mehl and C. David Benson, both of whom make passing reference to the *Seege* only to dismiss it from further consideration. Benson's judgement is typical: 'The *Seege or Batayle* might be entertainment for the common folk, but its crude unlearned approach disqualified it from claiming the attention of any serious audience' (Benson 1980, 134).

What Benson means by a serious audience needs, however, to be examined. The assumption which underlies all twentieth-century criticism of *The Seege of Troye* is that it was intended for a 'popular audience with little learning and less time' (Barron 1987, 118). Professional medievalists, today's serious audience for most medieval literature, find that the *Seege* runs counter to their aesthetic predispositions and thus postulate that it could not have sustained the interest of a similarly serious medieval audience. Unable to validate their own aesthetic imperatives, scholars create, *ex nihilo*, the image of an audience which, solely because it is an audience for the *Seege*, is the antithesis of the well-schooled academic. Adjectives of opprobrium highlight the distinguishing features of the putative medieval auditor: the vulgar, ignorant, brutish peasant. Yet, curiously, none of the vigour associated with the peasant's crude enjoyment of the energetic narrative is allowed to vitiate the critic's assessment of the poet as an intellectually emasculated *rédacteur*. Extant evidence for the audience of Middle English romance is notoriously inadequate, and, for a text like the *Seege*, which is poised at the intersection of the oral and written traditions,[4] the case is more complicated still. But one thing is certain: from the late fourteenth to the mid-fifteenth centuries the poem excited sufficient attention to have survived in four medieval copies. The *Seege* is the earliest Middle English treatment of the Trojan War, and, as its manuscripts attest, it enjoyed the attention of a diverse audience eager to exploit its generic fluidity.[5] No less than any other Middle English popular romance, it both deserves and rewards the attention of contemporary readers.

The purpose of this essay is to reopen critical debate on *The Seege of Troye*. When Nicholas Birns outlined the 'unintentional quasi-veracity' of medieval Britain's originary myth (Birns 1993, 54), he was referring to the archaeological discoveries which suggest that the linguistic and cultural genealogy of the West lies in the East, that the historical Trojans were closely related to our primal ancestors, the Indo-European Hittites. Other archaeological finds have profoundly influenced our understanding of the historicity of this originary battle. Since Montesquieu,[6] at least, Western commentators have urged that the mythic adventures of the Greek and Trojan heroes are elaborate fictions designed to mask the commercial heart of an imperialist desire to control the trade routes that link Europe to Asia.[7] The mythic battle over the possession of one beautiful woman is historically, the archaeologists tell us, a trade war, with the prosaic 'commodity' taking the place of the more inviting 'woman'. Although she does not mention the Trojan example, Gayle Rubin's attack on Levi-Strauss's glamorization of the exchange of women becomes an appropriate epigram for the pervasive myth: 'one of the greatest rip-offs of all time [is] the root of romance' (Rubin 1975, 201). More than any other medieval version of the story, *The Seege of Troye*, with its bald narrative and starkly formulaic compositional structure, validates a feminist figuration of the Trojan myth as a glorification of male hegemony expressed in terms of the power to exchange women. But the *Seege* goes one step further still: with remarkable clairvoyance, it exhibits an unintentional quasi-veracity of its own. Despite the prominence of women in the story, the *Seege* makes clear that the enterprising knight's real interest lies in the commodities (precious physical objects including, but by no means limited to, women) which he is able to gain by means of his extravagant adventures abroad. Scholars such as David Aers (1988) and Stephen Knight (1986a) have argued that romance is all about the concealment of male acquisitive aggression under the pleasing fiction of a knight's erotic pursuit of a lady. What is so remarkable about the *Seege*, however, is that the fiction is all but gone; the knight's desire to possess precious objects controls the narrative trajectory and the women who are collected along the way are barely visible beneath their glittering regalia.

Unlike other Middle English histories of Troy (the *Laud Troy Book*, the *Destruction of Troy* or Lydgate's *Troy Book*), the *Seege* is not a translation, or bowdlerization, of Guido delle Colonne's *Historia Destructionis Troiae*. It seems rather to be a fluid amalgam of Dares, Benoît and a version of the *Compendium Historiae Troianae-Romanae* or a schoolboy's Latin chronicle akin to the Rawlinson *Excidium Troiae* (perhaps the 'bokes of gramer' identified in the Harley version of the poem, H1791*p*). The poet has selected his material carefully, preserving a sense of the amplitude of Trojan history (the city's first and second destructions) while condensing and streamlining the twists and turns of a capacious plot. Extraneous detail is eliminated and the remaining material is compressed into a highly wrought and at times obtrusive structure. Two structuring devices, using the related motifs of battle and round-trip sea voyage, work simultaneously to propel the events towards a predetermined conclusion.

The linear motif of serial battles is initially signposted by reference to Dares who 'dude write hit ilke a bataile' (L18) and is followed through by counting out the battles one by one: 'Theo forme bataile this thenne was' (L195); 'Thus con ende theo secounde bataile' (L816); and so on, conveniently rounding off with 'Thus endith theo tenthe bataile' (L1851).[8] The enumerative process is a particularly conspicuous form of narrative punctuation and it is made even more so by the almost uniform addition of a prefatory address to the audience, 'lordyngis saun faile'. Less relentless, but equally fixed, is the underlying diptych structure into which is woven the cyclical motif of the round-trip sea voyage. The poem divides neatly into two parts (marked at A980: 'Her ys the haluyndell of our geste') and hinges on a highly formulaic, numerically precise account of the mobilization of the Greek navy in which the themes of battle and sea journey are united. Various pairings and doublets, highlighted by close verbal repetition, reinforce the binary nature of the diptych. The parallel portraits of Paris and Achilles – fair-unknown-style youth, revelatory experience which determines fitness for battle, love-longing for and fatal pursuit of a foreign woman – provide ballast (Paris dominates the first half, Achilles the second) and allow the poet to apportion the elaborated, and sometimes decorative, romance material evenly. Diptych narratives have a tendency to fold in on themselves, to find their end in their beginning,[9] and it is this predisposition for closure that is confirmed by the circular nature of the round-trip sea voyage. The action of the first half of the *Seege* is wholly subsumed in the continuous toing and froing of four such voyages, two Greek, two Trojan, while the action of the second half (eight of the ten battles) is framed by one outward journey and one return. The predetermined quality of the poem's linear narrative, signalled by the lines:

> Men of grece heolden gret bataile
> With the kyng of troye stout and grym
> And at theo laste they ouercome him
> (L12–14)

is compounded by the inexorable cyclic logic of the round-trip voyage – whatever goes out must come back.

The plot can be summarized as follows: Jason and the Argonauts sail to Troy in quest of the golden fleece;[10] the Trojan king Laomedon rebuffs them and they return to Greece offended and empty-handed. A second expedition is undertaken. The Greeks destroy Troy (battle number one), abduct Laomedon's daughter Hesione along with the golden fleece, and then return home to celebrate their victory. Priam goes to Troy, taking with him his three sons, Hector, Troilus, and Paris (who has been raised incognito as a swineherd); he rebuilds the city and sends a party of Trojans to Greece to demand Hesione's return. The Trojans are rebuffed and return home offended and empty-handed. The Trojans resolve to launch a military attack on the Greeks, and Paris, recounting his dream-like judgment of 'ffoure ladies of eluene land' (L508),[11] offers himself as the expedition's leader. Paris assaults Menelaus's citadel and abducts Helen (battle number two); the Trojans return home and celebrate their victory with Paris's marriage to Helen. Menelaus assembles an enormous Greek navy, sails to Troy and the siege begins. An initial Greek attack (battle number three) is matched by a Trojan retaliation (battle number four) and is followed by Hector's emergence as a peerless champion (battle number five). The Greeks, daunted by their indefatigable opponent, send for Achilles, who is found, disguised as a girl, in the court of Lycomedes. His true identity is revealed, and Achilles hastens to Troy; he enters the fray and demonstrates his prowess (battle number six). Hector and Achilles then meet face-to-face. Sorely wounded, Hector retreats, is distracted by a precious jewelled helmet, and is killed by Achilles as he attempts to retrieve it (battle number seven). Achilles visits Hector's grave, catches sight of Polyxena and falls in love; he offers Priam peace in exchange for the girl but is unable to gain Menelaus's consent; Achilles refuses to fight but is then persuaded to return to battle and kills Troilus (battle number eight). Tricked by Hecuba's duplicitous offer of marriage to Polyxena, Achilles enters the Trojan temple and is killed by Paris and his warriors (battle number nine). Enraged, the Greeks kill Paris (battle number ten). Priam attempts to rally the remaining Trojans while Antenor and Aeneas strike a deal with the Greeks to betray the city. The Greeks enter Troy freely and slay the remaining citizens, including Priam, Hecuba and Polyxena. Menelaus and Helen are reunited; the Greeks loot Troy and return home to celebrate their victory.

Three of the round-trip sea voyages which control the narrative's ebb and flow conclude with a celebration of victory; two do not. What constitutes victory in this romance, and thus what merits celebration, is the knight's successful completion of his quest, a triumph effected by his acquisition of the desired trophy. On the other hand, the knight's empty-handed return home marks his failure. There is nothing remarkable about this formulation of victory (or failure) or about the quest structure itself (except perhaps that there are so many quests); it is the stuff of romance. What is unusual, however, is the way in which the poem brashly formulates our understanding of the precise nature of the quest. The *Seege* begins, as romances do, with the promise of 'anturis' (L3) or 'aventures' (A3), the perilous journeys and encounters which are the very essence of the romance experience. *Aventure* signals generic identity for both the narrative and the protagonist. It is simultaneously the characteristic form of romance activity and the means by which the knight is able to achieve self-realization. When Auerbach writes that 'the very essence of the knight's ideal of manhood is called forth by adventure' (Auerbach 1953, 135), he acknowledges the absolute centrality of *aventure* to that narrative construct that we call the knight; by means of the adventure, the knight defines himself as both knight and man. The *aventure* is thus a crucial narrative determinant. It controls the man-knight's development and conditions his experience, and thereby shapes the 'meaning' of the romance.

The *Seege* opens quickly with a concise account of its initial *aventure*, the first round-trip sea voyage. That first event (a knight is sent to a distant land in pursuit of a marvel and returns home) functions effectively as an epitome of what will follow. A certain narrative economy is evident in the painstaking outline of the requisite features of, and rationale behind, round-trip sea voyage number one. As with many good stories, the audience is immediately thrust into the narrative's defining event and is provided with what seems to be an interpretive template, to be reapplied as necessary. Jason, a young knight conveniently endowed with all of the qualities necessary for heroic action ('corteis and hende, hardy and bold', L31), is dispatched by a

senior nobleman, his uncle Peleus, to win Troy's coveted treasure, a golden
sheep's skin; he sails to Troy with an army of celebrated warriors, fails to
win the fleece and returns home, 'ouer theo flod' (L94), disappointed. What
is most striking about this introductory event is the way in which Peleus sets
the parameters of the quest:

> 'Me is don,' he saide, 'to vndurstonde
> That the kyng of troie hath in his londe
> Theo koyntiste thyng aboue molde,
> That is, a schepis skyn of golde.
> Myghtest thou with thy coyntiste gyn
> And from heom that skyn wyn
> And brynge to me that skyn of gold,
> Thy trauaile qwyte the y wolde.'
>
> (L35–42)

In each of the four versions, Peleus's proposal, which conveniently sums up
what the quest means for Jason, is almost identical, except for the last line.
The details of how the young knight will be recompensed vary slightly from
version to version, but the variation is instructive. It illuminates exactly
what self-defining reward he can hope to gain through his *aventure*. L and E
agree that Jason will be recompensed for his 'travaile': 'Thy trauaile quyte
the [y] welde' (E42). The *MED* records the primary sense of 'travail' as
'hard physical labour, toil', in particular that associated with an assigned
job or daily work. 'Travail' can also be used to describe a 'feat of strength
or arms' or figuratively a 'knightly competition', and it is possible that the
poet may have intended one of these latter meanings. Yet the choice of lexis
in H ('Thy whyle shuld bene well I-yold', H42), with its emphasis on paying
Jason for his time ('whyle'), suggests that the promised recompense is closer
to the idea of wages in exchange for labour. Simple reciprocity is similarly
implied in A ('y schuld the avance wyth-oute any fayle', A42), where Peleus's
offer of an 'avance' characterizes the adventure as a socially expedient
endeavour for an upwardly mobile young man. Totally devoid of any sentiment of honour or hope of ethical achievement, this *aventure* is explicitly constructed as an economically driven enterprise. Peleus's naked self-interest
(his desire for a valuable commodity) prompts the quest; he engages the ser-
vices of a skilled labourer and offers him a decent wage as well as possible
social perks. Jason, no longer the inherently noble idealist, is reduced to a
simple mercenary. It is perhaps not too much of a simplification to suggest
that for the knights of the *Seege* the concept of adventure, as it is constructed
in this initial quest, is defined as a dangerous enterprise in pursuit of valuable merchandise.

The depiction of the *aventure* as a physical risk for material gain and of the knightly adventurer as something akin to a merchant voyager is reminiscent of Michael Nerlich's formulation of capitalist commerce as 'the most dynamic adventuresome activity' (Nerlich 1987, I, xx). In *Ideology of Adventure*, Nerlich asserts that the knights of medieval romance are the direct ancestors of capitalism's adventuring merchants. He argues not only that the medieval quest ethos is an idealization of acquisitive aggression, but that the very language of adventure, the vocabulary used in romance to describe the quest, is imbued with distinctly commercial significance. Nerlich cites evidence from as early as the thirteenth century to demonstrate that the term *aventure* was used to designate, among other things, 'output, earnings, income' and 'catch, booty, or harvest' (Nerlich 1987, I, 51–2), and he contends, along with economic historian E. M. Carus-Wilson, that the adoption in the fifteenth century of the name Merchant Adventurers by English merchants engaged in especially risky long-distance trade merely formalized the already common valence of the term (Carus-Wilson 1967, xv–xvi). The depiction of the knight in *The Seege of Troye* as just such an adventurer is signalled by the blatantly acquisitive dynamic of the initial *aventure*, and it is further underscored in the account of Hector's death.

Conventionally, Hector is killed by Achilles when he attempts to despoil a Greek warrior he has just slain. H preserves a version of the story that is closest to the sources: Hector decapitates a certain Sir Annys and while stooping to remove his victim's jewelled helmet is stabbed by Achilles. In LEA, however, the narrative is more familiarly stark and the detail of Hector's slaying of the Greek is omitted. Fleeing Achilles's assault, Hector espies a richly decorated treasure lying unclaimed on the field (in LE a helmet, in A a shield) and is killed as he attempts to seize it. The passage reads as follows:

> As Ector prikede apon his way,
> He sawgh an helm ther hit lay
> That was riche, for the nones,
> Al by-set with preciouse stones,
> And loth him was theo helm for-go.
> ffor-thy he loste worth the too;
> He loste his lyf for theo helmes sake;
> ffor Ector in Troye gret sorwe they makith.
> Ector to theo helm rod ryght –
> Ther-thorough dyede that doughty knyght.
> And leonede ouer his stedis mane
> Theo riche helm vp to tane;
> Achilles com rydyng verrement
> And smot him yn at the fondement

And to theo heorte smot him ryght;
And endith that doughty knyght.

(L1487–502)

Hector's victorious despoliation of a defeated enemy is here transformed into an act of sheer greed. His rapacity, stripped of all martial justification, is acquisitive desire at its most elemental. Like Peleus, Hector covets a precious physical object, and his struggle to possess it is marked off by the conventional phraseology of romance adventure. In this brief interlude, the formulaic opening ('Ector prikede apon his way') is brought to a rapid, and equally familiar, close ('And endith that doughty knyght'), while the essence of the *aventure* is contained in the line 'He loste his lyf for theo helmes sake'.[12]

These adventures, as Hector's death makes clear, are risky exploits designed to secure possession of treasures whose value is symbolized by their luminescence: the fleece, 'schyny[n]g ryght as golde' (A38), mirrors Sir Annys's precious jewel-studded war garb 'that shone as gold and Asure' (H1443*t*). In keeping with the rest of his unelaborated narrative, the poet provides only a perfunctory description of these prized commodities, but it is not insignificant that he represents them as a simple amalgam of precious metals and undifferentiated gemstones. The merest invocation of these basic ingredients, the starting point of all conventional treasure, is sufficient to convey the economic value of the desired object. The poet shows no interest whatsoever in sumptuous or decorative detail or any other by-product of sophisticated craftsmanship. The catalogue of the treasure's elemental composition is embellished, if at all, only by a passing reference to the way in which the metal or stone is able to catch and reflect light. This, as a fundamental quality of physical purity, is, crucially, reflective of economic value.

If, as Auerbach and others have argued, the *aventure* provides the structural foundation of medieval romance (determines events and orders their sequence) and defines the knight's experience both of the world and of himself, then there is little doubt that the dynamics of the mercantile venture and the ethos of appropriation are fundamental to the shape and meaning of the *Seege*. Yet, while the Argonautic expedition is the originary adventure (in terms of the *Seege*'s narrative trajectory and pseudo-historically),[13] and thus casts its long shadow over subsequent adventure-quests, not all of the poem's adventures claim gilded sheep or costly helmets as their prizes. Aside from the first two round-trip sea voyages (failure followed by success) and Hector's rash escapade, the *Seege*'s adventures are never quite so simply focused on the acquisition of precious, inanimate objects. When the Argonauts finally defeat Laomedon and capture the golden fleece, they greedily pillage Troy, taking from among its riches random treasures, armour and the king's daughter Hesione. The abduction of Hesione is traditionally an afterthought, a simple way of further humiliating the defeated Trojans. In the *Seege*, however, Hesione's abduction so takes over the narrative foreground that the woman quickly overshadows the fleece as the most prominent, if not most prized, symbol of the Greek victory:

> Ercules and his felawes alle
> Wenten and robboden that riche cite;
> Of mon no wommon they nade pite.
> The kyng of troye nade doughter bote an,
> And heo was hote dame vsian.
> When heo herde hire fadir was brought of lyf,
> Heo wente and hudde hire swithe;
> And Hercules was so stout,
> fful hastely he fond hire out
> And ladde hire to schip in hy;
> No wondur thaugh heo weore sory.
> Heo hadde sorwe and mukil thought,
> ffor hire fadir was to dethe brought,
> Hire threo bretheren and al hire kyn;
> Gret was the sorwe that heo was yn.
> Ercules wan the skyn al-so,
> ffor wham was wakened al this wo.
> They token tresour, armure al-so
> And duden heom in haste to schip go.
>   (L172–90)

In their moment of triumph, the fleece-hungry Greeks are transformed into undiscriminating marauders who pitilessly ravage the defeated city. The defining heroic event is not the seizure of Troy's famed and precious fleece, but Hercules' forceful abduction of a distraught, weeping woman. Hesione is the first in a series of women in the *Seege* whom men seize or otherwise attempt to appropriate. Significantly, she is never the subject of any erotic interest. No mystification of violence is needed to camouflage Hercules' predatory motivation. The virtue of the *Seege*'s bald narrative is that, for the most part, it tells things as they are. Hesione's abduction is a demonstration of physical dominance and political dominion, and the woman comes to stand for all that the Trojans have lost. The substitution of Hesione for the fleece is made complete when Priam's new Trojan parliament meets to determine what compensation will be required of the Greeks. Itemizing their losses (dead kinsmen and stolen goods), the counsellors ask only that Hesione, Priam's 'suster bryght' (L371), be returned.

In structural terms, the *Seege* has a fairly rigid grammar or syntax. The primary units of composition, the ten battles and five round-trip sea voyages, inflexibly control a sequence of causally related events. Once the system of narrative consequences is initiated (by Peleus's expression of desire for a rich foreign treasure), the romance's inexorable structural logic pushes the recapitulatory plot forward to its final resolution. Within this system, however, there are some compositional units which do allow for limited variation. These might be described as the units of incident, rather than of the macro-plot structure. For instance, although battles one to ten are predetermined events, the individual warriors who participate in them vary from fight to fight. Similarly, while each round-trip sea voyage is predicated on the pursuit of an object of value, a war trophy of sorts, the precise nature of that trophy is liable to change. These units of incident are flexible enough to allow one unit to be freely substituted for another, so long as the substituted unit is what structuralists would call homologous, that is, having a similar or analogous functional role.[14] The individual warriors (Hercules or Achilles, Paris or Hector) can, with reasonable freedom, be substituted one for the other in the various battle scenes because the function of each, as a man who fights against an enemy, is the same; the only limit to flexibility is that there must always be at least one Greek fighting one Trojan.

The functional roles of Hesione and the golden fleece are likewise the same. They are variant units of incident which operate in structurally identical ways within the macro-plot. In the guise of desiderata, Hesione and the fleece share narrative responsibility for the initiation of adventure. The fact that, in the conclusion to and aftermath of the first successful quest, the fleece can be effortlessly replaced by Hesione not only demonstrates this homology, but suggests that there are correspondences between the desiderata that go beyond the simple requirements of structural substitution. The exchange of a woman for a fleece seems to be occasioned by a shift in the nature of what men want. However, the absence of any expression of redefined desire (or of surprise that the Greeks and then Trojans want Hesione and not the fleece) implies that, in terms of the self-reflexive logic of the romance, the men's desire stays the same and the substitution goes virtually unnoticed. The *Seege*'s first adventure (comprising two round-trip sea voyages) begins as an expedition to appropriate the king of Troy's single most valuable treasure ('A wonder thyng that he loveth wele', H37); it is an opportunity for a young knight (Jason) to prove himself in predatory *aventure*. The expedition concludes with Hercules' successful (and, one might argue, self-defining) abduction of the king of Troy's only daughter (as well as, parenthetically, the fleece). The seamless substitution of Hercules for Jason as the heroic quester simply underscores the congruence of Hesione and the fleece as objects of appropriation.

The sequential substitution of one desideratum for another punctuates the narrative of the *Seege*. Five round-trip sea voyages are undertaken in quest of three objects of value. While it helps to provide the incident variation necessary to invigorate the repetitive plot, the substitution system can work effectively only if the substitution value of the various desiderata is the same. This implies that the golden fleece, Hesione, and Helen are structurally identical and share a number of correspondences in form and content. The yoking of the two women and the fleece as structural equivalents, all equally indispensable as initiators of *aventure*, runs counter, however, to conventional medieval (and modern) assumptions which follow Jerome, among others, in privileging Helen as the pre-eminent, if not the sole, cause of the Trojan war: 'on account of the rape of one foolish woman Europe and Asia are involved in a ten years' war'.[15] But *The Seege of Troye* is a remarkably self-contained romance. As is typical of Middle English popular romance, the poem constructs for itself a set of logical and self-justifying imperatives, the validation of which is strictly internal and predicated on values encoded in the text (Fewster 1987, 1–38). In the *Seege*, Helen, like the fleece and Hesione, is merely one in a sequence of things that questing men want; she exhibits few, if any, characteristics which distinguish her from other treasured commodities.

The substitution of Helen for Hesione as the next in a series of desiderata occurs after the Trojans' first unsuccessful attempt to secure the return of Priam's sister. The Trojan warriors reconvene to decide who is to lead the second expedition (round-trip sea voyage number four). Hector volunteers to 'stoutly brynge hom' Hesione 'theo pris' (L448), but Paris interjects. A marvellous interlude in the forest with 'ffoure ladies of eluene land' (L508) has convinced him of his own fitness for the quest. Priam's challenge 'on what maner hopest thou spede' (L480) prompts him to recount the judgment scene which concludes with Venus's promise:

> 'Bide thy fadir, as he is kyng hende,
> Graunte the to grece to wende,
> ffor nothyng schaltow ther drede;
> fful wel schaltow ther spede.
> Theo faireste lady that beorith lyf
> Thou schalt welde to thy wif.'
> (L609–14)

Hector's shrewd assessment of the danger of the expedition intimates that 'theo faireste lady that beorith lyf' has supplanted Hesione as the 'pris' of the proposed voyage:

> '. . . yf sir Alisaunder Parys
> Wende to Grece to wynne the prys
> And wynneth there through maistry
> Suche a ryall lauedy,
> The folk of Grece nyl dwell no stound
> Tyl that Troye be brought to ground.'
>
>   (E621–6)

Further confirmation of Helen's substitution for Hesione (who, like the fleece before her, disappears from the narrative after successfully initiating the *aventure*) is offered at the conclusion of Paris's successful voyage when the victor, in response to Priam's question 'how hastow sped' (L775), enumerates:

> 'The qwene y haue whyt so flour
> With alle theo maydenes of hire bour;
> Theo gold, theo seoluer, gret and smal,
> And the tresour of that contre al.'
>
>   (L781–4)

Success is here, as elsewhere, defined by the achievement of a desired 'pris', but the identity of the 'pris' is by no means stable. Just as Hesione fuses with and then takes the place of the fleece, so Helen, by a series of tiny verbal readjustments, merges with and then supplants Hesione as the object of the adventure. In many ways Helen is indistinguishable from Hesione. The scene of her abduction purposefully echoes the earlier one:

> And alisaunder tho the qwene nam
> And tok theo qwene in hire wede
> And sette hire by-fore him on his stede;
> Theo qwene grette and made gret cry
> And [he] ladde hire forth to schip in hy . . .
>
>   (L760–64)

And, like Hercules', Paris's achievement is one of physical dominance and political dominion: 'he tok her in-to hys powere' (A761).

Although Helen, unlike Hesione, is an eroticized figure, and both Paris and Helen experience perfunctory bouts of love-longing, there is little doubt that the erotic impulse is subordinate to the desire for 'theo maystry' (L473). In romance, the knight's quest for love is commonly expressed in terms of his ability to subjugate physically the obstacles that separate him from the object of his desire. In the *Seege*, however, the act of subjugation not only dominates the narrative but explicitly becomes, mediated through the figure of a woman, the object of desire itself. In its rather curiously reworked version of the Judgment of Paris,[16] Priam's youngest son is enjoined to arbitrate a dispute between four elf-queens, Saturn, Mercury, Jupiter and Venus. The women have found a golden ball which proclaims itself to be the property of the 'faireste wommon of al' (L519). Unable to decide who is the most beautiful among them, they elicit Paris's help. The passage begins as one of the most elaborate romance scenes in the poem with an engaging description of Paris's foray into the forest, his falling asleep under a tree, and the appearance of the four elf-women. When the group settles down to debate ownership of the golden ball, however, the tone and structure of the passage changes completely. Suddenly, alert to the governing ethos of com- mercial exchange, the ladies are transformed into astute businesswomen, each intent on winning Paris's favour by the promise of a profitable reward. Paris admits that the women are equally beautiful and so bases his judg- ment solely on the self-interest value of the proposed rewards.[17] He rejects the offers of Saturn ('richesse', L557), Mercury ('streynthe and myght', L567) and Jupiter ('bewte', L583) because he judges himself sufficiently wealthy, strong, and beautiful for his requirements. Venus, however, offers something more lucrative:

> 'Knyght, yef me theo bal for thy cortesy
> And thou schalt haue loue and wolde,
>
> . . . .
>
> Alle wymmen schole beo in thy pouste
> And alle schole they loue the.'
> (L590–98)

The allure of power combined with that of love, and expressed in terms of the ability to control women, proves irresistible and Paris 'hastely' (L601) gives the ball to Venus. Paris first reveals his fitness for knightly adventure as a child when he assumes the role of adjudicator at bull fights, crowning each winner with a victory garland (L281–8). His innate fitness comes to maturity when he assumes the predatory role himself and seeks to express his physical dominance by abducting a weeping, resistant woman.

Paris's part in the *Seege* is complemented structurally by that of Achilles; together the men form the paired halves of the narrative diptych. Just as Paris pursues Helen, so Achilles seeks to gain possession of Polyxena. The details of Achilles's attempt to secure the Trojan princess provide an inter- esting commentary on the process of desiderata substitution and reinforce our apprehension of Helen as little more than a convenient outlet for the appropriative impulse that, as Nerlich insists, is endemic to the desire for chivalric 'maystry'. Achilles espies Polyxena, much as Hector did the jewelled helmet, attractively decked out in precious metal at the side of the battle-field; here, weeping, she pays her respects at the tomb of her dead brother. Achilles immediately delineates a simple plan of exchange whereby he hopes to win Polyxena. Imagining the women as a coinage of sorts, he envisages that his receipt of Polyxena will balance the Greeks' loss of Helen. By paying their debt, the Trojans can secure peace:

> . . . for a wommon this weorre was waked,
> And for a womman pes schal beo maked.
> ffor Dame Elayne, the qwene of grece,
> Mony men han beon hewen to peces;
> Yef me his doughter; yef he wol swa,
> Schal beo mad pes for euer-ma.
>
> (L1543–8)

In Achilles's mind at least, the substitution value of Helen and Polyxena is identical.[18] His formulation of the exchange equation, an anaphoric couplet with parallel syntactic structure ('for a wommon this weorre was waked, / And for a womman pes schal beo maked'), makes explicit what has been implied elsewhere: in structural terms, one woman is exactly like another. But it is not only women who are implicated in this ultimately formulaic equation. When, at the end of all their journeying, the Greeks finally return home, the narrator offers a recapitulatory glance back to the beginning of the poem. Helen is again identified as a figure of initiation: 'And dame Elayne, his gode wyf, / ffor hire was wakened mukil stryf' (L2048–9). By the end of the poem, Helen has replaced the golden fleece as the object of risky *aventure*, but the very language in which her initiatory function is proclaimed identifies her coincidence with that costly treasure: 'Ercules wan the skyn al-so / ffor wham was wakened al this wo' (L187–8).

The relationship between women and treasure, however, is not simply one of formal equivalence. As the example of Polyxena demonstrates, there is a distinct tendency for the one to merge imperceptibly into the other. When Achilles first catches sight of Polyxena, he sees a woman clothed in gold and silver:

> Achilles stod and by-huld ryght,
> Theo maiden that was fair and bryght –
> How heo was dyght in seoluer and gold –
> And thoughte theo faireste may on molde
> And by-gan to loue theo maide so
> That nygh his heorte barst atwo.
>
> (L1531–6)

The syntax implies that Achilles's love is inspired as much by Polyxena's metallic radiance as by her womanly beauty; he notes both that she is 'fair and bryght' and 'how heo was dyght in seoluer and gold'. Indeed, the affiliation between 'bryght' Polyxena and her precious attire implies that her beauty is consonant with the shine of the costly metal that adorns her. The description of women in Middle English romance is often conventional in the extreme. A small number of formulaic tags are used over and over again. While the range of tag variation is traditionally attributed to the poem's metrical demands, some scholars have pointed to the 'associative value of romance formulae' (Fewster 1987, 12). David Aers, for instance, outlines the implication of the traditional association of women and flower imagery: 'Plucked flowers do not speak, let alone answer back and walk away' (Aers 1988, 127). The limited range of descriptive terms found in the *Seege* sets the poem firmly in the mould of conventional romance. Both men and women are uniformly 'curtays', 'freo', 'fair', 'gentyl' and 'noble', but some terms are gender-specific. Only women are described as 'bryght' or 'schene'; only women, that is, and treasure.[19] In the *Seege*, conventional imagery is enlivened by the analogy that is drawn between precious metals, gemstones and other treasured commodities (for instance, costly armour) and the various desired or abducted women. The repeated descriptions of Helen as 'bothe bryght and schene' (L672) and Polyxena as 'bryght and schene' (L2017) function as a kind of shorthand for the women's economic value. Like the golden fleece and Sir Annys's precious helmet, the women are identified as worthy objects of appropriation on account of their ability to catch and reflect light. The description in A of Achilles's first sighting of Polyxena notably omits the reference to her costly garb, but the recrafted passage highlights the efficacy of the conventional descriptive terminology:

> Apon a day he com [and] seye
> Wer that ector y-bured did lye;
> And by hym stod hys suster bryght,
> Pollexna that mayde bryght.
> . . . .
>
> Achilles then by-hul[d] ful ryght
> That damsel that was so bryght.
> Hys loue lyght on her tho;
> Hym thoughth hys hert brek ato.
> (A1525–36)

Polyxena's distinctive brightness convinces Achilles, literally dazzled, that the woman is worthy of appropriation. Bright women who shine, like costly treasures, incite the adventure-lust of ambitious men. They initiate the romance's distinctive activity and lead the knights to self-realization. Whether successful or not, the knights of the *Seege* find self-definition in their struggle to acquire costly treasures.

The version of *The Seege of Troye* that is found in the Harley manuscript has traditionally been read as a more than commonly sophisticated rendering of the original text (Pearsall 1965, 93). The omission of oral formulae, the elaboration of descriptive detail, the insertion of an occasional learned or pious digression, and the replacement of the 'ffour ladies of eluene land' by Venus, Juno and Minerva has given the poet-reviser the reputation of 'a man of creative ability . . . of learning and piety' (Barnicle 1927, lv). The revisions, while not sufficient to 'affect the trend of the story' or 'obscure the lines of the original poem', are credited by Barnicle as, for the most part, 'informative' (Barnicle 1927, lv). When Paris arrives in Greece determined to win Helen, the H reviser adds a curious detail. As in LEA, the Greeks question Paris about the purpose of his visit, but here he does not simply answer 'with wordis wis' (L654). The Trojan response in H is at once more calculated and more revealing: '"Marchauntis," they seyd, "that we be; / Out of the see Octaman comen wee"' (H654*a*–654*b*). The H revision strikes right at the heart of the romance. The implication that the poem's heroic adventurers are roving merchants is made explicit. The H-reviser, writing in the fifteenth century, may have gleaned this detail from the *Compendium Historiae Troianae-Romanae*[20] or from the account of Helen's abduction in Robert Mannyng of Brunne's *Chronicle* (*c*.1327–1338),[21] a popularized history of England that shows some evidence of having been influenced itself by the earlier versions of *The Seege of Troye* (Ehrhart 1987, 68). In the *Chronicle*, Venus advises Paris to make his assault on Helen in the guise of a merchant. She rightly suspects that Helen's passion for shopping will both lure her aboard the ship and keep her sufficiently occupied in the perusal of merchandise, for the Trojans to abduct her without incident. Masquerading as a jewel merchant, Paris wins his own prize and confirms the virtue of adventurous endeavour: '"Thou [Helen] was gyfen, that gyft I haue; / alle my trauaile I vouch it saue"' (I.693–4). Certainly both texts share the figure of the merchant adventurer, but in all other ways the episodes are quite different. Robert Mannyng's explanation of the rationale behind the merchant disguise is absent in the Harley *Seege*, and the latter text retains a full account of the Trojan assault on Menelaus's citadel (in the *Chronicle*, the success of the disguise obviates the need for military action). The very brevity with which the merchant interlude is interpolated into the Harley *Seege* suggests that the reviser did not judge it sufficiently intrusive to warrant comment. The depiction of Paris and his Trojan companions as foreign merchants engaged in overseas trade matches the image of the knight as an appropriative adventurer that is drawn so effectively elsewhere in the romance. As the *Seege* attests, adventure is after all an economic enterprise.

Notes

1 *The Seege or Batayle of Troye*, ed. M. E. Barnicle, EETS o.s. 172 (London: Oxford University Press, 1927). Barnicle edits the four extant versions of the poem: London, Lincoln's Inn 150 (L); London, British Library, Egerton 2862 (E); London, College of Arms, Arundel XXII (A); and London, British Library, Harley 525 (H). In this essay L is used as the base text; references are made to E, A, and H as necessary.

2 Thomas Warton judges the Troy story one of the 'most capital and favourite stories of romance' (Warton 1774–81, I, 124). His patronizing assessment of medieval romance – the 'feeble efforts of remote ages' (I, i), 'the rude origin and obscure beginnings' of 'our national poetry' (I, ii) – has had extraordinary longevity, nowhere more so than in scholarship's sporadic accounts of the *Seege of Troye*.

3 Both Barnicle and Severs assign the *Seege* to the period 1300–1325 (Barnicle 1927, xxx; Severs 1967, 116). Pearsall's later dating stems, solely it seems, from his desire to distance it from the 'vigorously professional' (Pearsall 1965, 97) products of the first growth of couplet romance (*c.*1280–1320).

4 See McGillivray 1990.

5 The *Seege* survives (in slightly different versions) in four manuscripts, two of which are roughly contemporaneous romance collections, Egerton 2862 (*c.*1400) and Lincoln's Inn 150 (early fifteenth century). Lincoln's Inn 150, the once-famous minstrel manuscript, is now thought to have belonged, like the Egerton anthology, to a 'moderately prosperous' provincial reader (Taylor 1991, 57). Arundel XXII (late fourteenth century), a more lavish volume associated (perhaps spuriously) with the Earls of Shrewsbury, configures the *Seege* as bona fide history (an apt introduction to a Geoffrey of Monmouth/Wace-inspired chronicle), and in Harley 525 (fifteenth century), the poem seems to have been selected, alongside *Robert of Sicily* and *Speculum Guy de Warewyke*, for its (morally) didactic potential. Read for moral and intellectual edification as well as for entertainment, the *Seege* resists easy classification, as does its audience.

6 In the eighteenth century, the letters of Dares and Dictys were proven, once and for all, to be forgeries (Benson 1980, 5). Renewed interest in the veracity of the Greek and Trojan myths sought to find a historical rationale for their prevalence. In 1748 Montesquieu wrote: 'Tout ce qu'Homère nous raconte des dangers de la navigation d'Ulysse: des Circés, des Lestrigons, des Cyclopes, des Sirènes, de Charybde et de Scylla, étoient des fables répandues dans le Monde et établies par des navigateurs qui, faisant commerce d'économie, vouloient dégoûter les autres peuples de la faire après eux.' (Everything that Homer tells us about the dangers of Ulysses' sea voyage: about the Circes, the Lestrigons, the Cyclopses, the Sirens, Scylla and Charybdis, all were fables spread about in the world and introduced by navigators who, engaged in commercial activity, wanted to discourage others from following them) (*Dossier de l'esprit des lois*, in *Oeuvres Complètes*, ed. Roger Caillois, 2 vols, Paris: Gallimard, 1976, II, 1087).

7   Wood 1996 offers a readable account of recent archaeological discoveries. Braund 1994 is indispensable for an understanding of the interplay of myth and history in the story of the Argonauts' pursuit of the golden fleece.

8   LEA agree that there are ten battles, but their numbering is not identical. The vagaries seem to result from the fluidity of a text that is, at least in part, the product of memorial transmission.

9   For a discussion of the diptych structure in *Horn, Havelok, Emaré* and other romances, see Fewster 1987, 14–22.

10 In the interest of narrative cohesion, Colchis is eliminated and the fleece becomes (ahistorically) a Trojan treasure. In Robert Mannyng of Brunne's *Chronicle*, ed. Idelle Sullens (Binghamton, NY: Medieval and Renaissance Texts and Studies, 1996), the fleece is also found in Troy.

11 The poet's substitution of the planetary deities Saturn, Mercury, Jupiter and Venus – all four presented as women – for the traditional triad (Venus, Juno and Pallas) has provoked derisive comments from scholars, yet aside from providing a little unintentional humour for the modern reader, it in no way mars the narrative.

12 In E the element of risk is further underscored by the choice of lexis: 'He *auentred* his lyf for the helmes sake' (E1493; italics mine).

13 Medieval commentators conventionally depicted the voyage of the Argonauts as history's first quest. Joseph of Exeter, who portrays this first long-distance sea voyage as the rape of Thetis, interprets Jason's motive as a self-aggrandizing greed for gold. *Trojan War I–III*, ed. and trans. A. K. Bate (Warminster: Aris & Phillips, 1986).

14 See Wittig 1978.

15 Jerome, *Adversus Jovinianum* (21), in Alcuin Blamires, with Karen Pratt and C. W. Marx (eds), *Woman Defamed and Woman Defended: An Anthology of Medieval Texts* (Oxford: Oxford University Press, 1992), 74.

16 See Ehrhart 1987 for a full account of medieval rewritings of the Judgment of Paris. Ehrhart notes that the *Seege* poet handles his material with 'almost complete freedom' and writes that 'the result was doubtless more effective for his purposes' (54), but she never discusses those purposes.

17 The commercial ethos which characterizes this reworking of the traditional Judgment scene is remarkably similar to what Sylvia Thrupp has identified as 'the distinctive mark of medieval merchant culture': 'the promotion of rational calculation as a means to the advancement of interest'. Thrupp elaborates: 'Rational calculation was certainly the heart of the formal education that was given to boys and is stamped on all the London merchants' political activity, on their business, on their angling for patronage and public appointments, and also on their guidance of government and judicial processes in their city' (Thrupp 1948, xi).

18 Menelaus does not, of course, agree to Achilles's proposal, but his reason for refusing to exchange peace for Polyxena is notably devoid of any reference to what we might assume to be Helen's superior value. Menelaus's rationale is, rather, in accord with the now familiar ethos of rational calculation: with

Hector dead, the Trojans are worthless ('ffor now Ector is to dethe falle, / y no yeue a sore for heom alle', L1579–80) and a Greek victory (with, it is implied, the attendant reward of all Trojan treasure, Polyxena and Helen included) is assured.

19   The one anomaly is the reference at A403 to Hercules' reputation: 'Sir Ercules hys name so bryght'.

20   See *Compendium Historiae Troianae-Romanae*, 243 for Paris's abduction of Helen. The *Compendium* includes the merchant disguise but shares few other details with the *Seege*. Atwood 1938b, 12–13 discusses the *Compendium*'s possible influence on Mannyng's *Chronicle*.

21   See n. 10 above.

CHAPTER NINE

Romance and Its Discontents in
*Eger and Grime**

ANTONY J. HASLER

... the anger of the Lady when her Knight went home without his little
finger is very amusing – considering into what hands he fell, she might
have been thankful that he made not greater losses.

> Charles Kirkpatrick Sharpe, cited by David Laing,
> *Early Metrical Tales* (1826)

Die Wunde schließt der Speer
Nur, der sie schlug.

(Only the spear that struck the wound can heal it)

> Wagner, *Parsifal*, Act III

Eger and Grime, also called *The History of Sir Eger, Sir Grahame and Sir Graysteel*,
is a romance about missing parts that is itself a missing part. That some
form of the story it tells was known in the later Middle Ages is attested by a
cluster of allusions, all Scottish, from the late fifteenth and sixteenth centuries. On 19 April 1497, James IV paid nine shillings to hear 'tua fithelaris
that sang Graysteil', and around 20 January 1508 he also gave five shillings
to 'Gray Steill, lutar', though whether 'Gray Steill' was the lutenist or the
work performed remains unclear (Purser 1996, 145).[1] In the didactic
Complaynt of Scotlande, 'syr egeir and syr gryme' is one of a number of 'pleysand
storeis' recited to enliven the pastoral leisure of some shepherds.[2] In the
1552 Cupar Banns to Sir David Lindsay's *Satyre of the Thrie Estaitis*, the
braggart soldier Fynlaw of the Fute Band brandishes the sword 'that slew
Gray Steill / Nocht half ane myle beyond Kynneill' (242–3),[3] while the

* My thanks to Joan Hart-Hasler, Gayle Margherita, and Ad Putter for their careful and perceptive
criticisms of various drafts of this essay.

protagonist of Lindsay's narrative poem *Squyer Meldrum* fights 'als weill / As did Sir Gryme aganis Graysteill' (1317–18).[4] Lindsay's play mentions the famous romance in a context of naked burlesque, while one of *Squyer Meldrum*'s recent critics has found in it a humanist and anti-chivalric 'scepticism about the validity of romance' (Riddy 1974, 26). These references suggest wide circulation, and in Lindsay's case sophisticated distance; for one contemporary, there was clearly something a little archaic about *Eger*.

We do not know, however, what version or versions of the narrative these early allusions describe, for the extant texts of the romance date from a much later period. One appears in British Library, Add. MS 27879, the seventeenth-century compilation known as the Percy Folio. The other was edited in 1826 by the Scottish antiquarian David Laing, one of whose copies eventually found its way into the Huntington Library; this so-called Huntington–Laing version is represented by three prints from the late seventeenth and early eighteenth centuries. To modern readers, the *Eger* known in the late Middle Ages has become archaic in ways that Lindsay could not have anticipated: it is a lost original, memorialized by some belated witnesses.

This is no more than apt, for *Eger* begins amid loss and reminiscence. One midnight, Eger, bloodied, weary and mutilated, furtively returns to the bedchamber he shares with his close friend Grime, and tells a story. Eger is a 'poore bachlour' (P 26).[5] ('Bachelor' here defines a young warrior knight who serves as retainer to a social superior, in this case an earl.) Seeking to impress his lord's haughty daughter Winglaine, he has ventured into a strange 'fforbidden countrye' (P 102) to fight its master, the mysterious, seemingly supernatural Graysteele. The result is harrowing: Eger is battered into a swoon from which he wakes to find his little finger hacked off, and the ministrations of the lady physician Loosepaine, at whose castle he finds help and whose own fiancé and brother have died at Graysteele's hands, do him little good. The resourceful Grime proposes to make good the standing Eger has lost in his lady's eyes by disguising himself as Eger, and setting out to defeat Graysteele while Eger lies at home recovering. Some cunning is needed to deceive both ladies, but the strategy of surrogacy succeeds: Grime kills Graysteele, and the poem in P ends in marriages between Eger and Winglaine, and Grime and Loosepaine. In HL, the story goes a little further. Grime dies shortly after the marriages, Eger, in a fit of guilt, reveals the trick that was played, an outraged Winglaine discards him, he leaves for Rhodes to fight the Saracens, Winglaine dies while he is away, and Eger returns to marry the widowed Loosepaine. The poem here ends in a prayer to 'Iesus Heavens King' to grant the surviving couple 'grace and good to spend, / And love ay while their latter end' (HL 2858–60).

The editors and critics of the poem in which Grime appears have joined him in devoting considerable attention to the difficulties caused by a lost object. As we have seen, *Eger* can be tied to several contexts of reception – late-medieval Scotland, seventeenth-century antiquarianism, the romance revival of the eighteenth and nineteenth centuries. Its date and place of origin, however, are uncertain, though linguistic evidence and some inconclusive geographical and historical hints suggest that it was composed in Scotland or northern England at some time, perhaps late, in the fifteenth century.[6] The nature of the relation between the two versions is also an open question. P has 1474 lines, and often seems fragmentary: 'incidents are strung together without articulation, the social background is universalised and stylised, archetypal motifs reintroduced, and sensational detail given obtrusive emphasis' (Pearsall 1977, 261). At 2860 lines, HL presents a fuller and more – though by no means wholly – coherent narrative. Some of P's readers have nevertheless found it tersely suggestive rather than messily over-packed, especially those who discern beneath its surface the looming shapes of themes from Celtic and Teutonic folklore and myth (French and Hale 1930, 671; Van Duzee 1963, 18–32). HL's advocates, on the other hand, believe that P's apparent incoherence can only be explained if we assume a more coherent lost original, to which HL brings us closer (the case is argued in detail in Reichel 1894). In this spirit, Derek Pearsall appropriates C. S. Lewis's approving general verdict on *Eger* – 'effortlessly and unobtrusively noble in sentiment' (Lewis 1954, 68) – for HL alone (Pearsall 1977, 261).

I should make it clear at this point that the present essay has no investment in deciding whether P or HL came first. Without firmer evidence, indeed, the debate surely tells us more about scholarly nostalgia than it does about *Eger*. For P's adherents, *Eger*'s ultimate source lies in the archetypes of a deep national past; for HL's, that source is a courtlier and better ordered – because lost – Ur-*Eger*. The modern reception of *Eger* neatly illustrates the tendency of medievalists to project their own ideological predilections on to the medieval text, generating a fantasized origin whose loss they then proceed to lament (Fradenburg 1990 and 1997; Margherita 1994). It might be observed in passing that such projection goes back a long way: the Percy Folio may have been a royalist compilation, and so itself a form of elegy for an absolute monarchy soon to be lost to history (Donatelli 1993, 129).

Eger's readers, however, are surely right to be preoccupied by loss, for it is central to the poem. Like the scholars who seek to historicize it, its main characters are confronted with the weird and disorienting phenomenon of a narrative that has somehow mislaid its beginning, and seek to construct a new narrative around the absence thus opened up. In what follows, I draw on the writings of the psychoanalytic theorists Jacques Lacan and Slavoj Žižek to argue first that loss and fantasy structure the narrative of *Eger*, and secondly that *Eger* strives to accommodate loss through reliance on a common romance pattern of *compagnonnage* or male companionship. This double movement becomes visible in *Eger*'s thematic concern with language and narration.

I am not the first reader to approach *Eger* as fantasy. It is also so labelled by Lee C. Ramsey, who assigns it to a category of Middle English 'fairy romances'. According to Ramsey, these romances voice the anxieties of a lesser nobility faced with the 'civilized' institutions of court and city. This group among the late-medieval aristocracy is, on Ramsey's showing, caught in an uncomfortable double bind. The court sustains it in many ways, but the monarch's arbitrary powers make the court a dangerous place. The city, the centre of trade, is 'necessary to the continuation of the lower nobility's perquisites', but since the labour involved in creating cities is essentially alien to its noble understanding, it thinks of them as 'having come into existence by magical, superhuman means', and regards the city's 'builders and maintainers' with suspicion and anxiety. For Ramsey, the 'fantasy solution' to the problems of these nobles

> was alliance with the makers and, ultimately, mastery of the civilization itself, but this process seemed beyond accomplishment by practical methods. It was necessary both to defeat and succumb to the makers. By a natural extension of the family-romance myth, this could be achieved by rejecting (slaying) the civilization emblemized as father and uniting oneself with it as emblemized by the mother-lover . . . All the adverse factors having been embodied in the abstract or father image, societal benefits can be concentrated and isolated in the figure of the fairy lover who brings riches and power.
>
> (Ramsey 1983, 146–7)

Ramsey's approach, of course, is a variation on Freud's well-known Oedipal family drama, in which a boy's incestuous longings for his mother must remain unsatisfied because of his father's prohibiting threat of castration. The boy is compelled to renounce his desire for the mother, but as a consequence of this sacrifice is granted entry into society and culture, his instincts now properly regulated. On this reading, the terrifying Graysteele, defending his forbidden land, is a 'father-figure', and Winglaine and Loosepaine, who finally bring their lovers 'riches and power', share the role of 'mother-lover' (Ramsey 1983, 140, 143). (The pattern, as Ramsey concedes, requires some stretching to fit *Eger*, for while Graysteele has superhuman qualities and there is an other-worldly aspect to Loosepaine's restorative skills, there are no fairies in the poem.) In Ramsey's picture of late-medieval civilization and its discontents, *Eger* is a story that some nobles tell themselves in order to hide from the real conditions of their historical existence. The Freudian family drama becomes the story of lovely mothers and forbidding fathers, and fantasy becomes cultural concealment.

More recent developments in theory offer, I think, less reductive ways of looking at fantasy, and for a different perspective we may turn to the work of Slavoj Žižek. Here is how Žižek describes fantasy:

> ... the psychoanalytic notion of fantasy cannot be reduced to that of a fantasy-scenario which obfuscates the true horror of a situation ... the relationship between fantasy and the horror of the Real it conceals is much more ambiguous than it may seem: fantasy conceals this horror, yet at the same time it creates what it purports to conceal, its repressed point of reference.
>
> (Žižek 1997, 7)

This passage clearly raises several questions, but the first point to note is Žižek's contention that fantasy does not, as Ramsey would have it, simply camouflage uncomfortable truths, but in some way brings to light the very thing it 'purports to conceal', even as it conceals it. For Žižek, fantasy is a form of narrative in which we both confront and disavow a loss that the writings of Jacques Lacan, on which Žižek draws, identify with castration. Taking the repressed as its point of departure, fantasy, in Žižek's words, actually 'stages the act of castration', providing the scene of a sacrificial renunciation which Žižek calls 'the very act of . . . installation . . . of the Law' (Žižek 1997, 14).

To what kind of 'castration' does Žižek refer, and what has it to do with 'the Law' and 'the horror of the Real'? To clarify Žižek's terms, we must first go back to Lacan. While Lacan's writings are notoriously complex, one way of describing his highly influential reading of Freud might be to say that he takes the Freudian story of the family drama which I have just outlined, and turns it into metaphor. In Lacan's account the father becomes – though he cannot be reduced to – a symbolic figure or metaphor, and the realm of society and culture over which he holds sway is a patriarchal 'symbolic order' bound up with the signifying structures of language itself. Culture becomes a system of regulatory metaphors which determines the positions of the subjects within it, including those positions which mark sexual difference (male, female). In this linguistic reworking of Freud, the interdiction proclaimed by Freud's castrating father appears as a governing metaphor, one that guarantees the male subject's place in the symbolic order through the institution of patrilineality, the transfer of power and privilege from fathers to sons.

Entry into language and the symbolic, however, comes at a cost. For Freud, we may recall, the threat of castration prohibited access to the mother. For Lacan, this estrangement from the mother's body is also alienation from the Real, the domain of bodily experience which cannot be symbolized in language. The subject who speaks is cut off from the Real, and is thus castrated, defined by lack. Yet the paternal prohibition also opens the door to desire, holding out the delusory promise of a return of the lost Real. It is in this sense that the 'primordial Law' (Lacan 1977, 66) of the father brings about the 'intervention of the cut of symbolic castration' (Žižek 1997, 14).

This 'intervention' cannot be pinned down to a specific moment in time, for we cannot simply say that Lacan's Real is a condition which in some way 'precedes' the acquisition of language. Because it is inaccessible to the subject within culture, the Real is *always already* lost, and its loss is thus, strictly speaking, a moment outside time. The status of this impossible, literally unthinkable moment is full of contradictions. The Real's return can be hallucinated as nostalgia, in which case it becomes the elusive origin that gives order and meaning to a particular chronology, the place to which we long to return. In this guise it lends authority to paternal narratives of legacy and descent, according to which history itself is read as inheritance, and the past as a smoothly continuous succession of events, Lacan's 'series of generations' (Lacan 1993, 320). But since the Real is also the carnal materiality, utterly alien to culture, that is repudiated by the entry into the symbolic, its return can appear as a nightmarish encounter which menaces those same patrilineal narratives with traumatic breakdown. The paradox is illustrated by the two ways in which the mother is most usually represented in Western culture: she is either nurturing, or monstrous, a womb which suffocates. Hence Žižek's emphasis on 'the horror of the Real' when he speaks of 'the primordial loss which allows the subject to enter the symbolic order' (Žižek 1997, 14).

We here come full circle back to Freud. As Ad Putter's essay in this collection notes, trauma for Freud is linked to the 'compulsion to repeat', which makes us recall and re-enact – involuntarily, even unknowingly – distressing past experiences which troublesomely refuse to stay in the past. This vulnerability to an overpowering 'compulsion' is yoked to what might seem its opposite, a drive to mastery, which drives the subject who has passively suffered a traumatic experience to tame the trauma by actively repeating it. This twofold impulse, to passive 'compulsion' and active 'mastery', sets the repetitive romance of *Eger and Grime* an extremely fraught task. For *Eger*'s aim is nothing less than to narrate the impossible 'lost event': to confront the danger it poses to masculine genealogy, and to master the material terrors of the Real by displacing the anxieties that surround it into the metaphoric terms of sexual difference. If this perspective, as I shall argue, brings into focus what is distinctive about *Eger*, it also reveals how far the poem is true to its genre. Indeed, we might say that the very purpose of romance, on the evidence of this romance, is to reassure by showing that if women can be kept in their place, all will be well for history.

Eger's Wound

Eger's first main event is what the narrative theorist Gérard Genette calls an analepsis, and we commonly term a 'flashback' – an 'evocation after the fact of an event that took place earlier than the point in the story where we are' (Genette 1980, 40). The poem opens not with a knight who rides out to seek adventure, but with a knight returned, who spends a good part of the total narrative telling of adventures already past.[7] He is, it should be said, not in a condition to do much else. Even before we hear of his missing finger, we are told that 'his kniffe was forth, his sheath was gone, / his scaberd by his thigh was done' (P 55–6). In P, his attempt to win 'worshipp' has failed; he has 'bought it deare & lost it soone!' (P 77–8). HL's Eger is more explicit:

> I am wounded and hurt full sore,
> And tint my man-hood for evermore.
>   Lost the Lady, for she is gone,
> Other Knights have stayed at home,
> Keeped their man-hood fair and clean,
> Will brook her now before mine een.
>
> (HL 75–80)

Eger is a knight torn from a virile world of action and chivalric display, who instead of being watched and admired must now watch other men 'brook' his Lady.

What are we to make of this episode? Ramsey sees in Eger's injuries a loss 'symbolically conveyed by the fact that Sir Gray-steel has cut off the defeated Eger's little finger and by the phallic imagery in the description of Eger's return' (Ramsey 1983, 138) – in short, literal castration. Yet this overlooks precisely what Lacan has taught us to observe, and what is surely one of this romance's most distinctive features – the strange temporality of its opening. For if castration and loss are to be found here, they cannot, as the poem soon makes clear, be separated from narration itself. The poem's beginning *in medias res*, and Eger's introductory analepsis, show us a knight and a text endeavouring to speak of an event lost to words.

Eger's quest, and his narration, founder because several things are missing. We have already learned that Eger's father is dead, and that the law of primogeniture is responsible for his younger son's powerlessness (Eger is poor because 'his elder brother was liuande, / & gouerned all his fathers Land', P 27–8). Now, unable to defend the flesh so savagely lacerated in his duel with Graysteele (P 124–80, HL 141–207), paternity fails Eger a second time over:

> My Habergion that was of Millaine fine, –
> first my fathers & then was mine,
> & itt had beene in many a thrust,
> & neuer a maile of itt wold burst; –
> my acton was of Paris worke,
> saued me noe more then did my sarke . . .
>
> (P 169–74)

(In HL 199, it is the 'actoun' that is assigned to the father.) The failure of lineal descent runs together with that of linear narrative, as Eger's tormented efforts to reconstruct the past hit an impasse. He awakens to find his little finger missing, his horse and another dead knight lying nearby, his weapons broken. The other knight's finger is also missing, and, says Eger,

> by that Knight I might well see
> that one man had delt both with him & me.
>
> (P 197–8)

The text both conceals and reveals the scene of Eger's mutilation, indicating it with a large 'X marks the spot' without actually describing it. Eger looks to the scattered signs of his demolished knightly ego – strewn armour, dead doubles of himself – and reads in them a deed already accomplished, the marks of a secret which is not available to representation. His wound lies deep within a retrospect, and even then it goes unnarrated, a 'repressed point of reference' indeed. It enacts the paradox of the entry into the symbolic, a narrative that begins by losing its beginning.

The violence of Eger's wound also shapes the part played in the poem by the unattainable lady of courtly romance. This figure shares in the two aspects under which the Real presents itself: she is desired, but she also embodies a terror which is forbidding in the most literal sense. Žižek, once again following Lacan, suggestively describes the lady as 'a spiritual, ethereal Ideal' – the object, indeed, of 'fantasy' as the term is commonly understood – but notes that this is 'strictly secondary' to her 'traumatic dimension', in which she appears as the dominatrix who subjects her lover to 'senseless, outrageous, impossible, arbitrary, capricious ordeals' (Žižek 1994, 90; cf. Lacan 1992, 139–54, 161–4). Winglaine, Eger's lady, is cast in this mould. Incidental assets such as gold, 'good' and 'highnese of . . . blood' (P 11–12) do not concern her. She is uninterested in any man 'without he would with swords dent / win euery battell where he went' (P 13–14), demanding martial aggression without logic or limit. She ceaselessly promises fulfilment, while continuing to defer that fulfilment by making it subject to equally endless preconditions. She thus personifies a law which in installing desire authorizes both endless enticement and endless demand. In Žižek's words, *'the Object of desire itself coincides with the force that prevents its attainment'* (Žižek 1994, 96).

Žižek's point, I think, makes it difficult to accept the validity for *Eger* of Ramsey's simple family drama, in which Graysteele is the cruel father and the ladies divide the role of good mother-lover. It may rather be said that Winglaine and Graysteele share the narrative function of interdiction: if she incites desire, he embodies prohibition. She demands uninterrupted ferocity; Graysteele slices off even the most apparently insignificant digits. Later in the poem, Winglaine's sardonic dismissal of Eger shows that she can clearly talk Graysteele's (body-) language of excess:

> You gave a finger to let you land,
> Now I am red ye leave an hand.
> (HL 995–6)

Winglaine and Graysteele are linked by a grotesquely carnal calculus.

The lady Loosepaine, at whose castle Eger stays, appears at first to promise escape from this circuit of desire and interdiction. She is, however, an ambivalent figure, for through her eyes Graysteele conquers a second time. After his combat with Graysteele, Eger was forced to clear his eyes of blood in order to recognize for the first time his own mutilation (P 189). Now, Loosepaine observes that Eger's armour conceals a defect:

> And when she saw mine hands barc,
> Then waxt mine anger far the mare,
> My glove was haile, my finger was tint,
>   She might well know it was no dint:
>   For Gray-steel he was of such pride,
>   And his word waxed ay so wide,
>   Of what countrey that he was commin,
> She might wit well I was overcommin.
> (HL 297–304)

She thus becomes the second reader, after Eger himself, of Eger's wound. Eger's bitterness at the ruin of his reputation is framed by the knowledge that he ascribes to Loosepaine as he watches her watching him ('She might wit well I was overcommin'). In medieval romance it is usually women, not men, who are looked at (Spearing 1993, 22–5); here the lady of courtly love looks back at a male observer. Eger interiorizes her look, and to his anguish it constitutes him as lacking, as castrated. Male self-perception is relayed through female eyes, and the result is a knight doubly 'overcommin', his identity damaged by a wound.

Loosepaine, in short, proves to be the final, and perhaps most lethal, in a trio of characters who deal in interdiction. Clad in the red and gold that also clothe Graysteele, she applies her medicinal skills. But in truth what she has to offer is a lure rather than a cure. The intact bodily surface restored by her healing arts will last only until Eger comes again in the presence of his lady:

> froe that loue make you once agast,
> your oyntments may noe longer last.
> (P 323–4)

Her words prove all too true, for Eger's homeward ride comes to a painful end:

> I fared full well all that while
> till I came home within 2 mile;
> then all my wounds wrought att once
> as kniues had beene beaten thorrow my bones . . .
> (P 337–40)

Eger's scars burst open with love; he draws close to his lady, only to find himself as far from physical union with her as ever. Loosepaine's labours have brought to light – by seeking to hide – the identity between the figurative wounds inflicted by the disdainful lady and the literal wounds received at Graysteele's hands, putting on display the connection between desire and prohibition which the two characters represent. Graysteele's wounds, quite simply, are the lady's wounds: the Object of desire itself coincides with the force that prevents its attainment. The lady's traumatic dimension – the literally shattering effect of the Real – is revealed in a body that explodes from within as if assaulted with 'kniues' from without.

The end of Eger's doomed quest confirms his predicament. A look from one lady revealed that something was missing beneath his glove. Now, his intimate conversation with Grime is overheard by another lady, Winglaine herself. In HL, she preserves a charged silence (HL 469–70). Her response in P is less equivocal:

> when shee heard that Egars bodye was in distresse,
> shee loued his body mickle the worse.
> (P 373–4)

Within the perspective of a listening woman, the words of Eger's long narration make his wound gape yet wider. The poem, however, now engineers a startling turn, for the language associated with loss and castration suddenly begins to exercise a shaping force on events. Eger and Grime's bedroom talk issues in a plot between men, whose aim is to reassert male symbolic authority.

Prowess by proxy

It will by now be clear that Žižek's model of fantasy has distinct critical advantages where *Eger* is concerned. We have already seen how well that model accounts for the temporality of the romance's opening scene. So too, if we see fantasy not as pure concealment but as the staging of the law's installation, we are better placed to make sense of the poem's gleefully exhibitionistic violence and fixation on severed body parts, registered in Lewis's characteristically perceptive remark that until he read the poem 'I never realized what fighting an enemy who wore full armour would be like' (Lewis 1954, 68). Concealment is further brought into the open in *Eger*'s breathtakingly flagrant plot of male deception and doubling.

If the fact that 'Eger is quite happy to win back his mistress in this fashion' (Faris 1981, 97) hardly bears out popular modern-day beliefs about how well medieval knights treated ladies, it also complicates recent critical claims that medieval romances specialize not in exposing but in disguising male complicity. The kind of male complicity at stake here is, as it happens, revealed early in *Eger*, where we are told that Eger and Grime are more than good friends:

> they keeped a chamber together att home;
> better loue Loved there never none.
>
> (P 47–8)

Though Eger and Grime both finally marry, their 'love' for one another is couched in superlatives that are never used to describe their other passions. The bond between Eger and Grime is clearly, in the sense made current by Eve Kosofsky Sedgwick, 'homosocial'. Sedgwick borrows the term from history and the social sciences, where it 'describes social bonds between persons of the same sex' and is 'obviously meant to be distinguished from "homosexual"'. However, her own usage connects the word with the idea of erotic desire 'to hypothesize the potential unbrokenness of a continuum between homosocial and homosexual . . .' (Sedgwick 1985, 1). The notion of homosocial desire suggests that what we commonly think of as 'male bonding' may rest on an – often disavowed – foundation of homoeroticism, which is an affective support for relations of male authority. Such relations entail 'the use of women as exchangeable, perhaps symbolic, property for the primary purpose of cementing the bonds of men with men' (Sedgwick 1985, 25–6). Sarah Kay has argued that homosociality underlies the romance motif of doubling, in which paired male characters, linked by blood, friendship, or patterns of structure and theme, function as mirror-images of one another. This is because homosocial desire plays a crucial part in shaping the entire semantic world of many medieval romances; Kay concludes that 'the most predictable impact' of bonds among male companions 'on the organization of meaning will be the representation of sameness as desirable' (Kay 1995, 145). Susan Crane, also borrowing Sedgwick's concept, suggests that the heterosexual courtship so central to medieval romances veils homoerotic desire by disavowing it, becoming a surface layer of meaning which 'overwrites masculine relations without fully obscuring them' (Crane 1994, 39).

Eger, however, is compelled to bring its homosocial plot of male deception to the fore by its unusual handling of the device of the double. Sometimes doubles are doubles because they are physically identical; in *Amis and Amiloun*, for example, the two heroes are so 'lyche . . . of syght' (88) that they cannot be told apart.[8] In *Eger*, such doubling is made not by nature but by man. While Eger stays at home, Grime must ride into the forbidden land and defeat Graysteele in his stead, all the while preserving the fiction that Eger is still the narrative protagonist. As a result, the second half of *Eger* repeats but also reverses the first. If for Eger speech was ultimately grounded in an absence, Grime's aim is to turn the gap between language and referent to narrative purpose, to become a romance author in his own text.

This begins in earnest when Grime tells his lord of Eger's injuries, and the court visit him:

> The Earl unto his chamber went,
> The Countess and her maidens gent,
> And they beheld him so deadly,
> He speaks not, what ever they say,
> Nor no language to them he had,
> But sir Grahame all the answer made:
> He said, yestreen when he came home,
> His tongue was not all from him gone . . .
>
> (HL 491–8)

Here, in HL, a series of displacements is at work. Eger told a story whose secret heart was a lost event. Grime's words here spell out, even as they hide, the link between the lost little finger and the speech that replaces it

– Eger's 'tongue was not all from him gone' (though something else certainly was). Now Eger's body has itself become the secret ground of narration. 'Deadly' in its silence, concealing a guilty secret, it becomes the matter for Grime's own romance, as he efficiently improvises a tale in which the wounds given by the lady and Graysteele are projected on to an anonymous force of political disorder, a band of thieves (P 429–38, HL 501–22). Now the bedbound Eger is in the place of the lady; as Eger left to fight for his lady, so Grime will leave to fight for Eger.

As the public display to deceive the court yields to more private dealings, Grime becomes the middleman in a series of exchanges between Eger and Winglaine. In HL, these interchanges brim with doubleness and erotic dissimulation, as Grime, like Chaucer's Pandarus, exploits the power of language to mediate between lovers. Winglaine, by now, has few words for an Eger who has so disgraced himself. If Eger knows she is cooling towards him it will be his death, so Grime reinterprets her brusqueness for his friend's ears:

> And on this wise, as with sir Grahame,
> So with the Lady on a time:
> On his foot with her would he gang,
> Then to his fellow would amang.
> And then told him a fern-years tale,
> And this while thus he wrought all hale . . .
> (HL 597–602)

Grime works to redeem male lack by making 'all hale' (whole) with his fictions, and those around him are successfully deceived: 'But all was fained each a deal, / Yet many said, he governd well' (HL 607–8).

The rhetorical figure that governs the development of Grime's plot is metaphor. Cicero speaks for an extended tradition of classical and post-classical rhetoric when he defines metaphor as 'a short form of simile, contracted into one word' which 'is put in a place not belonging to it as if it were its own place'.[9] Translated into narrative terms, metaphor, as Patricia Parker points out, generates plots turning on substitution, exchange, and the transgression of boundaries between identities; it constitutes 'a violation of the law that two bodies cannot occupy the same space at the same time' (Parker 1982, 138–9). Now, Grime produces new rivalries and alignments in a series of fictive substitutions. The result, in HL in particular, is that for the rest of the poem every other narrative decorum takes second place to the requirements of *compagnonnage*. The 'use of women as exchangeable . . . property for . . . cementing the bonds of men with men' comes to the fore, as the two knights slide into one another's love relations. *Amis and Amiloun* features a temporary exchange of wives as one of the factors which 'bond' its heroes, but *Eger* takes the same motif startlingly literally.

Grime's stratagem first blurs the bounds between friend and rival. When Winglaine reveals that she has overheard Eger's story and no longer cares for him, Grime jestingly ('into bourding', HL 681) responds to her with a double fiction, claiming both that Eger has met another woman and that he himself is interested in Winglaine ('You love not him, will you love me?', HL 680). He then pushes a reluctant Eger into assenting to his plan by claiming that Winglaine's thoughts have already turned to an alternative suitor, one Olyas (HL 761), whom Winglaine has contacted by 'A privie message' (HL 764) during Eger's sickness. These substitutions are repeated at the end of HL, as Eger finally steps into Grime's shoes. In this version the poem draws divine intervention into its orbit (Grime's death, Eger's repentance) to ensure that Eger eventually marries Loosepaine, Grime's widow.

The text of P participates in this obfuscation of identity. Grime's scheme to replace Eger depends on a moment of quick-change artistry which is enabled by reading. Eger must sit in a window and read romances to convince the court that he is up and healthy. Eger will then take his leave of the court, but it is Grime who will gallop off over the horizon. HL narrates this complex sequence of events at some length. This is as well, since P compresses it to eight near-incomprehensible lines:

> Early on the other day
> theese 2 knights did them array:
> into a window Sir Egar yeede,
> bookes of Romans for to reede
> that all the court might him heare.
> the Knight was armed & on steere;
> he came downe in to the hall,
> & tooke his leaue both of great & small.
> (P 625–32)

To some readers, this has seemed utterly absurd, and a prime instance of P's 'degeneracy' in relation to HL. With the information provided by HL it becomes possible to work out the reference of 'the Knight' and 'he': 'the Knight' refers back to Grime, who has got himself ready to ride off in Eger's armour; 'he' refers back to Eger, who publicly takes leave of the court as if *he* were about to ride out on adventure. But how is the reader of P, who does not have the benefit of HL's wisdom, to guess how the anaphoric reference works? For the textual antecedent of 'he' (which should be Eger) is in fact 'the Knight' (Grime), and the antecedent of 'the Knight' (which should be Grime) is in fact 'Sir Egar'. Now we might put this down, as Pearsall does, to a lamentable accident of textual transmission (Pearsall

1977, 261), but notice how the textual confusion answers to a certain tur-
bulence within the story. As the identities of Eger and Grime merge in the
plot, so P confounds Eger and Grime in discourse. P, in short, turns the
romance fiction of Grime's scheme into a screen between reader and tale,
realized within the narrative in an act of reading (Eger's) which we cannot
quite read.

If Graysteele left Eger half a man, Grime has now turned Eger into two
men, and this doubling of identity necessarily entails a doubling of plot.
However, the difference of identity also ensures repetition with a difference.
Grime now goes to recover the ground Eger lost, but its dangers have
diminished since his friend passed the same way. After the failure of Eger's
paternal weapons, Grime rides to meet Graysteele with a sword once owned
by Eger's uncle, as if to tap a fresh source of patrilineal authority (P 553–
76, HL 801–6). In the poem's first half, HL's Eger crosses a desolation:

> Ye shal be four dayes, and than
> That ye shal see no kind of man,
> Nor nothing but the fowles flyand,
> Wilderness and all wasted land . . .
> (HL 881–4)

He traverses the waste alongside a river, which merges with another (HL
891) and then with 'salt water' (896) and 'salt sand' (897). Several of *Eger*'s
readers have associated Graysteele's domain with the region about the
Solway Firth, that shifting territory which dissolves boundaries between
land and water and between England and Scotland.[10] However this might
be, borderlands are certainly in question here. The terrain, where clear-cut
distinctions fade, points to the precarious and permeable bounds of a masculine identity marked by prohibition, and to the body whose surfaces are
wounded when armour fails and fathers are absent.[11] In HL, it is 'The land
of doubt' (1447, 1864). For Grime, however, the country's strangeness has
recoiled; it is suddenly full of towers, towns and hospitable burgesses.

Perhaps the greatest transformation, however, is reserved for Graysteele
himself, who is shorn of his mystique by a simple shift of perspective. As his
sentries hasten to warn him of the new invader of his territory, Eger's
sinister and alien challenger, described by HL's Grime as 'uncannand' (HL
443), dwindles to a truculent knight amid his own *familia*. In P he has occult
powers, but they are limited as soon as they are mentioned: his strength
waxes until noon, then wanes (891–4). P, indeed, suggests that Graysteele's
secret weapon is not supernatural potency, but demystification. He knows
better than his opponent, rather tiresomely telling him that Eger's defeat
was due to flaws in his arms rather than his own weakness:

'& hee had beene weaponed as well as I,
he had beene worth both thee & mee.'
(P 1039–40)

Graysteele retells Eger's story of the earlier combat, and in so doing dispels
rumours of his own unearthly and matchless might. In the traumatic con-
frontations of Eger's quest, Winglaine was desired, and so Graysteele, the
force blocking that desire, was a powerful and terrifying figure. Since,
however, Winglaine is not Grime's lady, Graysteele is merely an irritating
windbag whose sole advantage lies in words. The relation between desire
and prohibition embodied in Winglaine and Graysteele remains rigorously
consistent: where Winglaine is not desired, Graysteele is easily overcome.

The episode of mutilation too is repeated, but with several variations.
Grime lodges with Loosepaine before the combat, and is able to deceive
her until she notices that he, unlike Eger, has a whole hand (P 803–10, HL
1259–78). This, however, is the last time she 'sees through' masculine disguise, for Grime, as if to stabilize Winglaine's fierce mathematics, cuts off
the dead Graysteele's hand and brings it back to Loosepaine, encased in its
glove, in token of victory. Both versions explicitly represent the severing of
the hand this time round, P's phrasing, indeed, insisting on its visibility: 'My
brother left a fingar in this land with thee', cries Grime, 'therfore thy whole
hand shall he see' (P 1107–8). Loosepaine's look too is repeated, but with
very different results. In HL, Loosepaine, laconically informed by Grime
'That in the glove there is an hand' (HL 1838), passes it to her maidservant;
the latter, noting the weight of the glove, opens it to look inside and its
contents fall at Loosepaine's feet. On seeing the hand that 'Had slain her
brother and her love', Loosepaine is first 'joyful' (1847), then turns pale
with remembered bitterness ('Such old malice made her to mean, / She
waxed cold, and syn to teen', 1851–2). P is typically starker:

he [Grime] gaue her the hand & the gloue gay,
& sayd, 'lay vp this till itt be day.'
shee took the gloue at him,
but shee wist not that they [sic] hand was in;
& as they stoode still on the ground,
the hand fell out therin that stond,
& when shee looked on that hand
that had slaine her brother and her husband.
noe marueill though her hart did grisse,
the red blood in her face did rise . . .
(P 1171–80)

Under Loosepaine's eyes, Eger was mortified by the loss of his finger; now
it is the lady's body that is exposed to male eyes, her complexion displaying

legible symptoms of her inner turmoil ('The knight he well perceived than, / That the Lady was in distress', HL 1854–5). While those symptoms differ between HL and P, both versions agree that the physiological response which reveals Loosepaine's emotions – now it is she who embodies loss – also inserts her into a male order in which she is named as sister and widow, a bearer of heredity rather than strange and subversive magical powers. In HL, this is promptly confirmed as Loosepaine, having already promised Grime that 'He that hath my marriage, / Shal have my fathers heritage' (1953–4), goes to her father's hall to tell him the news of Grime's victory (1996–2080). P, going a step further, has her carry with her the hand itself, in proof of Grime's success (1204–20).

The scene is the inevitable outcome of Grime's plot, in which it is the men who double up to confuse the women rather than (as in Eger's story) the other way around. Loosepaine, like the severed hand she holds, becomes a token passed between men to reconstruct masculine bonds, as will also be true of Winglaine. P, in fact, signals this in the heroines' names: the alternations of profit and pain, winning and losing, that mark the male subject's relation to chivalric culture, are finally dispelled as Eger wins Winglaine, and Loosepaine, it belatedly turns out, was only ever called Loosepaine because 'a better Leche was none certaine' (P 1408). Earlier, Loosepaine was insubordinate enough to perceive the absence marked by Eger's injury. Now, the hand that inflicted that wound, cut off but forcefully present, is possessed by Grime, and it is the pale, or blushing, Loosepaine who is consigned to subjection and lack. Grime's homosocial and metaphorical plot has replaced absence with presence: the poem's anxieties about castration and the body's materiality are refigured to male advantage, and the relations of power inscribed in the metaphors of sexual difference are safe again. The result, in the case of HL, is an immediate and unquenchable flow of narrative, as the story that started analeptically now moves to its end in leisurely fashion, across another eight hundred or so lines. The romance that had no beginning is suddenly unable to stop.

The scene just described typifies the way in which P, with its 'sensational detail', occasionally goes beyond HL in representing the bodily commitments of fantasy and in laying bare the homosocial economy that fantasy in *Eger* sustains. But how far does Grime's extemporized romance make good Eger's loss? Loosepaine reminds us that 'There is no Leech in all the land, / Can put a finger to an hand' (HL 1273–4). The scene's excesses, centred on the gory unwieldiness of Graysteele's hand, recall and amplify the disquiets they claim to resolve. In this sense they are characteristic of *Eger*: Loosepaine's ambiguously curative salves, which heal wounds only to reveal them again at the worst possible moment, can be read as a *mise-en-abîme*, an image within the text of its own workings. Žižek says that '*narrative as such* emerges in order to resolve some fundamental antagonism by rearranging its terms into a temporal succession' (Žižek 1997, 11). Fantasy cannot conceal or master the originary scene it repeats: it can only hallucinate it again and again, producing endlessly new narrative forms without bringing closure. Grime's generation of narrative from Eger's wound is above all an attempt to resituate what that wound figured: to celebrate lack and privation, in the struggle to repair the split between language and an impossible Real. Grime's labours as romance author have been replicated by scholars and critics, as the different versions of *Eger* themselves become Žižek's narrative 'terms' – one always faced, like Grime, with the burden of 'redeeming' the other's faults – and rival genealogies are constructed to repair loss and close unwanted gaps in the material state of the text. The discontents of romance, however, cannot be laid to rest by the toil of knights or of critics, for they are finally inseparable from the discontents of language itself.

Notes

1   *Compota Thesauriorum Regum Scotorum: Accounts of the Lord High Treasurer of Scotland*, ed. Thomas Dickson, Sir John Balfour-Paul and C. T. Innes, 12 vols (Edinburgh: H.M. General Register House, 1877–1916), I, 330; IV, 96.

2   Robert Wedderburn, *The Complaynt of Scotland (c.1550)*, ed. A. M. Stewart, STS 4th ser., 11 (Edinburgh: Blackwood and Sons, 1979), p. 50.

3   Sir David Lindsay, 'Proclamatioun maid in Cowpar of Fyffe', printed as an appendix to *Ane Satyre of the Thrie Estaitis*, ed. Roderick Lyall (Edinburgh: Canongate, 1989).

4   Sir David Lindsay, *Squyer Meldrum*, ed. James Kinsley (London: Nelson, 1959).

5   All references are to *Eger and Grime: A Parallel-Text Edition of the Percy and the Huntington–Laing Versions of the Romance*, ed. James Ralston Caldwell (Cambridge, MA: Harvard University Press, 1933). The Percy text is referred to as P, the Huntington–Laing text as HL. In the interests of consistency, I use throughout the characters' names as they appear in P: thus, HL's Grahame, Winliane and Liliane become Grime, Winglaine and Loosepaine respectively.

6   For a full recent survey of scholarly opinion on *Eger*'s provenance see Evans (forthcoming), who herself argues for a Cumbrian origin. I would like to thank Professor Evans for allowing me to read her article in typescript.

7   The same, it may be noted, is true of Chrétien de Troyes's *Yvain*, chosen by Erich Auerbach to demonstrate his claim that the paradigmatic action of romance occurs when, as the title of his famous essay puts it, 'The Knight Sets Forth' (Auerbach, 1953).

8   *Amis and Amiloun*, ed. MacEdward Leach, EETS o.s. 203 (London: Oxford University Press, 1937).

9   Cicero, *De oratore*, trans. E. W. Sutton and H. Rackham, 2 vols, Loeb Classical Library (Cambridge, MA: Heinemann, 1976), III, xxxix, 157.

10 George Ellis identifies 'Galias', ruled in HL by Loosepaine's father, with Galloway (Ellis 1811, 309, 348). For Sir Walter Scott the romance's 'scene is laid in Carrick, in Ayrshire', perhaps because Grime is lord of 'Garwicke': *Sir Tristrem: A Metrical Romance of the Thirteenth Century, by Thomas of Erceldoune, called the Rhymer*, ed. Walter Scott, 3rd edn (Edinburgh: Constable, 1811), lviii. For an extended argument that the poem is set in the so-called 'Debatable Land' of the Borders see Rickert 1967, xx–xxii.

11 Julia Kristeva notes that the male subject is defined by the 'uncertainty of his borders', which is 'all the more determining where the paternal function [is] weaker or non-existent' (Kristeva 1982, 63).

CHAPTER TEN

From Beyond the Grave: Darkness at Noon in *The Awntyrs off Arthure**

MARGARET ROBSON

In this essay, I shall offer a reading of *The Awntyrs off Arthure* which is based on a literal interpretation of the narrative of a return of a corpse from its resting place. Crucial to any interpretation of *The Awntyrs off Arthure* is an understanding of why the decomposing corpse of Guinevere's mother should appear to her daughter and Sir Gawain. This essay sets out to explore the phenomenon of the return of a corpse from its resting place, and then looks at some different ways in which the messages dead bodies bring can be read culturally.

The Awntyrs off Arthure is an alliterative poem which survives in four fifteenth-century manuscripts. There is no immediate source for the poem as a whole, but its stanza form and alliteration show affinities with other poems of the region of the north-west of England, most notably *Pearl* and *Sir Gawain and the Green Knight*. There are also links with the alliterative *Morte Arthure*.[1] Although the tale is usually included in the genre of romance, the first episode may equally well be read as an exemplum. Part of the problem of classification relates to the discussion of the tale's unity. A synopsis of the whole of the narrative will illustrate the point:

> One winter, Arthur and his knights are out hunting with Guinevere in Inglewood Forest, near Carlisle.[2] Guinevere and Gawain have become separated from the party when the hunt is interrupted by a storm so fierce that the sky turns black. They are then confronted by a demonic figure who appears from the tarn and, revealing itself to be Guinevere's mother,

* This essay owes both its inspiration and its existence to Dr Darryl Jones, without whose help the corpse would have stayed firmly in her grave. I would also like to express my thanks to Professor Felicity Riddy, Professor John Scattergood and Dr James R. Simpson.

proceeds to catechize both Guinevere and Gawain on the evils of the proud rich and the lustful, on the virtues of alms-giving, and on Arthur's greed. Finally, the figure predicts the downfall of Arthur's court, asks for charity to be done for her sake and for masses to be said for the sake of her soul. After the figure's departure, the weather clears up and the hunting party is reunited to return home for supper. Thus ends the first half of the tale (usually known as the *Awntyrs A*).

The second half (the *Awntyrs B*) begins when, at supper, a knight accompanied by a lady enters and asks for an adversary to step forward. His name is Galeron, and his grievance is against Arthur, who has stolen his lands and given them to Gawain. Gawain consents to defend his rights. The fight is a brutal one, with Guinevere weeping for the injured Gawain, and Galeron's lady pleading that Guinevere should intercede and stop the fight. Galeron and Gawain are satisfied, and the former gives up the right to the disputed territory. Arthur then gives Gawain great tracts of land and a dukedom, on the condition that Galeron is given the original lands. Galeron, also made a duke, weds his lady. The concluding stanza refers back to the first half, detailing the masses which Guinevere arranges to be said for her mother.

The tale has stimulated much critical debate on its status as a single, complete piece of work. Ralph Hanna actually divides his edition of the tale into two separate adventures (the *Awntyrs A* and the *Awntyrs B*), with the final stanza also included separately. His argument, that the two parts were composed by different authors and compiled by a third, is not one accepted by other notable critics of the poem such as Rosamund Allen, A. C. Spearing, and Helen Phillips.[3]

David Klausner argues that the tale should be read as though one part amplifies the other, although he begins by stating: 'It is clear that this tale was formed by the joining of two independent stories, and it will be convenient to consider each half of the narrative separately' (Klausner 1972, 309). This is a contradiction which other critics also fail to confront, although Thorlac Turville-Petre turns it into an argument for reading the poem as a unified work: 'Perhaps', he suggests, 'the poet's message lies in the very lack of connection between the two episodes' (Turville-Petre 1977, 65).

These critical arguments, however, rest on the assumption that, within the narrative, the events of *A* are known to the courtiers of *B*. However, we are never told that the courtiers are aware of the appearance of Guinevere's mother and of her prophecies. When Guinevere and Gawain are re-united with the others, there is only some conversation about the weather, after which everyone rides off to supper:

> The king his bugle has blowen and on the bent rides;
> His fair folk in the frith, they flokken in fere.
> And al the riall route to the quene rides
> And melis to hir mildlely on thaire manere.
> The wise of the wedres, forwondred they were.
> Prince proudest in palle,
> Dame Gaynour and alle,
> Rayked to Rondelesette Halle
> To the suppere.
>
> (330–8)

Except for the concluding stanza (703–15), the events of *A* are never mentioned again.[4]

We cannot, therefore, assume that the Arthur who gives away great tracts of land in *B* is doing so because he has been told that he is too covetous. I cannot see that the events of *B* are a direct consequence of the prophecies and admonishments of *A*: the only continuity between the two sections is that the narrative is still Arthurian and set in Cumbria. Assumptions as to the poem's unity are primarily based on the fact that these two seemingly disparate narratives are yoked together under the one title, *The Awntyrs off Arthure*. However, this title is the invention, not of the original author, but of Robert Thornton, the compiler of Lincoln Cathedral MS 91, the major manuscript in which the poem appears (Mills 1992, xxv).

There is another argument which militates against reading the tale as a whole, and that is the argument from boredom. Hanna politely remarks that 'a reader of the poem ought to be struck by the differing levels of poetic competence in the first and second halves of the poem' (Hanna 1970, 277). John Speirs simply ignores completely the fact that there is a second half: his penetrating analysis of the first half suggests a lack of interest in the second (Speirs 1967). Critics are united in finding the *B* episode 'stock', while the *A* episode, which has 'no apparent direct written source', is generally treated as though it provided the impetus for interpretation of *B* (Lowe 1980, 202). The contradictory and contrived positions which the critic who wishes to read this poem as a unified whole has to adopt are, in my view, sufficient reason for reading it as two separate narratives. Spearing's carefully counted explanation of the importance of Arthur, who sits at the midpoint of the poem, much as we would expect to see the seated figure of Christ at the apex of church porches or on tomb sculptures, relies on the reader accepting that 'in both episodes Arthur's role is of some importance' (Spearing 1982, 251).[5] I shall return to this question below; for the moment, suffice it to say that in the first half Arthur's role is limited to that of blowing the horn at the beginning and end of the hunt.

Phillips has recently suggested a different schema from the generally accepted bipartite model. She observes: 'None of the manuscripts simply divides the work into two halves to produce the binary structure that has become a standard assumption for modern critics' (Phillips 1993, 65). Her own reading focuses on the theme of mutability, seen less as the mortality of the flesh than as the transience of the 'kings and the territory-controlling élite' (79) with whom Guinevere's mother identifies. Although Phillips's argument is both cogent and interesting, I remain unconvinced of the coherence of the poem. Furthermore, it seems to me that the message and the knowledge carried by the decaying body in the *Awntyrs* are more powerful and disturbing than a simple reminder of the mutability topos. Nor, I think, does the figure which reveals itself to be Guinevere's mother derive either its authority or its prescience from her aristocratic lineage: the fact that this woman was a queen is of far less importance than the fact that she is now a corpse. It should also be remembered that Guinevere's mother has no place in any other piece of Middle English Arthurian literature.[6] Almost every other Arthurian mother can be identified at least by territory: they commonly come attached to places or family (Igrayne is Duchess of Cornwall, Morgawse is Queen of Lothian, Elaine is 'of Corbenic'). Here we have a mother who remains an otherwise anonymous body: we know neither her name, nor the land she may have controlled. It would seem to me odd that we should be expected to read an unknown, unnamed woman as a type for a narrative of 'The Fall of Princes'.

It is generally agreed that the *A* episode is analogous to *The Three Living and the Three Dead* and to *The Trental of Gregory*.[7] In the case of *The Three Living and the Three Dead*, both the setting and the public message are similar: indeed, Orme remarks that 'by the early fifteenth century a specific link had developed between the story and hunting' (Orme 1992, 144). In the *Trental*, the appearance of Gregory's mother with a personal message about adultery suggests some connection with the *Awntyrs A*. However, I want to argue that the singularity of the figure in the *Awntyrs*, coupled with the setting, opens up the possibility that the impetus for this section of the narrative was a local story of the discovery of a corpse in the tarn.

The mention of 'the Terne Wathelyn' in the poet's own introduction (1–2) and in the (modern) title of the romance implicitly acknowledges that the setting of the poem is as important as any of its characters (Hanna 1974, 32). I would go further and say that the tarn is the most important feature of the tale. Moreover, the setting does not fit easily into established interpretative models. This is not, or not primarily, the landscape of allegory, nor is it merely decorative; it is not even, simply, plausible as a setting for a hunting story. Phillips mentions the story's 'cosily localized setting' (Phillips 1993, 56), but it is difficult to imagine anything less cosy than an isolated, marshy tarn in a forest, especially when that tarn has a reputation for dire or supernatural events.[8] In general terms, as Speirs notes, there is an analogy to be drawn here with *Beowulf*, where a tarn also features as a locus for the appearance of 'monsters from the deep' (Speirs 1967, 255). More specifically, the poet here draws on local legends about this particular tarn as a notorious site for ghostly or unnatural apparitions, legends fostered by the region's notoriety as a hideout for murderers and criminal gangs.[9]

There are landscapes which are intrinsically hostile to human life, such as glaciers and deserts; there are also landscapes which are constructed as hostile according to cultural mores.[10] In this tale, we have a landscape which is hostile because of its association with events, events which are interpreted supernaturally. I want to suggest that this reputation was established because the geography of the tarn made it an eminently suitable place for the illicit disposal of dead bodies.

Normally, in Christian tradition, bodies are buried 'six feet under', with attendant rites and witnesses. Although not all cultures hide decaying bodies, some of the reasons for doing so were as apparent in the fourteenth century as they are in the twentieth, as witness the vividly described stench of the sixteen-week-old corpse in *Sir Amadace*.[11] It should be remembered that, when dealt with properly, bodies are not merely hidden from view, but prevented from coming to view.

Not all bodies, however, were buried. Relics were an important commodity in the Middle Ages, as Chaucer's Pardoner makes plain (*Pardoner's Prologue*, 347–51). The idea that the bodies of holy people retained power which could be transmitted to those who touched them was commonplace. Philippa Tristram writes:

> On his death in 1274, Aquinas was decapitated and his bones boiled by
> his fellow monks at Fossanuova, in order to secure his relics; the bones of
> St Louis were distributed to guests by his descendant, Charles VI, at a
> solemn feast in 1392. These crudities leave their mark even on relatively
> reticent and pious sensibilities. Lydgate is fond of such tales, and relates
> how five roses sprung from the eyes, ears and mouth of a dead devotee of
> the Virgin, each one inscribed with her name in gold. These stories may
> indeed endeavour to correct macabre terrors with the assurance that, if the
> evil stink in their decay, the good remain incorrupt and sweet-smelling.
>
> (Tristram 1976, 153)

The converse of the sweet-smelling, whole (and holy) corpse is the stinking, dissolving one, whose touch does not heal but causes decay. The leper is, of course, the living embodiment of such terror, decaying while still above ground and spreading infection. The unquiet dead, however, add metaphysical fear to the physical fear of the leper. Unless there are particular circumstances, such as an epidemic of pestilential illness, improper burial indicates some type of crime: the corpse is either that of a sinner (the murderer or suicide buried in unconsecrated ground) or that of a victim, disposed of in haste by the murderer. *Sir Orfeo* contains an account of such untimely or sinful dead (and undead), removed, in accordance with Celtic tradition, by the fairies, and preserved in their last earthly states:

> Than [Orfeo] gan bihold about al
> & seighe liggeand with-in the wal
> Of folk that were thider y-brought,
> And thought dede, & nare nought.
> Sum stode with-outen hade,
> & sum non armes nade,
> & sum thurth the body hadde wounde,
> & sum lay wode, y-bounde,
> & sum armed on hors sete,
> & sum astrangled as thai ete;
> & sum were in water adreynt,
> & sum with fire al for-schreynt.
> Wiues ther lay on child-bedde,
> Sum ded & sum a-wedde,
> & wonder fele ther lay bisides
> Right as thai slepe her vnder-tides,
> Eche was thus in this warld y-nome,
> With fairi thider y-come.
>
> (387–404)[12]

Chaucer's *Nun's Priest's Tale* provides an interesting, and roughly contemporary, example of the hurried disposal of a murder victim; and one, moreover, which employs several of the same motifs. The fact that the body is hidden, under cover of darkness, in a waggon-load of dung (which serves both to hide the smell of the body and to suggest its decay), is revealed in a dream, in which the victim himself visits his companion. The populace's comments on the discovery of the corpse insist that, when no other means of discovering a wrong is afforded, God empowers the dead to return (here through a vision) to reveal the crime:

> O blisful God, that art so just and trewe,
> Lo, how that thou biwreyest modre alway!
> Modre wol out
>
> (3050–2)

This same phrase, 'Modre wol out', also appears in the *Prioress's Tale* (576), again in the context of a returning murdered body. Here a Christian child, murdered by Jews, is hidden in a cesspit; the body is discovered when it is given the grace to sit up and sing the 'Alma redemptoris' (607–13).

The problems of the illicit disposal of bodies are many and various. Firstly, one has to dispose of the body without being seen. (I am working on the assumption that most murderers wish to escape detection, although this is not always the case.) In order to avoid detection, the body must be disposed of either under cover of darkness or in an isolated spot, and preferably both. Secondly, bodies must remain hidden long enough for murderers to make good their escape. If a body is buried quickly and in darkness, the disposer is unlikely to have time, or ground soft enough, to dig a six-foot pit and fill it in again. The shallow grave is, in itself, almost a sign of crime: and of course shallow graves yield up their bodies easily. Paul Barber, author of a study of the return of the corpse, cites a case from the *Los Angeles Times* where 'A hand protruding from an incline . . . led to the discovery of the badly decomposed body of an adult male' (Barber 1988, 134). Barber provides a forensic explanation for the well-known folklore motif that Stith Thompson names 'Hand of Sinner Sticks Out From Grave' (Thompson 1932–5, E 411.0.1). He further remarks:

> The event is not unusual – if it follows two other events: shallow burial and either erosion or the presence of scavengers (or both). This is because the scavengers dig down to the corpse and latch onto whatever part of it is most easily brought to the surface, which is most likely to be a hand. This could explain how the hand in the newspaper account quoted above came to the surface. Erosion could also account for this, since the dirt would have been loosened by digging, then raised higher than the dirt that surrounded the grave.
>
> (Barber 1988, 134–5)

Leaving the corpse *in situ* is not an option for those wishing to postpone the detection of their crime: as Hamlet remarks, even if the body were hidden, one would be able to find it soon enough by sniffing. In terrain which is rocky, or where tree-roots and undergrowth provide a significant obstacle to digging, an obvious solution is to dispose of the body in water. However, as bodies are buoyant, they must either be exceedingly heavily weighted (bodies have floated to the surface despite being attached to electricity generator casings or wholly sealed in lead pipes), or the water must be both standing (in order that tides or currents do not wash the body into public view) and isolated. A tarn, a small lake in the middle of a forest, is therefore a perfect location.

What the Tarn Wathelyn provides, in both its topography and its legends, is, in essence, a famous local murder-spot. 'Ghastly' figures are seen there, and indeed a decomposing body which has spent some time in water must qualify as 'ghastly' by anybody's standards. In fact, this decomposing body might look very much like the figure which reveals itself as Guinevere's mother. What I suggest is that the impetus for the narrative is the rumour, or legend, of a local murder story. Corpses do speak, as forensic medical examiners well know; they speak the language of the body and its decay. Those cultures without the benefit of modern pathology might offer other explanations as to why a corpse might rise from the dead. In the *Awntyrs* we are offered both a physical and a spiritual explanation for the presence of the figure.[13]

With this in mind, a physical explanation for the presence of the figure suggests itself. We are told that the narrative events occur in winter (it is the close season, September to February, 8); we are also told that the figure's appearance is heralded by a tremendous storm:

> The day wex als dirke
> As hit were mydnight myrke
> Thereof Arthur was irke
> And light on his fote.
>
> Thus on fote are they founde, these frekes vnfayn,
> And fleen to the forest fro the fawe felle.
> And to reset thei ronne for rydour of reyne,
> For the sneterand snawe that snaypped hem snell.
>
> (75–82)

The storm here is not only a literary signifier of troubled times, nor just an appropriate backdrop to a prophetic narrative: it is also a realistic feature. When it rains, the water-table rises, and with it anything in the marsh. All human bodies, living or dead, are naturally fairly buoyant; but this buoyancy increases with decomposition, as methane gas is produced within the body cavities. We are further told that the ghastly figure that appears to Guinevere and Gawain is preceded by a flame (83); read symbolically, this flame may represent the entrance to hell, read literally it betrays the presence of marsh gas.

The body that emerges from the tarn speaks. I shall examine what it says a little further on. The manner of its speech, however, also deserves comment:

> Hit waried, hit waymented, as a woman,
> But nauthyr on hide ne on huwe no heling hit hadde.
> Hit stemered, hit stonayde, hit stode as a stone;
> Hit marred, hit memered, hit mused for madde.
>
> (107–10)

Although this particular figure is represented as having unusual powers of speech and movement, it must be remembered that decomposing bodies do both move and make noises, which may be interpreted as moaning. The reasons for this are due to the processes of decomposition itself. Firstly, *rigor mortis* is not a permanent but a temporary condition, which passes in about thirty-six hours.[14] Secondly, as gases are emitted, tissues burst and this may be audible, even when the body is properly interred in the ground (Barber 1988, 127–8). The 'original' figure may, in actual, literal fact, have burst out of the marsh, moaning and squirming.

Naked and black, with glowing eyes, the figure is also hung with snakes and toads:

> Bare was the body and blake to the bone,
> Al biclagged in clay vncomly cladde.
>
> (105–6)

> On the chef of the cholle,
> A pade pikes on the polle,
> With eighen holked ful holle
> That gloed as the gledes.

> Al glowed as a glede the goste there ho glides,
> Vmbeclipped in a cloude of clethyng vnclere;
> Serkeled with serpentes that sat to the sides –
> To tell the todes theron my tonge wer full tere.
>
> (114–21)

Whatever their metaphorical significance, none of these features would be surprising in a real corpse. In the early stages of decomposition, the human body first becomes greenish, then darkens; if the body is supine, before liquefying the eyeballs will fill with blood, and thus show red. Critics have made much of the presence of toads on the body. Phillips notes:

> The toads and serpents in the *Awntyrs* thus have a complex ancestry: they belong to the *memento mori* tradition, demonstrating the dissolution of the corpse; they may also reflect tales and exempla of the 'adulterous mother' type, where toads and serpents symbolize illicit kisses and illegitimate children; but they also clearly represent the fiends of hell who, held at bay by baptism, have reclaimed the sinner after death.
>
> (Phillips 1989, 51)

What I would also emphasize, however, is that toads live in, or by, water, and eat flesh, as do snakes: they too are part of the natural process of decomposition. The figure, then, is neither unusual nor solely allegorical: this is what a decomposing corpse found in these circumstances would probably look like. This interpretation does not, of course, exclude metaphorical readings. The figure also looks as we would expect a demon to look: as Barber points out, the fat and healthy-looking figure does not form part of our nightmare ideas of dissolution.[15]

When a body 'returns from the dead', its presence has to be accounted for. Almost all the critics who have commented on the *Awntyrs* refer to the figure either as a ghost (Withrington 1991, 13; Krishna 1976, 11; Barron 1987, 163), an apparition (Spearing 1985, 134; Lowe 1980, 203), or a returned spirit (Hanna 1974, 24, although he also remarks on 'the ghost's earthiness', which he accounts for by saying that the figure is 'a reminder of the grave' (29)). Orme, by contrast, calls it a 'spectre [which] resembled a corpse' (Orme 1992, 144), and Speirs writes (though he does not pursue the comment): 'The full horror of the appearance is now visible at close quarters as a body risen from the grave, the body of what was a woman' (Speirs 1967, 256). Each of the critics, Speirs included, accounts for the figure in the same terms with which the author sought to account for it. Christian tradition, which naturally seeks an explanation in metaphysical rather than forensic terms, works on the assumption that a body comes back for a metaphysical reason. I have been arguing instead for the importance of acknowledging and understanding the literal existence of the figure as a decomposing body. Critics have ignored the material 'corpo-reality' of the figure: ironically, even when (or perhaps especially when?) describing it as a reminder of mortality. To read such a figure allegorically is to suppress its powerful message of physical decay.[16]

There are, however, ways of reading allegorically the ghastly figure in the *Awntyrs* that reinforce its import instead of diminishing it. In what follows, I shall attempt to construct (or reconstruct) the body's symbolic significance in the text. The temporal setting of the narrative is important here. The figure appears only after the day has turned dark: 'The day wex al dirke / As hit were nydnight myrke' (75–6). Lowe remarks that the idea of 'undern' as a dangerous time is a familiar trope in other Middle English works, and mentions its association with Gawain, whose mythic strength waxes and wanes with the sun (Lowe 1980, 213–15). Similarly, Friedman has discussed the significance in *Sir Orfeo* of the 'noon-day demon', whose danger is, typically, that of rape to unaccompanied women (Friedman 1966). In the *Awntyrs*, the danger lies not so much in the fact that it is 'undern', but that it is dark at this hour. The motif of 'darkness at noon' belongs, first of all, to the rhetoric of the Day of Judgment:

> Blow ye the trumpet in Zion,
> and sound an alarm in my holy mountain:
> let all the inhabitants of the land tremble:

> for the day of the Lord cometh,
> for it is night at hand.
> A day of darkness and of gloominess,
> a day of clouds and of thick darkness,
> as the morning spreads upon the mountains.
> (Joel 2.1–2; Authorized Version)

The climate and events of Good Friday echo those of Doomsday, as Langland describes:

> The lord of lif and of light tho leide hise eighen togideres.
> The day for drede withdrough and derk bicam the sonne.
> The wal waggede and cleef, and al the world quaved.
> Dede men for that dene came out of depe graves.
> (*Piers Plowman* B.18.59–62)

The blowing of Arthur's horn replicates the 'Last Trump' which will call all to judgment (1 Corinthians 15.51–2), and indeed Guinevere refers to this as 'my dethday' (98). The narrative thus images forth the events of the apocalypse, offering an interpretation of the figure's appearance in terms of a realized eschatology, and this for three reasons. Firstly, the return of a dead body is a type of apocalypse, in the sense that it reveals an event – a crime or sin – which needs judgment. Secondly and consequently, it is on the Day of Judgment that the dead shall arise from their graves. Thirdly, the dead know things that the living do not: the authority of the ghastly figure in the *Awntyrs*, the truth of her prophecies, rests on the fact that her knowledge comes from beyond the grave. It is easy to see why a returned body should be given an apocalyptic message, because such bodies know about the 'four last things': death, judgment, heaven and hell. Here, the poet's achievement is to have worked the 'natural' narrative (the events that really might surround the return of a corpse from a body of water) seamlessly in with the 'supernatural' interpretation of that narrative (a typological reading in which these events are types of Good Friday and Doomsday).[17]

According to her own account, Guinevere's mother was during her lifetime guilty of a number of sins. One of the principal among these, adultery, brings the *Awntyrs* into relation with other texts which deploy what we can call the 'Adulterous Mother' topos. In such narratives, the child is told that the dead mother is being punished in the afterlife because of her pride and lust. When we compare the *Awntyrs* more closely with its analogues, however, significant differences emerge. In *The Legend of Pope Gregory*, an analogue of *The Trental of Gregory*, Gregory's mother relates that she has had a child by her brother and then married her son.[18] In another analogue, the

legend of 'How a Son Delivered His Mother From Hell', the son is represented as being so holy that he prays to be sick for as long as it takes to
ensure his mother's deliverance from Purgatory, only to be told by an angel
that life is not long enough to redeem her.[19] What these 'Adulterous Mother'
narratives are essentially about is the holiness of male children and the
fleshly, evil nature of their mothers (and perhaps, by implication, of the
whole female sex). When Guinevere is informed of her mother's adultery,
however, the impact cannot be the same. Two principal features differenti-
ate the figure in the *Awntyrs* from other Adulterous Mothers: its place within
the Arthurian meta-narrative, and the female gender it shares with the
child to whom it appears. It is to these features that I shall now turn.

The *Awntyrs* differs most clearly from the Gregory narratives in its
Arthurian setting. This setting allows both for the courtly hunt which provides the naturalistic return of the corpse from the tarn, and for the tale's
apocalypticism. The Arthurian court is the epitome of that civilized, worldly
society whose downfall apocalyptic prophecies predict. Moreover, the wider
perspective of Arthurian history gives greater import to the gender of the
figure who in the *Awntyrs* speaks the apocalypse. The end of Arthur's reign
is marked by the reappearance of the Lady of the Lake, giver of the sword
Excalibur (source and symbol of Arthur's power): in Malory's version, after
the final, fatal battle, with Arthur mortally wounded, Sir Bedivere returns
the sword to the Lady:

> Than sir Bedwere departed and wente to the swerde and lyghtly toke hit
> up, and so he wente unto the watirs syde. And there he bounde the gyrdyll
> aboute the hyltis, and threw the swerde as farre into the watir as he myght.
> And there cam an arme and an honde above the watir, and toke hit and
> cleyght hit, and shoke hit thryse and braundysshed, and than vanysshed
> awaye the hande with the swerde into the watir.
>
> (III, 1240.1–7)

It is a part of the figure's apocalyptic resonance in the *Awntyrs* that she
provides a monstrous antitype to the Lady of the Lake.

The ghastly figure offers an interpretation of the reasons behind the
future downfall of the Arthurian world; and the story she tells is, first of all,
one of adultery. At one level, the choice to identify the figure in the *Awntyrs*
with Guinevere's mother may have been an expedient one: if the author
wanted to tell an Adulterous Mother story in an Arthurian setting, then
it was necessary to find a mother whose story was unknown, and whom
we could accept as adulterous. Guinevere is the only major Arthurian
figure whose mother allows for this interpretive openness. There are many

adulterous mothers in Arthurian narrative, starting with Arthur's and Gawain's, but they are accounted for; we know that they did not disappear mysteriously, to re-emerge from obscure tarns in Cumbria (Arthur's mother, Igrayne, meets an honourable end; Gawain's mother, Morgause, is – in one version at least – murdered by her sons for her adultery). About Guinevere's mother, however, we know virtually nothing (certainly not her name); about her death, we know absolutely nothing.

At another level, however, the choice of identity is much more significant. Mother and daughter are both intimately implicated in the text's account of the end of a kingdom; and it is an appreciation of this fact that leads us to the text's most profound resonances. The two female characters are, to many intents and purposes, identical. As Spearing points out, there is a transference of activities between mother and daughter (Spearing 1981, 193). The logic of medieval literary characterization means that, given her daughter's behaviour (her adulterous affair with Lancelot), we can accept Guinevere's mother as an adulteress; and indeed, the figure tells Guinevere to 'Muse on thi mirrour' (167). Furthermore, the pairing of beautiful woman and 'loathly lady', frequent in Middle English literature (for example, *Sir Gawain and the Green Knight*, 942–69), does not only depict 'Woman' under two guises, or two ages; not uncommonly, the women are revealed to be one and the same. The best-known example is Chaucer's *Wife of Bath's Tale*, itself an Arthurian narrative in which an unnamed knight marries a hag who on their wedding night becomes a beautiful woman. In two of the *Tale*'s analogues, *The Marriage of Sir Gawain* and *The Wedding of Sir Gawain and Dame Ragnell*, the knight is identified as Gawain. The presence at the visitation scene in the *Awntyrs* of Gawain, who has this repeated association with loathly-lady-and-beauty pairs, underlines a similar pattern. Guinevere and the ghastly figure identified as her mother are conflated by the text: Guinevere is faced with one (possible? inevitable?) version of her future self, the image of her fate should she continue along the path of adultery (as we, the readers, know she will).

Guinevere's function here is at once personal and political: the moral and physical corruption combined in the maternal figure symbolizes her own moral destiny as well as the decay predicted for Arthur's court. She is also told to mend her ways, as if this could avert the public tragedy, the end of an empire. This is not, however, the figure's only message, nor Guinevere's only role in this scene. Despite the apparent insistence on her adultery, and perhaps even on female nature, as a cause of Arthur's downfall, the *Awntyrs* in fact espouses a much more complex account. Guinevere's question-and-answer session with the figure, while making plain the evil consequences of adultery, is also concerned with right conduct toward the poor:

'Wysse me,' quod Waynour, 'som wey, if thou wost,
What bedis might me best to the blisse bring?'
'Mekenesse and mercy, thes arn the moost,
And haue pite on the poer, that pleses Heuenking.
Sithen charite is chef, and thew of the chaste,
And then almessedede ouer al other thing.
Thes arn the graceful giftes of the holy goste
That enspires iche sprete without speling.'

(248–55)

Guinevere and her mother articulate the plight of the poor and the action necessary to address it. These lines can be read as mere pious convention, or as part of the misogynistic agenda: as evidence of a typically feminine soft-heartedness that, far from suggesting moral seriousness in women, removes them from the domain of genuine ethical reflection (see, for instance, Chaucer's sentimental Prioress in the *General Prologue*, 143–50). A more radical, and feminist, reading is also possible: poverty is an important political issue that can lead to the downfall of states; indeed, in the real world, even that of the Middle Ages, it is much more likely to do so than is the adultery of a queen. Yet only the female characters in the text comment on and attempt to address this problem.[20] Guinevere's position is far from simple: the narrative conflation of Guinevere and the figure of her mother means that, in effect, it is given to Guinevere both to embody the ills of Arthur's rule *and* to speak as the sole conscience in the text that is aware and critical of those ills.

An examination of the role of Gawain supports the idea that the *Awntyrs* is poised between what we might call a 'romance' and a 'political' explanation of the fall of Arthur's kingdom. The romance version apportions blame to both Guinevere and Gawain: to Guinevere for her adultery with Lancelot, to Gawain for vowing enmity with Lancelot after the latter had killed Gareth and Gaheris. In the *Awntyrs*, by contrast, we have Guinevere and Gawain involved in a discourse which questions and criticizes Arthur's rule as well as their own role in his state. Like Guinevere's, Gawain's conversation with the ghastly figure focuses on Arthurian oppression:

'How shal we fare,' quod the freke, 'that fonden to fight,
And thus defoulen the folke on fele kinges londes,
And riches ouer reymes withouten eny right,
Wynnen worshipp and wele thorgh wightnesse of hondes?'

(261–4)

In an extremely interesting essay, Rosalind Field argues that the writers of alliterative verse bear comparison with the writers of Anglo-Norman verse, who, as Field notes, had no interest in praising Arthur. She writes:

The explanation for [the scant interest in Arthurian narrative in the Anglo-Norman period] would seem to be that Arthur, as a paradigm of kingly power, had been recognized as a valuable royal symbol as early as the time of Geoffrey of Monmouth, and was fostered as such by kings from Henry II to Henry VIII. Arthurian romance, therefore, like other manifestations of fashionable Arthuriana, archaeological or mimetic, was not, as it was on the continent, a fanciful amusement, but a deliberate expression of centralized royal power. That the cult of Arthur was encouraged by successive kings for their own purposes is generally accepted. That the converse might also hold good, that opposition to the monarchy could be one reason for the scarcity of Arthurian literature in England, has not, as far as I know, been suggested before.

(Field 1982, 64)

In the case of the alliterative romances it would be fair to say not only that Gawain is the hero, as Field notes, but that Arthur is generally presented in a way that displaces him as the central authority of the text. Either he is 'sumquat childgered' (*Sir Gawain and the Green Knight*, 86), or dependent on Gawain (*The Wedding of Sir Gawain*); at best he is 'ambiguous', 'both great king and aggressive imperialist', as in the alliterative *Morte Arthure* (Krishna 1976, 22). This ambiguity clearly fits with that of the second part of the *Awntyrs* (see the plot summary, p. 200 above); in the first part, which I have been discussing, Arthur is not a presence so much as a focus for hostile conversation.

Gawain completes the triangle formed by Guinevere and the figure. As noted earlier, the figure is an antitype of the Lady of the Lake. Like her, she has knowledge of the future, for she accurately predicts that Arthur's nemesis will be Mordred:[21]

> In riche Arthures halle,
> The barn playes at the balle
> That outray shall you alle,
> Derfely that day.
>
> (309–12)

In this narrative, the three most important figures of Arthur's world (or versions of them) unite to look forward to his doom, and to give an account of it which places the principal blame on his royal shoulders. The causes which will lead to the end of his empire are not ultimately, or not only, the unethical personal behaviour of his subjects whose unruly private lives spill over into the public domain. It is his government which is at fault. Social division and inequality, aggressive imperialism: these are the problems which bring down kingdoms. Spearing has commented: 'In both parts of the poem, the Arthurian civilization is faced with the challenge of an apparently hostile outsider: [this challenge is] supernatural in the first [part], in the form of Guinevere's mother' (Spearing 1981, 185). As I have suggested, however, the hostility is not external but internal in origin. The *Awntyrs* is not so crude a text as to engage in populist projection of conflict onto others.

Kathryn Kerby-Fulton comments that medieval apocalypticism calls on the individual to make a choice between good and evil, that it urges action, and suggests that any individual in the audience could make a difference to the outcome of events: that it is, in fact, a way of confronting the present (Kerby-Fulton 1990). Of course, the whole point of realized eschatology is to bring forward the end of the world – as this narrative does so effectively, with its resolutely apocalyptic resonances – in order to warn people, and here most particularly Arthur, that they must change their ways. I began this essay eschewing the idea that this poem is a 'revenge of the revenant' type; but what realized eschatology does, in figuring forth a horrible future for political and personal oppressors, is at least to predict the after-life revenge of those powerless to overthrow them in this world. Fichte has commented: 'The tale of Galeron [in the *Awntyrs B*] illustrates the reluctance of an independent lord to be assimilated into the scheme of royal power. The point of view we get here is decidedly English; the author's sympathies are with Gawain' (Fichte 1989, 134). In the first episode, 'the irresponsibility, extravagance, and foppish elegance of the court' (Moorman 1981, 85) are condemned, and not by an enemy but by her who, from the lake, is traditionally the giver of Arthur's power. The warning to Arthur, or to those who seek to invoke him as a figurehead, is clear: darkness can fall at any time, even at noon.

Notes

1 For details of the manuscripts, see Guddat-Figge 1976. For formal similarities between the *Awntyrs*, *Pearl* and *Sir Gawain and the Green Knight*, see Hanna 1974, 14–15 and Fein 1997. For links with *The Alliterative Morte Arthure*, see Krishna 1976, 11. All references here are to *The Awntyrs off Arthure at the Terne Wathelyn*, ed. Ralph Hanna (Manchester: Manchester University Press, 1974).
2 See Orme 1992 for details of the hunting seasons.
3 Allen 1985, 5; Spearing 1985, 141; Phillips 1989 and 1993. Allen's position, however, is not unproblematic. She begins by observing: 'Structurally, [the *Awntyrs*] is in two parts, which differ in content and to some extent in style.' Her reading of the poem relies on connections between these two parts, characters in *B* having knowledge of the events of *A*. She also remarks: 'As is now

recognized, there is organic unity in *The Awntyrs off Arthure*.' It is perhaps not surprising that, while I understand Allen's arguments as being on the side of unity, Phillips 1993, 64 places her on the side of disunity. In an earlier work, Spearing (1981, 184) concedes that there may have been more than one author. Barron 1987, 163 also argues for unity, suggesting that the second part demonstrates, in answer to the first, 'that knighthood is still socially valid'.

4 The only critic to comment upon this is Fichte 1989, 133.

5 For descriptions and illustrations of apocalyptic sculptures, see Mâle 1972, 355–74.

6 Mills 1992, 201 notes that while there is one narrative (the French prose *Lancelot*) which includes reference to Guinevere's unnamed mother, she does not figure in Middle English narratives.

7 The legend of *The Three Living and the Three Dead* is a *memento mori* tale. There are various versions, but all limit themselves to temporal concerns such as social station (in some versions the dead are kings) or age (in some the three represent old age, middle age and youth). The moral is always the same: the dead tell the living that this is what they will come to. For a discussion of these legends, see Tristram 1976, 159–67. *The Trental of Gregory*, which will be discussed on pp. 229–30, tells of the appearance to Gregory of his mother while he is praying in church. Suffering the pains of purgatory because she was an adulteress, she is covered in toads and serpents, and begs him to arrange for masses to be said for the repose of her soul. A year later, she appears to him again, but this time she is not a repulsive, earth-bound figure, but one so glamorous that she is mistaken for the Virgin Mary. Again, this is a widespread tale, which always focuses on the fact that the adulterous mother is made repulsive by her sins, and beautiful by the intercession of her holy son. The tales are always set in a church, and the child is always a son. For these tales, see Wells 1923, 172–3 and Hartung 1993, 3267–8.

8 See, for example, *The Avowing of King Arthur*, ed. Roger Dahood (New York: Garland, 1984), ll. 131–2.

9 There is considerable testimony to this: see, for example, Hanna 1974, 34–5; Withrington 1991, 11; Phillips 1993, 80.

10 The 'frightening' forest of medieval romance becomes the forest where Gothic heroines seek sanctuary, fleeing from the 'frightening' buildings. See, for example, the relationship between liberating exteriors and imprisoning interiors in 1790s Gothic, particularly the novels of Anne Radcliffe.

11 *Sir Amadace*, ed. Maldwyn Mills, *Six Middle English Romances*, Everyman (London: Dent, 1973), ll. 71, 91–3, 103–5, 117, 124–5.

12 *Sir Orfeo*, ed. A. J. Bliss (Oxford: Oxford University Press, 1966).

13 I use the word 'figure' here for Guinevere's mother to indicate the literal presence of the body, for this is not, in my reading, a 'ghost'.

14 See Barber 1988, 117–18, although the duration of *rigor mortis* is variable and depends on numerous factors, such as temperature.

15 Barber 1988, 2, 13. Barber points out that the revenant of folklore is radically different from the revenant of fiction, and that the description of the former is,

forensically, far more realistic than the latter. The revenant of the *Awntyrs* fits neither (and both) of the models, having as it does both forensic reasons for emerging from its resting place, and a general similarity to what literature expects a demon to look like. For details of the processes of decomposition, see Barber 1988, 106.

16 Those analogues of the *Awntyrs* that include the appearance of a dead mother to a child are notably different in this respect: in none of them does the setting allow the possibility of the literal, physical presence of a corpse.

17 For realized eschatology and apocalyptic typology in the Middle Ages, see Charity 1966.

18 *Gesta Romanorum*, ed. Sidney J. Herrtage, EETS e.s. 33 (London: Oxford University Press, 1879), pp. 250–63. In this version Gregory is not mentioned by name.

19 Ibid., pp. 401–2.

20 Gayle Margherita (1994, 100–28) similarly argues that Criseyde, far from standing for a 'feminine', private world, as many critics have believed, actually represents the public world of 'masculine' politics.

21 Kennedy 1986, 120, 123 notes that the Lady of the Lake has knowledge of future events; she also observes that emissaries from the lake are associated with supernatural events.

CHAPTER ELEVEN

Gender, Oaths and Ambiguity in
Sir Tristrem and Béroul's *Roman de Tristan*

JANE GILBERT

According to much modern critical opinion, *Sir Tristrem* typifies the worst aspects of Middle English popular romance.[1] It is a greatly condensed translation of an acknowledged masterpiece, an aristocratic and courtly French-language romance: Thomas of Britain's Anglo-Norman *Roman de Tristan*.[2] The process of translation into English, however, apparently involved a fall both in the literary quality of the text and in the social standing of the audience. Helaine Newstead's response is typical: '*Sir Tristrem* is unfortunately a much coarsened version of its subtle and moving original, significant chiefly because it preserves, however inadequately, the lost episodes of its source' (Severs 1967, 79). Among the rare positive readings of *Sir Tristrem*, two stand out: those of Thomas Rumble (1959) and Michael Swanton (1987, 203–15).[3] Rumble argued that in tightening and moralizing the narrative, the poet of *Sir Tristrem* was deliberately tailoring his source to suit the taste of his new audience. In Rumble's view, however, that audience was still 'relatively uncultured' (Rumble 1959, 223). By the standards of Anglo-Norman court society, perhaps, but not within the context of Middle English romance, as Swanton shows. The vocabulary of *Sir Tristrem* is often French in origin, signalling 'an aristocratic tone' (Swanton 1987, 204), while its social setting shows considerable class.[4] In this essay, I shall follow these two commentators in arguing that *Sir Tristrem* is not the simply incompetent poem it was once thought to be.

The full version of the story of Tristan and Yseut (Tristrem and Ysonde in the English poem) begins with Tristan's parents, and ends with the lovers' own deaths.[5] Due to the length and complexity of the narrative, I shall give only a brief contextualization of the parts most directly relevant to my argument. King Mark of Cornwall sends his nephew Tristan to Ireland to fetch Yseut, Mark's intended bride. On the way back to Mark's kingdom,

237

Tristan and Yseut fall in love as a result of accidentally drinking a love potion provided by Yseut's mother and meant to cement her daughter's marriage with Mark. The lovers begin an affair which for both will override all other considerations, and which will end only with their deaths many years later. A major theme of many of the medieval narratives is the adulterers' often highly ingenious attempts to enjoy their love while avoiding if not detection, at least punishment. The majority of the many surviving medieval versions are fragmentary, whether by design or accident, and this fact echoes the concerns of the texts with fragmentation and division: of love and allegiance, as the lovers are torn between their desire for each other, their respect for Mark, and their wish to fulfil their public roles with honour; of the king and his kingdom, as Mark is divided both between his love and need for his queen and for his best knight, and also between the beloved pair and his barons, who constantly threaten to rebel against the shame of a cuckolded king; of the female body, shared between two men; of signification, as facts do not give rise to their expected signs, while signs cannot unproblematically be traced back to facts; of knowledge and proof, as the lovers repeatedly escape those who want to catch them 'in the act'.[6] In this essay, I shall concentrate on one of the greatest moments of evasion: the episode of Yseut's equivocal oath.[7] This occurs when, convinced of the adulterous affair, Mark's barons oblige him to put his wife on trial. She must swear a judicial oath, before God and before the people, stating that she is innocent of the affair with Tristan. If she admits her guilt, she will be burnt alive, while if she lies, she will endanger her immortal soul. In fact, Yseut stage-manages the entire event, first engineering an encounter with the disguised Tristan, and then devising an oath whose ambiguous phrasing enables her, without uttering a downright lie, to disculpate herself publicly, even as she admits her infidelity to those in the know. By this means, both divine and human witnesses are satisfied.

This scene survives in *Sir Tristrem*, but not in its presumed source, Thomas's *Roman de Tristan* (which preserves only the end of the story: from Tristan's marriage while in exile to Queen Yseut's namesake, Yseut *aux blanches mains*, up to the lovers' deaths).[8] Another twelfth-century French poem, Béroul's mainly Norman French *Roman de Tristan*, does have the equivocal oath episode, however, and it is with this that I propose to compare *Sir Tristrem*.[9] To Tristan scholars, this comparison may seem counter-intuitive, because medieval Tristan romances have traditionally been divided into two categories, known generally as the *version courtoise* (Thomas and related versions) and the *version commune* (Béroul and derivatives).[10] Since *Sir Tristrem* is associated with Thomas's version, it is placed in the *courtois* category, but is then criticized for, precisely, its supposedly uncourtly qualities (such as coarseness, cheerful amorality and broad comedy), as well as for its incompetence (seen in its variations of tone and style, and departure from set generic models). Even though there is no evidence that the writer of *Sir Tristrem* knew Béroul's poem, and although it is clear that the narrative of *Sir Tristrem* is based on Thomas, there are reasons to suppose that a comparison with Béroul would illuminate the Middle English text.[11] Many of *Sir Tristrem's* 'uncourtly' and 'incompetent' (or 'popular') features are shared with Béroul's poem; but whereas they have been castigated in *Sir Tristrem*, recent readings of Béroul have interpreted them as creative challenges to literary convention.[12] It is time that the same charitable reading was extended to *Sir Tristrem*. Its Béroul-like changes of tone and humorous seeming-incongruities should be seen as positive literary strategies. Whether or not these strategies are ultimately judged to be successful, a close reading of the equivocal oath episode at least reveals a composer working intelligently and programmatically to alter – and even improve upon – his source material.

In *Sir Tristrem*, the scene of Ysonde's public disculpation occupies about fifty lines (2234–89). Tristrem, disguised and poorly clad, turns up at the place where Ysonde is to take her oath. In full sight of the court, Ysonde asks him to carry her out to a waiting ship. He stumbles, and falls on top of her; she is uncovered in the tumble, showing her body naked to the waist for the assembled company to see. When the knights wish to give Tristrem a ducking (or worse) for his clumsiness, Ysonde defends the poor man, who, she claims, is so faint with hunger he could not bear her weight. She then proceeds to her oath:

> Swete Ysonde sware
> Sche was giltles woman:
> 'Bot on to schip me bare,
> The knightes seighe wele than;
> Whatso his wille ware,
> Ferli neighe he wan,
> Sothe thing;
> So neighe com never man
> Bot mi lord, the King.'
> (2269–77)[13]

To prove the truth of her oath, she is given hot iron to carry; presumably she does so unscathed, since the culmination is that she is 'graunted clene' (2289).[14]

The parallel episode in Béroul's *Tristan* is staged in a quite different way. The text here extends over some one thousand lines (3283–4266). There is a lengthy description of how Tristan, disguised as a leper, sits by a marsh which those attending Yseut's trial must cross. He begs from the assembling audience, bandies words with Mark and with King Arthur (who is present to see fair play), and sends the three wicked barons, Yseut's accusers, floundering into the boggiest patch. When Yseut herself arrives, she commandeers the leper as a horse, and, in the sight of the whole company, rides over the marsh on his back. The following day, Yseut swears her oath, of which this is the essence:

> 'Or escoutez que je ci jure,
> De quoi le roi ci aseüre:
> Si m'aït Dex et saint Ylaire,
> Ces reliques, cest saintuaire,
> Totes celes qui ci ne sont
> Et tuit icil de par le mont,
> Qu'entre mes cuises n'entra home,
> Fors le ladre qui fist soi some,
> Qui me porta outre les guez,
> Et li rois Marc mes esposez.'
>
> (4199–208)

('Now hear what I swear here, may the king be reassured by it. So help me God and Saint Hilary, these relics and this reliquary, as well as all those relics which are not here and all holy things throughout the world, as no man ever entered between my thighs except the leper who acted as a packhorse and carried me over the ford, and King Mark, my husband.')

Yseut repeats four times her identification of the only two men who have been 'between her thighs'; it is repeated again in the anonymous murmurings of the crowd. Arthur offers to fight anyone who dares accuse Yseut further, and Mark accepts her vindication. There is no ordeal.[15]

In these scenes, the heroine's oath produces a clear division between the perspective of the audience of fictional characters inside the text (whom I shall call the intratextual audience) and that of the audience of readers and listeners to the poem (the extratextual audience). In the eyes of the former, the heroine has proved her innocence, while for the latter, she has confessed, even flaunted her guilt. Generally, when this scene is discussed, only the extratextual audience's perspective is considered. I want, however, to look also at the intratextual audience, and to analyse the similarities and differences between this and the extratextual perspective in each poem. How is the heroine constructed as guilty for the extratextual audiences of the poems, and what is the status of that guilt? How does she manage to convince her intratextual audience – Mark and his court – that she is innocent of adultery? My particular focus will be on gender, and on the

contribution the various configurations of gender make, both to the heroine's conviction for adultery and to her disculpation.

The Extratextual Audience

The situation of the extratextual audience is essentially the same in Béroul's
Tristan and in *Sir Tristrem*. It is determined by the literary experience of that
audience, and in particular by their expectations about the appearance of
equivocal oaths. In medieval literature (see the wide-ranging survey in Hexter
1975), by far the most common use of the equivocal oath motif is in circumstances where a woman, brought to trial for an illicit love affair, contrives
to swear an oath which at once proves her innocence to her intratextual
audience, and joyously declares her transgression to her co-conspirators;
thus she outwits the husband or father who supposedly controls her sexuality, and enjoys her chosen lover unpunished. This topos – which I shall
call the Equivocal Oath scenario – enshrines a particular version of sexual
difference: an essentialist identification of femininity with trickery.[16] The
origin of the trick (so enjoyed by the extratextual audience) always lies with
the woman. Often, it is she who designs the oath, but even when it is not,
her sexual trickery, her refusal to be bound sexually by society's laws, is the
fundamental premise. There are, of course, also unfaithful men present: the
situation requires a rogue male, the illicit lover. Even when he designs and
swears the oath, (as Lancelot does when defending Guinevere's reputation
in Chrétien de Troyes's *Chevalier de la Charrete*, or as Ami does in defending
Belissant, in *Ami et Amile*), however, no conclusion about masculine nature
is drawn.[17] At most, we can say that his behaviour is the aberration of an
individual; hers, by contrast, is presented as typically, generically feminine.
Feminine sexuality and feminine language are both designated as equivocal.

As far as the extratextual audience is concerned, the equivocal oath is
great fun. This audience embraces the heroine's adultery. It celebrates her
illicit love with her, glories in her hoodwinking of her husband and society,
loves the feistiness with which she refuses to be subjugated, the ingenuity
and wit with which she turns the male institutions against themselves. Yseut's
is a classic case. Much of the pleasure of the medieval *Tristan* texts, for the
reader and presumably also for the writer, lies in the deceit practised by the
lovers on their society, and in the tricks and equivocations by which they
evade entrapment. In both *Sir Tristrem* and Béroul's *Tristan*, therefore, the
extratextual audiences' pleasure in the equivocal oath is a pleasure in the
feminine, which includes a pleasure both in uncontainable feminine sexuality and in inexhaustible feminine wiliness.

The Intratextual Audience

Critics have concentrated on the pleasure that the extratextual audience gets from Yseut's craftiness. There is, however, another side to the story. For the intratextual audience, the heroine's adultery is a transgression deserving of severe punishment; her subversion of the judicial system only adds to her wickedness. The essentialist idea of femininity found in the Equivocal Oath scenario remains in place, but its value is inverted: what in the positive, extratextual perspective is a celebration of woman's intelligence and refusal to be subordinated, is in the negative, intratextual perspective a condemnation of her inevitable sexual and linguistic falsehood.[18] Extratextual 'ingenious, amusing trickery' turns into intratextual 'deceitful, damnable treachery'. In its negative version, the Equivocal Oath scenario endorses the same ideas embedded in the positive version: that all women are sexually unfaithful by nature (and if they have not actually been unfaithful yet, they will be as soon as they are given half a chance); and that any woman who appears faithful is to be approached with especial suspicion, as one engaged in an elaborate charade.

The fact that the Equivocal Oath account of femininity is essentialist does not mean that it was the only one available within the culture that produced it. Medieval culture and medieval literary texts put various femininities into circulation: it is largely context that determines which version of femininity predominates in any given circumstance. The possibility that faithful, truth-telling women might exist was not precluded, and many works show such women in action. Furthermore, medieval writers were capable of reflecting on the effects that the assumption of female sexual guilt and lies could have on women's lives. A faithful woman might find herself closely confined by a husband in mortal fear of cuckoldry: a man who 'knows' that all women are unfaithful by nature.[19] She might also – and this is particularly pertinent to my subject – find herself wrongfully accused of infidelity yet be unable to prove her innocence, due to her society's assumption of feminine deceit. Working from a belief in the possibility of feminine fidelity on the part of writer and audience, such texts critique the general prejudice. Put like this, it is clear that, whatever applause the heroine who flagrantly swears an equivocal oath may win, the Equivocal Oath scenario is also misogynistic, forming part of the great body of thinking that, from the classical period onwards, condemned women and promoted men.[20]

In the *Tristan* poems, the heroine faces the problem of establishing her innocence against an overwhelming presumption of guilt. Somehow, she must circumnavigate the Equivocal Oath scenario, which would condemn her outright. It is in the approach the heroine takes towards this problem that *Sir Tristrem* and Béroul's *Tristan* part company. In order to establish their innocence, both the English Ysonde and the French Yseut perform a version of gender, but the gender they perform and the way it signifies innocence are quite different.[21] Ysonde changes the script entirely, inverting the Equivocal Oath scenario into its literary opposite by playing the innocent; Yseut adopts a two-pronged approach, remaining within the Equivocal Oath scenario but, on the one hand, altering her gender so that she is seen in masculine, not feminine, terms, and, on the other, mimicking and self-consciously performing the part of the unfaithful trickster in such a way that her adoption of this role seems ironic.

Sir Tristrem

Ysonde addresses the problem of establishing her innocence (or more precisely, of making the accusation against her look groundless) by altering the literary scenario in which she finds herself. This she does essentially by manipulating her own image. She manages to make herself look not like an Equivocal Oath heroine, but like the heroine of a Calumniated Queen narrative.[22] Calumniated Queen narratives centre around 'an innocent, persecuted queen' and the story of her 'undeserved suffering at the hands of a persecutor or a credulous and suspicious husband' (Schlauch 1927, 3).[23] The heroine's persecution may take various forms; most commonly, it consists of an accusation of sexual transgression (infidelity or giving birth to monstrous offspring), or of murder. Despite the injustice of this accusation, nothing can be done to put it aside, and the heroine undergoes a long punishment before being rehabilitated. What I want to draw attention to is the fact that the intratextual audience in a Calumniated Queen narrative is guided by exactly the same assumptions as rule the extratextual audience in the Equivocal Oath scenario: that women on trial for their chastity are axiomatically unfaithful, and that any legal representation which makes them look innocent is not only highly suspect, but actually to be read as confirmation of guilt. Calumniated Queen narratives present in many ways the negative image of Equivocal Oath narratives, the situations of the extratextual and intratextual audiences being reversed: the latter convinced of the heroine's guilt, while the former knows her to be innocent.

These twin narrative scenarios thus encode completely opposite ideas of femininity: in the Equivocal Oath plot, woman is indisputably guilty, in that of the Calumniated Queen, indisputably innocent. So strongly is each version of femininity associated with its particular scenario, that the presentation of the heroine functions as a synecdoche for the type of narrative: only

create the look of the right heroine, and the appropriate structures of meaning – innocence or guilt – will fall into place around her. Ysonde sets out
to do precisely this: by evoking the Calumniated Queen type in the minds
of her intratextual audience, she will automatically appear as the opposite
of the Equivocal Oath heroine, and thus establish her innocence, for a
Calumniated Queen cannot, by definition, be guilty.

As mimicked by Ysonde, the Calumniated Queen has a variety of features. Several could be explored, but I shall confine my discussion to two
that Ysonde highlights. The Calumniated Queen is tender-hearted and
compassionate, identifying with the underprivileged and with those in danger. Ysonde demonstrates these qualities when she intercedes on behalf of
the supposed beggar with the knights who want to punish him for stum-
bling while carrying her:

> In water thai wald him sink
> And wers, yif thai may.
> 'Ye quite him ivel his swink,'
> The Quene seyd to hem ay.
> 'It semeth mete no drink
> Hadde he nought mani a day.
> For poverté, methenk,
> He fel, for sothe to say,
> And nede.
> Geveth him gold, Y pray;
> He may bidde God me spede.'
> (2256–66)

In claiming that the beggar falls for lack of food, Ysonde not only highlights
her womanly solicitude and sympathy for the underdog, but also emphasizes her own vulnerability by her intercessory stance.[24] She thus calls forth
her entourage's generic protectiveness: what romance knight could resist
the plea of a lady in distress?

The Calumniated Queen is also, of course, sexually pure. Ysonde emphasizes her own purity in her description of her adventure with the beggar:

> 'Whatso his wille ware,
> Ferli neighe he wan,
> Sothe thing.'
> (2273–5)

This is rich in implication: so far is Ysonde from even thinking a sexual
thought that she is uncertain as to how to interpret the behaviour of the
beggar who threw himself on top of her. She seems to intimate that only
men and unchaste women really understand sexual desire: she herself,

being a chaste woman, knows nothing of it. And yet, so scrupulous is this faithful queen's awareness of the proper boundaries to be maintained between body and body, that she feels that this 'ferly neighe' contact must be declared. The right to evaluate her encounter with the beggar is deferentially handed over to the upper-class males who witnessed it. They of course, having seen that 'nothing happened', will judge the episode to have been wholly innocent, and thus award her the seal of a purity which she appears almost too timid to claim for herself. Ysonde here presents herself as a punctilious and submissive wife, conscious that it is not for her to decide whether or not she has transgressed.

Ysonde's sexual purity is further emphasized in the scene that prepares the way for the oath. The major element in this scene is the revelation of her genitals:

> Tristrem hir bar that tide
> And on the Quen fel he
> Next her naked side
> That mani man might yse
> San schewe.
> Hir queynt aboven hir kne
> Naked the knightes knewe.
> (2249–55)

This immodest scene is cleverly turned into evidence of the heroine's modest nature. The intimate revelation appears to those who witness it to be wholly involuntary. Ysonde's genitals are on display 'that mani man might yse', but without apparently being shown ('san schewe').[25] The responsibility for this embarrassing revelation is thereby firmly placed with the men who witness it: they are to blame for looking when they should have been averting their eyes. Ysonde succeeds in casting herself as the innocent victim of the sexual gaze of men, who notice her genitals when no notice has been given. The narrator here colludes with his heroine in his use of language: there is a wonderful primness to the French 'san' (Modern French *sans*, 'without'), which mimics the heroine's demure appearance by a proceeding not unlike the modern novelistic technique of free indirect speech.

This coyness is evident also in the use of the word 'queynt' for Ysonde's genitals. 'Queynt' is a much discussed term within Middle English studies, and particularly in criticism of Chaucer. For long it was thought to carry an obscene register. Larry Benson, however, conclusively disproved that supposition, demonstrating that the use of 'queynt' for the female genitals was in Middle English a euphemism, with a sense approximating to 'elegant, pleasing thing' (Benson 1984, 38). Discussing two uses of the term by the Wife of Bath in her addresses to her husbands, Benson analyses the tone conveyed by 'queynt'. On the first occasion (*Wife of Bath's Prologue*, 332), the Wife is 'on her dignity', employing a 'formal, almost too correct tone' (Benson 1984, 44); on the second (*Wife of Bath's Prologue*, 444), she is 'talking cute', in 'wheedling baby talk' (Benson 1984, 43). Although addressing the possibility that Chaucer owes the euphemistic application of 'queynt' to the female genitalia to *Sir Tristrem* (cited by Benson as the sole recorded use in this sense before Chaucer's time), Benson clearly conceives of this debt as a parody on Chaucer's part of the older text (Benson 1984, 41–2), as if the use of 'queynt' in *Sir Tristrem* were entirely straightforward and unselfconscious.[26] In my opinion, this drastically understates the suitability of 'queynt' in the context in which it is deployed in *Sir Tristrem*. The tone implied by the use of 'queynt' is exactly the same as that of 'san schewe': the French-derived euphemisms conjure up the image of someone too prudish even to speak (or write) directly of the indelicacy that is sex.[27] This prude is not, however, the writer of *Sir Tristrem*; it is the Calumniated Queen Ysonde, the 'pure' woman. The narrator gives us the words she would have spoken, had she deigned discuss her exposure. Her tone is described perfectly by Benson's characterization of the Wife of Bath: both dignity and cuteness are implied in Ysonde's stance before her accusers. It is not Chaucer but Ysonde (and behind her, the poet of *Sir Tristrem*) who first parodies the euphemistic sensibility suggested by 'queynt'. The queenly dignity and child-like purity adopted by the Wife of Bath in her brawls with her husbands were earlier borrowed by Mark's adulterous wife.

The preceding discussion does not exhaust the appropriateness of 'queynt' to its context in *Sir Tristrem*. Benson's discussion of the term is framed as a refutation of the many critics who have seen an obscene pun in its every occurrence within Chaucer's works. Benson advances some rules of the pun: the punned upon word must have (at least) two distinct meanings, both current in contemporary language, and both of which fit the context (25–6). As Benson himself insists, the most commonly attested use of the term 'queynt' – its primary meaning – is not that of the female genitals; this sense is found, before Chaucer's time, only in *Sir Tristrem*. Since the sexual meaning was not current, the vast majority of those puns in which an obscene referent is detected behind Chaucer's use of the term 'queynt' must be invalidated. However devastating to seekers of Chaucerian obscenity, these rules are very useful in approaching *Sir Tristrem*. As Benson points out, the *MED* records only four uses of 'queynt' as a noun before 1400: 'three where the meaning is "trick" . . . and one where the meaning is "a clever or curious device or ornament," that from *The Wars of Alexander*: "A bedd . . . with koyntis and knopis of perle"' (Benson 1984, 37). Insofar as these few instances can constitute evidence, the primary meaning of 'queynt' seems to be 'trick'. And this sense is appropriate in the context of *Sir Tristrem*. When

Ysonde reveals her 'queynt', she bares not only her genitals, but also the trick with which she is in the process of deceiving her intratextual audience. Both the genitals and the trick are displayed, unashamedly, to the audience outside the text, that audience which anyway knows she is the heroine of an Equivocal Oath, and expects from her the pleasure of the 'queynt' (as trick).

The choice of the term 'queynt' thus skilfully delineates Ysonde's position in relation at once to the intratextual and to the extratextual audience. Although Benson sees in this episode of *Sir Tristem* the trademarks of a 'crude and unskilled' writer, he is willing to accept a similar pun in both uses of 'queynt' by the Wife of Bath. Since the Wife is defending herself mendaciously against her husbands' accusations of adultery, it is possible that the primary sense of 'queynt' as 'trick' is also present behind the contextually appropriate euphemism for the genitals, whose innocence she is at once asserting and connoting (Benson 1984, 44). Once again, we can suggest here that Chaucer is not parodying but imitating the practice in *Sir Tristrem*. If such a pun is indeed intended in *The Wife of Bath's Prologue*, it has a precedent in the popular romance so derided by modern critics.[28]

More than anything else, we may say, Ysonde's intimate revelation reminds those who witness it of the basic fact that she is female. In itself, however, this fact is nothing. Where it becomes important is in the cultural significance of femininity, the expectations of and beliefs about women held by those who look on. Any group of people has a variety of such beliefs. The double meaning of 'queynt' encapsulates the contrasting views of femininity enshrined in the Equivocal Oath and Calumniated Queen scenarios. In the Equivocal Oath scenario, woman is by nature sexually and linguistically deceitful. Femininity is identified with trickery. For the extratextual audience, who know themselves to be listening to a text of this sort, *Sir Tristrem* neatly encodes this identification at a lexical level by defining woman's sexual organs (the physical symbol at once of her femaleness and of her sexuality) as themselves a prank. When Ysonde uncovers her genitals, in this audience's eyes she reveals her feminine falsity, which is also the pleasure of the text. The intratextual audience, however, perceives her discovery in the mode of the Calumniated Queen, and thus sees the revelation of naked truth, an accident that certifies the heroine's innocence. 'Femininity', in this latter version, means not only innocence but the painful inability to represent that innocence, or to have it accepted when the whole weight of a culture is against it. Within the powerful context provided by the Calumniated Queen scenario, in establishing that she is a true *woman*, Ysonde will simultaneously establish herself as a *true* woman. Thus, although the revelation of the queen's genitals functions for both intratextual and extratextual audiences as the proof of her femininity, 'femininity' means something different for each audience.

Calumniated Queens appear exactly as Ysonde manages to do to her intratextual audience: they are sexually pure, vulnerable, merciful and meek, essentially bodily creatures, unable to manipulate the symbolic systems of their society, not stridently protesting their innocence but trusting that their male guardians will ultimately come, with God's help, to the right decision.[29] By mimicking the kind of femininity found in the Calumniated Queen romances, Ysonde manages to make her own situation look like that of their heroines, and thus to convince her intratextual audience that they should see in her only 'the steadfastness of sorely tried virtue' (Schlauch 1927, 3).

Béroul's *Tristan*

At first sight, the strategy of Béroul's Yseut seems the exact opposite of the Middle English Ysonde's. Where Ysonde emphasizes her femininity, Yseut presents herself as boyish – especially in the scene in which she arrives at the marsh. The onlookers wonder how she will cross without dirtying her clothes. Her solution is to dismount, send her horse across alone, and then insist on mounting the 'leper' (actually Tristan in disguise) who has been begging from the crowd, and force him to carry her over. When she ties up the trappings of her harness to stop them getting splashed, the narrator exclaims in admiration:

> Nus escuiers ne nus garçons
> Por le taier mex nes levast
> Ne ja mex nes aparellast.
> (3888–90)

(No squire or stable-lad could have lifted them better out of the way of the mud, nor ever have arranged them better.)

Yseut herself describes her behaviour in the same terms, as she declares her intention to mount astride the leper:

> 'Diva! malades, molt es gros!
> Tor la ton vis et ça ton dos;
> Ge monterai conme vaslet.'
> . . . .
> Yseut la bele chevaucha,
> Janbe deça, janbe dela.
> (3929–31, 3939–40)

('Go on! leper, you're very well-fed! Turn around; I'll mount like a lad.' . . . Lovely Yseut rode, one leg this side, one leg that side.)

At several points, then, Yseut presents herself as masculine, contrasting with the specific and exaggerated femininity of Ysonde.

Although her approach is different, Yseut is addressing the same problem as that faced by Ysonde. But whereas the English heroine exploited a duality within contemporary views of women (one definition of femininity against another), Yseut uses the symbolism of sexual difference (femininity against masculinity) in order to establish her innocence. It will be clear, therefore, that Yseut is not invoking the Calumniated Queen prototype in order to change the scenario through which her intratextual audience perceives her.[30] Instead, Yseut remains within the Equivocal Oath scenario, and exploits the models of gender inherent in that. Since the Equivocal Oath posits an equivocating, duplicitous woman, whose (essentially feminine) role is that of sexually unfaithful deceiver and false swearer, Yseut decides logically that to distance herself from that role she must apppear unfeminine; must look, in fact, like a man. Doing otherwise risks being caught in a trap of representation peculiar to the feminine: that a woman is most obviously guilty when she protests her innocence.

Yseut challenges head-on the assumptions that threaten her. She takes them on board, and fights them with their own weapons: in a world of equivocation, the faithful woman must take roundabout, indirect paths if she is to appear faithful. Yseut's performance at her trial dramatizes the difficulties that the faithful woman has in representing herself, by including in her self-presentation an element of corruption. This corruption, as the mark of a symbolic system biased against the whole idea of female fidelity, paradoxically becomes the sign of Yseut's innocence. I shall look at two examples of this mechanism in action: Yseut's exposure of the beggar as a fraud and her persistent bawdiness.

Yseut's treatment of the leprous beggar played by Tristan establishes her in an oblique relation to truth and faith. Like Ysonde, Yseut shows an understanding of the beggar; but in the French poem, there is none of the compassion for his plight displayed by the English heroine. At first glance, indeed, the two encounters seem diametrically opposed. When called upon by Arthur to pay the leper for his porterage, Yseut objects roughly that he is a con-man:

> 'Il est herlot, si que jel sai.
> Hui a suï bone pasture,
> Trové a gent a sa mesure.
> De moi n'en portera qui valle
> Un sol ferlinc n'une maalle.'
> Grant joie en meinent li dui roi.
>
> (3976–81)

('He is a good-for-nothing, I know it well. Today he's had good grazing, he's found people aplenty. He shan't carry away the value of a single farthing or penny of mine.' The two kings are highly amused by this answer.)

As one might expect, Yseut's asperity contributes to her masculinization: her brutal treatment of the leper contrasts with Ysonde's super-feminine empathy. In another light, the difference between the texts is not so great. Certain elements in the encounter with the beggar as it appears in Béroul's poem distinguish Yseut from privileged males such as Mark and Arthur and align her with marginalized masculinity. In Béroul's text, the alignment is expressed as one of rank: the masculinized Yseut and the fake leper share a status which is well below that enjoyed by the ruling males. The leper is described as 'fors de gent' ('outside of society', 3579), and terms proper to men of inferior status are likewise used to describe Yseut, both by Yseut herself and by the narrator (*escuiers* and *garçons*, 3888; *vaslet*, 3931). Yseut appears to use her self-proclaimed status as a 'low-ranking male' in order to claim that she understands the lowly leper, and understands that he is a liar and a cheat: since both occupy the same world, he becomes transparent to her, in a way, she implies, that he is not to the honourable kings. Class similarity does not bring solidarity, however. Whereas the leper exploits his difference from the kings in order to cheat them, the boy-woman is supposedly loyal to her masters: instead of being a liar like him, she will reveal his lies for what they are. In playing the informer for the ruling order, she does not wholly dissociate herself from deception, but presents herself as the decoder, not the producer, of deceptions. While Ysonde establishes an identification with the pilgrim based on shared vulnerability and piety, Yseut calls upon a common suspicion of the lower orders, and the idea that the appearances of poverty and illness they use to gain sympathy (and money) from the ruling classes are in truth dishonest masquerades. Her sophisticated awareness of masquerade and her scrupulousness in bringing the leper's exploitative use of it to her judges' attention make her appear honest but not naïve, struggling with a difficult situation in a dishonest world she knows only too well.

Yseut also displays a little sexual corruption. An obvious feature of Yseut's performance is the element of bawdy, the flaunting of a sexual relationship with the leper. Yseut constructs a sexually aware persona, and insistently foregrounds the presence of sexuality all around her – all very different from Ysonde's portrayal of sexual ignorance. Where the punctilious Ysonde seems uncertain about whether her interlude with the beggar counts as infidelity, Yseut is bold to declare it as a sexual relation. Whereas Ysonde's oath is premised on an accidental proximity, Yseut mounts and rides astride her leper in a deliberate and blatant sexual image. And yet, although this is an obviously sexual image, it is just that: an image. The intratextual audience sees the encounter, and sees that, at the literal, factual level which is all that the law is concerned with, it is not sexual. Thus, Yseut's declaration appears spectacularly, consciously ironic. Like Ysonde, Yseut draws attention to the ambiguity of her oath and, in both cases, the ambiguity is made to seem an incongruous effect of the audience's expectation that a woman in this generic situation will necessarily be unfaithful. This expectation is thereby satirized: the intratextual audience is expected to join, as sophisticated and humane people, in decrying it. In case the audience should be in any doubt, Béroul's text is carefully sprinkled with details that make the sexual interpretation seem incorrect. Leprosy was often thought in the Middle Ages to be a venereal disease, and the supposed leper has already told Mark that his leprosy is of this nature (3760–75).[31] Yseut, however, when ordering the beggar to carry her over the marsh, dismisses his reluctance in the following terms:

> 'Quides tu que ton mal me prenge?
> N'en aies doute, non fera.'
>
> (3924–5)

('Do you think your disease will infect me? Don't worry, it won't.')

Yseut's ambiguously constructed gender plays a part here, too: in the eyes of the intratextual audience, the fact that Yseut has not had sex with the leper is as obvious as the fact that she is not a man. Both the masculine and the sexual aspects of her self-presentation thus appear as deliberate, comic, courageous misrepresentations. Yseut's feisty flaunting of sexuality functions as the little element of sexual and linguistic corruption which, within the Catch-22 of the Equivocal Oath scenario, is necessary to establish her fidelity.[32] She mimics the brazen whore of the Equivocal Oath so perfectly, and yet with such apparent irony, that she disarms any attempt to identify her with that role.[33]

A further aspect of this bawdiness is, of course, Yseut's ambiguous oath. This depends on her beauty, the very feminine physical attractions which she emphasizes by her splendid clothing and trappings. This beauty is clearly aimed at stimulating desire in all her audiences, but not in order to satisfy it: romance heroines are no more available than movie stars. The innuendo of Yseut's declaration needs to be seen against this background of desire aroused and frustrated. Freud's discussion of 'smut' offers an interesting way of conceptualizing what Yseut is doing here (Freud 1960, 97–102). Freud envisages a situation in which a man is attracted to a woman, and makes overtures to her. If she does not respond positively (and in Freud's view, the chance that she will refuse increases with her level of education and of class: what he calls 'civilisation'), then the man's frustrated desire turns to aggression. He makes a joke that 'compels the person who is assailed to imagine the part of the body or the procedure in question and shows her that the assailant is himself imagining it' (Freud 1960, 98). The effect is redoubled if there is another man (or men) present to hear the joke. The intimacies of the woman's body are displayed publicly, shared among the men, in total disregard of her rejection. Thus the first man in some sense gets his desire, not at the literal level but at the still powerful imaginary one. Freud's analysis accounts for the discomfort and feeling of violation experienced by those who have been subjected to harassment of this jocular sort: 'a person who laughs at smut that he hears is laughing as though he were the spectator of an act of sexual aggression' (Freud 1960, 97).

When Yseut jokes that only two men have been between her thighs, and that the intratextual audience has seen one of those encounters, she is making a joke of precisely this sort, although at her own expense. She makes the audience imagine her genitals, and imagine her having sex with the leper.[34] This joke refers to the desire of the men in the audience for her, desire aroused by her beauty, and perhaps also by her situation. Her dual gender again contributes to this situation. On the one hand, as object of the joke, Yseut is feminine, the woman who refuses illicit male sexual desire. On the other hand, as the subject who tells the joke, Yseut is masculine, giving voice to the frustrated desire of the men looking at her. Both aspects work to reinforce the impression that she is chaste: the promiscuity that the joke ascribes to her is transformed into the nudge-nudge revenge of the spurned suitor. The implication is that the only way to achieve sexual access to this faithful wife is through dirty jokes of this sort. Thus Yseut's bawdy and blatant innuendo works indirectly, like the rest of her self-presentation, to convince her intratextual audience of her innocence. Just as in her 'exposure' of the beggar, cover is reinforced precisely by being ostentatiously blown. The laughter of the intratextual and extratextual audiences is very different: they laugh at the possibility of the queen having a sexual relationship, we laugh at them laughing it off.

On the basis of the previous argument, I should like to suggest a revaluation of the *Tristrem*-poet's project and achievement. Although we cannot know exactly what was in Thomas's poem, the evidence of Robert of Norway's *Tristrams saga ok Ísöndar*, generally considered to be a fairly faithful translation of Thomas, suggests that the *Tristrem*-poet altered his source in two important ways.[35] On the one hand, he appears to have deleted a sexually knowing joke which, in the *Saga*, the heroine makes to her entourage.[36] In deleting this joke, the *Tristrem*-poet has given his heroine a sexual purity which accords better with other known examples of the Calumniated Queen. On the other, *Sir Tristrem*'s blatant description of the heroine's nakedness – coyly implied, rather than baldly stated, in the *Saga* – is a very effective means of highlighting the ambiguity of that nakedness, its dual function in parallel constructions of femininity.[37] For the intratextual audience, the sight of Ysonde's genitals puts the seal on a version of woman as the innocent wrongly accused; for the extratextual audience, the name of *queynt* makes those genitals the symbol of woman as sexual and linguistic trickster. Both these alterations to the source – if alterations they be – are felicitous; far from being coarse and inadequate, *Sir Tristrem*, in its treatment of this episode at least, shows a sensitivity and skill which require us to take it seriously as a literary work.

Notes

1   *Sir Tristrem* is preserved only in the Auchinleck manuscript, probably produced around 1330 (see Pearsall and Cunningham 1977). The poem itself is generally dated to the late thirteenth century, making it one of the earliest English-language romances. The most recent and accessible edition is *Sir Tristrem*, ed. Alan Lupack, in *'Lancelot of the Laik' and 'Sir Tristrem'*, TEAMS (Kalamazoo, MI: Medieval Institute Publications, 1994). Quotations are from this edition. Lupack's punctuation and glossing are sometimes debatable; my own reading at times takes different paths. Lupack gives a bibliography, and a brief account of the poem's critical history, and also of the various views on its provenance (143–55). I disagree with Lupack's argument that *Sir Tristrem* should be seen as a parodic 'anti-romance' (147–52).

2   Thomas's text is known in nine fragments of varying length, shared among six manuscripts (only five still survive). One of these, the Carlisle fragment, was discovered only recently: see Benskin, Hunt and Short 1992–5. For a description of the better known manuscripts, see *Le Roman de Tristan par Thomas*, ed. Joseph Bédier, 2 vols, SATF (Paris: Firmin Didot, 1902–5), II, 1–9. A recent edition with parallel English translation is Thomas of Britain, *Tristran*, ed. Stewart Gregory (New York: Garland, 1991). The poet of *Sir Tristrem* refers to a 'Tomas' as his source (2, 10, 397, 412, 2787), but, since he places this poet in 'Ertheldoun' (1), the man in question seems to be Thomas of Erceldoune, a thirteenth-century poet and writer of prophetic works. Critics generally describe the *Sir Tristrem* poet as confusing Thomas of Erceldoune and Thomas of Britain; in view of the importance of namesakes within the narrative (there is a second Tristan, and a second Yseut), however, and the difficulties suffered by the characters of keeping a clean and clear distinction between these namesakes, it is possible that we should think more carefully about this 'confusion'.

3   Other commentators I have found useful are Flora Alexander, who discusses Ysonde along with other active English romance women (Alexander 1993),

and André Crépin, who gives a brief but valuable comparison with Thomas (Crépin 1982, 90–3).

4 For instance, the poem supposes 'an etiquette of polite dining-table conversation and washed hands', while 'the service of porters and ushers is taken for granted' (Swanton 1987, 205).

5 Recent comparative studies of medieval Tristan legends are Baumgartner 1987 and Ferrante 1973.

6 Critical readings focusing on fragmentation and division of various sorts include Huchet 1990; Burns 1993; McCracken 1993; Pensom 1995.

7 Depending on the version, this episode occurs in one of two places: in *Sir Tristrem* and other Thomas-based versions, it follows from Mark's obtaining circumstantial proof of the adultery (in the flour-on-the-floor episode), and precedes the lovers' exile in the forest. In Béroul and derived versions, the exile comes directly after the flour on the floor, and the equivocal oath comes after the lovers' return from exile.

8 Nevertheless, it is common in the criticism to discuss episodes of Thomas that are missing. Critics who do so generally refer to Joseph Bédier's reconstruction of the text's outlines on the basis of surviving versions (*Le Roman de Tristan*, I). Although a work of immense scholarship, Bédier's text is, in my view, ultimately a retelling, and cannot be held to represent Thomas's original.

9 Béroul's poem is preserved in a single manuscript of poor quality (Paris, BN f. fr. 2171) copied in the second half of the thirteenth century; see Béroul, *The Romance of Tristran*, ed. Stewart Gregory (Amsterdam: Rodopi, 1992). The poem itself is variously dated around 1160 or 1180, see Gregory (xxvii–xxix). References to the poem are to Gregory's edition, translations are my own.

10 For an illuminating exploration of this traditional distinction, see Frappier 1963. The most important of the many challenges is Jonin 1958, 177–335; for an assessment of this and the traditional view, see Wind 1960–61.

11 The exact provenance and circulation of Béroul's poem are problematic. The text contains the apparently English word 'lovendrant' ('love-drink', 2159); it uses English place names accurately; and it has a character with the English-derived name of Godoïne (Godwin). Dominica Legge, in her still useful historical siting of Thomas's and Béroul's poems, suggested that the latter may have had an English audience, as the former certainly did (Legge 1963, 44–59). Gregory points out that there is no concrete evidence for an English association (*Romance of Tristran*, xxiii–xxiv).

12 On the use of different genres in Béroul, see Varvaro 1972, 162–96; Sargent-Baur 1984; Kay 1985. On Béroul's poem as 'liminal' in a variety of ways, see Pensom 1995.

13 In preference to Lupack's punctuation of this passage, I have used that in the edition by George P. McNeill, *Sir Tristrem*, STS 8 (Edinburgh: Blackwood and Sons, 1886), 2269–77.

14 The ordeal is found in all the Thomas-derived versions. On the historical background to ordeals, see Bartlett 1986. In 1215, the Fourth Lateran Council issued a papal canon against ordeals. The speed with which this was adopted

by secular authorities varied throughout Europe, but England was among the first, with a royal ordinance in 1219 (Bartlett 1986, 127). Thus, although the ordeal was a flourishing legal practice at the time when Thomas was writing, it had been dead for at least half a century by the time *Sir Tristrem* was composed – although its imaginative value clearly saved it from oblivion.

15 Legally, the procedures of oath and of ordeal were alternatives: see Bartlett 1986, 24–33 and J. Hudson 1996, 72–7.

16 'Essentialist' in the sense that it posits an 'essence' of womanhood, to which all women supposedly conform. For a sophisticated discussion of essentialism of different sorts, see Fuss 1989.

17 Chrétien de Troyes, *Le Chevalier de la Charrete*, ed. Mario Roques, CFMA (Paris: Champion, 1983), 4971–84. *Ami et Amile: chanson de geste*, ed. Peter F. Dembowski, CFMA (Paris: Champion, 1987), 1415–30. Several critics have argued that Tristan should be seen as a trickster no less slippery than Yseut (for Béroul, see especially Regalado 1976; Blakeslee 1989, 113–26; Pensom 1995, 92–6; for *Sir Tristrem*, see Barnes 1993, 97–8).

18 McCracken 1993 highlights the negative, social view of adulterous queens, but neglects the positive, literary one.

19 Marie de France shows that this cruelty may itself provoke infidelity, as it does in *Guigemar* (*Les Lais de Marie de France*, ed. Jean Rychner, TLF (Geneva: Droz, 1966)). Similarly, as noted by Carolyn Dinshaw (1989, 130), the fifteenth-century French woman writer Christine de Pizan claimed that the misogyny of the *Roman de la Rose* caused men to beat their innocent wives. It should, nevertheless, be emphasized that Christine was writing as part of a literary polemic, and that her assertion cannot be taken as historical evidence of such beatings.

20 A recent anthology of misogynistic literature current in the Middle Ages, and of replies to it, is Alcuin Blamires, with Karen Pratt and C. W. Marx (eds), *Woman Defamed and Woman Defended: An Anthology of Medieval Texts* (Oxford: Oxford University Press, 1992). A wide-ranging and controversial discussion of misogyny and its relations to the idealization of women is Bloch 1991.

21 The idea that both femininity and masculinity are performed, rather than natural or even unconscious, has been influential in recent gender theory: see especially Butler 1990 and 1993.

22 Helaine Newstead (1969, 1982) suggested that 'Thomas' (in Bédier's reconstruction) presents Yseut's public trial in such a way that it 'strongly suggests similar ordeals in which falsely accused queens are vindicated'. For Newstead, this is a matter of the poet's choice, while I am treating it as a strategy on the part of the character herself.

23 Middle English romance examples are *The Earl of Toulous* and *Le Bone Florence of Rome*. Old French examples include *Parise la duchesse* and *La Belle Hélène de Constantinople*. For a full-length study of the type, see Schlauch 1927. There is also valuable material in Heffernan 1976, 30–8, and especially in Christophersen 1952 (which deserves to be much better known than it is). The group is also related to the types collected by Lillian Herlands Hornstein under the

umbrella title of 'Eustace-Constance-Florence-Griselda Legends' (Severs 1967, 120–32).

24 Paul Strohm (1992, 95–119) has shown how the idea of the queen as inter- cessor is essentially deferential, as the woman abjectly humbles herself before the source of true authority. He further notes that intercessory power is pre- mised on the queen's 'sympathetic self-identification with the threatened and oppressed', an intensely vulnerable position (102).

25 Lupack glosses 'san schewe' as 'without [their] noticing', which, in my view, misses the point.

26 Like 'lemman', 'queynt' was seen by Chaucer as 'old-fashioned, once elegant but now lower-class and therefore slightly humorous' (Benson 1984, 42). Chaucer's knowledge of *Sir Tristrem* and of other romances in the Auchinleck manuscript is apparent from his parodic *Sir Thopas*.

27 'Queynt', as noun and adjective, derives from the Old French adjective *cointe*, meaning 'skilful', 'ingenious', or 'malicious' (Godefroy, *Dictionnaire de l'ancienne langue française*).

28 Of Nicholas's wooing of Alisoun in *The Miller's Tale* (3275–6), Benson com- ments that 'there is a delightful disparity between the directness of action and the reticence of expression' (42): a phrase which could apply equally well to Ysonde's extratextual immodesty and intratextual coyness in *Sir Tristrem*.

29 All Calumniated Queen texts 'emphasize the virtue of a meek, Job-like faith' (Schlauch 1927, 120).

30 Newstead 1969, 1082 points out that, although Béroul does not employ the Calumniated Queen presentation in the oath scene, he had already used it in developing the flour-on-the-floor episode.

31 Brody 1974: on the medical idea of leprosy as venereal disease, 52–8; on leprosy as figuring the sin of carnality, 143–6; on leprosy in some versions of the Tristan narrative, 179–86.

32 In Jean Renart's thirteenth-century French romance *Le Roman de la Rose ou de Guillaume de Dole*, ed. Félix Lecoy, CFMA (Paris: Champion, 1979), the hero- ine Lïenor also deploys corruption in the service of innocence. She is slan- dered by the court steward who produces his knowledge of a rose-shaped birthmark on her thigh as proof that he has slept with her, when he has actually got the information from her mother. Lïenor plants certain intimate personal belongings of her own on the steward, then accuses him of rape. The steward is forced to undertake an ordeal, in which he swears that he has not had sex with her; thus she is vindicated of his original accusation.

33 Irigaray argues that women should mimic stereotypes of femininity: 'one must assume the feminine role deliberately'. This will 'convert a form of subordina- tion into an affirmation, and thus [. . .] begin to thwart it'. By mimicking, even exaggerating what is supposed to be 'natural' feminine behaviour, women can show how artificial that behaviour is. Their self-conscious mimicry shows that they have minds and consciousnesses beyond their traditional roles; it demonstrates that the conventional wisdom about femininity does not tell the full truth, for women *'also remain elsewhere'*. Furthermore, such mimicry can be

used to render women's unequal position obvious – whereas society tries to cover up this inequality, pretending it does not exist – and thereby to make it a subject for discussion. 'To play with mimesis is thus, for a woman, to try to recover the place of her exploitation by discourse, without allowing herself to be simply reduced to it' (Irigaray 1985, 76). Burns 1993 follows Irigaray in her reading of Béroul.

34 Yseut's joke thus exposes her sexual parts to the company's mind's eye no less graphically than Ysonde's 'accident' reveals her to its sight.

35 *Tristrams saga ok Ísöndar*, ed. Eugen Kölbing (Heilbronn: Henninger, 1878). An English translation is available: *The Saga of Tristram and Ísönd*, trans. Paul Schach (Lincoln: University of Nebraska Press, 1973). The equivocal oath episode occupies chs. 56–60.

36 This knowing witticism corresponds with the dirty joke in Béroul's *Tristan*, but in the *Saga* it is separated from the oath.

37 Both the knowing joke and the indirect expression of nudity are also found in the Middle High German adaptation of Thomas, Gottfried von Strassburg's *Tristan*, ed. Rüdiger Krohn, 3 vols (Stuttgart: Reclam, 1980). An excellent English translation is available: *Gottfried von Strassburg, 'Tristan', with the 'Tristran' of Thomas*, trans. A. T. Hatto (Harmondsworth: Penguin, 1960). The equivocal oath episode is in ch. 23. Bédier preserves a similar reading in his reconstruction of Thomas: *Le Roman de Tristan*, I, ch. 24.

CHAPTER TWELVE

Sir Orfeo: Madness and Gender*

A. C. SPEARING

Sir Orfeo is one of those short Middle English romances that identify themselves as Breton lays, English offshoots of the genre introduced into French in the twelfth century by Marie de France: relatively brief narratives with Breton settings, in which the story focuses on human emotions, often crystallized in some symbolic object, and magic or the supernatural frequently plays a crucial part (Rumble 1965, xiii–xxx; Stevens 1966; Finlayson 1985; Burgess 1987; Spearing 1990a). *Sir Orfeo* is an anonymous poem of some six hundred lines, perhaps of the early fourteenth century, certainly not later than 1330–40. It survives in three versions; the earliest, best and most authoritative of these, and the one in which the fairy element is most prominent, is the famous Auchinleck manuscript (National Library of Scotland, Advocates' 19.2.1), which contains many other Middle English romances, including two other Breton lays.[1] This manuscript was produced in the London area, and may once perhaps have passed through Chaucer's hands (Loomis 1941).

The story told by *Sir Orfeo* is as follows. Orfeo, the king of Winchester, loves harp music, and is a skilful harpist himself. One day when his beloved and beautiful wife Heurodis is relaxing with her maidens in an orchard, she falls asleep at midday beneath a grafted tree. When she wakes, she begins weeping and tearing at herself, behaving as if mad. Her maidens summon help, and Heurodis is put to bed, but she goes on crying and trying to escape. When Orfeo asks her what is wrong, she says they have to part,

* In earlier forms this paper was read at the Interdisciplinary Symposium in Medieval, Renaissance and Baroque Studies at the University of Miami in 1993; before the Department of English, Copenhagen University, in 1995; at Washington College, Maryland, in 1996; and at Washington and Lee University in 1997. It has benefited from suggestions made by the audiences on those occasions, and also from the comments of Rosalind Field, Mary Hamer, Barbara Nolan and Lisa Samuels.

because in her sleep armed knights came and summoned her to speak with their king. She refused, but the king came himself with more knights and beautiful ladies, and made her accompany him to his palace. He brought her back, but warned her that next day he would seize her from under the same tree, and make her live with him for ever, regardless of her wishes; if she failed to be there, she would be torn limb from limb. Next day Orfeo and his knights surround Heurodis beneath the tree, but their attempt to protect her is in vain, and she is snatched away regardless, 'With fairi forth y-nome' (193).[2] Orfeo falls into despair. He tells his barons that he is going to live in the wilderness with wild beasts, leaving his steward to rule in his place. If they learn of his death, they are to choose a new king. Despite the barons' protests, he departs, wearing only a mantle, taking with him only his harp. In the wilderness he endures great hardship, living on berries and roots; his body withers and his beard grows long. Sometimes he plays his harp and the beasts come to hear his music. Sometimes too he sees 'The king o fairy with his rout' (283) hunting, or companies of knights riding past, or knights and ladies dancing – all, evidently, fairy creatures. One day he sees sixty ladies hawking, and among them is Heurodis. They look at each other; neither speaks, but she weeps to see her husband in such wretchedness, until the other ladies force her away. Orfeo follows them; they ride into a rock, and inside there is a beautiful landscape and a castle glittering with precious stones. Admitted to the castle as a minstrel, he sees the bodies of people who were supposed dead but had really been brought there 'With fairi' (404) – wounded, drowned, burned, women in childbed, mad people, all as if asleep, and Heurodis among them. He enters the hall, sees the king and queen, introduces himself as one of those minstrels who visit lords' houses whether or not they are welcome, and plays his harp. The king is so delighted by his music that he offers to grant Orfeo anything he wishes. Orfeo asks for Heurodis, and the king first demurs and then grudgingly keeps his promise. Taking Heurodis by the hand, Orfeo leads her away and returns to Winchester, unknown. Borrowing a beggar's clothes, he enters the city as a minstrel and is welcomed by the steward because his master loved minstrels. Orfeo plays his harp, and though the steward does not recognize him, he recognizes the harp and asks where he got it. Orfeo tells a story of having found it in the wilderness beside a man who had been killed by lions and was being eaten by wolves. The steward faints from grief; and Orfeo remarks that *if* the king had returned in beggar's clothes, and had told this story to test him, and the steward had seemed pleased at Orfeo's supposed death, Orfeo would have thrown him out. Now the steward joyfully recognizes that this is his master, and throws himself at his feet. Orfeo and Heurodis are newly crowned, and reign in Winchester for a long time. After their deaths, the steward becomes king.

This story is obviously a version of the classical myth of Orpheus and Eurydice, but the processes by which it has been so strangely transformed remain uncertain, partly because no immediate source has been found for the English poem. It is generally thought that *Sir Orfeo*, like so many Middle English romances, must have had a French original, and references exist to a French *Lai d'Orphée* (Bliss 1966, xxxi–xxxiii, xl–xli), but that poem does not survive. By whatever means, the classical myth has been medievalized and (though the story is set in England) Celticized, with the fairy realm and its king replacing Pluto and the underworld, and it has also been combined with other traditional story-material, notably that of the absent ruler and the faithful steward. The best-known versions of the classical myth – those in Virgil's *Georgics*, Ovid's *Metamorphoses* and Boethius's *Consolation of Philosophy* – are tragic: as Orpheus leads his wife up from the underworld, he looks back at her when approaching the boundary with this world, and in doing so loses her again, this time for ever. The happy ending of *Sir Orfeo* may seem especially characteristic of medieval romances (Brewer 1978), though it is worth remembering that there had also been classical versions of the Orpheus myth that ended happily: Orpheus sometimes succeeded in rescuing Eurydice from the underworld (Dronke 1962).

It is hard to be certain what the *Orfeo* poet knew of earlier versions of the story and the ways in which they were interpreted. In late antiquity and the Middle Ages the Orpheus myth was read allegorically, with Orpheus interpreted sometimes as a figure of Christ descending into hell to retrieve human souls, sometimes as the human 'seeker after truth or spiritual enlightenment who, when he has almost gained his goal, looks backward to material concerns and so loses all the good he has gained' (Vicari 1982, 68), sometimes as a personification of eloquence, wisdom, or reason.[3] Most modern scholars have assumed that the *Orfeo* poet must have been familar with some at least of these learned interpretations. Many have proceeded to the further assumption that his poem must itself have been intended to convey an allegorical significance (such as that the fairy king represents Satan) or moral teaching derived from the tradition of allegorical interpretation (such as that when Heurodis is abducted from the orchard it is because of 'her love of sensual pleasures').[4] In one of the most thoughtful recent accounts of the poem, Jeff Rider notes that 'It is impossible to know exactly what versions and treatments of the Orpheus myth the *Orfeo* poet knew', but nevertheless asserts that 'it is *clear* he or she was well-versed in the Orpheus tradition', and adds, in a reversal of much recent reading, that 'the poet is *clearly* writing *against* the tradition of reductive Christian moralization' represented by Pierre Bersuire and the *Ovide moralisé* (Rider 1988, 355; my italics). Rider rightly sees *Sir Orfeo* as deeply and hauntingly mysterious, and recognizes that this mystery, centred in the poem's fairy element, makes modern allegorical interpretations arbitrary and undermines their claim to historical validity. It seems no clearer to me, however, that the poet was 'writing against the tradition of reductive Christian moralization' than that he was writing within it.

There is a problem here that scholarship has been reluctant to acknowledge. Once made, the suggestion that a writer possessed certain knowledge and alluded to it in his work remains current. Convincing counter-argument is rare, both for logical reasons (how is a negative case to be established?) and for institutional reasons (scholars earn their livings and gain prestige by explaining allusions rather than by denying that they exist to be explained).[5] I cannot prove that whoever composed *Sir Orfeo* did not belong to the medieval scholastic world in which classical myths were allegorized and moralized; I can only say that I think it very unlikely that he did. The Auchinleck manuscript contains Latin items alongside its large collection of English romances, but this is evidence as to the knowledge of its compiler and expected readers, not of the composer of any individual component text. The poet shows marked rhetorical skill in the verbal amplification of his story, as in the repeated relative constructions of lines 102–8 or the repeated contrasts between past luxury and present deprivation in lines 241–56, yet the figures he uses, while powerful in effect, are relatively simple and do not necessarily imply clerkly rhetorical training. (His opening reference to 'this clerkes' (2) implies that he did not claim to be one of them.) Again, he employs a few relatively learned or technical terms, such as 'butras' (361) and 'vousour' (363) in the description of the fairy king's castle, but these seem insufficient to indicate a scholastic background. On the other hand he displays 'a refreshing ignorance of classical mythology' (Severs 1961, 197) in stating that Orfeo's father was descended from Pluto and his mother from 'King Juno' (43–4) and that Winchester was once called Thrace (49–50). These could have been deliberate errors intended to amuse those who knew better, but it is hard to see how such jokes would serve his poetic purpose. I refer to the 'poet' and his 'poem' not because I believe him to have had contact with scholastic or humanist conceptions of *poetria*, but for convenience and in tribute to his unusual talent. I think it most likely that the Orpheus story came to him indirectly, probably through Celtic or French rather than Latin sources, and that he was unaware of his divergences from classical forms of the story and a fortiori of his divergences from the meanings attributed to the story by medieval scholars.

No interpretation of *Sir Orfeo* known to me that relates it directly either to the classical myth or to 'the tradition of reductive Christian moralization' seems to make it a better poem; rather the contrary. Moreover, such interpretations are often at odds with the literal sense of the Middle English poem. The classical myth is a story about death, its happy-ending version a fantasy of the power of human love to overcome mortality. Modern scholars sometimes suggest that 'the fairy kingdom represents death' (Ramsey 1983, 153), but the English poet undermines almost systematically the notion that death is the enemy defeated by Orfeo and Heurodis. He tells us that the hideous bodies Orfeo sees inside the fairy castle are 'thought dede' but 'nare nought' (390); when the steward recovers after learning of his master's supposed death, the barons remind him that 'It is no bot of mannes deth' (552); and at the end of the story Orfeo and Heurodis really die and the steward succeeds to the throne. The Christian moralizations show a strong tendency to blame Heurodis and (more rarely) Orfeo for the sufferings they undergo. They are punished, such interpretations suggest, for some identifiable moral failing: when Heurodis is abducted by the fairy king she gets what she deserves, because in relaxing in her orchard at midday she is indulging in the sin of sloth. Yet, as the *Orfeo* poet tells the story, it is precisely the unexpectedness and inexplicability of the fairy summons that make it so compelling. It is because we do not know what Heurodis would have to do, or what anyone would have to do, to avoid such a summons that it is disturbing and memorable. In medieval romances a major purpose of the fairy world is precisely to bring an element of the inexplicable into human life, to function as 'a metaphor for . . . unknowableness' (Pearsall 1996, 54). That is surely so in *Sir Orfeo*.

Sir Orfeo could be understood in many ways that would not insist on its relation to classical mythology or medieval mythography – I doubt, for example, whether its political implications have been fully explored – but, if we focus on the fundamentally inexplicable nature of what happens to Heurodis, it has obvious analogies with the kind of experience that modern readers would define as madness. Elizabeth Spearing and I first made this suggestion years ago,[6] and my aim now is to develop it further, taking account of a factor associated with madness but previously disregarded, namely gender. I need to begin with some recapitulation of our earlier proposal. *Sir Orfeo* contains several explicit references to madness. When Heurodis wakes from the apparent nightmare in her orchard, her behaviour is that of a madwoman – she cries out, rubs her hands and feet, scratches her face till it bleeds, tears her clothes – and the poet ends by saying openly that she was 'reueyd out of hir witt' (82). Her maidens too see her actions as symptoms of madness: they run to the palace in terror and exclaim that 'her quen awede wold' (87). The poem seems to describe the onset of what might now be called schizophrenia. Of the 'schizophrenic experience' R. D. Laing wrote as follows:

> The process of entering into *the other* world from this world, and returning to *this* world from the other world, is as natural as death and giving birth

or being born. But in our present world, that is both so terrified and so unconscious of the other world, it is not surprising that when 'reality', the fabric of this world, bursts, and a person enters the other world, he is completely lost and terrified, and meets only incomprehension in others.

(Laing 1967, 103)

That sounds very much like an account of Heurodis's experience, and I have been informed by psychiatrists of a less visionary persuasion than Laing that both her behaviour and her account of her experience in the orchard would now indicate a diagnosis of schizophrenia, the symptoms of which are generally thought to include hallucinations, delusions, and 'episodes of passivity in which the individual feels his thoughts or impulses to be under external control' (Showalter 1985a, 204). It is true that the categories in terms of which mental disorder is discussed do not necessarily have any permanent validity. Like the colour spectrum, the spectrum of mental behaviour can be divided up in many different ways, and schizophrenia may be no more than a cultural construct. On the other hand, historians of mental illness see schizophrenia, along with depression, as coming closer to being a universal phenomenon, with the same symptomatology over many centuries, than other forms of madness.

If Heurodis's initial symptoms indicate madness of some kind, then what happens to her afterwards may also correspond to what we would call going mad. She is snatched away despite anything that Orfeo and his knights can do to protect her, and transported to an alien realm that exists alongside the world of normality but cannot communicate with it except in extreme circumstances. When Orfeo too reaches that realm, there are more references to madness among the distorted, supposedly dead, apparently sleeping figures that he finds inside the castle wall:

> Sum stode with-outen hade,
> & sum non armes nade,
> & sum thurth the bodi hadde wounde,
> & sum lay wode, y-bounde,
> & sum armed on hors sete,
> & sum astrangled as thai ete;
> & sum were in water adreynt,
> & sum with fire al for-schreynt;
> Wives ther lay on child-bedde,
> Sum ded & sum awedde . . .
>
> (391–400)

The medieval fiction seems to correspond to a real experience that some cultures, though not necessarily all, would categorize as madness. However loving, and however dearly loved, the subject is cut off from human contact and absorbed despite herself into an alien world, an *inner* world that corresponds to the medieval *other* world – 'inner' and 'other' both being metaphorical ways of describing it. It is a terrifying world, but it also has a seductive glitter. Its king and queen are glamorous and powerful figures, and when Orfeo enters it he sees something more like the heavenly Jerusalem than the dimness of the classical underworld:

> Amidde the lond a castel he sighe,
> Riche & real & wonder heighe:
> Al the ut-mast wall
> Was clere & schine as cristal . . .
>   (355–8)

> Al that lond was euer light,
> For when it schuld be therk & night
> The riche stones light gonne
> As bright as doth at none the sonne.
>   (369–72)

As Virginia Woolf wrote in her diary after recovering from one of her bouts of mental illness: 'the dark underworld has its fascinations as well as its terrors' (Bell 1972, II, 84).[7]

Madness was traditionally regarded as a form of mental disharmony. In *King Lear* Cordelia prays to the gods to 'wind up' (that is, retune) Lear's 'untun'd and jarring senses' (IV.vii.15),[8] as though his mind was a musical instrument that had gone wrong. Music was therefore seen as the best remedy for madness – 'the best comforter / To an unsettled fancy', as Prospero puts it, calling for music to 'cure th[e] brains' of Alonso, driven mad by Ariel's magic (*The Tempest*, V.i.58–9). When Orfeo responds to his overwhelming loss by fleeing to the wilderness, he is doing what Lear does, under the impact of his daughters' rejection, when he leaves Gloucester's castle for the bare heath, and what the hero of any medieval romance might do in a comparable crisis: Chrétien de Troyes's Yvain, for example, also discards civilized dress after his wife rejects him, and he takes flight to the wilderness, abandoning cooked food and courtly manners, and letting his beard grow till he becomes unrecognizable. But whereas Heurodis was snatched away against her will, Orfeo does this voluntarily; and he takes his harp with him. In *Sir Orfeo*, as in the classical myth, the harp will tame wild beasts. It will also overcome the wildness of mental disorder. That idea of music's therapeutic value is retained in a ballad version of the story collected in nineteenth-century Shetland: the hero plays on the bagpipes a 'reel / Dat meicht ha made a sick hert hale' (Bliss 1966, l). The harp, emblem of the poet's own power, is one of those objects in which the meanings of Breton lays tend to be crystallized and made memorable.

Orfeo will confront the force that holds Heurodis prisoner, will use the harp to defeat it, and will bring her back, stage by stage, to normality. In our terms, he is a kind of psychotherapist; but he is not like the classic psychoanalyst, who sits hidden, detached from the patient's suffering, asking questions but giving no answers. Orfeo is more like the ideal psychotherapist postulated by Laing, who shares lovingly in his patient's experience, follows her into her inner wilderness, and has 'both quite exceptional authority and the capacity to improvise' (Laing 1967, 40). That improvisational capacity is crucial when Orfeo faces the fairy king: he has no preconceived plan for regaining Heurodis, but seizes the sudden opportunity of the king's rash promise, and instantly sees how he can force him to keep it.

Sir Orfeo tells a story about healing; it also has the capacity to heal its own listeners, to harmonize their discordant impulses, and to encourage them to believe that life's problems can be overcome, and that happy endings are possible, though only at the price of risk and suffering – and even ageing. Again a Shakespearean parallel suggests itself. In *The Winter's Tale*, Leontes' supposedly dead wife Hermione is restored to him after a sixteen-year gap when, apparently by magic, her statue seems to come to life. It is not really magic, though, and what makes the reunion especially poignant is Leontes' realization that the statue looks older than Hermione did when he last saw her: 'Hermione was not so much wrinkled', he says, 'nothing / So aged as this seems' (V.iii.28–9). Similarly in *Sir Orfeo*, Orfeo's 'ten yere & more' (264) of living rough in the wilderness leaves its marks on his body, and when he encounters Heurodis among the hawking ladies she weeps to see him so changed. That glimpse of ageing is uncommon in medieval romances, where time usually passes without affecting human bodies as it does in the real world.[9] In *Sir Orfeo* the couple are eventually restored to power, but nothing can restore the lost years, and they die childless. Both in Shakespeare's play and in the medieval romance, the optimism of fairy tale is tempered but also made more credible by this element of realism.

Like Freud's psychoanalytic fictions, which never achieved the objective physiological grounding he hoped to provide for them, or like Laing's fictions of liberation, *Sir Orfeo* is a winter's tale, a story of the kind we need to tell ourselves in order to help us face and overcome dangers we do not understand. The medieval poet and the founder of psychoanalysis are alike in offering the real possibility of healing by means of fictions about healing. 'Where id was, there ego shall be', Freud promised (Freud 1964, 80); and romances such as this (*Sir Orfeo* more obviously than others) propose personal and social integration as an achievable possibility – achievable only at a price, but still achievable. I must emphasize that I am not claiming that any of this is what the poet meant, only that the terrifying experience that he coded as being abducted by the fairies and then being brought back is one that we might code as going mad and being cured.

So far I have been sketching, with some revision, our earlier interpretation of *Sir Orfeo*. This discusses it as if the gender roles in the story might have been reversed: Orfeo might have been carried off by the fairies, and Heurodis might have brought him back. It is hard to imagine it being told like that, and not only because the reversal would have entailed representing the male as passive and the female as active. I have gained help in seeing why the actual gender roles are necessary to the meaning of *Sir Orfeo* from a somewhat unexpected source: a paper by Mary Ann Doane called 'The Clinical Eye: Medical Discourses in the "Woman's Film" of the 1940s' (Doane 1986). This is concerned with 'a cluster of films which depict female madness, hysteria, or psychosis. These films', Doane writes, 'manifest an instability in the representation of female subjectivity and situate the woman as the object of a medical discourse.' That medical discourse is invariably male; and though, as she says, 'In the majority of the films . . . the female character suffers from some kind of mental illness: depression, nervous breakdown, catatonia, amnesia, psychosis', Doane notes that even in cases where the illness is physical it is still associated with some disturbance in the woman's whole being (Doane 1986, 153). The films she discusses include *The Cat People, Beyond the Forest, Now Voyager, The Dark Mirror, A Stolen Life*, and others.

I called Doane's paper an unexpected source of light on *Sir Orfeo*, but there are reasons why its helpfulness should not be unexpected, for the narrative discourse of medieval English popular romance has many analogies to that of classic Hollywood film. The style of both is predominantly fast-moving, transparent and non-metaphorical, focusing on represented events and occluding the means of representation. Meaning and feeling are conveyed primarily by smooth progressions in what is 'seen' and 'heard', and the expressive devices employed belong to a code of representation so familiar as to remain unnoticed; it also lacks any coherent narrative 'I' and thus does not reveal a specific narratorial point of view.[10] Further, Hollywood 'woman's films', like Middle English popular romances, form a distinct and highly stylized group of texts, with constant repetition of narrative themes and formulas within the group (Wittig 1978). Most important for my purposes, the outlook of 1940s Hollywood had much in common with that of medieval culture, both popular and 'official', and one thing they shared was a marked essentialism in their conceptions of gender. For both, rational order was essentially male, fantasy essentially female. This implies that for both the female was the weak point in the kingdom of man.

Let me take *Beyond the Forest* as one instance. In this 1949 film Bette Davis plays Rosa, the unscrupulous wife of a dedicated family doctor in a small town in Wisconsin. She feels desperately constricted by her marriage and by small-town life; one of the film's most memorable lines (one that may now be better known through being quoted in Albee's *Who's Afraid of Virginia Woolf?*) is her contemptuous 'What a dump!' (Another is her husband's plaintive question, 'Why can't you be like other women?') Rosa longs to escape to the big city, in this case Chicago, for which a train leaves several times a day. She has an affair with a Chicago millionaire, she does run away, and then, when her lover decides to marry someone else, she returns to her husband. She turns out to be pregnant, presumably by her lover, and tries to induce an abortion. Though she is sick, she dresses and makes up her face, and desperately attempts to get to Chicago again; she ends by dying of peritonitis on the road by the railtrack as the train draws out. The small town has a saw-mill as its only industry, and Rosa's excessive desire is associated with the burning glow from the mill, shining in through her bedroom window, as well as with the crushing energy of the steam locomotive hauling the train to Chicago. The sickness from which she dies is as much mental as physical: it is a kind of madness, burning up her mind as the fever burns up her body. Her husband, though a doctor, trying to make objective sense of her sickness, remains outside her excessive desire and is unable to help her. I find the parallels with *Sir Orfeo* illuminating, if incomplete. Something drives Heurodis to escape from her husband's kingdom and her marriage – a marriage figured by the orchard, a cultivated space, at once protective and constricting. In the medieval romance, the something that drives Heurodis is evidently outside herself, though it first appears to her when she is sleeping; but in both cases the heroine suffers a compulsion that is threatening precisely because inexplicable. All that can be said of Heurodis is that she 'wold vp, & owy' (96), and, as she herself says to Orfeo, 'Do thi best, for y mot go' (126). Fortunately, her husband's response is less objectifying than that of Rosa's husband: Orfeo ventures into the realm of Heurodis's madness himself and is able to rescue her.

In *Beyond the Forest*, though Rosa's husband wishes she could be like other women, the subtext is that there is something distinctively female about her instability. *The Cat People* (the 1942 version directed by Jacques Tourneur) is an especially illuminating case, because there an instability associated with femaleness is given symbolic form by the heroine's recurrent metamorphosis into a wild animal, a panther. Orpheus tames wild animals; in *The Cat People* Irena (not just a woman but a foreign woman, played by a foreign actress, Simone Simon) becomes a wild animal. Or so it seems: we never witness her turning into a panther, and we cannot be quite certain that this is not a delusory symptom of her instability. Either way, dangerous animality and otherness are associated with female sexuality. Irena is obsessed by stories of people from her Sèrbian village who worshipped Satan and could turn into cats, and is convinced that if her American husband kisses her the same evil inside herself will escape from control. Not surprisingly, her husband tires of her rejection of him, and turns instead to his sensible, all-American office colleague Alice, who has loved him all along. Irena, apparently in panther form, makes two attempts to kill Alice. Her husband sends her to see a psychiatrist, who does not believe that she can turn into a panther, and falls in love with her. He kisses her, and she kills him, though at the same time he wounds her; then she goes to the zoo, where her husband first met her when she was sketching a panther. She releases the panther from its cage, and she dies.

This is obviously a quite different story from that of *Sir Orfeo*, but through its very excess in the attribution of mental illness to its heroine it reveals something about *Sir Orfeo* that I had not previously noticed. Feminist theory has seen, as Elaine Showalter notes, 'a fundamental alliance between "woman" and "madness"' and has sometimes gone so far as to affirm 'the impossibility of representing the feminine in patriarchal discourse as other than madness, incoherence, fluidity, or silence' (Showalter 1985a, 3).[11] Certainly, one type of mental instability was traditionally regarded as specifically female and called hysteria – Showalter suggests that its place as 'the female malady' has subsequently been taken by schizophrenia (Showalter 1985a, 203) – and I now see that the association between madness and femaleness assumed by patriarchy is to be found in the medieval poem. It is not by accident, I suggest, that it is Heurodis in whom there occurs 'the surfacing of the invisible, chaotic forces of instinct or the unconscious' (Doane 1986, 161). The orchard or garden where the surfacing happens – a place inhabited especially by women – symbolizes the delectable and vulnerable female body enclosed by man for his proper use and cultivation; this is so in texts from the Song of Songs or the story of Susanna and the Elders down to much more recent times, including medieval texts such as Chaucer's *Merchant's Tale* and *Franklin's Tale*. The garden is usually represented as surrounded by walls to contain and protect its female inhabitants – to keep the women in, under the control of the patriarchal regime of the household, and to keep intruders out (Lerer 1985, 95) – but in *Sir Orfeo* this is in vain, because the 'intruders' are already present. In terms of the interpretation I am suggesting, they belong to Heurodis's own unconscious. It is not by accident, either, that it is the man who is able to survive life in the wilderness 'With wilde bestes in holtes hore' (214), entering the realm of the 'invisible, chaotic forces' and challenging them on their own ground. Orfeo can tame wild beasts with his music: in this he is unlike the unfortunate psychiatrist in *The Cat People*, who is killed by the heroine in her wild beast role, and who resembles in this the fictional Orfeo of the story Orfeo tells to the steward – the one who was killed by wild beasts, leaving only his harp behind. That story gives a glimpse of an alternative ending to the romance, one in which the 'invisible, chaotic forces' would have triumphed over the rational order of civilization. But the real Orfeo can enter the very domain of these forces without being overwhelmed by them, and he can rescue his queen, thus restoring order to his kingdom.

The analogy with Doane's cases is fascinating, but it is not perfect, for two reasons. One is implied in what I have just said: in *Beyond the Forest* and *The Cat People* (unlike some other films that Doane discusses), female madness is merely destructive and self-destructive. These are not fictions of healing, but only warnings of a danger inherent in femaleness. The other reason is that the essentialism of Hollywood is not identical with that of the Middle Ages. Doane writes that in these films 'The doctor's work is the transformation of the woman into a specular object' (Doane 1986, 155). So indeed it had been in nineteenth-century attempts to define hysteria medically, for example by Charcot, whose carefully arranged theatrical displays of female hysterics at the Salpêtrière became a fashionable Parisian spectacle. But Orfeo, as I have noted, is not detached and objective in the manner of the traditional male doctor confronted by 'female madness, hysteria, or psychosis'. He is also a loving husband, and, by taking to the wilderness, where the boundary between the human and fairy worlds is especially permeable, he enters into his wife's experience himself. (In medieval romances the wilderness may often be thought of as an external projection of the unconscious.) Doane, discussing her 1940s films, refers to 'a narcissism purportedly specific to femininity' (Doane 1986, 156), and notes how there 'The illness of the woman is signaled by the fact that she no longer cares about her appearance' (155). (The mad Ophelia with her dishevelled hair is a familiar example in Shakespeare. In *Beyond the Forest*, this is taken to the opposite extreme: Rosa tries to make herself look attractive for her last attempt to escape to Chicago, but instead turns herself into a grotesque parody of the feminine. The same thing is sometimes done with Ophelia in modern productions of *Hamlet*.) This destruction of the outward markers of femininity is indeed paralleled in *Sir Orfeo*. The first sign of the intrusion of the fairies into Heurodis's life is that

> Sche crid, & lothli bere gan make:
> Sche froted hir honden & hir fet,
> & crached hir visage – it bled wete;
> Hir riche robe hye al to-rett . . .
>
> (78–81)

And this destruction of her beauty is the first thing Orfeo notices when he sees her after her initial encounter with the fairies, systematically contrasting her former immaculate appearance with its present ruin:

> Thi bodi, that was so white y-core,
> With thine nailes is al to-tore.
> Allas! thi rode, that was so red,
> Is al wan, as thou were ded;
> & al-so thine fingres smale
> Beth al blodi & al pale.
> Allas! thi louesome eyyen to
> Loketh so man doth on his fo!
>
> (105–12)

In medieval culture, though, the 'Great Masculine Renunciation' (Flugel 1930) having not yet taken place, narcissism is attributed to men as much as to women, and Orfeo is marked by the same collapse of narcissism when he follows his wife into the wilderness. He abandons his kingly robes and lets his body waste away and his beard grow long, and the fairy king describes him as 'lene, rowe & blac' (459). The recovery is signalled by a fresh toilet attributed to Orfeo rather than to Heurodis:

> To chaumber thai ladde him als biliue
> & bathed him, & schaued his berd,
> & tired him as a king apert.
>
> (584–6)

Narcissism, both male and female, is a necessity of the secular order, whether that of the ego or that of the social hierarchy, and both king and queen must once more become specular objects, bathed and newly clothed, and displayed before their subjects 'with gret processioun' (587), to indicate that normality is restored.

Yet it can be said that the story of *Sir Orfeo*, though it is Orfeo's story, arises out of what happens to – or in – Heurodis; and one way of interpreting it would be to say that Orfeo enters into female fantasy, into what is described in Freud and Breuer's *Studies on Hysteria* as 'systematic day-dreaming' (Freud and Breuer 1955, 22; cited by Doane 1986, 165). And he does so in order to overcome its power. The irresistible power that Heurodis attributes to the fairy world perhaps does not really exist except in her dangerous imaginings (just as in *The Cat People* the transformation of woman into panther perhaps belongs only to Irena's imaginings). The danger of fairy may *be* the power of female imaginings; and it is striking that when Orfeo confronts the fairy king face to face, he finds him to be a man like any other, one who cares about his reputation among other men and there-fore keeps his rash promise, with a gruffly masculine and distinctly ungraci-ous 'I wish you joy of her!':

> The king seyd: 'Sethen it is so
> Take hir bi the hond & go:
> Of hir ichil thatow be blithe!'
> (469–71)

It is through Heurodis that the fairy world can gain access to Orfeo's kingdom and disrupt it. But it is not as simple as that. Orfeo, as we have seen, has to share in Heurodis's fantasy (if that is what it is) in order to defuse its danger; yet without her fantasy there would be no story, nothing of interest for the poet to recount. It is striking, too, that unlike the silent Eurydice of Ovid and Boethius, Heurodis speaks of her own experience. The story the poet tells has in part already been told by her. More gener-ally, without female fantasy there would be none of the fascinatingly errant, transgressive story-material that forms the substance of so many medieval romances, story-material in which female characters often do speak for themselves. The kind of narrative that modern scholars define as romance, and especially perhaps the Celtic stories that nourished the medieval French courtly tradition, possesses features that in medieval culture were seen as characterizing Woman. Romance is wandering, elusive, transgressive – both in crossing the boundaries of the classical genres and in representing actions in which the crossing of boundaries is common and significant. (Crossing boundaries is certainly significant in *Sir Orfeo*, whether it is the fairy king intruding into the orchard or Orfeo crossing into and out of the realm of fairy itself.) Romance is fictional, and was condemned for its deceitfulness by clerical and ecclesiastical authorities who tended to criticize women on the same grounds (Kelly 1985, 74–81). Romance is fickle, evasive, hard to pin down in terms of genre or tone; it is what diverges from a norm that the official culture defined as masculine. Perhaps the sense of satisfaction given by *Sir Orfeo*, the sense that here one kind of Middle English romance has perfectly fulfilled its potential, derives from its reciprocal enactment of gen-der roles: man follows woman into the realm of female fantasy, woman follows man back into that of male order, and the mutual love that binds them ensures that both complete themselves by doing so. I am tempted to suggest that we might think of Orfeo not only as a psychotherapist but as a figure of the male poet of romance and a model for its male reader, explor-ing fantasies of the inexplicable in order to complete himself – fantasies that are inexplicable and, though frightening, desirable precisely because they lie outside the walls of masculine identity. This too, of course, cannot be what the poet consciously meant; it is at best a tribute to the inexhaustible power of the finest stories to generate new meanings. It seems clear, at least, that whether or not *Sir Orfeo* is read as a poem about madness, gender plays a crucial part in its effect.

Notes

1   1330–40 is the date assigned to the Auchinleck manuscipt. The other two manuscripts are British Library, Harley 3810 and Bodleian, Ashmole 61. For recent discussion of the versions and their manuscript contexts, see Evans 1995, 96–100. For the view that the three versions should be considered equally authentic variants of the poem, see Longsworth 1982; for objections, see Spearing 1987, ch. 3, n. 25, and Pearsall 1996, 52 and nn. 4–5.

2   *Sir Orfeo* is quoted from the Auchinleck version in the edition of A. J. Bliss (Oxford: Oxford University Press, 1966).

3   For valuable surveys of such interpretations, see Friedman 1970 and Vicari 1982. The quotation is from Vicari, adapting Friedman's account (90) of Boethius's interpretation.

4   For the former interpretation, see Friedman 1970, 184–90; for the latter, Doob 1974, 74–6. For critiques of the underlying assumptions, see Spearing 1987, ch. 3, and Rider 1988.

5   I argue this case more fully in Spearing 1990b.

6   Spearing and Spearing 1974, 41–9, elaborated in Spearing 1987, ch. 3. Pearsall 1996, in an article drafted in unawareness of these earlier readings, offers an encouragingly similar interpretation, but with 'important differences of detail and emphasis' (n. 2).

7   Mumford 1986 notes a similar ambivalence – 'the fairy-king's world . . . is both richer and more terrifying than our own' – and suggests that in Jungian terms it is 'the world of the *shadow*, the world of the unconscious' (297).

8   Shakespeare quotations and references are from *The Riverside Shakespeare*, ed. G. Blakemore Evans et al. (Boston: Houghton Mifflin, 1974).

9   Rosalind Field reminds me of a rare parallel in another Breton lay, Marie de France's *Milun*, where, as in *The Winter's Tale*, the story covers two generations. When the hero is unhorsed by his own son, his age is revealed by the white hair seen through his visor.

10 For attempts at fuller treatment of these analogies, see Spearing 1984 and 1987, ch. 2.

11 For an exemplary analysis of the association of woman with madness in a nineteenth-century text, Balzac's short story *Adieu*, see Felman 1975. See also Mazzoni 1996.

BIBLIOGRAPHY

Primary Sources

Alliterative Morte Arthure, ed. Valerie Krishna (New York: Franklin, 1976).

Ami et Amile: chanson de geste, ed. Peter F. Dembowski, CFMA (Paris: Champion, 1987).

Amis and Amiloun, ed. MacEdward Leach, EETS o.s. 203 (London: Oxford University Press, 1937).

Aucassin et Nicolette, ed. Mario Roques, CFMA (Paris: Champion, 1955).

Augustine, *De Civitate Dei*, ed. E. Huffman, Corpus Christianorum Series Latina 40 (Turnhout: Brepols, 1954–).

 Quaestiones in heptateuchum, ed. J. Zycha, Corpus Scriptorum Ecclesiasticorum Latinorum 28 (Vienna, 1895).

Avowing of Arthur, ed. Roger Dahood (New York: Garland, 1984).

Awntyrs off Arthure at the Terne Wathelyn, ed. Ralph Hanna (Manchester: Manchester University Press, 1974).

Ballad of Sir Aldingar: Its Origin and Analogues, ed. Paul Christophersen (Oxford: Oxford University Press, 1952).

Bataille Loquifer, ed. Monica Barnett (Oxford: Society for the Study of Mediaeval Languages and Literature, 1975).

Benoît de Sainte-Maure, *Le Roman de Troie*, 6 vols, ed. L. Constans, SATF (Paris: Firmin Didot, 1904–12).

Béroul, *The Romance of Tristran*, ed. and trans. Stewart Gregory (Amsterdam: Rodopi, 1992).

Blamires, Alcuin, with Karen Pratt and C. W. Marx (eds), *Woman Defamed and Woman Defended: An Anthology of Medieval Texts* (Oxford: Oxford University Press, 1992).

Chanson de Guillaume, ed. D. McMillan, 2 vols, SATF (Paris: Picard, 1949–50).

 Trans. Glanville Price, Lynette Muir and David Hoggan, *William, Count of Orange: Four Old French Epics*, Everyman (London: Dent, 1975).

Chastelaine de Vergi, ed. Gaston Raynaud, rev. Lucien Foulet, CFMA (Paris: Champion, 1921).

Chaucer, Geoffrey, *The Riverside Chaucer*, ed. Larry D. Benson et al. (Boston: Houghton Mifflin, 1987).

Chaucer Life-Records, ed. Martin M. Crow and Clair C. Olson (Oxford: Oxford University Press, 1966).

Chrétien de Troyes, *Le Chevalier de la Charrete (Lancelot)*, ed. Mario Roques, CFMA (Paris: Champion, 1983).

Cligés, ed. Alexandre Micha, CFMA (Paris: Champion, 1982).

Erec et Enide, ed. Mario Roques, CFMA (Paris: Champion, 1981).

Le Conte du Graal (Perceval), ed. Félix Lecoy, 2 vols, CFMA (Paris: Champion, 1973–5).

Cicero, *De oratore*, trans. E. W. Sutton and H. Rackham, 2 vols, Loeb Classical Library (Cambridge, MA: Heinemann, 1976).

Compendium Historiae Troianae–Romanae, ed. Henry Simonsfeld, *Neues Archiv der Gesellschaft für ältere deutsche Geschichtskunde* 11 (1886), 239–51.

Compota Thesauriorum Regum Scotorum: Accounts of the Lord High Treasurer of Scotland, ed. Thomas Dickson, Sir John Balfour-Paul and C. T. Innes, 12 vols (Edinburgh: H. M. General Register House, 1877–1916).

Dares, *Daretis Phrygii de excidio Troiae historia*, ed. F. Meister (Leipzig, Teubner, 1873).

Trans. R. M. Frazer, *The Trojan War* (Bloomington: Indiana University Press, 1966).

Destruction of Troy, ed. G. A. Panton and D. Donaldson, 2 vols, EETS o.s. 39, 56 (London: Oxford University Press, 1869, 1874).

Eger and Grime: A Parallel-Text Edition of the Percy and the Huntington–Laing Versions of the Romance, ed. James Ralston Caldwell (Cambridge, MA: Harvard University Press, 1933).

Emaré, ed. Anne Laskaya and Eve Salisbury, *The Middle English Breton Lays*, TEAMS (Kalamazoo, MI: Medieval Institute Publications, 1995).

Emaré, ed. Edith Rickert, EETS e.s. 99 (London: Oxford University Press, 1908).

Excidium Troiae, ed. E. Bagby Atwood and Virgil K. Whitaker (Cambridge, MA: Mediaeval Academy of America, 1944).

Folie Tristan d'Oxford, ed. Ernest Hoepffner (Paris: Belles Lettres, 1943).

Trans. Judith Weiss, *The Birth of Romance: An Anthology*, Everyman (London: Dent, 1992), 121–40.

Froissart, Jean, *Chronicles*, trans. Geoffrey Brereton (Harmondsworth: Penguin, 1968).

Gamelyn, ed. Walter W. Skeat, *The Tale of Gamelyn* (Oxford: Oxford University Press, 1884).

Gesta Romanorum, ed. H. Oesterley (Berlin: Weidmann, 1872).

Gesta Romanorum, ed. Sidney J. Herrtage, EETS e.s. 33 (London: Oxford University Press, 1879).

Gibbs, A. C. (ed.), *Middle English Romances* (London: Arnold, 1966).

Gottfried von Strassburg, *Tristan*, ed. Rüdiger Krohn, 3 vols (Stuttgart: Reclam, 1980).

Trans. A. T. Hatto, *Gottfried von Strassburg, 'Tristan', with the 'Tristan' of Thomas* (Harmondsworth: Penguin, 1960).

Gower, John, *Confessio Amantis*, in *The English Works of John Gower*, ed. G. C. Macaulay, EETS e.s. 89, 91 (London: Oxford University Press, 1900–01).

Graelent, ed. Alexandre Micha, *Lais féeriques des XIIe et XIIIe siècles* (Paris: Flammarion, 1992).

Guido delle Colonne, *Historia Destructionis Troiae*, ed. N. E. Griffin (Cambridge, MA: Mediaeval Academy of America, 1936).

Trans. M. E. Meek, *Historia Destructionis Troiae* (Bloomington: Indiana University Press, 1974).

Guillaume de Palerne: Roman du XIIe siècle, ed. Alexandre Micha, TLF (Geneva: Droz, 1990).

Guingamor, ed. Alexandre Micha, *Lais féeriques des XIIe et XIIIe siècles* (Paris: Flammarion, 1992).

Hartmann von Aue, *Gregorius*, ed. H. Paul, rev. B. Wachinger (Tübingen: Niemeyer, 1992).

Havelok, ed. G. V. Smithers (Oxford: Oxford University Press, 1987).

Hrólfs saga Kraka, ed. D. Slay, Editiones Arnamagnæanae Series B, I (Copenhagen: Munksgaard, 1960), 16–36.

Trans. Gwyn Jones, *King Hrolf and his Champions*, in *Eirik the Red and other Icelandic Sagas* (London: Oxford University Press, 1961), 234–50.

Joseph of Exeter, *Trojan War I–III*, ed. and trans. A. K. Bate (Warminster: Aris and Phillips, 1986).

King Alisaunder, ed. G. V. Smithers, 2 vols, EETS o.s. 227, 237 (London: Oxford University Press, 1952, 1957).

König von Reussen, ed. anon., in *Mai und Beaflor* (Leipzig: Göschensche Verlagshandlung, 1848).

Lai le Freine, ed. Margaret Wattie (Northampton, MA: Smith College, 1929).

'Lament for Sir John Berkeley', ed. Thorlac Turville-Petre, *Speculum* 57 (1982), 332–9.

Lancelot do Lac, ed. Elspeth Kennedy, 2 vols (Oxford: Oxford University Press, 1980).

Langland, William, *The Vision of Piers Plowman: A Critical Edition of the B-Text*, ed. A. V. C. Schmidt, 2nd edn, Everyman (London: Dent, 1995).

Laud Troy Book, ed. J. Ernst Wülfing, 2 vols, EETS o.s. 121, 122 (London: Oxford University Press, 1902, 1903).

Lindsay, Sir David, *Ane Satyre of the Thrie Estaitis*, ed. Roderick Lyall (Edinburgh: Canongate, 1989).

Lindsay, Sir David, *Squyer Meldrum*, ed. James Kinsley (London: Nelson, 1959).

Lybeaus Desconus, ed. Maldwyn Mills, EETS o.s. 261 (London: Oxford University Press, 1969).

Lydgate, John, *Troy Book*, ed. H. Bergen, 4 vols, EETS e.s. 97, 103, 106, 126 (London: Oxford University Press, 1906, 1908, 1910, 1935).

Malory, Thomas, *The Works of Sir Thomas Malory*, ed. Eugène Vinaver, rev. P. J. C. Field, 3 vols (Oxford: Oxford University Press, 1990).

Mannyng of Brunne, Robert, *The Chronicle*, ed. Idelle Sulens (Binghamton, NY: Medieval and Renaissance Texts and Studies, 1996).

Marie de France, *Les Lais de Marie de France*, ed. Jean Rychner, TLF (Geneva: Droz, 1966).

Trans. Glyn S. Burgess and Keith Busby, *The Lais of Marie de France* (Harmondsworth: Penguin, 1986).

275

Mills, Maldwyn (ed.), *Six Middle English Romances*, Everyman (London: Dent, 1973).

Mirk, John, *Instruction for Parish Priests*, ed. Gilles Kristensson (Lund: Bloms, 1974).

Montesquieu, Charles de Secondat, baron de, *Dossier de l'Esprit des Lois*, in *Oeuvres Complètes*, ed. Roger Caillais, 2 vols (Paris: Gallimard, 1976), II.

Octavian Imperator, ed. Frances McSparran (Heidelberg: Winter, 1979).

Paris, Matthew, *The Illustrated Chronicles of Matthew Paris: Observations of Thirteenth-Century Life*, ed. and trans. Richard Vaughan (Cambridge: Corpus Christi College, 1993).

Philippe de Beaumanoir (Rémi), *La Manekine*, ed. Hermann Suchier, *Oeuvres Poétiques de Philippe de Rémi*, 2 vols, SATF (Paris: Firmin Didot, 1884), I.

    Philippe de Rémi's 'La Manekine': Text, Translation, Commentary, ed. and trans. I. Gnarra (New York: Garland, 1988).

Renart, Jean, *Galeran de Bretagne*, ed. Lucien Foulet, CFMA (Paris: Champion, 1925).

    Le Roman de la Rose ou de Guillaume de Dole, ed. Félix Lecoy, CFMA (Paris: Champion, 1979).

Rymes of Robyn Hood: An Introduction to the English Outlaw, ed. R. B. Dobson and J. Taylor (Gloucester: Alan Sutton, 1989).

Sands, Donald B. (ed.), *Middle English Verse Romances* (New York: Holt, Rinehart and Winston, 1966).

Seege or Batayle of Troye, ed. M. E. Barnicle, EETS o.s. 172 (London: Oxford University Press, 1927).

Shakespeare, William, *The Riverside Shakespeare*, ed. G. Blakemore Evans et al. (Boston: Houghton Mifflin, 1974).

    The Winter's Tale, ed. J. H. Pafford, Arden Shakespeare (London: Routledge, 1963).

Sir Amadace, ed. Maldwyn Mills, in *Six Middle English Romances*, Everyman (London: Dent, 1973).

Sir Degaré, ed. G. Schleich, *Sire Degarre nach der gesamten Überlieferung und mit Untersuchungen über die Sprache und den Romanzenstoff* (Heidelberg: Winter, 1929), repr. and corrected in Nicolas Jacobs, *The Later Versions of 'Sir Degarre': A Study in Textual Degeneration* (Oxford: Society for the Study of Medieval Languages and Literature, 1995), 12–37.

Sir Degrevant, ed. L. F. Casson, EETS o.s. 221 (London: Oxford University Press, 1949).

Sir Eglamour, ed. Frances E. Richardson, EETS e.s. 256 (London: Oxford University Press, 1965).

Sir Ferumbras, ed. Sidney J. Herrtage, EETS e.s. 34 (London: Trübner, 1879).

Sir Gawain and the Green Knight, ed. J. R. R. Tolkien and E. V. Gordon, rev. Norman Davis (Oxford: Oxford University Press, 1967).

Sir Isumbras, ed. Harriet Hudson, in *Four Middle English Romances*, TEAMS (Kalamazoo, MI: Medieval Institute Publications, 1996).

Sir Isumbras, ed. Maldwyn Mills, in *Six Middle English Romances*, Everyman (London: Dent, 1973).

Sir Launfal, ed. A. J. Bliss (London: Nelson, 1960).

Sir Orfeo, ed. A. J. Bliss (Oxford: Oxford University Press, 1966).

Sir Tristrem, ed. Alan Lupack, '*Lancelot of the Laik*' and '*Sir Tristrem*', TEAMS (Kalamazoo, MI: Medieval Institute Publications, 1994).

Sir Tristrem, ed. George P. McNeill, STS 8 (Edinburgh: Blackwood and Sons, 1886).

Sir Tristrem: A Metrical Romance of the Thirteenth Century, by Thomas of Erceldoune, called the Rhymer, ed. Walter Scott (Edinburgh: Constable, 1811).

Thomas of Britain, *Le Roman de Tristan par Thomas*, ed. Joseph Bédier, 2 vols, SATF (Paris: Firmin Didot, 1902, 1905).

    Tristran, ed. and trans. Stewart Gregory (New York: Garland, 1991).

Tristrams saga ok Ísöndar, ed. Eugen Kölbing (Heilbronn: Henninger, 1878).

    Trans. Paul Schach, *The Saga of Tristram and Ísönd* (Lincoln, NE: University of Nebraska Press, 1973).

Vie du Pape Grégoire: 8 versions françaises médiévales de la légende du Bon Pécheur, ed. H. B. Sol (Amsterdam: Rodopi, 1977).

Weber, H. (ed.), *Metrical Romances*, 3 vols (Edinburgh: Constable, 1810).

Wedderburn, Robert, *The Complaynt of Scotland (c.1550)*, ed. A. M. Stewart, STS 4th ser., 11 (Edinburgh: Blackwood and Sons, 1979).

Wedding of Sir Gawain and Dame Ragnell, ed. John Withrington (Lancaster: Lancaster Modern Spelling Texts, 1991).

William of Palerne, ed. G. H. V. Bunt (Groningen: Bouma's Boekhuis, 1985).

William of Palerne, ed. Walter W. Skeat, EETS e.s. 1 (London: Trübner, 1867).

'*Ywain and Gawain*', '*Sir Percyvell of Gales*', '*The Anturs of Arther*', ed. Maldwyn Mills, Everyman (London: Dent, 1992).

Facsimile editions

The Auchinleck Manuscript: National Library of Scotland, Advocates' MS 19.2.1, ed. Derek Pearsall and I. C. Cunningham (London: Scolar Press, 1977).

Cambridge University Library, MS Ff.2.38, ed. Frances McSparran and P. R. Robinson (London: Scolar Press, 1979).

The Thornton Manuscript (Lincoln Cathedral MS 91), ed. Derek Brewer and A. E. B. Owen (London: Scolar Press, 1975).

Secondary Sources

Adams, Robert P. (1959), '"Bold Bawdry and Open Manslaughter": The English New Humanist Attack on Medieval Romance', *Huntington Library Quarterly* 23, 33–48.

Aers, David (1988), *Community, Gender and Individual Identity: English Writing, 1360–1430* (London: Routledge).

(1992), 'A Whisper in the Ear of Early Modernists, or, Reflections on Literary Critics Writing the "History of the Subject"', in *Culture and History: Essays on English Communities, Identities, and Writing*, ed. David Aers (Detroit: Wayne State University Press), 177–200.

Alexander, Flora (1993), 'Women as Lovers in Early English Romance', in *Women and Literature in Britain 1150–1500*, ed. Carol M. Meale (Cambridge: Cambridge University Press), 24–40.

Allen, Rosamund (1987), 'Some Sceptical Observations on the Editing of *The Awntyrs off Arthure*', in *Manuscripts and Texts: Editorial Problems in Later Middle English Literature*, ed. Derek Pearsall (Woodbridge: Brewer), 5–25.

Archibald, Elizabeth (1990), 'Women and Romance', in *Companion to Middle English Romance*, ed. Henk Aertsen and Alasdair A. MacDonald (Amsterdam: VU Press), 153–69.

—— (1991), *Apollonius of Tyre: Medieval and Renaissance Themes and Variations* (Woodbridge: Brewer).

—— (1996), 'Contextualizing Chaucer's Constance: Romance Modes and Family Values', in *The Endless Knot*, ed. R. F. Yeager and M. Teresa Tavormina (Woodbridge: Brewer), 161–75.

Armstrong, Elizabeth Psakis (1990), 'The Patient Woman in Chaucer's *Clerk's Tale* and Marie de France's *Fresne*', *Centennial Review* 34, 433–48.

Ashley, Bob (1997) (ed.), *Reading Popular Narrative: A Source Book*, rev. edn (London: Leicester University Press).

Atwood, E. Bagby (1938a), 'The *Excidium Troie* and Medieval Troy Literature', *Modern Philology* 35, 115–28.

—— (1938b), 'Robert Mannyng's Version of the Troy Story', *Texas University Studies in English* 18, 5–13.

—— (1941), 'The Youth of Paris in the *Seege of Troye*', *Texas University Studies in English* 21, 7–23.

—— (1942a), 'The Judgement of Paris in the *Seege of Troye*', *PMLA* 57, 343–53.

—— (1942b), 'The Story of Achilles in the *Seege of Troye*', *SP* 39, 489–501.

Auerbach, Erich (1953), *Mimesis: The Representation of Reality in Western Literature*, trans. Willard R. Trask (Princeton: Princeton University Press).

Bakhtin, Mikhail (1984), *Rabelais and his World*, trans. Hélène Iswolsky (Bloomington: Indiana University Press).

Barber, Paul (1988), *Vampires, Burial, and Death: Folklore and Reality* (New Haven: Yale University Press).

Barnes, Geraldine (1993), *Counsel and Strategy in Middle English Romance* (Woodbridge: Brewer).

Barnicle, M. E. (1927) (ed.), *Seege or Batayle of Troye*, EETS o.s. 172 (London: Oxford University Press).

Barron, W. R. J. (1982), 'Alliterative Romance and the French Tradition', in *Middle English Alliterative Poetry and its Literary Background*, ed. David Lawton (Woodbridge: Brewer), 75–80.

—— (1987), *English Medieval Romance* (London: Longman).

Barthes, Roland (1968), 'L'effet de réel', *Communications* 11, 84–9.

Bartlett, F. C. (1970), *A Study in Experimental and Social Psychology* (Cambridge: Cambridge University Press).

Bartlett, Robert J. (1986), *Trial by Fire and Water: The Medieval Judicial Ordeal* (Oxford: Clarendon).

Baugh, Albert C. (1950), 'The Authorship of the Middle English Romances', *Annual Bulletin of the Modern Humanities Research Association* 22, 1–28.

—— (1959), 'Improvisation in the Middle English Romance', *Proceedings of the American Philosophical Society* 103, 418–54.

—— (1967), 'The Middle English Romance: Some Questions of Creation, Presentation, and Preservation', *Speculum* 42, 1–31.

Baum, Paull F. (1916), 'The Medieval Legend of Judas Iscariot', *PMLA* 31, 481–563.

Baumgartner, Emmanuèle (1987), *Tristan et Iseut: De la légende aux récits en vers* (Paris: Presses Universitaires de France).

Beer, Gillian (1970), *The Romance* (London: Methuen).

Bell, Quentin (1972), *Virginia Woolf: A Biography*, 2 vols (London: Hogarth Press).

Bellamy, John G. (1973), *Crime and Public Order in England in the Later Middle Ages* (London: Routledge & Kegan Paul).

—— (1985), *Robin Hood: An Historical Enquiry* (Bloomington: Indiana University Press).

—— (1989), *Bastard Feudalism and the Law* (Portland, OR: Areopagitica).

Bennett, Michael (1979), *Community, Class and Careerism: Cheshire and Lancashire Society in the Age of 'Sir Gawain and the Green Knight'* (Cambridge: Cambridge University Press).

Benskin, Michael, Hunt, Tony and Short, Ian (1992–5), 'Un nouveau fragment du *Tristan* de Thomas', *Romania* 113, 289–319.

Benson, C. David (1980), *The History of Troy in Middle English Literature* (Woodbridge: Brewer).

Benson, Larry D. (1976), *Malory's 'Morte Darthur'* (Cambridge, MA: Harvard University Press).

—— (1984), 'The Queynte Punnings of Chaucer's Critics', *Studies in the Age of Chaucer Proceedings* 1, 23–47.

—— (1993) (ed.), *A Glossarial Concordance to the Riverside Chaucer*, 2 vols (New York: Garland).

Birns, Nicholas (1993), 'The Trojan Myth: Postmodern Reverberations', *Exemplaria* 5, 45–78.

Blakeslee, Merritt R. (1989), *Love's Masks: Identity, Intertextuality, and Meaning in the Old French Tristan Poems* (Woodbridge: Brewer).

Blanchfield, Lynne S. (1991), 'The Romances of Ashmole 61: An Idiosyncratic Scribe', in *Romance in Medieval England*, ed. Malwyn Mills, Jennifer Fellows and Carol M. Meale (Woodbridge: Brewer), 65–87.

—— (1996), 'Rate Revisited: The Compilation of the Narrative Works in MS Ashmole 61', in *Romance Reading on the Book: Essays in Medieval Narrative Presented to Maldwyn Mills* (Cardiff: University of Wales Press), 208–20.

Blessing, James (1960), *A Comparison of Some Middle English Romances with the Old French Antecedents*, diss. Stanford University.

Bliss, A. J. (1958), 'Thomas Chestre: A Speculation', *Litera* 5, 1–6.

(1960) (ed.), *Sir Launfal* (London: Nelson).

(1966) (ed.), *Sir Orfeo* (Oxford: Oxford University Press).

Bloch, Marc (1961), *Feudal Society*, trans. L. A. Manyon, 2 vols (London: Routledge & Kegan Paul).

Bloch, R. Howard (1983), *Etymologies and Genealogies: A Literary Anthropology of the French Middle Ages* (Chicago: University of Chicago Press).

(1991), *Medieval Misogyny and the Invention of Western Romantic Love* (Chicago: University of Chicago Press).

Bloch, R. Howard and Nichols, Stephen G. (1996) (eds), *Medievalism and the Modernist Temper* (Baltimore: Johns Hopkins University Press).

Bogdanow, Fanni (1966), *The Romance of the Grail* (Manchester: Manchester University Press).

Bollas, Christopher (1989), *Forces of Destiny* (London: Free Association Books).

Boswell, John (1989), *The Kindness of Strangers: The Abandonment of Children in Western Europe from Late Antiquity to the Renaissance* (New York: Pantheon).

Bourdieu, Pierre (1984), *Distinction: A Social Critique of the Judgement of Taste*, trans. Richard Nice (London: Routledge).

Bradbury, Nancy Mason (1994), 'Literacy, Orality, and the Poetics of Middle English Romance', in *Oral Poetics in Middle English Poetry*, ed. Mark C. Amodio, with the assistance of Sarah Gray Miller (New York: Garland), 39–69.

Brandt, William J. (1966), *The Shape of Medieval History: Studies in Modes of Perception* (New Haven: Yale University Press).

Braswell, Laurel (1965), '*Sir Isumbras* and the Legend of St Eustace', *MS* 27, 128–51.

Braund, David (1994), *Georgia in Antiquity: A History of Colchis and Transcaucasian Iberia, 550 BC – AD 562* (Oxford: Oxford University Press).

Brereton, Georgine E. (1950), 'A Thirteenth-Century List of French Lays and Other Narrative Poems', *MLR* 45, 40–45.

Brett, Guy (1986), *Through Our Own Eyes: Popular Art and Modern History* (London: GMP).

Brewer, Derek (1978), 'The Nature of Romance', *Poetica* 9, 9–48.

(1980), *Symbolic Stories: Traditional Narratives of the Family Drama in English Literature* (Woodbridge: Brewer).

(1988), 'Escape From the Mimetic Fallacy', in *Studies in Medieval English Romances*, ed. Derek Brewer (Woodbridge: Brewer), 1–10.

Brewer, D. S. and Owen, A. E. B. (1975) (eds), *The Thornton Manuscript (Lincoln Cathedral MS 91)* (London: Scolar Press).

Brody, Saul Nathaniel (1974), *The Disease of the Soul: Leprosy in Medieval Literature* (Ithaca: Cornell University Press).

Bruckner, Matilda Tomaryn (1993), *Shaping Romance: Interpretation, Truth, and Closure in Twelfth-Century French Fictions* (Philadelphia: University of Pennsylvania Press).

Brundage, James A. (1969), *Medieval Canon Law and the Crusader* (Madison: University of Wisconsin Press).

(1976), 'Holy War and the Medieval Lawyers', in *The Holy War*, ed. Thomas Patrick Murphy (Columbus: Ohio State University Press), 99–140.

(1987), *Law, Sex, and Christian Society in Medieval Europe* (Chicago: University of Chicago Press).

(1995), *Medieval Canon Law* (London: Longman).

Brunner, Karl (1961), 'Middle English Metrical Romances and their Audience', in *Studies in Medieval Literature in Honor of Professor Albert Croll Baugh*, ed. MacEdward Leach (Philadelphia: University of Pennsylvania Press), 219–27.

Brusendorff, Aage (1925), *The Chaucer Tradition* (London: Oxford University Press).

Bunt, G. H. V. (1984), 'Patron, Author and Audience in a Fourteenth-Century English Alliterative Poem', in *Non Nova, Sed Nova*, ed. Martin Gosman and Jaap van Os (Groningen: Bouma's Boekhuis), 25–36.

Burgess, Glyn S. (1987), *The Lais of Marie de France: Text and Context* (Manchester: Manchester University Press).

Burns, E. Jane (1983), 'How Lovers Lie Together: Infidelity and Fictive Discourse in the *Roman de Tristan*', *Tristania* 8, 15–30.

(1993), 'Why Beauty Laughs: Iseut's Enormous Thighs', in her *Bodytalk: When Women Speak in Old French Literature* (Philadelphia: University of Pennsylvania Press), 203–40.

Burrow, J. A. (1986), 'Romance', in *The Cambridge Chaucer Companion*, ed. Piero Boitani and Jill Mann (Cambridge: Cambridge University Press), 109–24.

(1987), '*The Avowing of King Arthur*', in *Medieval Literature and Antiquities: Studies in Honour of Basil Cottle*, ed. Myra Stokes and T. L. Burton (Woodbridge: Brewer), 99–109.

Butler, Judith (1990), *Gender Trouble: Feminism and the Subversion of Identity* (New York: Routledge).

(1993), *Bodies That Matter: On the Discursive Limits of 'Sex'* (London: Routledge).

Bynum, Caroline Walker (1984), 'Women's Stories, Women's Symbols: A Critique of Victor Turner's Theory of Liminality', in *Anthropology and the Study of Religion*, ed. Robert E. Moore and Frank L. Reynolds (Chicago: Chicago University Press), 105–25.

Caldwell, James Ralston (1933) (ed.), *Eger and Grime: A Parallel-Text Edition of the Percy and the Huntington–Laing Versions of the Romance* (Cambridge, MA: Harvard University Press).

Calin, William (1994), *The French Tradition and the Literature of Medieval England* (Toronto: Toronto University Press).

Cannon, Christopher (1993), 'Raptus in the Chaumpaigne Release and a Newly Discovered Document Concerning the Life of Geoffrey Chaucer', *Speculum* 68, 74–94.

Cantor, Norman F. (1991), *Inventing the Middle Ages: The Lives, Works, and Ideas of the Great Medievalists of the Twentieth Century* (New York: Morrow).

Carruthers, Mary J. (1990), *The Book of Memory: A Study of Memory in Medieval Culture* (Cambridge: Cambridge University Press).

Carus-Wilson, E. M. (1967), *Medieval Merchant Venturers: Collected Studies* (London: Methuen).

Casson, L. F. (1949) (ed.), *Sir Degrevant*, EETS o.s. 221 (London: Oxford University Press).

Chandler, Alice (1970), *A Dream of Order: The Medieval Ideal in Nineteenth-Century English Literature* (Lincoln, NE: University of Nebraska Press).

Charity, A. C. (1966), *Events and their Afterlife: The Dialectic of Christian Typology in Dante and the Bible* (Cambridge: Cambridge University Press).

Chaytor, H. J. (1966), *From Script to Print: An Introduction to Medieval Literature* (Cambridge, MA: Harvard University Press).

Chinca, Mark (1997), *Gottfried von Strassburg, Tristan* (Cambridge: Cambridge University Press).

Christophersen, Paul (1952) (ed.), *The Ballad of Sir Aldingar: Its Origin and Analogues* (Oxford: Oxford University Press).

Cooper, Helen (1977), *Pastoral: Medieval into Renaissance* (Ipswich: Brewer).

Crane, Susan (1986), *Insular Romance: Politics, Faith, and Culture in Anglo-Norman and Middle English Literature* (Berkeley: University of California Press).

— (1994), *Gender and Romance in Chaucer's Canterbury Tales* (Princeton: Princeton University Press).

Crépin, André (1982), 'Position de *Sir Tristrem*', in *La Légende de Tristan au moyen âge*, ed. Danielle Buschinger (Göppingen: Kümmerle Verlag), 89–108.

Curtius, Ernst Robert (1953), *European Literature and the Latin Middle Ages* (Princeton: Princeton University Press).

Dannenbaum, Susan Crane (1984), '*Guy of Warwick* and the Question of Exemplary Romance', *Genre* 17, 351–74.

Davenport, W. A. (1998), *Chaucer and his English Contemporaries: Prologue and Tale in the 'Canterbury Tales'* (London: Macmillan).

Davies, R. P. (1978), *Lordship and Society in the March of Wales: 1282–1400* (Oxford: Oxford University Press).

Davis, Nick (1985), 'Narrative Composition and Spatial Memory', in *Narrative: From Malory to Motion Pictures*, ed. J. Hawthorn (London: Arnold), 25–39.

Denholm-Young, Noel (1978) (ed. and trans.), *Vita Edward II* (London: Nelson).

Dickins, Bruce (1933), 'The Date of the Ireland Manuscript', *Leeds Studies in English* 2, 62–6.

Dinshaw, Carolyn (1989), *Chaucer's Sexual Poetics* (Madison: University of Wisconsin Press).

— (1992), 'Quarrels, Rivals and Rapt in Gower and Chaucer', in *'A Wyf Ther Was': Essays in Honour of Paule Mertens-Fonck*, ed. Juliette Dor (Liège: Université de Liège), 112–22.

Doane, Mary Anne (1986), 'The Clinical Eye: Medical Discourses in the "Woman's Film" of the 1940s', in *The Female Body in Western Culture: Contemporary Perspectives*, ed. Susan Rubin Suleiman (Cambridge, MA: Harvard University Press), 152–74; repr. in Doane, *The Desire to Desire: The Woman's Film of the 1940s* (Bloomington: Indiana University Press, 1987).

Donatelli, Joseph (1993), 'The Percy Folio Manuscript: A Seventeenth-Century Context for Medieval Poetry', *English Manuscript Studies, 1100–1700* 4, 114–33.

Donovan, Mortimer J. (1974), 'Middle English *Emaré* and the Cloth Worthily Wrought', in *The Learned and the Lewed: Studies in Chaucer and Medieval Literature*, ed. Larry D. Benson (Cambridge, MA: Harvard University Press), 337–42.

Doob, Penelope (1974), *Nebuchadnezzar's Children: Conventions of Madness in Middle English Literature* (New Haven: Yale University Press).

Doyle, A. I. and Parkes, M. B. (1978), 'The Production of Copies of the *Canterbury Tales* and the *Confessio Amantis* in the Early Fifteenth Century', in *Medieval Scribes, Manuscripts and Libraries: Essays Presented to N. R. Ker*, ed. M. B. Parkes and Andrew G. Watson (London: Scolar Press), 163–210.

Dronke, Peter (1962), 'The Return of Eurydice', *Classica et Mediaevalia* 23, 198–215.

Du Bois, Arthur E. (1937), 'Not Sans Peur', *Sewanee Review* 45, 115–22.

Duby, Georges (1964), 'Dans la France du nord-ouest au XIIe siècle: les "jeunes" dans la société aristocratique', *Annales ESC* 19 (1964), 835–46.

Dunn, Charles (1960), *The Foundling and the Werwolf: A Literary-Historical Study of Guillaume de Palerne* (Toronto: Toronto University Press).

Dyer, Christopher (1989), *Standards of Living in the Later Middle Ages: Social Change in England c.1200–1520* (Cambridge: Cambridge University Press).

Eadie, John (1983), 'Two Notes on *The Anturs of Arther*', *English Language Notes* 21, 3–7.

Edwards, A. S. G. (1991), 'Middle English Romance: The Limits of Editing, the Limits of Criticism', in *Medieval Literature: Texts and Interpretation*, ed. Tim William Machan (Binghampton, NY: Medieval and Renaissance Texts and Studies), 91–104.

Ehrhart, Margaret (1987), *The Judgement of the Trojan Prince Paris in Medieval Literature* (Philadelphia: University of Pennsylvania Press).

Ellis, George (1805) (ed.), *Specimens of the Early English Metrical Romances*, 3 vols (London: Longman).

—— (1811), *Specimens of Early English Metrical Romances*, 3 vols (London).

Evans, Deanna Delmar (forthcoming), 'Re-evaluating the Case for a Scottish *Eger and Grime*', in *The European Sun*, ed. Graham Caie and Ken Simpson (East Linton: Tuckwell Press).

Evans, Murray J. (1995), *Rereading Middle English Romance: Manuscript Layout, Decoration, and the Rhetoric of Composite Structure* (Montreal: McGill-Queen's University Press).

Everett, Dorothy (1955), *Essays on Middle English Literature*, ed. Patricia Kean (Oxford: Oxford University Press).

Faris, David E. (1981), 'The Art of Adventure in the Middle English Romance: *Ywain and Gawain, Eger and Grime*', *Studia Neophilologica* 53, 91–100.

Fein, Susanna Greer (1997), 'Twelve-Line Stanza Forms in Middle English and the Date of *Pearl*', *Speculum* 72, 367–98.

Felman, Shoshana (1975), 'Woman and Madness: The Critical Phallacy', *Diacritics* 5.4, 1–10.

Fentress, James and Wickham, Chris (1992), *Social Memory* (Oxford: Blackwell).

Ferrante, Joan M. (1973), *The Conflict of Love and Honor: The Medieval Tristan Legend in France, Germany and Italy* (The Hague: Mouton).

Fewster, Carol (1987), *Traditionality and Genre in Middle English Romance* (Woodbridge: Brewer).

Fichte, J. O. (1989), '*The Awntyrs off Arthure*: An Unconscious Change of the Paradigm of Adventure', in *The Living Middle Ages: Studies in Medieval Literature and its*

Tradition, ed. Uwe Böker, Manfred Marcus and Reiner Schönerling (Stuttgart: Belser Wissenschaftlicher Dienst), 129–36.

Field, P. J. C. (1979), 'Malory's Minor Sources', *N&Q* n.s. 26 (1979), 107–10.

(1982), 'Malory and the *Wedding of Sir Gawain and Dame Ragnell*', *Archiv für das Studium der neueren Sprachen und Literaturen* 219, 474–81.

(1991), 'Malory and Chrétien de Troyes', *RMS* 17, 19–30.

(1998), *Malory: Texts and Sources* (Woodbridge: Brewer).

Field, Rosalind (1982), 'The Anglo-Norman Background to Alliterative Romance', in *Middle English Alliterative Poetry and its Literary Background*, ed. David Lawton (Woodbridge: Brewer), 54–69.

Finlayson, John (1979), '*Sir Gawain* and the Expectations of Romance', *Genre* 12, 1–24.

(1980–81), 'Definitions of Middle English Romance', *ChR* 15, 168–81.

(1985), 'The Form of the Middle English *Lay*', *ChR* 19, 352–68.

Flugel, J. C. (1930), *The Psychology of Clothes* (London: Hogarth).

Foster, Edward E. and Gilman, Gail (1973), 'The Text of *William of Palerne*', *NM* 74, 481–2.

Foulon, Charles (1978), 'L'Éthique de Marie de France dans le lai de *Fresne*', in *Mélanges Jeanne Lods du moyen âge au XXe siècle*, 2 vols (Paris: École Normale Superiéure de Jeunes Filles), I, 203–12.

Fowler, Elizabeth (1995), 'Civil Death and the Maiden: Agency and the Conditions of Contract in *Piers Plowman*', *Speculum* 70, 760–92.

(1998), 'Chaucer's Hard Cases', in *Medieval Crime and Social Control*, ed. Barbara A. Hanawalt and David Wallace (Minneapolis: University of Minnesota Press).

(1999), 'The Rhetoric of Political Forms: Social Persons and the Criterion of Fit in Colonial Law, *Macbeth*, and *The Irish Masque at Covrt*', in *Form and Reform in Renaissance England: Essays in Honor of Barbara Kiefer Lewalski*, ed. Amy Boesky and Mary Thomas Crane (Newark: University of Delaware Press).

Fradenburg, Louise O. (1990), '"Voice Memorial": Loss and Reparation in Chaucer's Poetry', *Exemplaria* 2, 169–202.

(1991), *City, Marriage, Tournament: Arts of Rule in Late Medieval Scotland* (Madison: University of Wisconsin Press).

(1997), '"So That We May Speak of Them": Enjoying the Middle Ages', *New Literary History* 28, 205–30.

Frappier, Jean (1963), 'Structure et sens du *Tristan*: version commune, version courtoise', *CCM* 6, 255–80 and 441–54.

Freeman, Michelle (1987), 'The Power of Sisterhood: Marie de France's *Le Fresne*', *French Forum* 12, 5–26.

French, Walter Hoyt and Hale, Charles Brockway (1930) (eds), *Middle English Metrical Romances* (New York: Prentice-Hall).

Freud, Sigmund (1955), 'Beyond the Pleasure Principle' (1920), *SE* XVIII, 1–61.

(1957), 'On Narcissism: An Introduction' (1914), *SE* XIV, 67–102.

(1959a), 'Family Romances' (1909 [1908]), *SE* IX, 235–41.

(1959b), *Inhibitions, Symptoms and Anxiety* (1926), *SE* XX, 75–175.

(1960), *Jokes and their Relationship to the Unconscious* (1905), *SE* VIII.

(1964), *New Introductory Lectures on Psychoanalysis* (1933 [1932]), *SE* XXII, 1–182.

Freud, Sigmund and Breuer, Josef (1955), *Studies on Hysteria* (1893–5), *SE* II.

Friedman, John Block (1966), 'Eurydice, Herodis and the Noon-Day Demon', *Speculum* 41, 22–9.

—— (1970), *Orpheus in the Middle Ages* (Cambridge, MA: Harvard University Press).

Frye, Northrop (1976), *The Secular Scripture: A Study of the Structure of Romance* (Cambridge, MA: Harvard University Press).

Fuss, Diana (1989), *Essentially Speaking: Feminism, Nature and Difference* (London: Routledge).

Genette, Gérard (1980), *Narrative Discourse*, trans. Jane E. Lewin (Oxford: Blackwell).

Gerould, Gordon H. (1904), 'Forerunners, Congeners, and Derivatives of the Eustace Legend', *PMLA* 19, 335–448.

Gibbs, A. C. (1966), *Middle English Romances* (London: Arnold).

Girouard, Mark (1981), *The Return to Camelot: Chivalry and the English Gentleman* (New Haven: Yale University Press).

Gravdal, Kathryn (1991), *Ravishing Maidens: Writing Rape in Medieval French Literature and Law* (Philadelphia: University of Pennsylvania Press).

Green, Richard Firth (1998), *A Crisis of Truth: Literature and Law in Ricardian England* (Philadelphia: University of Pennsylvania Press).

Greenblatt, Stephen (1982), 'Introduction', *Genre* 15, 3–6.

Griffiths, Lavinia (1985), *Personification in Piers Plowman* (Woodbridge: Brewer).

Guddat-Figge, Gisela (1976), *Catalogue of Manuscripts Containing Middle English Romances* (Munich: Fink).

Guilbert, L. et al. (1972) (ed.), *Grand Larousse de la Langue Française* (Paris: Larousse).

Hall, Bert S. (1997), *Weapons and Warfare in the Renaissance: Gunpowder, Technology and Tactics* (Baltimore: Johns Hopkins University Press).

Hall, Stuart (1981), 'Notes on Deconstructing "The Popular"', in *People's History and Socialist Theory*, ed. Raphael Samuel (London: Routledge), 227–40.

Hall, Stuart and Whannel, Paddy (1964), *The Popular Arts* (London: Hutchinson).

Hanna, Ralph (1970), '*The Awntyrs off Arthure*: An Interpretation', *Modern Languages Quarterly* 31, 275–9.

—— (1974) (ed.), *Awntyrs off Arthure at the Terne Wathelyn* (Manchester: Manchester University Press).

Hardman, Philippa (1978), 'A Medieval Library *in Parvo*', *MAE* 47, 262–73.

Hartung, Albert E. (1993) (ed.), *A Manual of the Writings in Middle English, 1050–1500*, vol. IX: *Proverbs, Precepts and Monitory Pieces; English Mystical Writings; Tales* (New Haven: Connecticut Academy of Arts and Sciences).

Havelock, Eric (1963), *Preface to Plato* (Cambridge, MA: Harvard University Press).

Hay, Douglas (1975), 'Poaching and the Game Laws on Cannock Chase', in *Albion's Fatal Tree: Crime and Society in Eighteenth-Century England*, ed. Douglas Hay (New York: Pantheon), 189–253.

Heffernan, Carol Falvo (1976) (ed.), *Le Bone Florence of Rome* (Manchester: Manchester University Press).

Héritier, Françoise (1995), *Les Deux sœurs et leur mère: anthropologie de l'inceste* (Paris: Jacob).

Hexter, Ralph (1975), *Equivocal Oaths and Ordeals in Medieval Literature* (Cambridge, MA: Harvard University Press).

Hicks, Michael (1995), *Bastard Feudalism* (London: Longman).

Hilton, R. H. (1975), *The English Peasantry in the Later Middle Ages* (Oxford: Oxford University Press).

—— (1976) (ed.), *Peasants, Knights and Heretics: Studies in Medieval English Social History* (Cambridge: Cambridge University Press).

Hirsh, John C. (1969), 'Providential Concern in the "Lay le Freine"', *N&Q* n.s. 16, 85–6.

—— (1977), 'Additional Notes on MSS Ashmole 61, Douce 228 and Lincoln's Inn 150', *NM* 78, 347–9.

Hoepffner, E. (1938), *La Folie Tristan d'Oxford* (Paris: Belles Lettres).

Holland, William E. (1973), 'Formulaic Diction and the Descent of a Middle English Romance', *Speculum* 48, 89–109.

Holmes, G. A. (1957), *Estates of the Higher Nobility in Fourteenth-Century England* (Cambridge: Cambridge University Press).

Holt, J. C. (1972), 'Politics and Property in Early Medieval England', *Past and Present* 57, 3–52.

—— (1989), *Robin Hood*, rev. edn (London: Thames & Hudson).

Hoops, Reinald (1929), *Der Begriff 'Romance' in der mittelenglischen und früneuenglischen Literatur* (Heidelberg: Winter).

Hopkins, Andrea (1990), *The Sinful Knights: A Study of Middle English Penitential Romance* (Oxford: Oxford University Press).

Huchet, Jean-Charles (1990), *Tristan et le sang de l'écriture* (Paris: Presses Universitaires de France).

Hudson, Harriet (1984), 'Middle English Popular Romances: The Manuscript Evidence', *Manuscripta* 28, 67–78.

—— (1996) (ed.), *Sir Isumbras*, in *Four Middle English Romances*, TEAMS (Kalamazoo, MI: Medieval Institute Publications).

Hudson, John (1996), *The Formation of the English Common Law: Law and Society in England from the Norman Conquest to Magna Carta* (London: Longman).

Hume, Kathryn (1974), 'The Formal Nature of Middle English Romance', *Philological Quarterly* 54, 158–80.

Hunt, Tony (1981), 'The Significance of Thomas's *Tristan*', *RMS* 7, 41–61.

Irigaray, Luce (1985), *This Sex Which is Not One*, trans. Catherine Porter with Carolyn Burke (Ithaca, NY: Cornell University Press).

Jacobs, Nicolas (1970), 'Old French "Degaré" and Middle English "Degarre" and "Deswarre"', *N&Q* n.s. 17, 164–5.

—— (1982), '*Sir Degarré, Lay le Freine, Beves of Hamtoun* and the "Auchinleck Bookshop"', *N&Q* n.s. 29, 294–301.

—— (1995), *The Later Versions of 'Sir Degarre': A Study in Textual Degeneration* (Oxford: Society for the Study of Medieval Languages and Literature).

Jameson, Fredric (1981), 'Magical Narratives: On the Dialectical Use of Genre Criticism', in his *The Political Unconscious: Narrative as a Socially Symbolic Act* (Ithaca, NY: Cornell University Press), 103–50.

Jardine, Alice A. (1985), *Gynesis: Configurations of Women and Modernity* (Ithaca, NY: Cornell University Press).

Johnson, James Turner (1981), *Just War Tradition and the Restraint of War: A Moral and Historical Inquiry* (Princeton: Princeton University Press).

Johnston, Arthur (1964), *Enchanted Ground: The Study of Medieval Romance in the Eighteenth Century* (London: Athlone Press).

Jonin, Pierre (1958), *Les Personnages féminins dans les romans français de Tristan au XIIe siècle: Etude des influences contemporaines* (Gap: Ophrys).

Kaeuper, Richard W. (1983), 'An Historian's Reading of *The Tale of Gamelyn*', *MAE* 52, 51–62.

Kane, George (1951), *Middle English Literature: A Critical Study of the Romances, the Religious Lyrics, 'Piers Plowman'* (New York: Barnes & Noble).

(1988) (ed.), *Piers Plowman: The A Version* (London: Athlone Press).

Kay, Sarah (1985), 'The Tristan Story as Chivalric Romance, Feudal Epic and Fabliau', in *The Spirit of the Court*, ed. Glyn S. Burgess and Robert A. Taylor (Woodbridge: Brewer), 185–95.

(1995), *The 'Chansons de Geste' in the Age of Romance: Political Fictions* (Oxford: Oxford University Press).

Keen, Maurice (1961), *The Outlaws of Medieval Legend* (Toronto: University of Toronto Press).

(1984), *Chivalry* (New Haven: Yale University Press).

Kelly, Douglas (1985), 'Romance and the Vanity of Chrétien de Troyes', in *Romance: Generic Transformation from Chrétien de Troyes to Cervantes*, ed. Kevin Brownlee and Marina Scordilis Brownlee (Hanover, NH: University Press of New England), 74–90.

Kennedy, Edward D. (1981), 'Malory and his English Sources', in *Aspects of Malory*, ed. Toshiyuki Takamiya and Derek Brewer (Woodbridge: Brewer), 27–55.

Kennedy, Elspeth (1986), *Lancelot and the Grail* (Oxford: Oxford University Press).

Kerby-Fulton, Kathryn (1990), *Reformist Apocalypticism and 'Piers Plowman'* (Cambridge: Cambridge University Press).

Kermode, Frank (1983), *The Art of Fiction* (London: Methuen).

Kettle, Arnold (1951), *Introduction to the English Novel* (London: Hutchinson).

Kierkegaard, Søren (1983), *Fear and Trembling; Repetition*, ed. and trans. Howard V. Hong and Edna H. Hong (Princeton: Princeton University Press).

Klausner, David (1972), 'Exempla and *The Awntyrs off Arthure*', *MS* 34, 307–25.

Knight, Stephen (1969), 'The Oral Transmission of *Sir Launfal*', *MAE* 38, 164–70.

(1986a), *Chaucer* (Oxford: Blackwell).

(1986b), 'The Social Function of the Middle English Romances', in *Medieval Literature: Criticism, Ideology and History*, ed. David Aers (New York: St Martin's Press), 99–122.

(1994), *Robin Hood: A Complete Study of the English Outlaw* (Oxford: Blackwell).

Kozicki, Henry (1968), 'Critical Methods in the Literary Evaluation of *Sir Degaré*', *Modern Language Quarterly* 29, 3–14.

Krishna, Valerie (1976) (ed.), *The Alliterative Morte Arthure* (New York: Franklin).

Kristeva, Julia (1982), *Powers of Horror*, trans. Leon S. Roudiez (New York: Columbia University Press).

Krueger, Roberta L. (1993), *Women Readers and the Ideology of Gender in Old French Verse Romance* (Cambridge: Cambridge University Press).

Lacan, Jacques (1977), 'The Function and Field of Speech and Language in Psychoanalysis' (1953), in his *Ecrits: A Selection*, trans. Alan Sheridan (London: Tavistock), 30–113.

(1992), *The Seminar of Jacques Lacan, Book VII: The Ethics of Psychoanalysis (1959–60)*, ed. Jacques-Alain Miller, trans. Dennis Porter (London: Tavistock).

(1993), *The Seminar of Jacques Lacan, Book III: The Psychoses (1955–6)*, ed. Jacques-Alain Miller, trans. Russell Grigg (New York: Norton).

Ladurie, Emmanuel Le Roy (1987), *The French Peasantry, 1450–1660*, trans. Alan Sheridan (London: Scolar Press).

Laing, R. D. (1967), *The Politics of Experience and the Bird of Paradise* (Harmondsworth: Penguin).

Landry, Donna and MacLean, Gerald (1996) (eds), *The Spivak Reader: Selected Works of Gayatri Chakravorty Spivak* (New York: Routledge).

Lawton, David (1980), 'Middle English Unrhymed Alliterative Verse and the *South English Legendary*', *English Studies* 61, 390–96.

(1982), 'Introduction', in *Middle English Alliterative Poetry and its Literary Background*, ed. David Lawton (Woodbridge: Brewer).

Leavis, Q. D. (1932), *Fiction and the Reading Public* (London: Chatto & Windus).

Legge, M. Dominica (1963), *Anglo-Norman Literature and its Background* (Oxford: Oxford University Press).

Lerer, Seth (1985), 'Artifice and Artistry in *Sir Orfeo*', *Speculum* 60, 92–109.

Lewis, C. S. (1954), *English Literature in the Sixteenth Century, Excluding Drama* (Oxford: Oxford University Press).

(1960), *The Four Loves* (London: Bles).

Longsworth, Robert M. (1982), 'Sir Orfeo, the Minstrel and the Minstrel's Art', *SP* 79, 1–11.

Loomis, Laura H. (1940), 'Chaucer and the Auchinleck Manuscript', in *Essays and Studies in Honor of Carleton Brown*, ed. W. P. Long (New York: Columbia University Press), 111–28.

(1941), 'Chaucer and the Breton Lays of the Auchinleck Manuscript', *SP* 38, 14–33.

(1942), 'The Auchinleck Manuscript and a Possible London Bookshop of 1330–40', *PMLA* 57, 595–627.

Loth, J. (1912), *Contributions à l'étude des Romans de la Table Ronde* (Paris: Champion).

Lowe, Virginia A. P. (1980), 'Folklore as a Unifying Factor in *The Awntyrs off Arthure*', *Folklore Forum* 13, 199–223.

Lupack, Alan (1994) (ed.), *'Lancelot of the Laik' and 'Sir Tristrem'*, TEAMS (Kalamazoo, MI: Medieval Institute Publications).

Lynch, Andrew (1990), 'Good Name and Narrative in Malory', *Nottingham Medieval Studies* 34, 141–51.

Maddicott, J. R. (1978a), 'The Birth and Setting of the Ballads of Robin Hood', *English Historical Review* 93, 276–99.

(1978b), *Law and Lordship: Royal Justices as Retainers in Thirteenth- and Fourteenth-Century England* (Oxford: Past and Present Society).

Maddox, Donald (1991), 'Specular Stories, Family Romance, and the Fictions of Courtly Culture', *Exemplaria* 3, 299–326.

Mahoney, Dhira B. (1980), 'Narrative Treatment of Name in Malory's *Morte D'Arthur*', *ELH* 47, 646–56.

Mâle, Emile (1972), *The Gothic Image: Religious Art in France of the Thirteenth Century*, trans. Dora Nussey (New York: Harper and Row).

Mann, Jill (1992), 'Langland and Allegory', published as *The Morton W. Bloomfield Lectures on Medieval English Literature, II* (Kalamazoo, MI: Medieval Institute Publications).

Maréchal, Chantal (1992), 'Le Lai de *Fresne* et la littérature édifiante du XIIe siècle', *CCM* 35, 131–41.

Margherita, Gayle (1994), *The Romance of Origins: Language and Sexual Difference in Middle English Literature* (Philadelphia: University of Pennsylvania Press).

Mazzoni, Cristina (1996), *Saint Hysteria: Neurosis, Mysticism, and Gender in European Culture* (Ithaca, NY: Cornell University Press).

McCracken, Peggy (1993), 'The Body Politic and the Queen's Adulterous Body in French Romance', in *Feminist Approaches to the Body in Medieval Literature*, ed. Linda Lomperis and Sarah Stanbury (Philadelphia: University of Pennsylvania Press), 38–64.

McGillivray, Murray (1990), *Memorization in the Transmission of the Middle English Romances* (New York: Garland).

McIntosh, Angus (1989), 'Is *Sir Tristrem* an English or a Scottish Poem?', in *In Other Words: Transcultural Studies in Philology, Translation, and Lexicology Presented to Hans Heinrich Meier*, ed. J. Lachlan Mackenzie and Richard Todd (Dordrecht: Foris), 85–95.

McKisack, May (1959), *The Fourteenth Century* (Oxford: Oxford University Press).

McSparran, Frances (1979) (ed.), *Octavian Imperator* (Heidelberg: Winter).

McSparran, Frances and Robinson, P. R. (1979) (eds), *Cambridge University Library, MS Ff.2.38* (London: Scolar Press).

Meale, Carol M. (1994), ' "gode men, / Wiues, maydnes and alle men": Romance and its Audiences', in *Readings in Medieval English Romance*, ed. Carol M. Meale (Woodbridge: Brewer), 209–25.

Mehl, Dieter (1968), *The Middle English Romances of the Thirteenth and Fourteenth Centuries* (London: Routledge and Kegan Paul).

Mertes, Kate (1988), *The English Noble Household, 1250–1600* (Oxford: Blackwell).

Mills, Maldwyn (1962), 'The Composition and Style of the "Southern" *Octavian*, *Sir Launfal*, and *Libeaus Desconus*', *MAE* 31, 88–109.

    (1969) (ed.), *Lybeas Desconus*, EETS o.s. 261 (London: Oxford University Press).

    (1973) (ed.), *Six Middle English Romances*, Everyman (London: Dent).

    (1992) (ed.), *'Ywain and Gawain', 'Sir Percyvell of Gales', 'The Anturs of Arther'*, Everyman (London: Dent).

    (1994), '*Sir Isumbras* and the Styles of the Tail-Rhyme Romance', in *Readings in Medieval English Romance*, ed. Carol M. Meale (Woodbridge: Brewer).

Mitchiner, Michael (1986), *Medieval Pilgrim and Secular Badges* (London: Hawkins).

Modell, Arnold H. (1968), *Object Love and Reality: An Introduction to a Psychoanalytic Theory of Object Relations* (New York: International Universities Press).

Moi, Toril (1992), '"She Died Because She Came Too Late . . .": Knowledge, Doubles and Death in Thomas's *Tristan*', *Exemplaria* 4, 105–33.

Moorman, Charles (1981), 'The English Alliterative Revival and the Literature of Defeat', *ChR* 16, 85–100.

Mumford, Marilyn R. (1986), 'A Jungian Reading of *Sir Orfeo* and *Orpheus and Erudices*', in *Scottish Language and Literature, Medieval and Renaissance*, ed. Dietrich Strauss and Horst W. Drescher (Frankfurt: Lang), 291–302.

Mustanoja, Tauno F. (1970), 'The Suggestive Use of Christian Names in Middle English Poetry', in *Medieval Literature and Folklore Studies: Essays in Honour of Francis Lee Utley*, ed. Jerome Mandel and Bruce A. Rosenberg (New Brunswick: Rutgers University Press), 51–76.

Nelson, Deborah (1978), 'The Implications of Love and Sacrifice in *Fresne* and *Eliduc*', *South Central Bulletin* 38, 153–5.

Nerlich, Michael (1987), *Ideology of Adventure: Studies in Modern Consciousness, 1100–1500*, trans. Ruth Crowley, 2 vols (Minneapolis: University of Minnesota Press).

Newstead, Helaine (1969), 'The Equivocal Oath in the Tristan Legend', in *Mélanges offerts à Rita Lejeune*, 2 vols (Gembloux: Duculot), II, 1077–85.

Nolan, Barbara (1996), 'The *Tale of Sir Gareth* and the *Tale of Sir Lancelot*', in *A Companion to Malory*, ed. Elizabeth Archibald and A. S. G. Edwards (Woodbridge: Brewer), 153–81.

Orme, Nicholas (1984), *From Childhood to Chivalry* (London: Methuen).

—— (1992), 'Medieval Hunting: Fact and Fancy', in *Chaucer's England: Literature in Historical Context*, ed. Barbara Hanawalt (Minneapolis: University of Minnesota Press), 133–53.

Parker, Patricia A. (1982), 'The Metaphorical Plot', in *Metaphor: Problems and Perspectives*, ed. David S. Miall (Brighton: Harvester), 133–57.

Parry, Milman (1971), *The Making of Homeric Verse*, ed. Adam Parry (London: Oxford University Press).

Patterson, Lee (1987), *Negotiating the Past: The Historical Understanding of Medieval Literature* (Madison: University of Wisconsin Press).

Pearsall, Derek (1965), 'The Development of Middle English Romance', *MS* 27, 91–116.

—— (1977), *Old English and Middle English Poetry* (London: Routledge).

—— (1981), 'The Origins of the Alliterative Revival', in *The Alliterative Tradition in the Fourteenth Century*, ed. Bernard S. Levy and Paul Szarmarch (Kent, OH: Kent State University Press), 1–24.

—— (1982), 'The Alliterative Revival: Origins and Social Background', in *Middle English Alliterative Poetry and its Literary Background*, ed. David Lawton (Woodbridge: Brewer), 34–53.

—— (1985), 'Middle English Romance and its Audience', in *Historical and Editorial Studies in Medieval and Early Modern English for Johan Gerritsen*, ed. Hanneke Wirtjes and Hans Jansen (Groningen: Bouma), 37–47.

—— (1992), *The Life of Geoffrey Chaucer* (Oxford: Blackwell).

(1996), 'Madness in *Sir Orfeo*', in *Romance Reading on the Book: Essays on Medieval Narrative Presented to Maldwyn Mills*, ed. Jennifer Fellows, Rosalind Field, Gillian Rogers and Judith Weiss (Cardiff: University of Wales Press), 51–63.

Pearsall, Derek and Cunningham, I. C. (1977) (eds), *The Auchinleck Manuscript: National Library of Scotland, Advocates' MS 19.2.1* (London: Scolar Press).

Pellegrini, Silvio (1967), 'Tabù del Nome Proprio nei Romanzi di Chrestien de Troyes', *Giornale Italiano de Filologia (Napoli)* 20, 243–7.

Pensom, Roger (1995), *Reading Béroul's 'Tristran': A Poetic Narrative and the Anthropology of its Reception* (Bern: Lang).

Phillips, Helen (1989), 'The Ghost's Baptism in *The Awntyrs off Arthure*', *MAE* 59, 49–58.

(1993), '*The Awntyrs off Arthure*, Structure and Meaning: A Reassessment', in *Arthurian Literature* 12, 63–90.

Pollock, Frederick and Maitland, Frederic William (1959), *The History of English Law Before the Time of Edward I*, 2nd edn (Washington, DC: Lawyers' Literary Club).

Powell, Edward (1989), *Kingship, Law, and Society: Criminal Justice in the Reign of Henry V* (Oxford: Oxford University Press).

Purser, John (1996), 'Greysteil', in *Stewart Style, 1513–1542: Essays on the Court of James V*, ed. Janet Hadley Williams (East Linton: Tuckwell Press), 142–52.

Putter, Ad (1995), *'Sir Gawain and the Green Knight' and French Arthurian Romance* (Oxford: Oxford University Press).

(1996), *An Introduction to the 'Gawain'-poet* (London: Longman).

Quinn, William A. and Hall, Audley S. (1982), *Jongleur: A Modified Theory of Memorial Transmission and its Effects on the Performance and Transmission of Middle English Romance* (Washington, DC: University Press of America).

Radway, Janice A. (1984), *Reading the Romance: Women, Patriarchy and Popular Literature* (Chapel Hill: University of North Carolina Press).

Ramsey, Lee C. (1983), *Chivalric Romances: Popular Literature in Medieval England* (Bloomington: Indiana University Press).

Regalado, Nancy F. (1976), 'Tristan and Renart: Two Tricksters', *Esprit Créateur* 16, 30–38.

Reichel, Georg (1894), 'Studien zu der schottischen Romanze: *The History of Sir Eger, Sir Grime and Sir Gray-Steel*', *Englische Studien* 19, 1–66.

Reichl, Karl (1991), 'The Middle English Popular Romance: Minstrel versus Hack Writer', in *The Ballad and Oral Literature*, ed. Joseph Harris (Cambridge, MA: Harvard University Press), 243–68.

Reiss, Louise Horner (1986), 'Tristan and Isolt and the Medieval Ideal of Friendship', *Romance Quarterly* 33, 131–7.

Richardson, Frances E. (1965) (ed.), *Sir Eglamour*, EETS e.s. 256 (London: Oxford University Press).

Rickert, Edith (1908) (ed.), *The Romance of Emaré*, EETS e.s. 99 (London: Kegan Paul).

(1967) (ed.), *Early English Romances: Romances of Friendship* (New York: Cooper Square).

Riddy, Felicity (1974), '*Squyer Meldrum* and the Romance of Chivalry', *YES* 4, 26–36.

(1987), *Sir Thomas Malory* (Leiden: Brill).

Rider, Jeff (1988), 'Receiving Orpheus in the Middle Ages: Allegorization, Remythification and *Sir Orfeo*', *Papers on Language and Literature* 24, 343–66.

Robson, Margaret (1996), '*Cloaking Desire: Re-Reading Emaré*', in *Romance Reading on the Book: Essays on Medieval Narrative Presented to Maldwyn Mills*, ed. Jennifer Fellows, Rosalind Field, Gillian Rogers and Judith Weiss (Cardiff: University of Wales Press), 64–76.

Rogers, Gillian (1991), 'The Percy Folio Manuscript Revisited', in *Romance in Medieval England*, ed. Maldwyn Mills, Jennifer Fellows, and Carol M. Meale (Woodbridge: Brewer), 39–64.

Ross, Charles (1997), *The Custom of the Castle: From Malory to Macbeth* (Berkeley, University of California Press).

Rubin, David C. (1995), *Memory in Oral Traditions* (New York: Oxford University Press).

Rubin, Gayle (1975), 'The Traffic in Women: Notes on the "Political Economy" of Sex', in *Toward an Anthropology of Women*, ed. Rayna R. Reiter (New York: Monthly Review Press), 157–210.

Rumble, Thomas C. (1959), 'The Middle English *Sir Tristrem*: Towards a Reappraisal', *Comparative Literature* 11, 221–8.

(1965) (ed.), *The Breton Lays in Middle English* (Detroit: Wayne State University Press).

Russell, Frederick H. (1975), *The Just War in the Middle Ages* (Cambridge: Cambridge University Press).

Sargent-Baur, Barbara (1984), 'Between Fabliau and Romance: Love and Rivalry in Béroul's *Tristran*', *Romania* 105, 292–311.

Saul, Nigel (1981), *Knights and Esquires: The Gloucestershire Gentry in the Fourteenth Century* (Oxford: Oxford University Press).

(1983), 'The Social Status of Chaucer's Franklin: A Reconsideration', *MAE* 52, 10–26.

Scattergood, John (1994), '*The Tale of Gamelyn*: The Noble Robber as Provincial Hero', in *Readings in Medieval English Romance*, ed. Carol M. Meale (Woodbridge: Brewer), 159–94.

Schelp, Hanspeter (1967), *Exemplarische Romanzen im Mittelenglischen* (Göttingen: Vandenhoeck and Ruprecht).

Schlauch, Margaret (1927), *Chaucer's Constance and Accused Queens* (New York: New York University Press, repr. 1973).

Schwake, H. (1970), 'Zur Frage der Namenssymbolik im höfischen Roman', *Germanisch-Romanische Monatsschrift* n.s. 20, 338–53.

Sedgwick, Eve Kosofsky (1985), *Between Men: English Literature and Male Homosocial Desire* (New York: Columbia University Press).

Severs, J. Burke (1961), 'The Antecedents of *Sir Orfeo*', in *Studies in Medieval Literature in Honor of Professor Albert Croll Baugh*, ed. MacEdward Leach (Philadelphia: University of Pennsylvania Press), 187–207.

(1967) (ed.), *A Manual of the Writings in Middle English, 1050–1500, I: The Romances* (New Haven: Connecticut Academy of Arts and Sciences).

Shannon, Edgar F., Jr (1951), 'Mediaeval Law in *The Tale of Gamelyn*', *Speculum* 26, 458–64.

Shepherd, Stephen H. A. (1989), 'The Ashmole *Sir Ferumbras*: Translation in Holograph', in *The Medieval Translator*, ed. Roger Ellis (Woodbridge: Brewer), 103–22.

Shepherd, M. (1990), *Philippe de Rémi's 'La Manekine' and 'Jehan et Blonde': A Study of Form and Meaning* (Amsterdam: Rodopi).

Shippey, T. A. (1969), 'The Fairy Tale Structure of *Beowulf*', *N&Q* n.s. 16, 2–11.

(1988), 'Breton Lais and Modern Fantasies', in *Studies in Medieval English Romances: Some New Approaches*, ed. Derek. Brewer (Woodbridge: Brewer), 69–91.

(1996), '*Robin Hood*: A Legend in Text, Film and Popular Consciousness', *ScriptOralia* 84, 409–23.

Shonk, T. (1985), 'A Study of the Auchinleck Manuscript: Bookmen and Bookmaking in the Early Fourteenth Century', *Speculum* 60, 71–91.

Showalter, Elaine (1985a), *The Female Malady: Women, Madness, and English Culture, 1830–1980* (New York: Pantheon).

(1985b) (ed.), *The New Feminist Criticism: Essays on Women, Literature and Theory* (New York: Pantheon).

Simpson, James (1997), 'Ageism: Leland, Bale and the Laborious Start of English Literary History, 1350–1550', in *New Medieval Literatures* 1, 213–35.

Skeat, Walter W. (1884) (ed.), *The Tale of Gamelyn* (Oxford: Oxford University Press, 1884).

Slover, C. H. (1931), 'Sir Degare: A Study of a Mediaeval Hack Writer's Methods', *Texas Studies in English* 11, 5–23.

Smithers, G. V. (1957) (ed.), *King Alisaunder*, 2 vols, EETS o.s. 227, 237 (London: Oxford University Press).

Spearing, A. C. (1981), '*The Awntyrs off Arthure*', in *The Alliterative Tradition in the Fourteenth Century*, ed. Bernard S. Levy and Paul E. Szarmach (Kent, OH: Ohio State University Press), 183–202.

(1982), 'Central and Displaced Sovereignty in Three Medieval Poems', *Review of English Studies* 33, 247–61.

(1984), 'Medieval Narrative Style', *Poetica* 17, 1–21.

(1985), *Medieval to Renaissance in English Poetry* (Cambridge: Cambridge University Press).

(1987), *Readings in Medieval Poetry* (Cambridge: Cambridge University Press).

(1990a), 'Marie de France and her Middle English Adapters', *Studies in the Age of Chaucer* 12, 117–56.

(1990b), '*Troilus and Criseyde*: The Illusion of Allusion', *Exemplaria* 2, 263–77.

(1993), *The Medieval Poet as Voyeur: Looking and Listening in Medieval Love-Narratives* (Cambridge: Cambridge University Press).

Spearing, A. C. and Spearing, J. E. (1974), *Poetry of the Age of Chaucer* (London: Arnold).

Speirs, John (1967), *Medieval English Poetry* (London: Faber).

293

Spivak, Gayatri Chakravorty (1993), *Outside the Teaching Machine* (London: Routledge).

Stallybrass, Peter and White, Allon (1986), *The Politics and Poetics of Transgression* (Ithaca, NY: Cornell University Press).

Stevens, John (1966), 'The *granz biens* of Marie de France', in *Patterns of Love and Courtesy: Essays in Memory of C. S. Lewis*, ed. John Lawlor (London: Arnold), 1–25.

Stock, Brian (1983), *The Implications of Literacy: Written Language and Models of Interpretation in the Eleventh and Twelfth Centuries* (Princeton: Princeton University Press).

Stones, E. L. G. (1957), 'The Folvilles of Ashby Folville, Leicestershire, and their Associates in Crime', *Transactions of the Royal Historical Society* 5th ser. 7, 117–36.

Storey, John (1993), *An Introductory Guide to Cultural Theory and Popular Culture* (New York: Harvester Wheatsheaf).

Strohm, Paul (1971), '*Storie, Spelle, Geste, Romaunce, Tragedie*: Generic Distinctions in the Middle English Troy Narrative', *Speculum* 46, 348–59.

(1977), 'The Origin and Meaning of Middle English *Romaunce*', *Genre* 10, 1–28.

(1980), 'Middle English Narrative Genres', *Genre* 13, 379–88.

(1992), *Hochon's Arrow: The Social Imagination of Fourteenth-Century Texts* (Princeton: Princeton University Press).

Suchier, Hermann (1884) (ed.), *Oeuvres Poétiques de Beaumanoir*, 2 vols, SATF (Paris: Firmin Didot).

Swanton, Michael (1987), *English Literature Before Chaucer* (London: Longman).

Tatlock, J. S. P. (1929), review of *The Seege or Batayle of Troye*, *MLR* 24, 74–5.

Taylor, Andrew (1991), 'The Myth of the Minstrel Manuscript', *Speculum* 66, 43–73.

(1992), 'Fragmentation, Corruption, and Minstrel Narration: The Question of Middle English Romances', *YES* 22, 38–62.

Thompson, John J. (1983), 'The Compiler in Action: Robert Thornton and the Thornton Romances in Lincoln Cathedral MS 91', in *Manuscripts and Readers in Fifteenth-Century England: The Literary Implications of Manuscript Study*, ed. Derek Pearsall (Woodbridge: Brewer), 113–24.

(1987), *Robert Thornton and the London Thornton Manuscript* (Woodbridge: Brewer).

(1994), '*The Cursor Mundi*, the "Inglis tong", and "Romance"', in *Readings in Medieval English Romance*, ed. Carol M. Meale (Woodbridge: Brewer), 99–120.

(1996), 'Looking Behind the Book: MS Cotton Caligula A.ii, part 1, and the Experience of Its Texts', in *Romance Reading on the Book: Essays on Medieval Narrative Presented to Maldwyn Mills*, ed. Jennifer Fellows, Rosalind Field, Gillan Rogers and Judith Weiss (Cardiff, University of Wales Press), 171–87.

Thompson, Stith (1932–5), *Motif-Index of Folk Literature*, 6 vols (Copenhagen: Rosenhilde and Bagger).

Thrupp, Sylvia (1948), *The Merchant Class in Medieval London* (Ann Arbor: University of Michigan Press).

Tierney, Brian (1997), *The Idea of Natural Rights* (London: Scolar Press).

Tigges, Wim (1990), 'Romance and Parody', in *Companion to Middle English Romance*, ed. Henk Aertsen and Alasdair A. MacDonald (Amsterdam: VU Press), 129–51.

Todorov, Tzvetan (1969), *Grammaire du Décaméron* (The Hague: Mouton).

Tristram, Philippa (1976), *Figures of Life and Death in Medieval English Literature* (London: Elek).

Tubach, F. (1969), *Index Exemplorum: A Handbook of Medieval Religious Tales* (Helsinki: Suomalainen Tiedeakatemia).

Tuck, Richard (1979), *Natural Rights Theories: Their Origin and Development* (Cambridge: Cambridge University Press).

Turville-Petre, Thorlac (1974), 'Humphrey De Bohun and *William of Palerne*', *NM* 75, 250–52.

    (1977), *The Alliterative Revival* (Woodbridge: Brewer).

    (1983), 'Some Medieval Manuscripts in the North-East Midlands', in *Manuscripts and Readers in Fifteenth-Century England: The Literary Implications of Manuscript Study*, ed. Derek Pearsall (Woodbridge: Brewer), 125–41.

    (1996), *England the Nation: Language, Literature, and National Identity, 1290–1340* (Oxford: Oxford University Press).

Van Duzee, Mabel (1963), *A Medieval Romance of Friendship: Eger and Grime* (New York: Franklin).

Varvaro, Alberto (1972), *Beroul's 'Romance of Tristran'*, trans. John C. Barnes (Manchester: Manchester University Press).

Vicari, Patricia (1982), '*Sparagmos*: Orpheus among the Christians', in *Orpheus: The Metamorphoses of a Myth*, ed. John Warden (Toronto: University of Toronto Press), 63–83.

Vitz, Evelyn Birge (1989), *Medieval Narrative and Modern Narratology* (New York: New York University Press).

Ward, Jennifer (1995), *Women of the English Nobility and Gentry: 1066–1500* (Manchester: Manchester University Press).

Warton, Thomas (1774–81), *The History of English Poetry from the Close of the Eleventh to the Commencement of the Eighteenth Centuries*, 3 vols (London: Dodsley et al.).

Wells, J. E. (1916–51) (ed.), *A Manual of the Writings in Middle English, 1050–1400*, 7 vols (New Haven: The Connecticut Academy of Arts and Sciences).

Williams, Raymond (1958), *Culture and Society, 1780–1950* (London: Chatto & Windus).

    (1983), *Keywords: A Vocabulary of Culture and Society*, rev. edn (London: Fontana).

Wind, Bartina (1960–61), 'Eléments courtois dans Béroul et dans Thomas', *Romance Philology* 14, 1–13.

Winnicott, D. W. (1989), 'Fear of Breakdown', in his *Psycho-Analytic Explorations*, ed. Clare Winnicott, Ray Shepherd and Madeleine Davis (Cambridge, MA: Harvard University Press), 84–95.

Withrington, John (1991) (ed.), *The Wedding of Sir Gawain and Dame Ragnell* (Lancaster: Lancaster Modern Spelling Texts).

Wittgenstein, Ludwig (1953), *Philosophical Investigations*, trans. G. E. M. Anscombe (Oxford: Blackwell).

Wittig, Susan (1978), *Stylistic and Narrative Structure in the Middle English Romances* (Austin: University of Texas Press).

Wood, Michael (1996), *In Search of the Trojan War* (Harmondsworth: Penguin).

Zeeman, Nicolette (1996), 'The Schools Give a License to Poets', in *Criticism and Dissent in the Middle Ages*, ed. Rita Copeland (Cambridge: Cambridge University Press), 151–80.

Žižek, Slavoj (1991), *Looking Awry: An Introduction to Jacques Lacan through Popular Culture* (Cambridge, MA: MIT Press).

(1994), *The Metastases of Enjoyment: Six Essays on Woman and Causality* (London: Verso).

(1997), *The Plague of Fantasies* (London: Verso).

NOTES ON CONTRIBUTORS

ELIZABETH ARCHIBALD is Associate Professor of English at the University of Victoria, British Columbia. She is the author of *Apollonius of Tyre: Medieval and Renaissance Themes and Variations* (1991), co-editor of *A Companion to Malory* (1996), and has published several essays on Chaucer, Malory, and the incest theme in medieval literature. A book on the subject of incest in medieval literature is forthcoming.

ARLYN DIAMOND is Professor of English at the University of Massachusetts at Amherst. She has published widely on Chaucer, medieval romance, and women's studies, and she is the co-editor of *The Authority of Experience: Essays in Feminist Criticism* (1977). She is currently working on issues of gender and social power in Middle English romances.

ELIZABETH FOWLER is Associate Professor of English at the University of Virginia. Her work on the representation of person in medieval and early modern poetry has appeared in a number of journals and essay collections and is forthcoming in her book, *The Human Figure in Words: The Arguments of Chaucer, Langland, Skelton, Spenser*.

JANE GILBERT is Lecturer in French at University College, London. She works on medieval French and English literature, both separately and in comparison, and has published on *Sir Gawain and the Green Knight, Aucassin and Nicolette*, and other romances. Her forthcoming book deals with the double in medieval narrative. Her ongoing research project is on the figure of the child as a focus for social tensions in the Middle Ages.

ANTONY J. HASLER is Assistant Professor in the Department of English at Saint Louis University. He has published essays on late medieval English and Scottish poetry, and on nineteenth-century Scottish literature. He is the co-editor of James Hogg's novel *The Three Perils of Woman* (1995). His current projects include a book-length study of early Tudor poetry entitled *Allegories of Authority*, and a translation of poems by Georg Heym.

NICOLA MCDONALD is Lecturer in English at the University of York. She is the author of articles on Chaucer's *Legend of Good Women* and Gower's *Confessio Amantis*. She is completing a book on representations of Medea in the later medieval period, and is editing a collection of essays on Middle English romance entitled *Unpopular Popular Romances*.

AD PUTTER is Lecturer in the English Department and the Centre for Medieval Studies at the University of Bristol. He has published several articles and books on medieval romance, including *An Introduction to the Gawain-Poet* (1996). One of his present research projects is a study of the meanings embodied in the literary conventions of popular romance.

MARGARET ROBSON studied at Goldsmith's College and the Centre for Medieval Studies, University of York, where she wrote her doctoral dissertation on women's viewpoints in the Middle English Breton lays. She has taught at the universities of York, Aberystwyth and NUI Maynooth. Publications include essays on *Emaré* and *Sir Gowther*. Her research interests are medieval romance and feminist and psychoanalytic theory.

TOM SHIPPEY holds the Walter J. Ong SJ Chair at Saint Louis University. His publications include critical books on and editions of Old English poetry and a number of essays on Middle English romances and Breton lays. He has recently brought out the *Beowulf* volume in Routledge's Critical Heritage series, and is working on a study of speech acts and oral skills in early Germanic poetry.

JAMES SIMPSON is Professor of Medieval and Renaissance English at the University of Cambridge and Fellow of Girton College. He has published widely on medieval literature, and is the author of *Piers Plowman: An Introduction to the B-Text* (1990) and a book on traditions of medieval humanism, *Sciences of the Self* (1995). He is writing a book on English literature, 1350–1550, for the Oxford English Literary History series.

A. C. SPEARING is William R. Kenan Professor of English at the University of Virginia and Life Fellow of Queens' College, Cambridge. He is the author of many books and articles on medieval literature, including studies of Middle English romances, published in such books as *The Gawain-Poet: A Critical Study* (1970), *Readings in Medieval Poetry* (1987), and *The Medieval Poet as Voyeur* (1993). He is currently working on a study of textual subjectivity in the Middle Ages and on a new translation of *The Cloud of Unknowing*.

MYRA STOKES is Senior Lecturer in English at the University of Bristol. She is the author of *Justice and Mercy in Piers Plowman* (1984) and *The Language of Jane Austen* (1991), and various essays on medieval topics. She is currently working with Ad Putter on an edition of the works of the *Gawain*-Poet for the Penguin English Poets series.

INDEX

This index contains references to medieval texts and people, manuscripts, placenames (only where relevant) and modern thinkers. It does not include references to medievalists, unless they are mentioned in the text.